# DIGITAL HUMANITIES
# PEDAGOGY

# Digital Humanities Pedagogy: Practices, Principles and Politics

Edited by

Brett D. Hirsch

http://www.openbookpublishers.com

As with all Open Book Publishers titles, digital material and resources associated with this volume are available from our website at:

http://www.openbookpublishers.com/product/161

ISBN Hardback: 978-1-909254-26-8
ISBN Paperback: 978-1-909254-25-1
ISBN Digital (pdf): 978-1-909254-27-5
ISBN Digital ebook (epub): 978-1-909254-28-2
ISBN Digital ebook (mobi): 978-1-909254-29-9

Typesetting by www.bookgenie.in

Cover image: © Daniel Rohr, 'Brain and Microchip', product designs first exhibited as prototypes in January 2009. Image used with kind permission of the designer. For more information about Daniel and his work, see http://www.danielrohr.com/

All paper used by Open Book Publishers is SFI (Sustainable Forestry Initiative), and PEFC (Programme for the Endorsement of Forest Certification Schemes) Certified.

Printed in the United Kingdom and United States by
Lightning Source for Open Book Publishers

# Contents

# Acknowledgments

This collection began as a result of my time at the University of Victoria, British Columbia, where I spent a year as a postdoctoral research fellow and, despite shipping my entire library of English Renaissance literary studies in the expectation (perhaps naïve) of teaching it, found myself tasked with designing and teaching undergraduate courses in digital humanities.

Thankfully, support and guidance was always close to hand. In particular, the "Three Musketeers" of the Humanities Computing and Media Centre—Greg Newton, Stewart Arneil and Martin Holmes—fielded my many questions with good humor and shaped my understanding and appreciation of the subject. Michael Best's expertise is matched only by his generosity, and I am eternally grateful for his ongoing mentorship and friendship. Michael Joyce, Cara Leitch, Tassie Gniady, Kim S. Webb, Meagan Timney, Paul Caton and other past members of the Electronic Textual Cultures Lab were always willing to share their ideas, assistance and commiserations. Other members of the Faculty of Humanities, Elizabeth Grove-White, Janelle Jenstad, Erin Kelly, Gary Kuchar and Jon Lutz were equally welcoming and supportive.

My time in North America afforded me additional valuable opportunities to discuss ideas with digital humanists from further afield, such as Richard Cunningham, Alan Galey, Ian Lancashire, Alan Liu, Kenneth Price, Geoffrey Rockwell, Stan Ruecker, Stéfan Sinclair and Kirsten Uszkalo. Back in the Antipodes, conversations with Toby Burrows, Hugh Craig, Willard McCarty, Jo McEwan, Jenna Mead, Philip Mead, Harold Short, Margaret Stevenson and Chris Wortham have been instructive. A Research Development Award from the University of Western Australia generously supported my own humble contributions to this collection.

Open Book Publishers has been a pleasure to work with, and I thank Alessandra Tosi, Corin Throsby and Samuel Moore for enthusiastically guiding this volume into its print and electronic manifestations. We are delighted to be a part of this exciting publishing venture, and fully support its vision.

I am also grateful to Daniel Rohr, a talented product designer based in Darmstadt, Germany, for generously allowing me to use a photograph of his stunning *Brain and Microchip* project for the volume's cover.

We have all heard the joke that bringing together academics to produce a collection such as this is like herding cats. Thankfully, I could not have hoped for a better lineup of contributors—practical, principled and political. No cats were herded in the making of this volume.

B.D.H.

Perth, July 15, 2012

# Notes on Contributors

**Olin Bjork** is a lecturer in English at Santa Clara University, "the Jesuit University in Silicon Valley," where he teaches first-year writing courses as well as upper-division courses in Internet culture and technical writing. His research interests include Computers and Writing, Digital Humanities, John Milton, and Textual Studies. In 2010, he completed a three-year post doc at Georgia Tech's School of Literature, Media and Communication, were he taught courses in technical communication and Web design. He received his PhD in English from the University of Texas at Austin, where in addition to teaching literature and composition courses he served as assistant director of the Digital Writing and Research Lab, then known as the Computer Writing and Research Lab, worked as the English department's webmaster, and collaborated on digital "audiotext" editions of John Milton's *Paradise Lost* (http://www.laits.utexas.edu/miltonpl) and Walt Whitman's *Leaves of Grass* (http://www.laits.utexas.edu/leavesofgrass) for UT-Austin's Liberal Arts Instructional Technology Services. His current research centers on print and digital interface design for editions of literature and other texts.

**Vicki Callahan** is an associate professor of Cinema Practice at the University of Southern California's Institute for Multimedia Literacy (IML) in the School of Cinematic Arts. She is the author of *Zones of Anxiety: Movement, Musidora, and the Crime Serials of Louis Feuillade* (Wayne State University Press, 2004) and the editor for the collection, *Reclaiming the Archive: Feminism and Film History* (Wayne State University Press, 2010). Vicki is the author/organizer of the *Feminism 3.0* website (http://www.feminismthreepointzero.com/) and, with Lina Srivastava, she co-authors *Transmedia Activism* (http://www.transmedia-activism.com/). Her interests in silent cinema, feminist theory, and digital media intersect around questions of emergent/disruptive technologies, new modes of writing, social justice, and alternative or counter narrative forms.

**Tanya Clement** is an assistant professor in the School of Information at the University of Texas at Austin. She has a PhD in English Literature and Language and an MFA in fiction. Her primary area of research is the role of scholarly information infrastructure as it impacts academic research libraries and digital collections, research tools and (re)sources in the context of future applications, humanities informatics, and humanities data curation. Her research is informed by theories of knowledge representation, information theory, mark-up theory, social text theory, and theories of information visualization. She has edited multiple digital editions of the poetry of Elsa von Freytag-Loringhoven and published pieces on digital humanities in several books and on digital scholarly editing, text mining, and modernist literature in *Journal of the Text Encoding Initiative, Literary and Linguistic Computing*, and *Texas Studies in Literature and Language*. She is the co-director of the Modernist Versions Project, and associate editor of the Versioning Machine (http://v-machine.org).

**Estelle Clements** is a PhD student in media at the Dublin Institute of Technology, where she is completing her dissertation on digital civics in pedagogy on an ABBEST scholarship. A former high school teacher and theatre director, she completed a Master's degree in the history of medicine at Newcastle University in 2007 on a Wellcome Trust Scholarship. Estelle also holds Bachelor's degrees in education, classics, and theatre from Acadia University, Nova Scotia.

**Richard Cunningham** is a professor of early modern English literature, rhetoric, and digital humanities in the Department of English and Theatre at Acadia University, Nova Scotia. He has published on Shakespeare, John Foxe, and on a variety of digital humanities topics. Since 2008, he has been the director of the Acadia Digital Culture Observatory. He is the administrative lead of, and a researcher on, the Textual Studies team, and a member of the executive board of the Implementing New Knowledge Environments (INKE) research initiative. He and a colleague in Acadia's Psychology Department are engaged in a long-term project researching the point at which the cognitive overhead necessary to a reader of any material reaches overload when reading in a digital environment.

**Diane Favro** is a professor of architecture and urban design at the University of California, Los Angeles (UCLA), and former president of the Society of Architectural Historians. She is the author of *The Urban Image of Augustan Rome* (Cambridge University Press, 1996), as well as numerous articles on ancient architecture and urban design, the pedagogy of architectural history, and the impact of real-time simulations of historic environments on disciplinary inquiries. Diane headed the scientific committees for the UCLA Cultural VR Lab, which developed virtual reality models of historic environments for research and education, including the internationally acknowledged Rome Reborn Project (http://www.romereborn.virginia.edu/). Currently, she is director of the succeeding digital lab, the Experiential Technologies Center, which promotes the critical incorporation of new technologies into research and teaching as evident in the National Endowment for the Humanities (NEH) sponsored Digital Karnak Project (http://dlib.etc.ucla.edu/projects/Karnak/), for which she is co-director, and the NEH Summer Institute "Models of Ancient Rome."

**Christiane Fritze** is a senior researcher at the Research and Development Department of the Göttingen State and University Library. Currently she is working as the scientific coordinator of the German chapter of the European Infrastructure Initiative DARIAH (Digital Research Infrastructure for the Arts and Humanities) and consults various research projects in their application of TEI. Before that, she worked as a research associate at the Berlin-Brandenburg Academy of Sciences and Humanities in several Digital Humanities projects such as the TELOTA Initiative and the German Text Archive. Christiane regularly teaches in the field of Digital Humanities at several German universities and co-organizes summer schools with a particular focus on XML technologies, TEI and digital edition-related matters.

**Matthew K. Gold** is an associate professor at NYC College of Technology (English) and the Graduate Center of the City University of New York (Liberal Studies and Interactive Technology and Pedagogy). At the Graduate Center, he serves as advisor to the provost for Master's Programs and Digital Initiatives, acting executive officer of the MA Program in Liberal Studies, director of the GC Digital Scholarship Lab, director of the CUNY Academic Commons, and co-director of the CUNY Digital Humanities Initiative. He is editor of *Debates in the Digital Humanities* (Minnesota, 2012) and has published work in *The Journal of Modern Literature, Kairos,* and *On* *the Horizon*, as well as in the edited collections *From A to <A>: Keywords of Markup* (Minnesota, 2010), *Learning Through Digital Media: Experiments in Technology and Pedagogy* (iDC, 2010), and the *Johns Hopkins Guidebook to Digital Media and Textuality* (Johns Hopkins, 2013). His digital humanities projects include "Looking for Whitman" and "The Commons in a Box," supported by grants from the NEH Office of Digital Humanities, the National Science Foundation, the US Department of Education, the Alfred P. Sloan Foundation, and the Ford Foundation. He serves on the Executive Council of the Association for Computers and the Humanities.

**Cathy Moran Hajo** is the associate editor of the Margaret Sanger Papers (http://www.nyu.edu/projects/sanger/), a scholarly editing project located at New York University. She has worked as a documentary editor for over twenty years, specializing in the publication of historical materials in digital form, and participating in scholarly conferences and meetings on digital issues. Cathy is a past president of the Association for Documentary Editing and the author of several articles on documentary editing. She teaches two courses for the archives and public history program at NYU, History and New Media and Creating Digital History.

**Brett D. Hirsch** is a university postdoctoral research fellow in medieval and early modern studies at the University of Western Australia. He is coordinating editor of the Digital Renaissance Editions (http://digitalrenaissance.uvic.ca/), co-editor of the Routledge journal *Shakespeare*, and vice president of the Australian and New Zealand Shakespeare Association (2010-2012). Brett's research has appeared in *The Ben Jonson Journal, Digital Studies, Early Modern Literary Studies, Early Theatre, Literature Compass*, and *Parergon*, in edited collections for Brepols and Palgrave, and in the forthcoming Cambridge *World Shakespeare Encyclopedia*. In addition to his involvement with digital projects like The Map of Early Modern London (http://mapoflondon.uvic.ca/) and The Lost Plays Database (http://www.lostplays.org/), he is currently working an electronic critical edition of *Fair Em* (with Kevin Quarmby), and a series of computational stylistics studies of English Renaissance drama (with Hugh Craig).

**Chris Johanson** is an assistant professor in the Department of Classics at the University of California, Los Angeles (UCLA). His research applies the tools and techniques of digital humanities and the analytical methodologies of classics to social historical problems. Chris is the associate director of the UCLA Experiential Technologies Center, and has worked for or collaborated on cultural mapping projects set in Bolivia, Peru, Albania, Iceland, Spain, Italy, and Turkey. He is currently developing a hybrid geotemporal publication entitled *Spectacle in the Forum: Visualizing the Roman Aristocratic Funeral of the Middle Republic*, which is a study of material and literary contexts set within a digital laboratory. Chris's work explores the evolution of scholarly tools and engages in the development of new methods of historical visualization, knowledge representation, and geotemporal argumentation.

**Esther Katz** is the editor and director of the Margaret Sanger Papers (http://www.nyu.edu/projects/sanger/), a scholarly editing project located at New York University. She is an experienced documentary editor and project director who has served on the resident faculty for the Institute for the Editing of Historical Documents of the National Historical Publications and Records Commission (NHPRC) and as president of the Association for Documentary Editing. Esther previously worked on the printed editions of *The Papers of William Livingston* (New Jersey Historical Commission, 1979–1988), *The Letters of William Lloyd Garrison* (Harvard University Press, 1971–1981), and the microfilm edition of the National Women's Trade Union League Papers (Schlesinger Library, 1981). At New York University she teaches twentieth-century United States and women's history courses, as well as the seminar on Historical Editing in the Electronic Era for the archives and public history program.

**Melanie Kill** is an assistant professor of English at the University of Maryland, College Park. Her scholarship is in digital rhetorics and rhetorical genre theory, with specific interests in the relationships between genre change and new writing technologies, as well as social change and rhetorical innovation. Her work has appeared in *College Composition and Communication*, *JAC: A Journal of Rhetoric, Culture, and Politics*, and the book *Genre: An Introduction to History, Theory, Research, and Pedagogy* (Parlor Press, 2010). In 2011, she joined an interdisciplinary team of scholars for the Wikimedia Summer of Research, which produced WikiHadoop (https://github.com/whym/wikihadoop/) and a range of findings about new Wikipedia editors. She teaches courses on web authoring, information design, digital writing, and Internet culture, and has been incorporating Wikipedia-based assignments into her courses since 2007.

**Virginia Kuhn** serves as associate director of the Institute for Multimedia Literacy (IML), and assistant professor at the University of Southern California's School of Cinematic Arts. She directs the IML's Honors in Multimedia Scholarship program and teaches a range of undergraduate and graduate courses, all of which marry theory and practice. Her most recent work centers on large-scale video analytics. With an award from the National Science Foundation's Extreme Science and Engineering Discovery Environment, her multi-institutional team is creating processes to harness both machine analytics and crowd-sourced tagging, in order to make sense of massive video archives that arise on a daily basis. Virginia serves on the editorial boards of *Kairos: A Journal of Rhetoric, Technology, and Pedagogy*; *PRE/TEXT: A Journal of Rhetorical Theory*; and *The Journal of Interactive Technology and Pedagogy*. Her work can also be found in *Enculturation: A Journal of Rhetoric, Writing and Culture*; *ebr (electronic book review)*; the *International Journal of Learning and Media*; and *Academic Commons*. She also co-chairs the Media Literacy and Pedagogical Outreach Scholarly Interest Group of the Society for Cinema and Media Studies. In 2005, Virginia successfully defended one of the first media-rich, born-digital dissertations in the United States, challenging archiving and copyright conventions. Her dissertation, *Ways of Composing: Visual Literacy in the Digital Age*, was created in *TK3*, the precursor to the USC-based, open source media-authoring program, *Sophie* (http://sophieproject.cntv. usc.edu/). Committed to helping shape emergent tools for scholarly endeavors, she recently published the first article created in the authoring platform, *Scalar* (http://scalar.usc.edu/).

**Simon Mahony** is a teaching fellow at the Centre for Digital Humanities at University College London. His research interests are in the application of new technologies to the study of the ancient world, using new web-based mechanisms and digital resources to build and sustain learning communities, and collaborative and innovative working. He is active in the field of distance learning and a member of the University of London's Centre for Distance Education. He is one of the founders of the Digital Classicist (http://www.digitalclassicist.org/), organizing its summer seminar series and various conference panels. He is also an editor at the Stoa Consortium weblog (http://www.stoa.org/) and an associate fellow of the Institute of Classical Studies, University of London.

**Willard McCarty** is professor of humanities computing at King's College London, and a professor within the School of Computing, Engineering, and Mathematics at the University of Western Sydney. He is editor of the British journal, *Interdisciplinary Science Reviews* (2008–), founding editor of the online seminar *Humanist* (1987–), and founding convener of the London Seminar in Digital Text and Scholarship (2006–). He is recipient of the 2005 Canadian Award for Outstanding Achievement (Computing in the Arts and Humanities) as well as the Rockefeller Foundation 2006 Richard W. Lyman Award. He is editor of *Text and Genre in Reconstruction* (Open Book Publishers, 2010) and author of the first comprehensive theoretical treatment of his field, *Humanities Computing* (Palgrave, 2005). He lectures widely in Europe, North America and Australia. For more details, see his website (http://www.mccarty.org.uk/).

**Elena Pierazzo** has a PhD in Italian Philology. Her expertise is in Italian Renaissance texts and text encoding, and she has published and presented papers at international conferences in Renaissance literature, digital critical editions, text encoding theory and Italian linguistics. She is currently a lecturer at the Department of Digital Humanities at King's College London, where she chairs the Teaching Committee and is director of the MA in Digital Humanities. Elena is also teacher of XML-related technologies at both undergraduate and master's level, and was formerly a researcher at the University of Pisa, engaged in both teaching and research. She is actively involved in the TEI user community, with a special interest in the transcription of modern and medieval manuscripts. She serves as TEI Chair for the 2012-13 term.

**Todd Presner** is an associate professor of Germanic languages at the University of California, Los Angeles (UCLA), and is chair of the faculty advisory committee for the Center for Digital Humanities. He is the author of two books and director of two digital mapping projects that utilize geographic information systems (GIS) to explore the layered cultural histories of city spaces: Hypermedia Berlin (http://www.berlin.ucla.edu/) and HyperCities (http://www.hypercities.com/). Todd's current research and teaching focus on the development of the geospatial web, augmented reality, issues of temporality and GIS, and the technical media that enable visualizations of complex city spaces. At UCLA, he directs an initiative called Media, Technology, and Culture, which is charged with creating new intellectual tools, pedagogical and curricular practices, research methodologies, and disciplinary paradigms for the humanities in the twenty-first century.

**Stephen Ramsay** is an associate professor of English and a fellow at the Center for Digital Research in the Humanities at the University of Nebraska–Lincoln. He is the author of *Reading Machines: Toward an Algorithmic Criticism* (University of Illinois Press, 2011), and has written and lectured widely on subjects related to text analysis, visualization, and software design for the digital humanities. An experienced software developer, Stephen has worked on a number of digital projects in the humanities since the early nineties, including, most recently, the MONK Project (http://www.monkproject.org/).

**Malte Rehbein** is an assistant professor of history and faculty fellow of the Center for Digital Research in the Humanities at the University of Nebraska-Lincoln. He was previously director of the Center for Digital Editing at the University of Würzburg, where he taught courses in the BA in Digital Humanities. He studied history and mathematics at the University of Göttingen, where he also received his doctorate in history with a digital edition of the *Göttinger kundige bok*, a late medieval town law book. After his studies, Malte worked for several private companies as a software developer, project manager, and consultant, before turning to digital humanities. He concluded a two-year Marie Curie Research Fellowship with the Transfer of Expertise in Technologies of Editing (TEXTE) Project at the National University of Ireland, Galway. He is an active member of the special interest group on "Genetic Editions" of the Text Encoding Initiative (TEI), an elected member of the steering committee of *Digital Medievalist* (http://www.digitalmedievalist.org/), and editor-in-chief of the *Digital Medievalist Journal*.

**Janice Reiff** is an associate professor of history and statistics at the University of California, Los Angeles (UCLA). Her interests in cultural and conceptual mapping, geographic information systems, and the use of digital technologies in teaching reach back to her dissertation, for which she mapped settlement and migration patterns in nineteenth-century Seattle. Her first book, *Structuring the Past: the Use of Computers in History* (American Historical Association, 1991), introduced historians to quantitative and geographic analysis and also shaped her next two projects: developing the database for an archeological dig at

Tell Nimrin, Jordan; co-editing an atlas entitled *The Settling of North America* (Macmillan, 1995; with Helen Tanner, Dirk Hoerder, John Long, and Henry Dobyns). Janice co-edited the *Encyclopedia of Chicago* (http://encyclopedia.chicagohistory.org/), a project of the Newberry Library, with James R. Grossman and Ann Durkin Keating. The University of Chicago Press published the *Encyclopedia* in print in 2004, while the Chicago Historical Society published it online in 2005.

**Geoffrey Rockwell** is professor of philosophy and humanities computing at the University of Alberta. He was previously director of the Humanities Media and Computing Centre (1994–2004) at McMaster University. He is the author of *Defining Dialogue: From Socrates to the Internet* (Humanity Books, 2003), associate interactive media editor for *Digital Humanities Quarterly*, and was the project leader for the Text Analysis Portal for Research (TAPoR) project. He is currently the Director of the Kule Institute for Advanced Study.

**Jon Saklofske** is an associate professor in the Department of English and Theatre at Acadia University, Nova Scotia. His specialization in the writing of the British Romantic period and continuing interest in the ways that William Blake's composite art illuminates the relationship between words and images on the printed page has inspired current research into larger correlations between media forms and cultural perceptions. In addition, he is actively pursuing the use of digital games in university-level research and learning. Recent and forthcoming work includes a reconsideration of virtual world design principles and the development and implementation of NewRadial (http://sourceforge.net/projects/newradial/), a digital visualization tool that promotes collaborative scholarship relating to William Blake's composite art.

**Stéfan Sinclair** is an associate professor of digital humanities at McGill University. His research focuses primarily on the design, development, and theorization of tools for the digital humanities, especially for text analysis and visualization. He has led or contributed significantly to projects such as Voyeur Tools, Simulated Environment for Theatre, and BonPatron. Other professional activities include serving as associate editor for *Literary and Linguistic Computing* and *Digital Humanities Quarterly*, as well as serving on the executive boards of SDH/SEMI, ACH, ADHO, and centerNET.

**Lisa Spiro** is director of National Institute for Technology in Liberal Education (NITLE) Labs, where she works with the liberal arts community to explore emerging educational technologies and develop collaborative approaches to integrating learning, scholarship and technology. Lisa has presented and published widely on the digital humanities, including contributions to *Debates in the Digital Humanities* (2012), *#alt-academy: Alternate Academic Careers for Humanities Scholars* (2012), *Collaborative Approaches to the Digital in English Studies* (2011), and *The American Literature Scholar in the Digital Age* (2010). She is the founding editor of the *Digital Research Tools* (DiRT) wiki and authors the *Digital Scholarship in the Humanities* blog. Before coming to NITLE, Lisa directed the Digital Media Center at Rice University's Fondren Library, where she oversaw the campus' central multimedia lab, led workshops on topics such as digital storytelling and digital research tools, and contributed to digital library projects. Lisa serves on the Executive Council for the Association of Computers and the Humanities and the Program Committee for the Joint Conference on Digital Libraries.

**Joshua Sternfeld** has served since 2009 as a senior program officer at the National Endowment for the Humanities Division of Preservation and Access in Washington, DC. Prior to his arrival at the Endowment, Josh served as assistant director and postdoctoral scholar for the UCLA Center for Information as Evidence and the Information Studies Department from 2007–2009. He holds a BA in History from Princeton University and received his PhD in 2007 from UCLA. While at UCLA, he worked as program manager for the first annual Archival Education and Research Institute (AERI), an international gathering of faculty and doctoral students in archival studies. He also conducted a series of original graduate seminars that explored the methodological, theoretical, and practical considerations of digital history from a multi-disciplinary perspective. Joshua has conducted workshops and delivered papers on digital history and its intersection with archival and new media theory. His many interests include digital preservation, digital humanities, jazz and American studies, modern German studies, sound technology and history, oral history, and cultural heritage.

**Elaine Sullivan** is a postdoctoral fellow in the Department of Near Eastern Languages and Cultures at the University of California, Los Angeles (UCLA). Currently, she is the project coordinator of the W. M. Keck Program for Digital Cultural Mapping. Elaine is also the project coordinator of the Digital Karnak Project (http://dlib.etc.ucla.edu/projects/Karnak/), a National Endowment for the Humanities funded online teaching and learning resource with virtual reality models and instructional materials documenting the ancient Egyptian temple of Karnak. She is currently developing an undergraduate research class for the Keck program that will use geographic information systems to analyze viewsheds between funerary monuments at the ancient Egyptian necropolis of Saqqara.

**Willeke Wendrich** is an associate professor of Egyptian Archaeology at the University of California, Los Angeles (UCLA). She is the editor-in-chief of the UCLA Encyclopedia of Egyptology (http://uee.ucla.edu/), an award-winning digital encyclopedia supported by the National Endowment for the Humanities. Since 2005, Willeke has served as the director of the UCLA Digital Humanities Incubator Group, where she is closely involved with developing faculty research projects, many of which involve undergraduate students.

**Peter J. Wosh** directs the graduate program in archives and public history at New York University, where he has taught since 1994. His archival career has included positions at the American Bible Society in New York (1984–1994) and at Seton Hall University and the Roman Catholic Archdiocese of Newark in South Orange, New Jersey (1978–1984). His research and writing interests involve both archival topics and American religious history, and his books include *Waldo Gifford Leland and the Origins of the American Archival Profession* (Society of American Archivists, 2011), *Covenant House: Journey of a Faith-Based Charity* (University of Pennsylvania Press, 2005), *Privacy and Confidentiality Perspectives: Archivists and Archival Records* (Society of American Archivists, 2005) with Menzi Behrnd-Klodt, and *Spreading the Word: The Bible Business in Nineteenth-Century America* (Cornell University Press, 1994). Within the Society of American Archivists, he has served on the Governing Council and as editor of Print and Electronic Publications. He is a fellow of the Society of American Archivists and a recipient of the 2000 Fellows' Ernst Posner Award for an outstanding essay in the *American Archivist*.

# Introduction

# </Parentheses>: Digital Humanities and the Place of Pedagogy

*Brett D. Hirsch*

It is fitting that this collection of essays on "digital humanities"[1] pedagogy should have its roots in discussions that followed the 2009 Digital Humanities Summer Institute at the University of Victoria, British Columbia, where I was then a postdoctoral fellow. In the course of his plenary lecture, "How to Win Friends," Donald Bruce noted how little focus there was on teaching in the extant critical literature on the digital humanities. To test this observation, after the lecture I turned to two volumes deservedly recognized as reference works in the "field,"[2] namely, the Blackwell *Companion to Digital Humanities* and *Companion to Digital Literary Studies*.[3] Indeed, despite their exhaustive

---

1 While I am aware of the arguments championed by some scholars, particularly Patrik Svensson, that there is an epistemological distinction to be made between "digital humanities" and "humanities computing," I treat the terms synonymously throughout this introduction. See Patrik Svensson, "Humanities Computing as Digital Humanities," *Digital Humanities Quarterly* 3, no. 3 (2009), http://digitalhumanities.org/dhq/vol/3/3/000065/000065.html.

2 I use the term "field" to describe digital humanities broadly as a "field of inquiry," to denote "an area or sphere of action, operation or investigation; a (wider or narrower) range of opportunities, or of objects, for labour, study or contemplation; a department or subject of activity or speculation" (OED, "field, n." III.15.a.). My purpose is to allow for an inclusive conception of digital humanities, whether as a discipline (in the institutional and intellectual sense) and/or a set of methodologies shared between the humanities, computer science, and library and information sciences.

3 Susan Schreibman, Ray Siemens, and John Unsworth, ed. *A Companion to Digital Humanities* (Malden: Blackwell, 2004), and Ray Siemens and Susan Schreibman, ed. *A Companion to Digital Literary Studies* (Malden: Blackwell, 2007). Both volumes are freely available online at http://digitalhumanities.org/companion/ and http://digitalhumanities.org/companionDLS/ respectively.

treatment of an equally impressive array of topics by leading experts, the focus of both volumes is primarily on the theories, principles, and research practices associated with the digital humanities—past and present—and not on issues of pedagogy. Consider, for example, the comparative frequencies with which the words "pedagogy" and "research" (and their synonyms and variant forms) appear in the *Companion to Digital Humanities* (Table 1).

| Word | Instances |
|------|-----------|
| research | 504 |
| scholarship | 99 |
| researchers | 73 |
| teaching | 66 |
| learning | 60 |
| training | 39 |
| researcher | 35 |
| education | 32 |
| educational | 29 |
| pedagogical | 14 |
| pedagogy | 8 |
| teach | 7 |
| teachers | 7 |
| taught | 6 |
| teacher | 5 |
| teaches | 4 |
| learners | 3 |
| researching | 2 |
| self-taught | 2 |
| learner | 1 |
| Corpus total | 297, 399 |
| Unique words | 20, 906 |

**Table 1.** Frequency of words in *A Companion to Digital Humanities* (Blackwell, 2004) produced using Voyant Tools (http://www.voyant-tools.org/).

As shown in Table 1, out of a corpus of 297, 399 words (of which 20, 906 are unique), "research" occurs 504 times, whereas "teaching" and "pedagogy" occur 66 and 8 times respectively.[4] A more comprehensive survey of recent

---

4   Of course, word frequencies are only suggestive of a trend of usage and are not offered here as exhaustive or conclusive evidence in and of themselves.

literature, gleaned from articles published in *Computers and the Humanities, Digital Humanities Quarterly, Digital Studies/Le champ numérique, Literary and Linguistic Computing, TEXT Technology,* and elsewhere, as well as in the growing body of scholarly monographs in the field, suggests a more telling trend; one that I will refer to as "bracketing."

By "bracketing" I refer to the almost systematic relegation of the word "teaching" (or its synonyms) to the status of afterthought, tacked-on to a statement about the digital humanities after the word "research" (or its synonyms), often in parentheses. For example, in his recent discussion of "What is Digital Humanities and What's it Doing in English Departments?" Matthew G. Kirschenbaum concludes,

> Whatever else it might be then, the digital humanities today is about a scholarship *(and a pedagogy)* that is publicly visible in ways to which we are generally unaccustomed, a scholarship *and pedagogy* that are bound up with infrastructure in ways that are deeper and more explicit than we are generally accustomed to, a scholarship *and pedagogy* that are collaborative and depend on networks of people and that live an active 24/7 life online.[5]

While Kirschenbaum's paper seeks to provide only a brief overview of the state of the digital humanities and is directed at a particular readership of English faculty, the concluding paragraph quoted above is the only instance where pedagogy is mentioned. Of course, we should be just as concerned about the pervasiveness with which pedagogy is excluded from discussions of digital humanities entirely, but the result of these practices is the same. To bracket pedagogy in critical discussions of the digital humanities or to completely exclude it from these discussions reinforces an antagonistic distinction between teaching and research, in which the time, effort, and funding spent on the one cannibalizes the opportunities of the other. Although there have been suggestions to the contrary,[6] research remains the principal vehicle for professional nobility and mobility—that is, for garnering the esteem (or envy) of colleagues, as well as increasing the

---

5   Matthew G. Kirschenbaum, "What is Digital Humanities and What's It Doing in English Departments?" *ADE Bulletin* 150 (2010): 55, 60, my emphasis.

6   The relative value accorded to research and teaching is an issue of perennial concern in the academic profession. Consequently, literature on the topic has become a genre unto itself, frequently appearing in scholarly journals and more professional venues. Representative examples include Lionel S. Lewis, *Marginal Worth: Teaching and the Academic Labor Market* (New Brunswick: Transaction, 1996); James J. F. Forest, *I Prefer to Teach: An International Study of Faculty Preferences for Teaching* (New York: Routledge, 2002); Michael Bernard-Donals, "It's Not about the Book," *Profession* (2008): 172–84; and, Cathy N. Davidson, "Research is Teaching," *ADE Bulletin* 149 (2010): 53–60.

chances of successful bids for funding, tenure, and promotion—in the digital humanities. Even so, we owe it to ourselves (and indeed to our students) to pay more than lip service to pedagogy in our field. Whether as a student or an educator, pedagogy should not be parenthetical to the experience of higher education. If we acknowledge that pedagogy is important, our goal should be to ensure that the primary disciplinary sites in the digital humanities—our journals, conferences, books and book series—reflect this privileged status. The primary aim of this collection then, is to contribute to this ongoing project to move pedagogy beyond the brackets, out of marginalization and exclusion, to the fore of the digital humanities.

## The Pedagogical (Re-)Turn

"To invoke the importance of pedagogy," Henry A. Giroux has remarked, "is to raise questions not simply about how students learn but also about how educators (in the broad sense of the term) construct the ideological and political positions from which they speak."[7] In any field, these ideological and political positions shift over time to meet new challenges and changing expectations, both within and outside of the academy. The increasing need to justify the relevance and value of the humanities, with an attendant focus on quantifiable "research outputs" and pressure to publish, is an important example of such a change, but one that goes only so far to explain why pedagogical issues have been consistently overshadowed by those of research in our journals, conferences and books. Even as the drive for greater publication opens up more and more field-specific avenues to do so,[8] the gap between the available literature on pedagogy and research in the field, paradoxically, is widening.

This has not always been the case. From the late 1980s through the mid 1990s, pedagogy held pride of place in the digital humanities–if the emergence of "Teaching Computers and the Humanities" workshops and conferences sponsored by the Association for Computers and the

---

7   Henry A. Giroux, "Rethinking the Boundaries of Educational Discourse: Modernism, Postmodernism, and Feminism," in *Margins in the Classroom: Teaching Literature*, ed. Kostas Myrsiades and Linda S. Myrsiades (Minneapolis: University of Minnesota Press, 1994), 45.

8   For example, in addition to the journals noted before, the field now boasts dedicated book series such as Digital Research in the Arts and Humanities (Ashgate), Topics in the Digital Humanities (University of Illinois Press), and the digitalculturebooks Digital Humanities series (University of Michigan Library and University of Michigan Press).

Humanities (ACH),[9] and the establishment of the annual Computers and Teaching in the Humanities (CATH) conference are any indication.[10] This period of growing interest in digital humanities pedagogy culminated with the 2001 conference on "The Humanities Computing Curriculum/ The Computing Curriculum in the Arts and Humanities" at Malaspina University-College.[11] It is only relatively recently that pedagogy has resurfaced as a focus in digital humanities conferences and panel sessions at broader disciplinary meetings, for example, at the second Texas Institute for Literary and Textual Studies (TILTS) symposium on "Digital Humanities: Teaching and Learning" in 2011,[12] and the acceptance of two proposed roundtable sessions on the topic for the 2012 annual meeting of the Modern Languages Association of America (MLA) in Seattle.[13] Vassar College, the venue of the first "Teaching Computers and the Humanities Courses" workshop back in 1986, was an appropriate institutional host for the first THATCamp Pedagogy, which took place in October 2011.[14] Likewise, chapters on aspects of digital humanities pedagogy have recently appeared in edited collections such as *Teaching Literature and Language*

---

9  These include the "Teaching Computers and the Humanities Courses" Workshop, Vassar College, Poughkeepsie (New York, July 31–August 2, 1986); "Computers in Liberal Arts Education" Conference, York College, City University of New York (New York, March 26–27, 1987); "Teaching Computers and the Humanities Courses" Conference of the ACH, Oberlin College, Oberlin (Ohio, June 9–11, 1988); and "Teaching Computers and the Humanities" Conference of the ACH, Fordham University, New York (New York, June 23–25, 1990).

10  These include "Computers and Teaching in the Humanities" CATH conference, Southampton University (April 10–11, 1987); "Redefining the Humanities" CATH conference, Southampton University (December 13–15, 1988); "From Rhetoric to Reality" CATH conference, University of St Andrews (St Andrews, April 2–5, 1990); "Strategies for Implementation" CATH conference, University of Durham, Durham (December 16–18, 1991); "Teaching with Computers: Experiences and Opportunities" CATH conference, Manchester Metropolitan University, Manchester (December 15–17, 1992); "Courseware in Action" CATH conference, Glasgow University (Glasgow, September 10–12, 1994); and "Computers and the Changing Curriculum" CATH conference, Royal Holloway, University of London (London, September 5–7, 1995).

11  "The Humanities Computing Curriculum / The Computing Curriculum in the Arts and Humanities" Conference, Malaspina University-College, Nanaimo (British Columbia, November 9–10, 2001).

12  "Digital Humanities: Teaching and Learning." The Texas Institute for Literary and Textual Studies Symposium, University of Texas at Austin (Texas, March 10–12, 2011).

13  These roundtable sessions include "Digital Pedagogy: An Electronic Roundtable," proposed and chaired by Katherine D. Harris, and "Building Digital Humanities in the Undergraduate Classroom: An Electronic Roundtable," proposed and chaired by Brian Croxall and Kathi Inman Berens.

14  THATCamp Pedagogy, Vassar College, Poughkeepsie (New York, October 15–16, 2011), http://pedagogy2011.thatcamp.org/.

*Online* in 2009,[15] *Debates in the Digital Humanities* and *Learning through Digital Media* in 2011,[16] and *Hacking the Academy* in 2012.[17]

We may well ask why it is that pedagogy seems to fall in and out of prominence in the conferences and critical literature—the formal sites for knowledge transfer—within our field, but I am only able to speculate in this introduction. Perhaps, as has been witnessed in other disciplines, it is the result of administrative developments to support digital humanities pedagogy. It cannot be coincidental that the peak period of formal interest in the late 1980s through the mid 1990s corresponds with the emergence of dedicated digital humanities centers and institutes, under the auspices of which undergraduate and graduate training could be (and still is) developed and delivered. For example, the Center for Computing in the Humanities at the University of Toronto and the Humanities Media and Computing Centre at McMaster University were founded in 1986; the Centre for Literary and Linguistic Computing (CLLC) at the University of Newcastle in 1989; the Centre for Computing in the Humanities (now the Department of Digital Humanities) at King's College London in 1991; the Archaeological Computing Laboratory at the University of Sydney and the Institute for Advanced Technology in the Humanities (IATH) at the University of Virginia in 1992; the Center for History and New Media at George Mason University in 1994; the Humanities Advanced Technology and Information Institute (HATII) at the University of Glasgow in 1997 and the Maryland Institute for Technology in the Humanities at the University of Maryland in 1999—to note but a few. Willard McCarty's chapter in this collection offers a case study of this symbiotic relationship between dedicated administrative centers and digital humanities pedagogy, in which he describes the historical development of the world's first PhD in Digital Humanities program out of the Centre for Computing in the Humanities (now the Department of Digital Humanities) at King's College London.[18]

---

15   Ian Lancashire, ed., *Teaching Literature and Language Online* (New York: Modern Language Association of America, 2009).

16   Matthew K. Gold, ed., *Debates in the Digital Humanities* (Minneapolis: University of Minnesota Press, 2012); Trebor Scholz, ed., *Learning Through Digital Media: Experiments in Technology and Pedagogy* (New York: Institute for Distributed Creativity, 2011), http://www.learningthroughdigitalmedia.net/.

17   Dan Cohen and Tom Scheinfeldt, ed., *Hacking the Academy: The Edited Volume* (Ann Arbor: University of Michigan Press, 2012). See also the originating website: *Hacking the Academy* (May 21–28, 2010) http://hackingtheacademy.org/.

18   See also Geoffrey Rockwell and Stéfan Sinclair's chapter, "Acculturation and the Digital Humanities Community" for case studies of the undergraduate program in multimedia

Dedicated centers such as these, however, are not the result of Aristotelian spontaneous generation; rather, they arise out of the recognition and endorsement of a critical mass of active researchers in a given field as a collective entity by their home institutions. Similarly, courses don't teach themselves but rely on the availability of suitable teaching staff. It is also important to distinguish between the delivery of digital humanities courses, which may be maintained by as few teaching staff as a single instructor, and the promotion of dedicated digital humanities degrees and structured teaching programs, which require not only deliberate sponsorship at the departmental or faculty level, but also the efforts of multiple teaching, support, and administrative staff. Since dedicated digital humanities degrees require far more institutional and administrative investment to maintain, it is not surprising that there are still so few undergraduate and graduate degrees in digital humanities offered at universities worldwide— the majority of these programs made possible only through the support of digital humanities research hubs.[19] As more dedicated digital humanities departments, centers, and institutes emerge, the administrative and institutional capacity for promoting, teaching, and maintaining field-specific degree programs will increase.

The peak in formal interest in digital humanities pedagogy during the late 1980s and mid-1990s might also be explained by changes in humanities curricula during this time. As was noted in the 1999 Advanced Computing in the Humanities (ACO*HUM) report,

> Whereas research in the field of humanities computing has a long history, beginning with projects in automatic translation as far back as 1947, its inclusion within official courses in humanities curricula is relatively recent.[20]

---

at McMaster University and the MA in Humanities Computing at the University of Alberta.

19  Representative examples of existing dedicated digital humanities degrees include the MA in Digital Humanities programs at Loyola University Chicago (supported by the Center for Textual Studies and Digital Humanities); the National University of Ireland, Maynooth (supported by An Foras Feasa, the Institute for Research in Irish Historical and Cultural Traditions); and the University of Virginia (supported by the Institute for Advanced Technology in the Humanities); the MA in Humanities Computing at the University of Alberta (supported by the Canadian Institute for Research in Computing and the Arts); the MA/MSc in Digital Humanities at University College London (supported by the UCL Centre for Digital Humanities); and the MA and PhD in Digital Humanities at King's College London (supported by the Department of Digital Humanities).

20  Tito Orlandi, Joseph Norment Bell, Lou Burnard, Dino Buzzetti, Koenraad de Smedt, Ingo Kropac, Jacques Souillot, and Manfred Thaller, "European Studies on Formal Methods in the Humanities," in *Computing in Humanities Education: A European Perspective,*

The development of digital humanities curricula, at both undergraduate and graduate levels, has been better surveyed elsewhere and will not be addressed here; the reader is directed to the ACO*HUM report quoted above,[21] Willard McCarty and Matthew G. Kirschenbaum's article on "Institutional Models for Humanities Computing"[22] and the discussion of undergraduate curricula in Tanya Clement's "Multiliteracies in the Undergraduate Digital Humanities Curriculum," another chapter in this collection.

In addition to the administrative and curricular developments outlined above, growing support from institutions, professional organizations, and granting agencies has undoubtedly reshaped the pedagogical landscape of the digital humanities. The inauguration of organizations and advocacy groups at national and international levels, such as the Association for Computers and the Humanities (ACH; founded 1973), the Association for Literary and Linguistic Computing (ALLC; founded 1978), the Society for Digital Humanities/Société pour l'étude des médias intractifs (SDH-SEMI; founded 1986), the Alliance of Digital Humanities Organizations (ADHO; founded 2002), and more recently the Australian Association for Digital Humanities (AADH; founded 2011) and the Japanese Association for Digital Humanities (JADH; founded 2011), among others, showcase an increasing professionalization of the field and support for primary disciplinary sites like conferences and formal venues for publication; they also represent key players in the promotion of secondary disciplinary sites—that is, training workshops, skills seminars, and summer schools.

Some of these—such as the Princeton–Rutgers Center for Electronic Texts (CETH) Summer Seminar (from 1992 to 1997), the Digital Humanities Summer Institute at the University of Victoria (founded in 2001), the Digital Humanities Observatory Summer School at the Royal Irish Academy (from 2008 to 2011) and the European Summer School "Culture & Technology" at the Universität Leipzig (founded in 2009)—were, or still are, annual fixtures in the digital humanities calendar, offering opportunities both to

---

ed. Koenraad de Smedt, Helen Gardiner, Espen Ore, Tito Orlandi, Harold Short, Jacques Souillot, and William Vaugh (Bergen: University of Bergen, HIT Centre, 1999), 13–62.

21  Koenraad de Smedt, Helen Gardiner, Espen Ore, Tito Orlandi, Harold Short, Jacques Souillot, and William Vaugh, ed., *Computing in Humanities Education: A European Perspective* (Bergen: University of Bergen, HIT Centre, 1999), http://www.hd.uib.no/AcoHum/book/.

22  Willard McCarty and Matthew G. Kirschenbaum, "Institutional Models for Humanities Computing," *Literary and Linguistic Computing* 18, no. 4 (2003): 465–89. The printed list has since been superseded by a wiki-based listing of centres, societies, tools, discussion groups and publications, available at http://digitalhumanities.pbwiki.com/.

teach and learn digital humanities methods and skills.[23] As with formal conferences and symposia, these workshops, training seminars, and summer schools could not be possible without substantial support from their host institutions.

Granting agencies, too, are becoming increasingly important sources of funding to support research and development in digital humanities pedagogy. In the United States, after establishing the Digital Humanities Initiative (now the Office of Digital Humanities), the National Endowment for the Humanities (NEH) in 2007 introduced the "Digital Humanities Start-Up Grants" program to fund, among other things, initiatives exploring "innovative uses of technology for public programming and education using both traditional and new media."[24] The following year, the NEH launched the "Institutes for Advanced Topics in the Digital Humanities" program to support "training programs for scholars and advanced graduate students to broaden and extend their knowledge of digital humanities" and to "enable humanities scholars in the United States to incorporate advances like these into their scholarship and teaching."[25] In the United Kingdom, the Joint Information Systems Committee (JISC) offers a number of funding programs for which projects in digital humanities pedagogy are directly suited. These include an "e-Learning" program to enable the "development and effective use of digital technologies to support learning and teaching,"[26] an "e-Content" program to "encourage partnerships for the clustering and enriching of existing digitized content and engaging the wider community in the co-creation of digital content,"[27] projects to "increase the use of geospatial tools, infrastructure (data and services) and information for learners, teachers and researchers,"[28] and grants to support

---

23  For a discussion of the teaching and learning experience at one of these summer schools, see Malte Rehbein and Christiane Fritz's chapter, "Hands-On Teaching Digital Humanities: A Didactic Analysis of a Summer School Course on Digital Editing."

24  Office of Digital Humanities, "Institutes for Advanced Topics in the Digital Humanities," National Endowment for the Humanities, November 3, 2010, http://www.neh.gov/grants/guidelines/IATDH.html.

25  JISC Learning and Teaching Committee, "e-Learning Programme," Joint Information Systems Committee, May 13, 2011, http://www.jisc.ac.uk/whatwedo/programmes/elearning.aspx.

26  JISC Infrastructure and Resources Committee, "e-Content Programme 2011," Joint Information Systems Committee, March 2, 2011, http://www.jisc.ac.uk/whatwedo/programmes/digitisation/econtent11.aspx.

27  JISC Infrastructure and Resources Committee, "e-Content Programme 2011," Joint Information Systems Committee, March 2, 2011, http://www.jisc.ac.uk/whatwedo/programmes/digitisation/econtent11.aspx.

28  JISC Learning and Teaching Committee, "Learning and Teaching Innovation Grants," Joint Information Systems Committee, May 19, 2011, http://www.jisc.ac.uk/whatwedo/programmes/elearning/ltig.aspx.

projects "dealing with any aspect of e-learning."[29] Dedicated programs such as these promote and validate pedagogical work in our field, and it is in our interest as digital humanists to champion their adoption by other granting agencies.[30]

## The Importance of Pedagogy

As the recent growth in institutional, curricular and funding support outlined above makes clear, there is an increasing recognition of the importance of pedagogy in our field. But why is pedagogy important? What opportunities might a critical pedagogy offer our field? What is at stake? According to the 1999 ACO*HUM report, "Humanities computing is most clearly in need of institutional stabilization."[31] For the authors of the ACO*HUM report, institutional stabilization might address a critical problem in our field: since "few of its followers are sufficiently aware of its long and rich tradition," we are often unaware that "many of today's perennial questions" were, in fact, answered long before. "Every now and again," the report continues,

> A fresh wave of discussion is ignited by authors or theoreticians who simply assume that they can ignore [the then] forty years of tradition and start from scratch. This lack of perception is particularly unfortunate for the individual

---

29   JISC Learning and Teaching Committee, "Learning and Teaching Innovation Grants," Joint Information Systems Committee, May 19, 2011, http://www.jisc.ac.uk/whatwedo/programmes/elearning/ltig.aspx.

30   Many national granting agencies continue to focus primarily on research-orientated projects, without dedicated programs for pedagogy and research training. For example, while the Social Sciences and Humanities Research Council of Canada/Conseil de recherches en sciences humaines du Canada (SSHRC-CRSH) has named "digital media" as a priority area for funding under its new "Insight" and "Connection" programs, both the priority area statement and the program guidelines are directed at funding "research and related activities." Without any explicit mention of pedagogy or research training in the documentation, it is unclear what "related activities" might include in this context ("Digital Media Priority Area," Social Sciences and Humanities Research Council of Canada/Conseil de recherches en sciences humaines du Canada, May 5, 2011, http://www.sshrc-crsh.gc.ca/funding-financement/programs-programmes/priority_areas-domaines_prioritaires/digital_research-recherche_numerique-eng.aspx). Although SSHRC-CRSH promises to announce new "Workshops and Conference Grants" and "Outreach and Tools Grants" under the "Connection Program" in 2012, it is equally unclear at this early stage whether these grants will support pedagogical projects in addition to research projects ("Connection Program," Social Sciences and Humanities Research Council of Canada/Conseil de recherches en sciences humaines du Canada, May 5, 2011, http://www.sshrc-crsh.gc.ca/funding-financement/umbrella_programs-programme_cadre/connection-connexion-eng.aspx).

31   Orlandi et al., "European Studies on Formal Methods in the Humanities."

researcher, as it usually means that newcomers to the field have to painfully rediscover ancient solutions simply because they have not been adequately transmitted through the generations.[32]

For a field that can trace its roots to research undertaken in the 1940s and boasts specialization in areas of humanities data archiving, preservation, and management to remain unable to adequately document, retrieve, and incorporate our own findings—our own histories—is a particularly embarrassing state of affairs.[33]

Whether the ACO*HUM report is an exaggeration for rhetorical effect or not, it is time that we begin to recover and write our histories—histories not of answers but histories that better illuminate the questions[34]—and begin to teach them as well. There is no better way to stabilize a field than through pedagogy. The foundations of any field or discipline in the humanities are its canons, and canons are, according to Roland Barthes' aphorism, "what gets taught." Questions of value and the scholarly debates over the origins, consequences, and appropriateness of canons in the humanities are far too complex to adequately address in this introduction. Suffice to say, regardless of how we might feel about them—love them, hate them, revise them, reify them—canons play an integral role in shaping and reshaping our fields. It is foolish to think that a digital humanities canon does not already exist; we could all readily list those volumes, collections, articles, and conference papers that are most frequently cited (and sighted) in papers and syllabi alike. It is prudent for us, as a field, to start thinking critically not only about what we teach under the banner of "digital humanities" and how we teach it, but also to consider the broader institutional implications and political consequences, of doing so. As Roger Simon has observed,

"[P]edagogy" is a more complex and extensive term than "teaching," referring to the integration in practice of particular curriculum content and design, classroom strategies and techniques, a time and space for the practice of

32  Orlandi et al., "European Studies on Formal Methods in the Humanities." Of course, the authors' reference to "ancient solutions" is an exaggeration for rhetorical effect, given the (relative) infancy both of digital humanities as a field and of humanities as a discipline.
33  The particular complaint of the ACO*HUM authors is, however, the failure of Anglophone digital humanities scholars to read (and, more importantly, cite) the work of their non-Anglophone counterparts. This is a valid concern for a "global" field like digital humanities. For a representative example of this concern as expressed by non-Anglophone scholars, see Tito Orlandi, "The Scholarly Environment of Humanities Computing: A Reaction to Willard McCarty's Talk on The Computational Transformation of the Humanities," n.d., http://rmcisadu.let.uniroma1.it/~orlandi/mccarty1.html.
34  I am indebted to Willard McCarty for this notion.

those strategies and techniques, and evaluation purposes and methods. [...] In other words, talk about pedagogy is simultaneously talk about the details of what students and others might do together and the cultural politics such practices support. To propose a pedagogy is to propose a political vision. In this perspective, we cannot talk about teaching practice without talking about politics.[35]

Before embarking upon a consideration of the politics of digital humanities pedagogy, it is instructive to consider the analogous case of English studies.[36] In her provocative study, *Professing and Pedagogy: Learning the Teaching of English*, Shari Stenberg argues, "Valuing pedagogy, making pedagogy central to professing, requires more than scholarly efforts and more than improved training practices." What is needed is "a rethinking of entrenched notions of the discipline that determine the relationship of teaching to scholarship and reinforce a limited conception of who the professor is and should be."[37] We are the inheritors of a nineteenth-century university model based on the German *Wissenschaft* ideal, in which "the professor is not a teacher" but is instead "a specialist [...] responsible only for the quality of his instruction" whose "duty begins and ends with himself."[38] Such a model promoted the distinction between the acts of scholarship and teaching, between the roles of professor and teacher. As Stenberg notes, "the new research university also gave way to a new conception of disciplinarity, conceived as a static body of specialized (not utilitarian) knowledge, made and extended by 'experts' and transported by 'teachers'."[39] As a result, "research is supported by public mechanisms" while "teaching is privatized."[40] In turn, this fostered what Louise Wetherbee Phelps has called "an ethic of radical individualism," which "discourages classroom visits as intrusions threatening a private space of autonomy, intimacy and power."[41]

---

35   Roger Simon, "Empowerment as a Pedagogy of Possibility," *Language Arts* 64 (1988): 371.

36   Shari Stenberg, *Professing and Pedagogy: Learning the Teaching of English* (Urbana: National Council of Teachers of English, 2005), 8.

37   The reader will indulge my decision to take English studies as a test case. While arbitrary, since any humanities discipline could serve the same purpose, English is my own disciplinary background. Moreover, as Kirschenbaum has noted, there are a number of reasons why "English departments have historically been hospitable settings" for work in digital humanities (Kirschenbaum, "What is Digital Humanities," 59–60).

38   James Morgan Hart, *German Universities: Narrative of Personal Experience* (New York: G. P. Putnam's Sons, 1874), 264. Hart, a professor of English language and literature at Cornell, visited Germany in 1861 to study and reported his experiences.

39   Stenberg, *Professing and Pedagogy*, 8.

40   Shari Stenberg and Amy Lee, "Developing Pedagogies: Learning the Teaching of English," *College English* 64, no. 3 (2002): 335.

41   Louise Wetherbee Phelps, "Practical Wisdom and the Geography of Knowledge in Composition," *College English* 53, no. 8 (1991): 866.

For Stenberg, a reevaluation of the function of the English professor as "more than one who transmits particular knowledge" is required, expanding the role to include that of "a facilitator of student projects, a co-inquirer, a learner." In order to do so, we must "give up the idea that our authority stems (solely) from our certainty, from the knowledge areas in which we have demonstrated achievement," and "exchange [this] foundational knowledge and transmission-based pedagogy for socially constructed knowledge and activity-centered learning."[42]

I would argue that the digital humanities is in a better position to undertake this transition than English studies, precisely because digital humanities is not, on the whole, characterized by the same "ethic of radical individualism." Whether it is conceived as a discipline in its own right or as a set of shared methodologies across a number of disciplines, the digital humanities embrace a hacker ethos. In this light, to paraphrase Tad Suiter, the digital humanities might be conceived as a field that "looks at systemic knowledge structures and learns about them from making or doing" in a way that employs "playful creation to enrich knowledge of complex systems."[43] As Gilbert Ryle maintained in *The Concept of Mind* (1949), knowing *how* and knowing *that* are epistemologically distinct;[44] digital humanities is about learning *by* doing and, as Cathy N. Davidson and David Theo Goldberg have urged, echoing Ryle, our wider university pedagogy should reflect this shift from vertical to horizontal structures of learning, "from learning *that* to learning *how*, from content to process."[45]

However, to characterize the digital humanities as a hacker culture is potentially misleading.[46] Much as we might fantasize about it, digital humanists are not hackers in the Gibsonian sense of the term—lone

---

42  Stenberg, *Professing and Pedagogy*, 2, 3.

43  Tad Suiter, "Why 'Hacking'?" in *Hacking the Academy: The Edited Volume*, ed., Cohen and Scheinfeldt. See also the additional essays in the "More Hacking" section of *Hacking the Academy*, May 21–28, 2010, http://hackingtheacademy.org/more-hacking/.

44  Gilbert Ryle, *The Concept of Mind* (Chicago: University of Chicago Press, 1949), 27–32. I am indebted to Willard McCarty for alerting me to this reference.

45  Cathy N. Davidson and David Theo Goldberg, *The Future of Learning Institutions in a Digital Age*, John C. and Catherine T. MacArthur Foundation Reports on Digital Media and Learning (Cambridge: MIT Press, 2009), 27, my emphasis original. Similarly, for Alan Liu, "one of the most remarkable differences" offered by digital humanities pedagogy is that teaching with—and through—new technologies allows us to "supplement the usual closed discursive circuit of the instructor-talking-to-the-student (and vice versa) with an open circuit of the instructor—*and*—student talking to others"; see "Digital Humanities and Academic Change," *English Language Notes* 47, no. 1 (2009): 20.

46  On hacking in the digital humanities, see the essays in Cohen and Scheinfeldt, *Hacking the Academy: The Edited Volume*.

"console cowboys" and "data jockeys" who roam the Wild West of cyberspace.[47] Unlike their traditional colleagues, some digital humanists are not lone rangers, but engage in "explicitly co-operative, interdependent and collaborative research."[48] This kind of research introduces a new mode of work into the humanities: hacking together, not alone.[49]

The teaching–research relationship, therefore, appears to be more symbiotic in the digital humanities than it is in other fields because our research, like our teaching, is founded on collectivity and collaboration in the pursuit and creation of new knowledge.[50] By extension, the capacity for research practices to inform and transform teaching, and vice versa, is—at least theoretically—more readily apparent in digital humanities than in other fields.[51] Whether horizontal or vertical, through self-learning, peer-to-peer learning, or more formal institutional structures of learning, pedagogy is at the heart of the digital humanities. If we were to formally acknowledge this more frequently, the gap between research and pedagogy in our primary disciplinary sites—our digital humanities journals, conferences, and books—might not appear so vast.

To reflect critically about pedagogy is to reflect critically about what it is that we *do* as digital humanists. To paraphrase Colin Irvine, do we

---

47   On the contested identity of the "hacker" and the history of the hacking subculture, see Douglas Thomas, *Hacker Culture* (Minneapolis: University of Minnesota Press, 2002).

48   For an in-depth discussion of the topic of collaboration in the digital humanities, see the essays in *Collaborative Research in the Digital Humanities*, ed. Marilyn Deegan and Willard McCarty (Farnham: Ashgate, 2012). See also Cathy N. Davidson, "What If Scholars in the Humanities Worked Together, in a Lab?" *The Chronicle of Higher Education*, May 28, 1999, http://chronicle.com/article/What-If-Scholars-in-the/24009; and, Lisa Spiro, "Collaborative Authorship in the Humanities," *Digital Scholarship in the Humanities*, April 21, 2009, http://digitalscholarship.wordpress.com/2009/04/21/collaborative-authorship-in-the-humanities/.

49   On the notion of "hacking together" to promote open learning communities in digital humanities pedagogy, see Matthew K. Gold's chapter "Looking for Whitman: A Multi-Campus Experiment in Digital Pedagogy."

50   I agree with Harold Short, who has argued against the assertion that "the digital humanities is a temporary phenomenon whose existence will end when it becomes the norm for all humanities scholars to understand and be able to apply advanced computational tools and techniques in their research." For Short, the imperative of digital humanities work is collaboration: even if humanities scholars were trained to program, there would still be need for collaboration with dedicated expert programmers and software developers, in addition to myriad other academic and technical specialists, for many projects typical in the digital humanities. By necessity, specialization and expertise in one discipline comes at the opportunity cost of another. What distinguishes digital humanists from traditional humanists, perhaps, lies in a willingness to embrace collaboration as a mode of research. See Harold Short, "The Digital Humanities: A Collaborative Discipline" (paper presented at the Oxford e-Research Centre, Oxford, May 18, 2010).

51   Colin Irvine, "Moving Beyond the Binaries: A Learning-Centered Approach to Pedagogy," *Pedagogy* 6, no. 1 (2006): 149.

*teach* digital humanities? Do we *profess* it? Do we *profess* to teach it? Or, do we *teach* (courses like computer-assisted text analysis and others surveyed in this collection and beyond) so that we might *profess* (our scholarly understanding of the digital humanities as the intersection of humanities and computing)?[52] However seemingly simple the question "what do we do?" may be, we do a disservice to our field and ourselves if we fail to consider the importance of pedagogy when it comes to answering such questions, no matter how commonsensical they might at first appear. As Irvine concludes, "despite being a college English professor as opposed to a high school English teacher," he "would nonetheless assert that 'I teach English,'" in the knowledge that such a "simple assertion can and should mean I am likewise a professor in the *process* of learning to enact my profession."[53]

## Terms and Conditions

Daniel Rohr's *Brain and Microchip*, a limited edition of table and chair designs pictured on the cover of this volume, eloquently captures the spirit of the essays that follow.[54] Rohr's designs symbolically bring the technological and the human together, reflecting the critical intersections between the humanities and computing at the heart of our field. Pedagogy in digital humanities, like any other discipline, is an ongoing, iterative process. As such, the present collection cannot claim to have the final word. Just as Rohr's empty tables and chairs invite users to sit and participate in an open dialogue, the chapters in *Digital Humanities Pedagogy* aim to open up critical discussion about pedagogy in our field. Like any work, it is the product of its particular historical and technological moment, a condition all the more important in a fast-paced, technologically driven field such as digital humanities. This collection, like any critical work of its kind, is also an assertion of value. This volume demonstrates that pedagogy is central to what we do as digital humanists and it is important enough to justify the critical attention it receives in the chapters that follow.

The present volume also cannot claim to be exhaustive in its treatment of the subject matter. Despite the range of topics addressed, the variety

---

52  Colin Irvine, "Moving Beyond the Binaries: A Learning-Centered Approach to Pedagogy," *Pedagogy* 6, no. 1 (2006): 149.

53  Irvine, Moving Beyond the Binaries," 153.

54  Daniel Rohr's *Brain and Microchip* are limited edition product designs for coffee tables and ottoman stools, first exhibited as prototypes in January 2009 at PASSAGEN (Interior Design Week Köln), Germany's largest design event. For more information about Rohr's designs, see http://www.danielrohr.com/.

of disciplines represented and the diversity of geographical, cultural, and institutional locales included, the chapters that follow are, by necessity, selective and limited. For example, self-directed learning, an important and under-theorized aspect of our field, is not addressed directly in this collection. Similarly, other specific (but nonetheless topical) issues, however pressing, such as the assertion of copyright over digital humanities syllabi,[55] are addressed only as part of a broader discussion, such as in Lisa Spiro's proposal for an open education model for digital humanities.[56]

The contents of the present collection are arranged under three broad, intersecting categories—practices, principles, and politics—as outlined below.

## Practices

If, as Mas'ud Zavarzadeh and Donald Morton have argued, "all discursive practices are pedagogical,"[57] then those practices associated with the digital humanities should be no different. Taken as a whole, the contents of the "Practices" section offer a critical, historical survey of digital humanities as taught, both formally at the undergraduate and graduate level and informally at summer schools. Individual chapters offer case studies from leading educators and institutions in North America and Europe, and cover a range of disciplines. These case studies not only offer compelling reading but also serve as models on which to build new, or extend existing, programs of study.

Chapters in the "Practices" section are therefore distinguishable from recent works, which focus on the use of particular digital tools and their

---

55   A series of Twitter posts following the DH2012 conference is representative of this topical issue. Jon Christensen tweeted "Oh, I love the idea of CC [Creative Commons] licenses & citation practices for syllabi. I often feel guilty about 'plagiarizing' syllabi" (June 21, 2012), to which Tom Scheinfeldt replied, "Like recipes, it'd be nice to establish syllabi as just plain uncopyrightable" (June 21, 2012). Like myself, Matthew K. Gold believes that "syllabi can and should be shared openly" and that "they should be treated with respect and that citations should be made when material is repurposed/reused" (personal communication, June 23, 2012).

56   In her chapter "Opening up Digital Humanities Education," Lisa Spiro argues that, "as much as possible, digital humanities educational resources should be released with Creative Commons attribution licenses so that they are credited to the original author and can easily be adapted, remixed and reused."

57   Mas'ud Zavarzadeh and Donald Morton, "Preface," *Theory/Pedagogy/Politics: Texts for Change*, edited by Donald Morton and Mas'ud Zavarzadeh (Urbana: University of Illinois Press, 1991), vii.

application in the humanities classroom.[58] While these are important in the promotion, development, and shaping of pedagogical strategies in digital humanities, they are not the focus of the present collection. On the one hand, there is the concern, aptly articulated by Charles Ess, to avoid "letting the technological tail wag the pedagogical dog."[59] On the other hand, as Lynette Hunter has noted, "practical skills are needed to start with," so that "at some point, sooner rather than later, criticism," that is, a critical pedagogy "may come."[60] The aim of the present collection, to use Hunter's term, is to contribute towards the timely inauguration of such a critical pedagogy.

In the opening chapter, Willard McCarty documents the historical development of the world's first PhD program in digital humanities, established in 2005 at what was then the Centre for Computing in the Humanities (CCH) at King's College London. Since then, the CCH has become the Department of Digital Humanities (DDH) and the PhD program, similarly, has been rebranded "to give the existing degree multiple names, one for each discipline or disciplinary area," such as a PhD in Digital Historical Studies or in Digital Musicology, and so forth. McCarty's chapter describes the origins of the PhD program, its application and admission processes, and a brief survey of current PhD projects ranging from the stylometric analysis of Shakespeare and digital palaeography of medieval Norwegian manuscripts through to narratological geography and the socio-philosophy of digital traces. To conclude, McCarty reflects on the nature of the PhD in Digital Humanities, arguing that the degree "is not just a framework for research, providing supervisory support and ensuring quality, but is itself empirical research into the best framework with which to further develop the intellectual culture of the digital humanities."

Our focus shifts from formal to informal instruction, from the PhD in Digital Humanities at King's College London to the second Europäische

---

58 Representative examples include edited collections, such as *Learning Through Digital Media: Experiments in Technology and Pedagogy*, ed., Trebor Scholz, *Teaching Language and Literature Online*, ed. Ian Lancashire, and *Teaching the Humanities Online: A Practical Guide to the Virtual Classroom*, ed. Stephen J. Hoffman (New York: M. E. Sharpe, 2011); special issues of journals, such as the August 2000 special issue of *Computers and the Humanities* on "Computers in Humanities Teaching and Research"; and single-author works on individual digital tools and humanities teaching applications, such as John Martin Mannion's *History Teaching with Moodle 2* (Birmingham: Packt Publishing, 2011).

59 Charles Ess, "Wag the Dog? Online Conferencing and Teaching," *Computers and the Humanities* 34, no. 3 (2000): 298.

60 Lynette Hunter, "Alternative Publishing in Canada," in *Difference and Community: Canadian and European Cultural Perspectives*, ed. Peter Easingwood, Konrad Gross, and Lynette Hunter (Amsterdam: Rodopi, 1996), 52.

Sommeruniversität "Kulturen & Technologien" (or European Summer School on "Culture & Technology") at the Universität Leipzig, July 26–30, 2010. In their chapter, "Hands-On Teaching Digital Humanities," Malte Rehbein and Christiane Fritze critically reflect upon the teaching strategies employed in their course on digital editing. Rehbein and Fritze argue against the use of discrete exercises and distinct materials in favor of a holistic learning-by-project approach, in which the same materials are progressively enriched in successive iterations. "The driving philosophy," they write, "was to get the students involved in the complete process of creating and publishing a digital edition, from the first encounter with the material until its web presentation." Like McCarty, Rehbein and Fritze discuss the background of the course, and reflect upon its participants and their varied academic and cultural backgrounds. While McCarty presents a bird's eye view of a broad range of projects undertaken in the PhD program, Rehbein and Fritze offer a detailed analysis of their digital editing course, from the identification of learning goals in course planning to data modeling and project management, from teaching strategies and methods to digital tools and infrastructure. After mapping the desired learning goals to the evaluation and practical outcomes of the course in terms of educational theory, Rehbein and Fritze reflect upon their successes and failures, concluding that the learning-through-project approach succeeds in teaching students "a better sense of what digital editing as a holistic process involves."

The importance of digital skills in archives and public history curricula is the focus of the next chapter, authored by Peter J. Wosh, Cathy Moran Hajo, and Esther Katz. As "digital technology has fundamentally altered the archival, public history, and editing landscapes," and "new media have, in many ways, promoted a convergence of these various fields," Wosh, Hajo, and Katz describe how

> All three professions are confronting the challenges of mastering new media, working collaboratively and effectively with information technology staff without allowing such services to drive their programs, and ensuring the long-term preservation of born-digital materials.

As a result, the task of preparing students for careers in these fields has also become far more demanding, requiring instructors to become familiar with digital tools and methods that are "becoming more diverse, more challenging, and rapidly changing" and to pass on this new knowledge effectively. However, in line with other contributors to this collection, the authors maintain that "students need more than a basic grounding in digital tools" and that "educators need to carefully balance theoretical, practical, and digital skills in their programs." In their chapter, Wosh, Hajo and Katz offer a detailed discussion of how to put this ideal balance into practice, taking the reconfiguration of a long-standing archives and public history program at New York University to integrate digital skills throughout its curriculum as a case study. The chapter considers the importance of institutional and external partnerships, the use of capstone projects and internships, and the challenges of successfully integrating digital skills and methodologies into existing programs of study, from overcoming issues of infrastructure to meeting different levels of technical expertise.

From technical expertise to technical writing, the next chapter considers the relationship of digital humanities to the first-year writing course. Olin Bjork argues that "composition studies is moving toward digital humanities even as it moves away from the material humanities, or that the humanities, in becoming digital, have moved toward composition studies." To support this claim, Bjork outlines the affinities and differences between projects representative of digital humanities, new media studies, and composition studies, and charts a new direction for the field of computers and writing, in which quantitative methods imported from digital humanities "serve as a corrective" to the primarily qualitative focus of composition. A critical discussion of implementing this convergence model takes up the remainder of the chapter, in which Bjork offers a case study of teaching digital humanities in the writing classroom, reporting on the integration of digital, quantitative methods (such as electronic text analysis) into extensively qualitative, writing projects. As such, "digital humanities [...] provides a rationale and opportunity for composition instructors to expose their students to aspects of technical writing processes" in conjunction with "the argumentative and expository writing processes practiced in the discipline of English studies."

In "Teaching Digital Humanities through Digital Cultural Mapping," a contingent of authors based at the University of California, Los Angeles (UCLA)—Elaine Sullivan, Janife Reiff, Diane Favro, Todd Presner and Willeke Wendrich, headed by Chris Johanson—tackles three pressing pedagogical questions:

> How does one teach students the digital tools to address [...] a wide variety of projects without neglecting traditional discipline-specific issues

of research formulation and data collection? How can one honestly and effectively evaluate student projects for content that lies outside one's domain expertise? While fully acknowledging that teaching a technological skill set can lead students to ask new and original questions of cultural data, when and in what instances must we nonetheless start with a domain-specific research question, and then move to teaching the digital?

In their chapter, the authors outline the processes employed over a three-year period to address these questions whilst developing a multi-track digital humanities program—now successfully expanded into an undergraduate minor—at UCLA. In addition to showcasing student projects in topics as disparate as Los Angeles history and Roman architecture, the authors critically identify the myriad obstacles to teaching digital skills and methods, and offer a series of case studies illustrating their integration into existing humanities courses. As with the chapter by Wosh, Hajo, and Katz preceding it, the UCLA "Digital Cultural Mapping" chapter provides a detailed analysis of the processes by which digital humanities skills, methods, and mindsets can be integrated into existing courses of study in a variety of humanities disciplines, offering insightful discussion of the challenges faced and solutions tried and tested. While the disciplinary foundations may differ, the desired outcomes of such convergences at the undergraduate level are the same: to produce a "budding digital humanist," armed "with broad training in his or her domain-specific discipline" able to "approach a traditional problem in a radically new way or conceive of an entirely fresh approach to the traditionally defined field."

Matthew K. Gold's chapter extends the preceding discussions about practical collaborations across various departments in the design and delivery of digital humanities (wholly or inflected) courses to collaborations across different geographical locations, campuses and countries. In this chapter, Gold describes the design, delivery, successes, and failures of the Looking for Whitman project, which brought together classes from four academic institutions in the United States and Serbia "in a collaborative digital environment that emphasized place-based learning and progressive educational techniques" in the pursuit of knowledge about Walt Whitman's life, works, and legacy. For Gold, the project's director, the Looking for Whitman project "set[s] forth a new model for aggregated, distributed, collaborative, and open learning techniques" and as such "serve[s] as an important example of digital pedagogy for the digital humanities community."

With this new model for networked pedagogy and online learning as its principal focus, Gold's chapter critically reflects upon the opportunities available to digital humanities through an embrace of open education pedagogy and the fostering of online learning communities to create "a shared landscape rather than a walled garden" of educational content. As with other chapters in the "Practices" section of the collection, Gold provides insightful theoretical considerations and useful practical suggestions to educators and course developers on how to apply the proposed model for linked digital humanities courses across campuses.

In "Acculturation and the Digital Humanities Community," Geoffrey Rockwell and Stéfan Sinclair close the "Practices" section by considering the much neglected and under-theorized issue of acculturation—that is, professionalization—in digital humanities curricula. Given the range of professional opportunities available in the digital humanities, including non-academic jobs or alternative academic ("alt-ac") jobs, for Rockwell and Sinclair the question is "how can digital humanities programs prepare students for a breadth of careers including, but not exclusively, academic careers?" What follows is an incisive assessment of the field—of what we really do as digital humanists—and provocative arguments for explicitly integrating professionalization into our pedagogy. To "illustrate how acculturation can be woven holistically into curriculum at both the undergraduate and graduate level," Rockwell and Sinclair offer two detailed case studies: the undergraduate program in multimedia at McMaster University; and the MA in Humanities Computing at the University of Alberta. In addition to these case studies, Rockwell and Sinclair offer timely and astute practical advice for students who are thinking about professionalization, and for educators wishing to integrate acculturation into their existing or developing digital humanities curriculum.

# Principles

In many ways, chapters in the "Practices" and "Principles" sections are interchangeable: all consider pedagogical strategies and methodologies and, with few exceptions, all offer case studies to illustrate their application. Chapters in both sections similarly reflect a diverse range of traditional humanities disciplines, as well as a breadth of institutional and geographical context, since their authors work across North America and Europe. While the contents of both sections certainly intersect in these ways, they are distinguishable by a matter of degree. The primary focus shifts from practical applications to the theoretical principles that underlie them.

Through a shared focus on principles, whether digital humanities or pedagogical, the chapters that follow set out to promote what Koenraad de Smedt has characterized as "more important than the use of machines" in the digital humanities—that is, "new ways of thinking."[61] To inculcate new ways of thinking into digital humanities pedagogy, Martyn Jessop has noted, "academic training in humanities computing must go well beyond skills-based courses" to "concentrate on the cognitive abilities of thinking both with and against the machine."[62] Thus, the "Principles" section begins appropriately with a broad discussion of this fundamental need to teach research methodologies in the digital humanities. As Simon Mahony and Elena Pierazzo argue, "[technological] skills training is not research training," since "the knowledge gained is [as] transient" as the tools themselves, whereas "[critical] thinking skills are the most important because they are the most deeply embedded and the most transferable." Through philosophical reflection and critical discussion of case studies, Mahony and Pierazzo's chapter concludes by endorsing Robert L. Oakman's adage, itself echoing Marshall McLuhan, that "the method is more important than the message."[63]

"Give someone a program, frustrate them for a day," or so the joke goes, "teach someone to program, frustrate them for a lifetime." In "Programming with Humanists," Stephen Ramsay argues for the necessity to teach programming in the humanities. His case is founded on more than utilitarian grounds: while "the ability to participate in the design and creation of new media is at least relevant if not exactly incumbent upon all," particularly for those "in a set of disciplines still primarily concerned with artifacts of communication" like the humanities, Ramsay suggests that programming and software design, "like writing [...] provides a way to think in and through a subject." After detailed discussion of the challenges

---

61    Koenraad de Smedt, "Some Reflections on Studies in Humanities Computing," *Literary and Linguistic Computing* 17, no. 1 (2002): 92.

62    Martyn Jessop, "Teaching, Learning and Research in Final Year Humanities Computing Student Projects," *Literary and Linguistic Computing* 20, no. 3 (2005): 307.

63    Robert L. Oakman, "Perspectives on Teaching Computing in the Humanities," *Computers and the Humanities* 21, no. 4 (1987): 232.

and benefits associated with such a teaching program, with case studies from courses taught at the University of Nebraska–Lincoln, Ramsay concludes,

> The center of digital humanities, after all, is not the technology, but the particular form of engagement that characterizes the act of building tools, models, frameworks, and representations for the traditional objects of humanistic study.

In 1991, Christian Koch argued that the key to integrating computer science into the humanities "is to develop and promote projects and courses for which the involvement of the computer is integral rather than secretarial."[64] For Koch, and as illustrated by Ramsay's chapter, "in order to increase the stature of computational courses in the humanities, a new wave of sophisticated courses needs to be introduced into liberal arts curricula."[65] The introduction of new, dedicated digital humanities courses is one thing. However, as we have already seen in the "Practices" section, much of the training in our field is accomplished by the integration of digital humanities methods and skills into existing, traditional humanities courses. In their second contribution to the present collection, "Teaching Computer-Assisted Text Analysis," Stéfan Sinclair and Geoffrey Rockwell make the case for teaching text analytics and offer strategies for including them in existing humanities curricula. To accomplish this, Sinclair and Rockwell not only propose a series of models ranging from out-of-the-box text and tool combinations to building a custom corpus for analysis, but also introduce a collection of "Recipes" that, "rather than starting with the technologies of analytics and their jargon," like cooking recipes they "start with something a humanist may want to do, like identifying themes in a text." The chapter concludes with a discussion of literate programming, and the importance of inculcating good research documentation skills in digital humanities students. After reading Ramsay's and Sinclair and Rockwell's chapters, you and your students could be cooking with code and text analytics.

In the next chapter, we exchange code-cooking aprons for whatever it is that digital historians wear, as Joshua Sternfeld addresses the interdisciplinary challenges and pedagogical opportunities associated with digital history. In "Pedagogical Principles of Digital

---

64 Christian Koch, "On the Benefits of Interrelating Computer Science and the Humanities: The Case of Metaphor," *Computers and the Humanities* 25, no. 5 (1991): 290.
65 Koch, "On the Benefits of Interrelating," 294.

Historiography," Sternfeld argues that "digital history has the capacity to reshape our conception of history, to generate new lines of inquiry" and to "challenge entrenched theories," but that such potential demands "a theoretical and methodological framework" and "a common language and a set of theoretical principles." In his chapter, Sternfeld introduces such a theory, dubbed *digital historiography*, defined as the "interdisciplinary study of the interaction of digital technology with historical practice." After further theoretical reflection on the burgeoning field of digital history, Sternfeld turns to a discussion of "a preliminary set of pedagogical principles that apply to digital historiography at all educational levels," followed by a detailed case study of a graduate seminar developed on the basis of these principles, and concluding with a consideration of their wider application across the humanities.

Virginia Kuhn and Vicki Callahan close the "Principles" section with their chapter, "Nomadic Archives," which offers a provocative re-conceptualization of interdisciplinarity in digital humanities pedagogy and research. For Kuhn and Callahan, the digital humanities "represents no less than an opportunity for a new form of interdisciplinary engagement," one that extends beyond the "horizontal" notion of interdisciplinarity—the "linking [of] fields without any fundamental change to the formal structures or logic of any one discipline"—to the "vertical." To embrace vertical interdisciplinarity, according to Kuhn and Callahan, is to overcome traditional (disciplinary) assumptions about how we understand and implement the materials we study—to reject, for example, the widely-held assumption that information encoded in images and audio materials is "aligned almost exclusively with creative/aesthetic expression" and is treated as "different or distinct from textual materials and critical thought/writing." The "radicality" of the digital humanities lies in its capacity for "a successful vertically integrated praxis," in which "these diverse materials and disciplinary strategies" are used "to engage across and within media, tools, formats and philosophical categories, with each component in ruthless interrogation of every possible formal boundary." After further reflection on the notion of vertical interdisciplinarity, the chapter offers case studies illustrating several possibilities for its integration in digital humanities pedagogy.

# Politics

As Roger Simon has argued, "to propose a pedagogy is to propose a political vision."[66] Indeed, while all of the contents of the present collection may be political inasmuch as they represent an assertion of value—namely, the place of pedagogy in the digital humanities—the chapters in this final section are more explicit about their "political vision" for the field. The sense of the political that emerges from the essays in this section, however, might strike some readers as circumscribed. Recent challenges have drawn attention to the tendency in digital humanities to brush aside assumptions of class, disability, ethnicity, gender, race, and sexuality, as well as the limited diversity among its practitioners.[67] The opportunities for pedagogy to bring these issues into useful discussion—and for digital humanities classrooms to create a more inclusive, diverse environment—remain largely unexplored. Although the collection initially included essays addressing issues of gender and race in digital humanities pedagogy, the contributors withdrew before going to press. Such contingencies are unfortunate, and unfortunately unavoidable. However, as the emergence of #transformDH (http://transformdh.org/) suggests, questions of diversity in all its forms within digital humanities research, practice and pedagogy are unlikely to remain marginalized for long.[68]

---

66  Simon, "Empowerment as a Pedagogy of Possibility," 371.
67  Representative examples include: Bethanie Nowviskie, "What Do Girls Dig?" *Bethany Nowviskie*, April 7, 2011, http://nowviskie.org/2011/what-do-girls-dig/; Alexis Lothian, "Conference Thoughts: Queer Studies and the Digital Humanities," *Queer Geek Theory* (October 18, 2011), http://www.queergeektheory.org/2011/10/conference-thoughts-queer-studies-and-the-digital-humanities/; Charlie Edwards, "The Digital Humanities and Its Users," in *Debates in the Digital Humanities*, ed. Matthew K. Gold (Minneapolis: University of Minnesota Press, 2012), 213–32; Tara McPherson, "Why Are the Digital Humanities So White? Or Thinking the Histories of Race and Computation," in *Debates in the Digital Humanities*, ed. Matthew K. Gold (Minneapolis: University of Minnesota Press, 2012), 139–60; George H. Williams, "Disability, Universal Design, and the Digital Humanities," in *Debates in the Digital Humanities*, ed. Matthew K. Gold (Minneapolis: University of Minnesota Press, 2012), 202–12; Matthew K. Gold, "Whose Revolution? Towards a More Equitable Digital Humanities," *The Lapland Chronicles* (January 10, 2012), http://mkgold.net/blog/2012/01/10/whose-revolution-toward-a-more-equitable-digital-humanities/; and Miriam Posner, "Some Things to Think About Before You Exhort Everyone to Code," *Miriam Posner*, February 29, 2012, http://miriamposner.com/blog/?p=1135.
68  Christine L. Borgman, "The Digital Future is Now: A Call to Action for the Humanities," *Digital Humanities Quarterly* 3, no. 4 (2009), http://digitalhumanities.org/dhq/vol/3/4/000077/000077.html.

In "They Have Come, Why Won't We Build It?" Jon Saklofske, Estelle Clements, and Richard Cunningham probe the question why, in an age of ubiquitous computing, "have we not yet developed and implemented curricula more appropriate to today's digital reality and tomorrow's digital prospects," as opposed to "the Gutenberg-era world in which most currently employed university faculty grew up?" With the premise that "it is past the time at which widespread introduction of digital humanities curricula would have been a timely intervention" in higher education, the authors address the issue by offering a provocative analysis of the academy and its resistance to digital culture, particularly in the arts and humanities, followed by an insightful discussion of the educational "hopes and fears raised by the prospect of immersion in digital culture." Saklofske, Clements, and Cunningham also consider the philosophical issues and practical obstacles associated with the adoption of digital humanities into new and existing curricula. The authors conclude with a call for digital humanists to lead the charge in convincing university administrators that the "needs, desires, and proclivities" of the Net Generation student are to be "recognized as an opportunity," and not "resisted as simply another assault on the *status quo*."

"The syllabus and curriculum of Humanities Computing," as Melissa Terras observes, "has never really been decided."[69] In "Opening Up Digital Humanities Education," Lisa Spiro extends the discussion of *what* is taught under the rubric of the digital humanities curriculum to consider *how* teaching programs are delivered. Faced with the question of how to provide a "flexible" and "inexpensive way" for budding digital humanists "to develop key skills, demonstrate their learning and participate in the digital humanities community," Spiro proposes a "networked, open digital humanities certificate program." By careful consideration of the practical and theoretical issues involved—from the establishment of a curriculum to its community-based teaching, assessment, and certification; from day-to-

---

69   On the origins of #transformDH, see: Amanda Phillips, "#transformDH – A Call to Action Following ASA 2011," *HASTAC*, October 26, 2011, http://hastac.org/blogs/ amanda-phillips/2011/10/26/transformdh-call-action-following-asa-2011/. For a critique of the movement, see: Roger T. Whitson, "Does DH Really Need to be Transformed? My Reflections on #mla12," *Roger T. Whitson, Ph.D.*, January 8, 2012, http://www. rogerwhitson.net/?p=1358; for a defense, see: Natalia Cecire, "In Defense of Transforming DH," *Works Cited*, January 8, 2012, http://nataliacecire.blogspot.com/2012/01/in-defense-of-transforming-dh.html. As evidence of growing community interest in diversity issues, a proposed roundtable on "Representing Race: Silence in the Digital Humanities" was accepted for the 2013 Meeting of the MLA.

day management and administration to securing funding and promoting growth—Spiro offers no less than a blueprint for the creation of such a certificate program. Through its development, according to Spiro, "the digital humanities community could spark innovations in teaching and research, share educational practices and resources, bring in new members, and cultivate a shared sense of mission." Spiro's vision for digital humanities pedagogy is truly egalitarian. Through the certificate program "the digital humanities community would create materials of benefit to all institutions with digital humanities programs, open or not," and such an endeavor would "produce both a community of trained digital humanists and broader knowledge about open education."

In "The Digital Future is Now," Christine L. Borgman urges the humanities to follow the sciences in promoting "initiatives to enable students to use data" and to do so early in the curriculum—"in the primary grades where feasible"—because

> If students can explore cultural records from the early grades and learn to construct their own narratives, they may find the study of humanities more lively. By the time they are college students, they will have learned methods of collaborative work and the use of distributed tools, sources and services.[70]

Tanya Clement takes up Borgman's charge in her chapter, "Multiliteracies in the Undergraduate Digital Humanities Classroom," in which she sketches out the prospect of just such a "curriculum infused with the pedagogical concerns reflected in digital humanities," in which "undergraduates learn to think about the cultural work done by and through digital media." After a brief history of digital humanities in the undergraduate classroom and an extensive survey of existing programs, Clement reflects on the role of undergraduate digital humanities curricula in inculcating multiliteracies and in sustaining the field. In recognizing its importance, Clement argues that much work remains to be done to "consider how the logistics of departments, the crossing paths of curricular development, and the allocation and reallocation of essential resources shape how we teach undergraduate programs." Like Borgman, Clement urges that "now is the time" to make this work "transparent" and available to "others who wish to continue, broaden, and support" its development.

---

70   Melissa Terras, "Disciplined: Using Educational Studies to Analyze 'Humanities Computing,'" *Literary and Linguistic Computing* 21, no. 2 (2006): 235.

The present collection closes with Melanie Kill's chapter on "Teaching Digital Rhetoric," in which she makes the case for using Wikipedia (http://www.wikipedia.org/) as "an environment for collaborative inquiry and skill building with tremendous potential to enrich student learning in courses across the humanities." Given the emphasis on collaboration in the digital humanities, Kill's chapter is a timely reminder of the "pedagogical affordances offered by the model of action, interaction, and knowledge-based community" that platforms like Wikipedia provide to digital humanities educators. Kill's political vision for digital humanities pedagogy shares much with Spiro's, as both champion the use and creation of open-access resources and the embrace of networked, collaborative models of learning. For Kill, Wikipedia serves as much more than a working model of the explicitly collaborative project of knowledge-creation. As a platform for teaching students digital rhetoric, Wikipedia offers students in the humanities an invaluable opportunity to become active participants in their own digital "social futures," to "integrate visions of writing as a platform of individual inspiration with understandings of writing as an arena of social action." With its message about the importance of digital humanities pedagogy in shaping our students into informed, civic-minded, digital participants in their "social futures," Kill's chapter is a fitting conclusion to *Digital Humanities Pedagogy*.

# I. Practices

# 1. The PhD in Digital Humanities

*Willard McCarty*

---

> The dream of every cell is to become two cells.
> —François Jacob

## Overview

The PhD in Digital Humanities was established at King's College London in 2005. By 2010 experience had persuaded us that collaborative supervision of interdisciplinary work is the norm for doctoral research in our subject. This, you might think, is obvious, but we had created the PhD deliberately without constraining what students might make of it. (More on origins and developments later.) Discussion with students and colleagues led us to suspect that—despite the obvious popularity of nearly anything that the adjective "digital" may be attached to and despite the relative success of the degree program in attracting students—its title remained an impediment. We reasoned that as the identifier for a doctoral program in a departmentalized world, "digital humanities" implies its own subject and so by implication excludes others. In a sense, creating this problem in categorization is a positive result from many years of struggle for recognition, but at the same time, it leads to a serious issue. In effect, the rubric requires a potential student to infer that the humanities subject that most interests him or her can be studied with critical involvement of digital tools and methods. No amount of qualifying prose, we thought, could overcome what the rubric seems to imply. The name of our degree was in effect hiding the interdisciplinary collaboration that our experience had shown was of the essence—and the most compelling, indeed innovative aspect of the degree.

Hence, in Autumn 2010 I began negotiations with the academic departments in the School of Arts and Humanities to create multiple synonyms of the "PhD in Digital Humanities," one for each discipline or disciplinary area: thus PhD programs in Digital Classics; Cultural Research; English and American Studies; Film; French; Hispanic and Portuguese Studies; History; Late Antique and Medieval Studies; Musicology; Theology and Religious Studies. (Creating multiple names for the same program rather than multiple programs was a far simpler and quicker to accomplish administratively.) The idea was to make the possibilities of the PhD in Digital Humanities explicit, rather than keep them concealed under a name that is paradoxically both popular and obscure.

The resulting programs were launched with the renaming of my department, from the Centre for Computing in the Humanities to the Department of Digital Humanities—CCH to DDH—in Spring 2011. At the same time we retained the "PhD in Digital Humanities" to denote studies of technical, methodological or behavioral subjects mostly in our field—or in subject-areas for which a collaborating department is not available but which we could support internally. The scheme was designed so that applications to all the degrees share the same process of evaluation, described below. Since the scheme of one degree under many names began a year ago, it has chiefly brought in new students for the collaborating departments but in one instance taken on a student who began in another department but discovered he needed a significant digital component to his degree.

# Origins

In 2005, the CCH established its PhD program when an MA student of the department showed keen interest in pursuing doctoral studies. In comparison to the process in some other countries, this happened quickly and with very little effort, since administrative procedures for creating a doctoral program in the UK are much simpler than they are, for example, in North America. In the UK, as Holm and Liinason have noted, "it is easy to set up courses and degrees in disciplines that can demonstrate market demand."[1] Indeed, anticipated market demand may be sufficient

---

1    Ulla M. Holm and Mia Liinason, "Disciplinary Boundaries between the Social Sciences and the Humanities: Comparative Report on Interdisciplinarity" (report prepared for the Research Integration: Changing Knowledge and Disciplinary Boundaries Through Integrative Research Methods in the Social Sciences and the Humanities project,

if a plausible case for such demand can be made.

As it happened the initiating student dropped out after a year, but two others joined in 2006. Since then, the program has grown at an accelerating pace, especially within the last academic year (2011–12). At the time of writing there are fifteen students enrolled and in progress, two of which are likely to finish before the end of 2012; seven who have been offered a place in the program and are expected to enroll in Autumn 2012; eight in the final stages of application, all of which are highly likely to be offered a place and subject to funding to accept for Autumn 2012; and fifteen in the initial stages. In total, therefore, there are currently forty-five students and potential students involved. I will review the projects undertaken by the cohort of fifteen students below. The queue of seriously interested students fluctuates but tends to maintain the current level.

## The Process of Application and Admission

The nature of the British PhD has necessarily shaped the degree program. In particular, unlike the North American PhD, the British is research-only, spanning a maximum of four years full-time (eight part-time). Students begin with MPhil status; after approximately a year of full-time work or its equivalent, they submit application for upgrade to the PhD. The upgrade interview does not constitute a comprehensive examination of the student's disciplinary knowledge, as in North America, rather the ability to carry out doctoral-level research within the scope of his or her project, or as the Australians denote it, a confirmation of candidature. Throughout the program, before and after the upgrade, reports of progress are now required biannually.

The brevity of allotted time for a research-only degree means that a well-developed, cogent research proposal is the primary focus for admission. Partly because the subject is new and partly because it is highly interdisciplinary, we have found that most students need a significant amount of help developing their proposals before formal application. Usually a student contacts the Director of the Doctoral Program with little more than a notion, sometimes not even what might be called a research problem. If the notion is plausible and the student undeterred by the commitment to doctoral work and its costs—approximately 20% survive

---

University of York, May 2005), 7.

to this point—he or she is encouraged to write a draft of roughly two pages (reduced in size from the much longer document formerly required). Through a cycle of commentary and revision, often iterated several times, perhaps over months, either a cogent proposal emerges or the weakness of the idea becomes obvious. If the proposal is sufficiently strong and if adequate supervision can be provided within or beyond the Department, the student is encouraged to apply. The process is laborious and may indeed be trimmed with the greater number of applicants we expect, but to date it has pushed us to discover potential dimensions of the PhD that we might not otherwise have seen.

In a few cases to date informal arrangement for co-supervision has been made with academics in institutions beyond the College. Arrangements with cultural institutions in London or nearby are certainly possible though none have yet been successfully made. A mechanism for formalizing such arrangements is now being put into place with the approval of the School of Arts and Humanities. Discussion is also ongoing with a Canadian institution about the possibilities for close ties that would establish cross-institutional co-supervision, perhaps a joint degree. Although paid employment cannot be directly related to the degree, part-time students can benefit more than financially from a job in an organization whose work is in the same area. Currently, for example, one student has such a job with an open-access publisher in parallel with his PhD at King's.

In the UK the PhD is slowly moving somewhat closer to a North American model by providing instruction in research-related skills for the first year, e.g. at King's through the UK Doctoral Training Centre scheme and through courses offered by the Graduate School.[2] For the PhD in Digital Humanities and its derivatives the department itself offers modules in its MA programs to which new students may be assigned by their supervisors.

No minimum requirements for a specific level of technical knowledge have been set, thus leaving room for a merely instrumental use of existing tools and for a purely speculative or theoretical project. Where such knowledge is absent, demand is placed on critical use of off-the-shelf tools or meticulously careful, intellectually sophisticated reflection on manifestations of computing. An acceptable dissertation

2  I teach one of these courses, on interdisciplinary research, which emerged from my experiences in pursuing the digital humanities wherever it might lead. Interested readers should contact me for more information.

must contribute to the digital humanities as a whole, at minimum by surveying previous work in an area, extending it to new areas of application and reflecting critically on what the dissertation has achieved. Speculation on computing in its cultural significance and influence, without engagement with past and/or current research in the digital humanities, is discouraged.

The norm for the PhD remains full-time study. Typically the student is resident in London, but compelling cases for non-resident study have resulted in the "semi-distance PhD," as we have called it. The practice would seem to be quite common now, especially for an institution located in an expensive city—but even more for a minority discipline that needs doctoral students in order to grow. Basically, a student wishing to take up the semi-distance option must agree with his or her supervisor on a schedule of visits, which of course can include those carried out on the internet or by telephone.

Funding remains a problem for many students. One of ours who has been especially clever raising funds from unexpected sources has co-authored (and sells) a booklet, *The Alternative Guide to Postgraduate Funding*, to help address the problem.[3] Otherwise, we are actively looking into building studentships into research project applications (as a staff member, Dr Peter Stokes, has already done for a digital palaeography project—further information on this below) and other fund-raising ventures. But the fact that all but a few of the students, past and present, have funded themselves or come with non-UK funding underscores the level of students' commitment to the idea of this degree. From the beginning, it has been demand-driven. But what is the idea?

## The Originating Idea of the PhD

Unaware of any precedents, we began more with questions than with a scheme or set of criteria, as I indicated earlier. We wanted to discover if a PhD on the subject was possible, indeed, if the idea itself made sense, and if it was both conceivable and possible, what it might involve and how it might be structured.

From the outset, its primary objective was clear: to produce culturally literate and critically as well as digitally adept scholars. Furthermore, we knew we wanted to equip them to pursue compelling research questions

---

3   For more information, see "GradFunding", http://www.gradfunding.co.uk/.

with computing, and whenever possible to do this not just in their disciplines of origin but wherever those questions might lead, including into the methodological heartland of our subject. We were much less clear about the kinds of knowledge and experience we might require of applicants, about existing models of research we might adapt and about the mixtures of practical, conceptual and theoretical work that might prove best. We did not proceed strictly from our competencies and interests to specify the range of subjects a student might undertake, nor did we limit applications to pre-existing studentships, but rather deliberately left the boundaries undefined and the possibility of self-funding open. We preferred to see what might happen, then adapt ourselves to the demand, if any, and perhaps eventually make these boundaries explicit.

The openness of the PhD in Digital Humanities already puts considerable demand on the teaching and research staff of the DDH to match incoming doctoral research projects with adequate technical and non-technical support. But in a market-driven academic economy, as ours is, this demand creates exactly the kind of problem one wishes to have, whatever the temporary discomfort.

## Current Projects

At the time of writing collaborative supervision is ongoing within the disciplines of these Departments and Programs: Classics; Culture, Media and Creative Industries; English and American Studies; Hellenic Studies; History; Music; Philosophy; Portuguese; Theology and Religious Studies; with a professor at University College London, Translation Studies; with a researcher in the Darwin Correspondence Project, Cambridge; with the Director of the Women Writers Project, Brown, and a professor in Communication and Media Studies at the Royal Institute of Technology, Stockholm; and with a lecturer in History, Brasenose College Oxford. The cohort of enrolled students whose projects are sketched here numbers fifteen, as I noted above. In addition, I include some mention of the projects likely to begin in Autumn 2012.

Of the projects of enrolled students, seven center on or are seriously involved with verbal language (one with gender), ten history, one musicology, one social anthropology and historical geography, one philosophy, one palaeography and two computational methods. Of these five involve textual encoding, two textual editing, three relational database technology, four corpus-linguistic methods and one statistical analytics. In two projects, the students are designing and building their own modeling software. The projects yet to begin include interests in digital literature, gendered language, music, museums, social networking and communications.

For the sake of brevity, the following includes only the projects of enrolled students.

## Projects in Language

The first of seven projects under this heading is a detailed analysis of how a translator's awareness of linguistic features in the original text affects his or her strategies of translation and so alters the meaning of the rendered text. It considers three twentieth-century American novels recently translated into Lithuanian. Corpus linguistic techniques and XML markup are certain; as of yet the extent to which statistical tools will prove relevant is unknown. For support on the Lithuanian side a senior professor in Vilnius has agreed to collaborate, and for support with translation theory another senior professor from University College London, as just noted. From the digital side the primary question here remains the powers and limits of text-analysis, which despite several decades of work are still not entirely clear and indeed still capable of surprising us.

In another project, stylometric analysis is applied to possible co-authorship of *Titus Andronicus*, usually attributed solely to William Shakespeare but possibly involving George Peele. Sentence-patterns are to be used as the primary discriminator. A senior professor and his research associate in the Institute of English Studies, London, have agreed to collaborate informally on the supervision, as has another senior professor in Australia. Colleagues in stylometrics were involved in evaluating the research proposal for admission. It is at first glance a fairly standard kind of authorship study, but as always the devil is in the detail: what patterns are revealed with what approaches, and how persuasively?

A project in what might be called interoperable bibliography is underway in collaboration with a professor of computational linguistics in the Department of Philosophy. The primary question is the extent to which fully automated techniques can pick out canonical references to classical Greek sources from secondary literature. Here the student is writing the software, which is an integral part of his research; it has potential use well beyond the doctorate, e.g. with bibliographies such as *L'Année philologique*. Further questions pertain to the effects of the tight interlinking of resources that could result from application of such tools across the discipline. The hard problem of interoperability is central, as noted.

An editorial project, co-supervised with Classics, is comparing current work on the digital side with editorial practices in printed critical editions of Homer, using the first book of the *Odyssey* as its focus. The student is considering *The Chicago Homer* and *Homer Multitext* as well as other digital products. The questions here are obvious but difficult: what do scholars of Homer want from an edition that the digital medium can better provide than the codex? What does Homer have to teach designers of digital editions? What accomplishments of the printed critical edition are at least currently beyond the reach of a digital edition? The specific focus on a single work places the questions of design precisely at the level at which scholars work.

A project in the analysis of gendered language takes as its data Swedish dramatic texts from a large archive of historical literature. Its central research problem is how questions of gender can be explored in this archive. Two obvious technical approaches are corpus linguistic methods to discover the workings of gendered language and text encoding to provide for retrieval.

Developing tools for aggregation and analysis of textual corpora is the object of another project. It begins in a survey of current corpus tools in light of the uses to which they are put and their perceived limitations, then moving on to implementation of prototypes designed to overcome these limitations and iterative trials. The audience for these trials will be researchers with a range of computing skills working in a variety of languages and disciplines. The project will take into account previous iterations of questioning the state of text-analysis but, unlike so much of previous debate, is undertaking its questioning of possibilities systematically.

The final project under this category is probing the interconnections between changes in publishing and changes in the humanities that stem from digital transformations of the book. It examines not only effects on text and how we relate to it when reading but also how the processes and mechanics of the publishing industry shape the digital text. What is needed, the student argues, is grounding in the concrete realities of the publishing industry, the situations of authors and readers and all the ways in which text is made available for reading. The problematic notion of de-materialized text—of information that moves unchanged through various media—plays a central role in this research.

Two additional projects in analysis of language are primarily historical and are described below.

## History by Prosopography, by Text-Analysis and by Palaeography

Of the ten projects that work with historical materials, seven are chiefly historical studies. One of these involves a study of political language; one of language used to characterize a particular subculture; two involve prosopography, i.e. history derived from the historical actors, and two manuscript studies. The prosopographical and one of the manuscript projects use relational database technology, and one of these uses mapping software. The two studies of language use corpus techniques. All are co-supervised with colleagues at King's.

One of the prosopographical projects focuses on the fourth- to early fifth-century *Ecclesiastical History* by Socrates Scholasticus. Its aim is to analyze biases and interests of the author and to chart the embedded geographical information. This project continues in the footsteps of the Prosopography of the Byzantine World, developed at King's, and seeks on the computing side to refine our understanding of digital prosopography by critiquing earlier ones as well as by exhibiting new approaches.

The other prosopographical project concentrates on high officials of the Portuguese court under the reign of John III (1521–57). It uses correlated assertions about these officials to enquire into the commonplace but incompletely understood notions of courtly service, social mobility, power and social reproduction. It asks if the group of individuals in service constitute a homogeneous group, whether patterns of social promotion can be discerned and a number of other questions to which answers are currently unknown. Categories of roles and typologies of interrelation, enforced by database entry, are themselves research questions. As with all such projects, the question of technological adequacy is forced by the normal intractability of historical data. This project also uses relational database technology.

One of the two manuscript projects is palaeographical; the other is concerned with illuminations.

The palaeographical project involves analysis of 6000–7000 Norwegian manuscript fragments from the period c.1000–1300 in order to investigate ecclesiastical connections between England and Norway. To date, the corpus has proven too large for manual analysis. For this reason the student will use digital methods under development in the department, as part of Dr Stokes' DigiPal Project, and within Scandinavia. These methods will be applied to suggest heretofore-unnoticed relationships, such as between letterforms and layout, and to identify fragments that were likely produced by the same scribe or scriptorium, or indeed were once part of the same book. In turn, these relationships will help to address key questions about English influence in Norway, ecclesiastical links between the two countries, and English script types in Norwegian scriptoria and their influence on Norwegian vernacular styles. The student is also planning to create an online resource that makes some of this research available to scholars and the general public. The dissertation is also intended to promote links between the digitization projects in Scandinavian and at King's College London.[4]

The project on illuminations centers on Hebrew manuscripts in medieval Portugal, questioning the originality and identity of specifically Portuguese illumination. It is investigating the iconographic features of Hebrew-Portuguese illumination, the salient features of the known illuminators and/or scribes, the iconographic relation between Portuguese and Castilian Hebrew book illumination and the connection between documented technical knowledge of pigments and other painting materials and the corpus under investigation. Using analytic and descriptive computer-assisted techniques it is attempting thus to characterize the main features of the ca. thirty manuscripts of the corpus.

Of the two corpus-linguistic projects, one is studying late nineteenth- to early twentieth-century grassroots politics in East Anglia through an analysis of speeches as transcribed in local newspapers. The student has laboriously built his own million-word corpus of election speeches, 1880–1910, and has to hand two larger reference corpora. From his corpus,

---

4    For the project, see "Digital Resource for Palaeography," King's College London News and Events, December 7, 2010, http://www.kcl.ac.uk/newsevents/news/newsrecords/2010/Dec/DigitalResourceforPalaeography.aspx.

using simple concordancing tools and elementary statistics, he argues quite persuasively for the close fit between the language of electioneering and the capabilities of the tools we have. He shows the inadequacy of remembered instances and broad generalizations drawn from long familiarity with historical data. Here, digitally, is an extension of known methods to a relatively unexplored kind of language, demonstrating their utility and power. Historically it demonstrates how close attention to the data upsets received knowledge.

The other corpus project focuses on perceptions of the Irish immigrant population in London from 1801 to 1820, in the period between the Acts of Union and beginnings of the campaign for Irish emancipation. Its central question, to be pursued by a corpus-analytic study of text from London newspapers and magazines, is how the historical print media shaped the vulnerable local communities of the Irish in London for better or for worse. It asks how were the Irish perceived in the relatively quiet period before emancipation became a prominent issue? What roles did the popular media play?

## Musicological Editing

The question here begins with the same dilemma as the Homeric edition: the still fluid and hotly debated nature of digital textual editing. The focus, however, is on the strongly performative dimension of musicological editions; several difficult but fascinating technological issues are faced, including development of recommendations from the Music Encoding Initiative. The student has begun with these recommendations but is writing his own software to model forms of the musical text. As expected, this project involves collaborative supervision with the Department of Music, but the student is also working closely with the Carl-Maria-von-Weber-Gesamtausgabe or WeGA project (http://www. weber-gesamtausgabe.de/) in Paderborn on a digital edition of Carl Maria von Weber's opera *Der Freischütz*.

## Narratological Geography

In this project, the student is investigating the differences between verbal and cartographic information for geographical purposes, asking, "What is the difference between a text and a map?" His project is supported informally by three scholars in Norway as well as by colleagues in the department at King's. He is using testimony of Norwegian and Sami people along the border with Sweden/Finland in the mid 18th Century as collected and transcribed by an army major at the behest of the Danish government. From this testimony, which was printed in the mid twentieth century, he has produced an XML-encoded text. He is using the encoded text to model the kinds of information contained in the verbal testimony to see if, as he suspects, words tell more than maps, or at least do so differently. Historical, philosophical, geographical and anthropological investigations thus sit alongside software modeling techniques. Each informs the other.

## Socio-Philosophy of Digital Traces

The basic premise of this project (currently in suspension while the student completes engineering-related doctoral work in Japan) is that a new meaning of identity has arisen out of the prevalence of mobile digital devices and the frequency with which they are used. On the social scientific side, the student proposes to track the actual behaviors of selected people; on the philosophical side, he is examining the idea of personal identity phenomenologically; on the technological side, he has been involved in designing and constructing devices. He has also written software for the iPhone to monitor such behaviors. Originally, the philosophical questions had priority, but with the engineering work it has become obvious that these questions need to be postponed until the behaviors they seek to illumine are more adequately manifested.

## Philosophical Questions of Performance

In research begun about a year ago, the student is examining the ontological questions raised by the involvement of dance with digital technology. Considering the multiple technological interfaces with which we engage when watching recorded performance, she is investigating the ontological repercussions for dance of this new mode of watching. She is concerned with the metaphysical nature of online performances in their multiple forms. Looking at full-length documentations, edited representations, performances made for the screen and specifically for the Internet, she is assessing the differing ontological status of these multiple formats and working towards an understanding of how multiplicity of representations impacts on the ontology of dance.

# Conclusions

What may we conclude from these last seven years of the PhD in Digital Humanities? Again, it seems obvious that the degree is defensible from a scholarly perspective as well as attractive to students, who from the outset have driven its development. By the end of the 2011–12 academic year, however, only one student had completed this degree; only two are in the final "writing up" phase; and only seven of the current fifteen enrolled students have converted from initial MPhil to PhD status. In other words, as should be clear from the discussion, we still have quite a bit to learn, perhaps even more than our students do.

One lesson we have learned concerns what one student has called "the openness of the program," that is, the license it gives to do research of any kind that involves critical work with digital tools and methods. The generosity of this license is by design, which is in turn a response to the plasticity of computing studied methodologically. However, it would not be practical to offer were it not for the supervisory talent provided by a major research institution located in one of the principal cities of the world. It would never have flourished were it not for the remarkably collegial academic culture in the School of Arts and Humanities at King's and the understanding built up over many years that the discipline we now call digital humanities is no less nor more than one among many.

Taken together, the projects I have described (and a number of others likely to begin in Autumn 2012 that I have not mentioned) show no sign of providing a map of the digital humanities. Rather their variety suggests, like Turing's design, an indefinite expansiveness. Inevitably, as the program grows, they will show the limitations of subject and approach that the Department of Digital Humanities at King's College London can properly cover and that British academic culture favors. Such a program in Australia, for example, would look rather different; so also would one in Germany. Nevertheless, the openness of the program to anything that we can support and that the culture favors, placing no other restrictions on it, seems appropriate for such a young and expansive discipline.

It is also perhaps worth mentioning that approximately half of the current students in the program are women.

So far the results of the program are largely unsurprising though very gratifying, especially to someone who has been arguing for the last quarter century that our subject is genuinely and independently academic at the highest levels. Perhaps the most important result is that a PhD in the digital humanities makes sense. But, crucially, the sense-making has in its first six years been almost entirely the work of the students. Earlier I said that the development of the PhD has been from the outset demand-driven, but neither "demand" nor "driven" are the right words to describe these students' contribution to our discipline. It is not demand that has driven but desire that is creating. "Real scientific research," John Ziman has written, "is very like play. It is unguided, personal activity, perfectly serious for those taking part, drawing unsuspected imaginative forces from the inner being, and deeply satisfying."[5] Partially subtract "scientific" and, for now, "unguided" to name what our students are doing.

What, then, is the PhD in Digital Humanities, exactly? The simple fact is that we do not have a stable answer, but all the evidence suggests that the intelligent desire powering its evolution will provide us with one. The simple fact is that this PhD is not just a framework for research, providing supervisory support and ensuring quality, but is itself empirical research into the best framework to adopt in order to further develop the intellectual culture of the digital humanities. Meanwhile, advertised jobs in the field are proving difficult to fill because qualified applicants are in short supply. Demand, need, desire and ability to produce them are not, however. It is too early to say anything useful about placement of students in jobs. Watch this space.

---

5   John Ziman, "Puzzles, Problems and Enigmas," in *Puzzles, Problems and Enigmas: Occasional Pieces on the Human Aspects of Science* (Cambridge: Cambridge University Press, 1981), 3. Ziman's essay originated as a BBC Radio broadcast in January 1972 as part of the science curriculum of the Open University.

# 2. Hands-On Teaching Digital Humanities: A Didactic Analysis of a Summer School Course on Digital Editing

*Malte Rehbein and Christiane Fritze*

This chapter discusses the rationale behind a week-long summer school course on digital editing in detail: its background, learning objectives, course content, methods, tools and media employed and the outcome of the course. It analyzes this approach by juxtaposing the course objectives with outcomes from a didactic perspective—that is, from the educational perspective of teaching the course. This chapter covers two areas of investigation: first, summer schools (or similar workshops and seminars *en-bloc*), as opposed to university teaching with face-to-face teaching every week, and second, digital editing through a holistic approach, rather than as a course focusing on particular aspects such as text encoding. The chapter is intended to present documentation as well as critical analysis that we hope will provide some guidance for similar enterprises.

## Motivation

Summer schools and workshops are common formats of conveying skills in digital humanities because regular curricula on university level do not exist in any comprehensive way and due to the fact that such skills are becoming more and more relevant as part of members of faculty's further training and for projects in the humanities.

In comparison to other aspects of digital humanities, digital editing appears to be a particularly collaborative and comprehensive process, requiring a wide range of skills. As Peter Shillingsburg has noted,

> Creating an electronic edition is not a one-person operation; it requires skills rarely if ever found in any one person. Scholarly editors are first and foremost textual critics. They are also bibliographers and they know how to conduct literary and historical research. But they are usually not also librarians, typesetters, printers, publishers, book designers, programmers, web-masters, or systems analysts. In the days of print editions, some editors undertook some of those production roles, and in the computer age, some editors try to program and design interfaces.[1]

What Shillingsburg implies here is the need for specific training in this area—that the required skills need to be taught—and this has to be reflected in didactics: the required skills *need to be taught*. The complex nature of the underlying process of digital editing requires a comprehensive educational approach encompassing a broad range of learning objectives.

The idea of designing a course on digital editing following these considerations had a second motivation derived from our experience of teaching digital humanities topics in both summer schools/workshops and in university curricula. This experience led us to the experimental "learning-by-project" approach that we are going to discuss in this chapter.

Our experience persuaded us that the practices of text encoding and data modeling, in particular, could be frustrating for students. It was always difficult to explain the rationale for certain tasks (such as creating a metadata model or encoding texts) and to illustrate their place within scholarly activity. This is because these tasks can only be understood abstractly aside from their place in the production of a digital resource in general and a digital edition in particular. Single exercises accompanying each step of the whole process could not establish the necessary connection for understanding and left students dissatisfied with their grasp of the topic. Hence, we decided to offer a learning-by-project approach aiming at group work to devise a small-scale edition, with the support of an out-of-a-box digital editing system. Participants were encouraged to collaborate with each other and to contribute their particular competencies and interests.

---

1   Peter Shillingsburg, *From Gutenberg to Google: Electronic Representations of Literary Texts* (Cambridge: Cambridge University Press, 2006), 94.

The driving philosophy was to get the students involved in the complete process of creating and publishing a digital edition, from the first encounter with the material to its web presentation. Through this holistic approach we hoped not only to convey a better understanding of the process but also to evoke an intrinsic motivation by completing a "real" (not only educational) project, to create something tangible and yet unpublished.

The innovation in this approach was two-fold: firstly, it did not focus on particular aspects of digital editing, such as TEI-based text encoding, but covered the complete life-cycle from planning the project to publishing. Secondly, we did not work with discrete exercises unrelated to the project but with one set of data that was enriched gradually during the course of the week—a format that would ideally serve as a model for a "real" project.

# Background

## ESU Summer school

The second Europäische Sommeruniversität "Kulturen & Technologien" or European Summer School on "Culture & Technology" (ESU) took place from July 26 to 30, 2010, at Leipzig University. It aimed to bring together postgraduates and early- career researchers in the arts, humanities, engineering, and computer sciences to foster cross-disciplinary networking and encourage future collaboration. The initiator of the ESU, Elisabeth Burr, describes its ongoing mission as

> Seek[ing] to offer a space for the discussion and acquisition of new knowledge, skills and competences in those computer technologies which play a central role in Humanities Computing and which increasingly determine [...] the work done in the Humanities and Cultural Sciences, as well as in Libraries and Archives everywhere.[2]

The week-long schedule of the Summer School was dominated by parallel workshops with a maximum of 20 participants each. The workshops were accompanied by plenary presentations of selected participants' projects in the afternoons as well as invited lectures by digital humanities specialists in the evenings. Each workshop comprised 15 sessions of 90 minutes, hence three sessions each day, and was led by two international instructors. The workshop From Document Engineering to Scholarly Web Projects looked behind the scenes of scholarly web publishing. Digital History and

---

2   Elizabeth Burr, "Mission," ESU Culture & Technology, University of Leipzig, October 15, 2010, http://www.culingtec.uni-leipzig.de/ESU/en/index_en.php?content=mission.

Culture: Methods, Sources and Future Looks stressed digital methods, tools and theory of online history projects. Methods in Computer-Assisted Textual Analysis dealt with the basic corpus linguistic methods using statistical software. This chapter treats the outcomes of the workshop taught by the authors on Introduction into the Creation of a Digital Edition.

## Participants

The Summer school was designed for an international clientele. The majority of the participants came from Central and Western Europe, but graduates and young researchers from Eastern Europe, India, Sri Lanka, and Brazil also attended the Summer University. The prospective candidates had to apply for participation and specify one workshop; the course instructors reviewed their applications.

Our class was finally attended by ten participants from Germany, Poland, France, Italy, Canada, the USA and China.[3] The cultural background of the participants differed significantly and so too did their level of graduation. About half of them were still graduate students whereas the other half comprised of young and advanced researchers in the humanities.

Disciplinary backgrounds were heterogeneous as expected but, in principle, all of the students came from the cognate fields of philology, language and literature studies. Of course, the languages and major areas of interest differed: 60% of the students planned to start editorial work, focusing for instance on fifteenth century manuscripts or on indigenous and *mestizo* chroniclers in colonial Mexico or on a Russian émigré's journal; 40% of the participants had in mind a linguistic analysis of the edited texts later on. The level of familiarity with the process of editing, on the one hand, and the use of digital humanities methods, on the other, showed a similarly wide range. The average age of the participants was 29 years, ranging from 23 to 40 years old; 70% were female, 30% male.

Overall, we expected student characteristics to vary in terms of prior knowledge, intellectual abilities and epistemological level. We also expected different learning styles and anticipated catering for these by a blend of learning methods. Our general assumption was that of a heterogeneous group of students with backgrounds in different fields in the Humanities but new or fairly new to digital humanities.

---

3   The authors wish to thank all participants of the workshop for their contribution and their willingness to participate in this experimental approach: Federico Caria, Claudia Di Fonzo, Małgorzata Eder, Natalia Ermolaev, Marc Andre Fortin, Jun Han, Marco Heiles, Stefanie Janßen, Julia Krasselt, and Annegret Richter.

# The Course on Digital Editing

## Course Objectives

The course was announced on the ESU website as an introduction to the "techniques and methods of a digital editing project … designed as an interactive experiment in which we work on a small corpus of manuscripts and bring it to online publication." The announcement noted the course's "learning-by-doing approach," in which the "typical processes in the creation of a digital edition are experienced by the participants" that are expected "to collaborate which each other during the workshop and to bring in their particular competencies and interests." The topics to be covered in the course included conceptualizing the editorial project; document analysis; data modeling; transcription, annotation and encoding; quality assurance; transforming and visualizing textual data; and online publication.[4] The main emphasis of the course was to be determined in consultation with the participants, with material provided by the instructors. The practical part of the workshop was estimated at 75% of the total time.

For the purposes of the workshop, a "digital edition" was understood as a scholarly edition not only *created* with the support of digital methods and tools but also one to be distributed by digital media—in this case, the internet.[5] The learning objectives of the workshop were shaped around this definition. Students would learn about the process of digital editing as a whole or, more generally speaking, about the application of digital methods for creating online resources. For this, we chose as a basis the reference model illustrated in Figure 1 and discussed in greater detail below. The workshop also had a second-order objective that was actually to create such a resource or edition and prepare it for publication as far as possible, i.e. to finish a small-scale project.

---

4  "Introduction into the Creation of a Digital Edition," ESU Culture & Technology, University of Leipzig, October 15, 2010, http://www.culingtec.uni-leipzig.de/ESU/en/index_en.php?content =../ESU_2010/en/workshops_2010.

5  According to Edward Vanhoutte's typology, this meant *creating* a digital edition rather than *digitizing* an existing analog/print edition or *generating* the edition from a set of data; see Edward Vanhoutte, "Traditional Editorial Standards and the Digital Edition," in *Learned Love: Proceedings of the Emblem Project Utretch Conference on Dutch Love Emblems and the Internet (November 2006)*, ed. Els Stronks and Peter Boot (The Hague: DANS Symposium Publications, 2007), 157–74. Compare Thomas Stäcker, "Creating the Knowledge Site—Elektronische Editionen als Aufgabe einer Forschungsbibliothek," in *Digital Edition und Forschungsbibliothek*, ed. Franz Fischer, Christiane Fritze, Patrick Sahle, and Malte Rehbein (special issue of *Bibliothek und Wissenschaft*, forthcoming), and Fotis Jannidis, "Digitale Editionen," in *Literatur im Medienwechsel*, ed. Andrea Geier and Dietmar Till (Bielefeld: Aisthesis, 2008), 317–32.

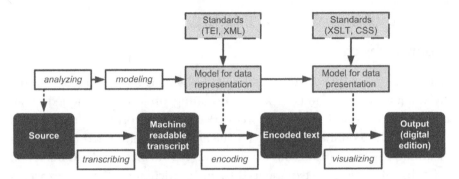

**Figure 1.** Reference model for digital editing.

Scholarly editing in general, comprising textual criticism, however, was not the primary concern of the workshop. However, we did consider the variety of the group's prior knowledge, especially regarding philology, and included a very basic introduction into the main principles of scholarly editing.[6]

The workshop also served as a test-run for our claim to combine learning objectives with project-like objectives. We expected this goal to be very demanding but wanted to see what progress we could make. The didactic, that is, educational objectives had priority, however. The experimental character of the workshop was not a hidden agenda. It was announced in the workshop description and clearly communicated to the participants in advance.

## Learning Goals

In preparation for the workshop, we defined the following learning goals (Table 1).

Most of these learning goals focus on knowledge and cognition. However, the last (but not least) objective—to experience collaborative work—has also a strong affective aspect, especially taking into account the heterogeneity of the group and the fact that members did not know each other beforehand. We stressed collaborative work by making it a learning goal, as traditional work in the humanities (too) often appears as a solitary enterprise while digital humanities projects are often conducted in groups.[7]

---

6   For a more general introduction to teaching the scholarly editing of German texts, see Bodo Plachta, "Teaching Editing—Learning Editing," *editio* 13 (1999): 18-32.

7   Compare Shillingsburg, *From Gutenberg to Google*, 94.

| Goal | Learning Outcome |
|:---:|---|
| 1 | To understand chances and challenges of the digital medium for scholarly editing. |
| 2 | To understand digital editing as a holistic process and to know typical phases in a digital editing project, methods and technologies applied and standards used in each phase. |
| 3 | To know typical infrastructural requirements for a digital editing project and to use such an infrastructure. |
| 4 | To know the definition and purpose of data modeling, to understand its importance in a project and to apply modeling techniques in simple editorial projects. |
| 5 | To apply the Guidelines of the Text Encoding Initiative (TEI) to encode "easy" texts and to use the Guidelines for further self-study |
| 6 | To be able to apply Cascading Style Sheets (CSS) for simple data representation. |
| 7 | To experience collaborative work. |

**Table 1.** Learning goals.

# Course Set-Up

This section deals with the didactic principles and the overall planning of the course. The following section analyzes the "performance" that actually took place in the classroom.

*Content:* Developing the content of the course was based on the two prevailing conditions: first, to cover the editorial process as a whole, beginning with the selection of the material and ending only with the publication on the internet, and second, rather than using separate exercises, for the single parts to employ one object of study and process it through the various stages of what we regarded as a typical workflow. This required that the results of one phase should influence the course as a whole, by becoming the input for the next phase. For instance, the agreement on a model for encoding textual features needs to be observed in the actual encoding; the definition of metadata made within the course provides the basis for the customization of the database etc.

As a model for the project workflow, we followed the digitization process used by the Brown University Women Writers Project or WWP (http://www.wwp.brown.edu/), in many ways typical of XML-based digital humanities projects, and modified it to suit the particular needs and scope of the workshop (Figure 2).

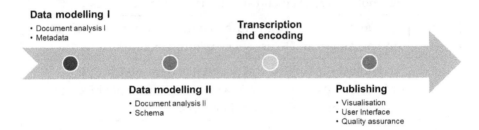

**Data modelling I**
• Document analysis I
• Metadata

**Transcription and encoding**

**Data modelling II**
• Document analysis II
• Schema

**Publishing**
• Visualisation
• User Interface
• Quality assurance

**Figure 2.** Reference process for digital editing.

*Data Modeling:* This is understood as the core process aimed at creating digital resources, such as an edition.[8] In our model workflow, data modeling occurs in two phases:[9] one models the *representation*[10] of the source data as input (in this case, texts and images of the documents) into the digital medium (i.e. it describes the "real world"), and the other models the presentation of the data as *output* (Learning Goal 4).[11] Here we follow Willard McCarty's definition:

> By "modeling" I mean *the heuristic process of constructing and manipulating models*; a "model" I take to be either *a representation of something for purposes of study,* or *a design for realizing something new.*[12]

Modeling the representation of data means analyzing the material with the project's objectives and deriving from both—by applying modeling techniques such as abstraction and generalization—the rules

---

8   Theorizing data modeling, developing models and managing the workflow around them can be regarded as the main reasoning behind digital humanities as a discipline.

9   See also Figure 1 in which we differentiate the outcome of the two modeling phases also technically: the XML schema for the representation of the source data and (mainly) the stylesheets (XSLT, CSS) for the presentation of the texts in the web (or any other medium).

10   For a definition of data representation and presentation in digital editing, see Patrick Sahle, "Zwischen Mediengebundenheit und Transmedialisierung. Anmerkungen zum Verhältnis von Edition und Medien," *editio* 24 (2010): 30.

11   In the German language, model theory distinguishes nicely between the two functions of models: an *Abbild* (of the reality)—the model of—on the one hand, and a *Vorbild* (the blueprint)—the model for—on the other; see Herbert Stachowiak, *Allgemeine Modelltheorie* (Wien: Springer, 1973).

12   Willard McCarty, "Modeling: A Study in Words and Meanings," in *A Companion to Digital Humanities*, ed. Susan Schreibman, Ray Siemens, and John Unsworth (Malden: Blackwell, 2004), 255, emphasis original.

for transforming the material into the digital medium. This includes its metadata, to cover the corpus of letters and to allow for database integration, as well as defining rules for text encoding.

In data modeling, a two-step approach suggested by Alexander Mehler and others was envisaged.[13] Beginning with the analysis of the material and the requirements, we would develop a *conceptual model* (expressed in natural language) and derive from this a *formalized (logical) model* (expressed in a formal language). We decided on entity-relationship models for metadata and XML-schema for textual data.[14]

*Transcription and Encoding:* In the context of this course, we understand transcription as the process of transforming the texts carried in the letters as physical objects into machine-readable format, basically as a sequence of characters. Encoding is the next step of enriching this (raw) data into processable information by making explicit structural and semantic features.[15] We chose to use the P5 Guidelines of the Text Encoding Initiative as the basis for both encoding metadata and text,[16] and to enable us to teach their basics (Learning Goal 5).

*Publishing:* This encompasses the design of the to-be-created digital edition in terms of data presentation or visualization (Learning Goal 6) and the interaction between the user and the data by means of a user interface (human-computer interaction). We used the WWP as a reference and, following its strong emphasis on quality assurance in the model, we took this also as part of the publishing workflow.

Modeling the presentation of the data necessitates analyzing (or reconsidering) the models developed for data representation as well as the project's objectives in order to identify the design of the online resource, i.e. to create a blueprint for the digital edition. The purpose of a digital edition consists in the interplay of these two models: "modeling of something readily turns into modeling for better or more detailed knowledge of it."[17] These considerations led us to emphasize data modeling strongly in this course.

---

13  See Peter Langmann, "Einführung in die Datenmodellierung in den Geisteswissenschaften," *xlab*, n.d., http://www.xlab.at/wordbar/definitionen/datenmodellierung.html.

14  On the entity-relationship model, see Peter Pin-Shan Chen, "The Entity-Relationship Model: Toward a Unified View of Data," *ACM Transactions on Database Systems* 1, no. 1 (1976): 9–36.

15  For a more elaborate definition of transcription and text encoding in the context of the creation of electronic texts, see Allen H. Renear, "Text Encoding," in *A Companion to Digital Humanities*, ed., Susan Schreibman, Ray Siemens, and John Unsworth, 218–39.

16  TEI Consortium, *TEI P5: Guidelines for Electronic Text Encoding and Interchange*, version 1.9.1, March 5, 2011, http://www.tei-c.org/release/doc/tei-p5-doc/en/html/.

17  McCarty, "Modeling," 257.

*Digital Editing Infrastructure:* This infrastructure is meant to support the whole workflow as much as possible. This includes the production of the digital edition as well as serving as the "host" for its publication. The role such infrastructure plays in both the production and publication process must be taught (Learning Goal 3).

The outline of the course contents helped us to sharpen learning goals so that in addition to the main objectives (as described in the previous section) some second-order goals (documented in Table 2) could be achieved.

| Goal | Learning Outcome |
|------|------------------|
| 8 | To gain insight into the different approaches of digital editing, to know selected sample projects and to assess them in terms of claim, audience, functionality, methods of data representation, data presentation and human-computer interaction. |
| 9 | To know selected tools supporting the various phases in digital editing. |
| 10 | To know some of the major principles as well as basic techniques of data modeling. |
| 11 | To learn fundamentals of Entity-Relationship modeling and to be capable of applying this method to an easy example. |
| 12 | To understand transcription as part of a digitization process and to know different approaches and their advantages and disadvantages. |
| 13 | To understand XML as a means for data representation and XSLT as a means for data presentation. |
| 14 | To know and be able to apply the principles and basic rules of XML; |
| 15 | To learn the main principles of the TEI and to gain insight into selected chapters of the TEI guidelines. |
| 16 | To become aware of the necessity to agree on and use standards. |
| 17 | To understand the necessity of quality assurance in a scholarly project. |

**Table 2.** Second-order learning goals.

To provide the students with an appropriate background, we decided to teach the additional theoretical lessons as documented in Table 3.

| Lesson | Description |
|--------|-------------|
| 1 | History and types of (scholarly) editions since the eighteenth century. |
| 2 | Examples of digital editions: the German Text Archive (http://www.deutschestextarchiv.de/), the kundige bok digital edition (http://kundigebok.stadtarchiv.goettingen.de/), the Thomas MacGreevy Archive (http://www.macgreevy.org/), and the Diary of Robert Graves 1935-39 (http://graves.uvic.ca/graves/). |
| 3 | Digital editions based on the SADE-infrastructure. |
| 4 | Modeling in general (following Stachowiak 1973) and its principles (such as classification, structuring, abstraction), modeling as a process, and entity-relationship modeling as an example (Chen 1976). |
| 5 | Basic principles and rules of XML. |
| 6 | Functionality of oXygen XML editor as an example of specialized XML editing software. |
| 7 | History and scope of the Text Encoding Initiative, and essential rules of the TEI Guidelines. |
| 8 | Schema, ODD, and ROMA. |
| 9 | Metadata according to TEI (teiHeader). |
| 10 | Pros and cons of different transcription approaches (e.g. OCR, double-keying). |
| 11 | Transcription of primary sources according to TEI. |
| 12 | Theory of information visualization and its role in digital editing. |
| 13 | Examples of visualizing textual data: the Republic of Letters project (http://toolingup.stanford.edu/rplviz/), Wendel Piez's Overlapping project (http://www.piez.org/wendell/dh2010/clix-sonnets/), and Ben Fry's Preservation of Favoured Traces visualization of Darwin's On the Origin of Species (http://www.benfry.com/traces/). |

**Table 3.** Additional theoretical lessons.

All these considerations led to the outline of the course as shown in Table 4. Each module was initially assigned a session of 90 minutes. We started with some "team building" to get to know each other and to learn more about the cultural and disciplinary background of the participants and then introduced the course design and the material. Most of the time in the workshop was spent with a series of theoretical, methodological and practical sessions that went step-by-step through the intended digital editorial process. The workshop concluded with project consultations and a course evaluation.

| Module | Title | Learning Goal | Content |
|--------|-------|:-------------:|---------|
| M1 | Introduction | | Course objectives and outline (T) Team building (P) Introducing the material (T) Document analysis I (P) |
| M2 | Digital Editing | | Exemplary overview of printed and digital editions Discussing the project's (Ehrlich letters) objectives (P) Phases in digital editorial projects (T) |
| M3 | Digital Editing Infrastructure I | 3 | The SADE infrastructure I (T) Overview of techniques / technologies involved in digital editing (T) Accessing SADE (P) |
| M4 | Data Modeling I | 4 | Theory of data modeling I (T) Document analysis II: Metadata (P) Developing the metadata (P) |
| M5 | Text Encoding I | 5 | XML Basics (T) Tools for encoding (P) TEI Basics I (T) |
| M6 | Data Modeling II | 4 | Document analysis III: text (P) Theory of data modeling II (T) Schema development (P) |
| M7 | Text Encoding II | 5 | TEI Basics II (T) Transcribing and encoding (P) |

| M8 | Text Encoding III | 5 | TEI Basics III (T)<br>Transcribing and encoding (P) |
|---|---|---|---|
| M9 | Text Encoding IV | 5, 7 | Transcribing and encoding (P)<br>Quality assurance (P)<br>Discussion of selected problems (T) |
| M10 | Digital Editing Infrastructure II | 3 | The SADE infrastructure II (T)<br>Putting it all together (P) |
| M11 | Visualization | 6 | Theory of information visualization (T)<br>Introduction to CSS (P)<br>CSS Visualization (P) |
| M12 | User Interface | 3 | Implementation of functionality into SADE (T/P) |
| M13 | Quality Assurance | 7 | Quality assurance (P) |
| M14 | Wrap-Up | | Recommendations for further reading and practice (T)<br>Feedback and discussion (T) |
| M15 | Project consultation | | Project consultation (P)<br>Conclusion (P) |

**Table 4.** Course set-up details, indicating theory (T) and practical (P) sessions.

## The Object of Study

Keeping these comprehensive learning goals in mind, careful consideration was required in order to find the appropriate materials to build the workshop. The following criteria, derived from the learning goals and the given constraints (number of participants, language, diverse backgrounds, prior knowledge and time for the workshop), guided our search:

- The materials should not be too comprehensive so as not to discourage the students with unrealistic goals.
- The corpus needed to be dividable into smaller portions, ideally equal in length and difficulty, so that students could work on their own portion of the whole corpus.
- The complexity of the source material in terms of textual features and the length of texts should be moderate; not too simple but not exaggerated.

- As we were not teaching paleography, we also had to ensure that the sources could be transcribed without special skills.

- The material should be comprehensible by all students; as the teaching language was English, English texts were preferred.

- Ideally, the material should not have been published yet as we hoped to increase students' motivation by doing something new.

- Copyright issues should not play a role.

Finally, thanks to the support of the special collections of the Universitätsbibliothek Würzburg, we came across a small corpus of letters from Paul Ehrlich that we found appropriate. These letters fulfill most of our criteria: the level of complexity of the letter-genre can be scaled according to the learning goals and the length of the single texts is moderate in such a way that each student or a small group can work on a clear-cut resource that still has a connection to the work of the other students. In the international context of the summer school, there is a drawback, however, as the language of that material is German.

The chosen collection (UB Würzburg, Paul Ehrlich Nachlass/1) consists of twenty typewritten and two handwritten letters with a length between one and six pages. The typewritten letters (see Figure 3 for an example) show some handwritten corrections and additional notes by their author, Paul Ehrlich. Other noticeable characteristics are the well-set letterheads and opener lines, attachments, colored passages, page numbers and marginal notes.

Paul Ehrlich (1854–1915) was a highly celebrated German scientist who conducted research in the fields of immunology and serology from the late 1870s until his death in 1915. In 1908 he became a Nobel Prize laureate in Medicine together with Ilya I. Mechnikov. All letters of the collection in question are addressed to Bodo Spiethoff. Spiethoff studied medicine in Berlin and Jena and, during the time of this correspondence, was an associate professor at the Universität Jena and practitioner in dermatology.

This correspondence between Ehrlich and Spiethoff took place between 28 June 1910 and 30 April 1914. The discussion between the two scientists was mainly about the further testing of the first effective chemotherapeutical remedy, the *Salvarsan-Kur* (the so-called "606" or Arsphenamine treatment) against syphilis.[18] Unfortunately, only the letters from Ehrlich to Spiethoff

---

18   This exchange of letters took place during the time when *Salvarsan* was officially marketed by Hoechst and introduced in 1910; see Amanda Yarnell, "Salvarsan," *Chemical & Engineering News* 83, no. 25 (2005): 16. It also covers the time of the introduction of *Neosalvarsan* by Ehrlich in 1912, which he mentions in letters 18 (dated May 20, 1912) and 20 (dated November 7, 1913).

are extant, at least in this collection; the content of Spiethoff's letters to Ehrlich can only be projected. In view of the educational objectives of the course, this is a negligible drawback. For publication and future research of this material, however, and discussion between the two scientists in the field of history of medicine, it remains a desideratum.

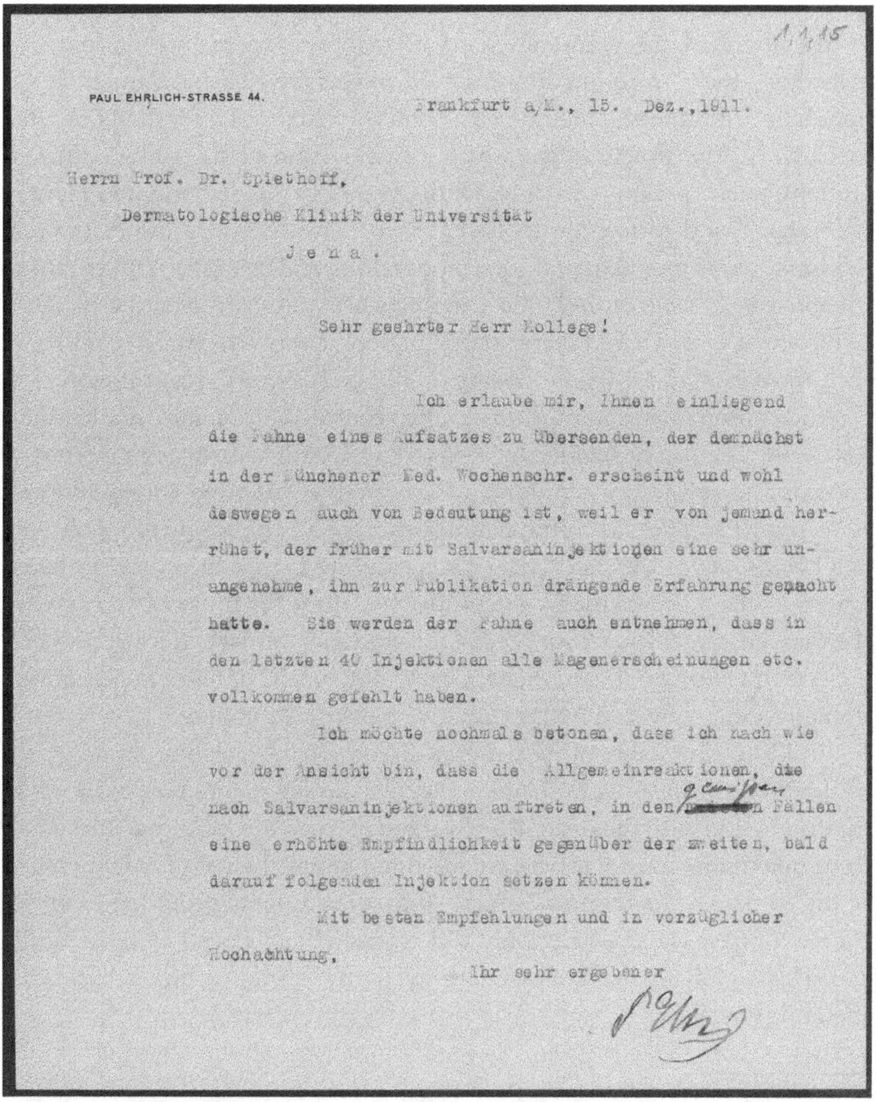

**Figure 3.** Sample letter (Paul Ehrlich to Bodo Spiethoff, dated December 15, 1910) from the Paul Ehrlich Nachlass (UB Würzburg Nachlass Ehrlich 1,1,15). Reproduced by kind permission of Universitätsbibliothek Würzburg.

## Didactics: Teaching Strategy and Methods

In order to find the best teaching methodology to bring this enterprise to a success, it soon became clear that we needed, first, a blend of didactic methods to cater for the heterogeneity of the group as well as for the wide range of learning objectives, and second, that each session should consist of both a theoretical and a practical part.

We intended the theoretical part of each session mainly to comprise lecturing—the "traditionally favored university teaching method"[19]— instructive discourses, demos and other (visual) presentations by the instructors. The practical parts of the workshops would allow sufficient student participation and interaction to apply the techniques learned beforehand and to use the tools that were introduced by the instructors, whose role was then that of tutors, moderators, and coaches. With regard to the the overall ratio of theoretical and practical parts, or from the students' perspective, passive and active participation, it was envisaged that 75% of the time allocated for the workshop would be spent on practical work.

All chosen methods address the cognitive domain of learning. Following the categorization by Diana Laurillard,[20] our teaching strategy encompasses all four main domains: discursive, adaptive, interactive and reflective. It is *discursive* as the establishment of a "discussion environment" is a key aspect of the theoretical parts; *adaptive* by the interplay of theory and practicing; particularly *interactive* as "students must act to achieve the task goal"; and *reflective*, i.e. as the students "must reflect on the task goal, their action on it, and the feedback they received" with the latter two domains being covered by the practical parts of the course.[21]

Building upon this more general discussion of teaching strategy, we decided on the best methods for achieving the six major course objectives in conjunction with the content we wanted to convey. One in particular had to be taken into consideration: we intended to use the results of one phase of the course—data models developed by the students provided input for the next phase—and so not only did course content need to be carefully coordinated but we needed to determine a corresponding blend of didactic methods (Table 5).[22]

---

19    Diana Laurillard, *Rethinking University Teaching*, 2nd edn (New York: Routledge, 2002), 92.
20    Laurillard, *Rethinking University Teaching*, 62ff.
21    Laurillard, *Rethinking University Teaching*, 78.
22    Compare Donald Clark, "Learning Strategies," *Big Dog & Little Dog's Performance Juxtaposition*, July 5, 2010, http://www.nwlink.com/~donclark/hrd/strategy.html.

| Content | Description of learning method / instructional strategy | Primary cognitive domains addressed | Learning goal(s) |
|---|---|---|---|
| Introduction | Lectures, visual demonstrations, Socratic didactic method | Understanding | 1 |
| Data Modeling | Work in small teams followed by presentation and discussion | Analyzing | 4, 7 |
| Transcription and Encoding | Practice by doing, coached by instructors | Applying | 5, 7 |
| Publishing | Use in real situation, coached by instructors | Creating | 6, 7 |
| Digital Editing Infrastructure | Demonstration | Understanding | 2, 3, 7 |

**Table 5:** Teaching methods employed for practical sessions.

## Tools and Media

The course was to be taught via local facilities: in a computer lab of the Faculty of Philology of the Universität Leipzig, which is equipped with a data projector, white board and flipchart. In preparation of the course we set up a wiki using MediaWiki (http://www.mediawiki.org/) and later encouraged the students to document the results of discussions and the joint development of concepts within this wiki (see Figure 7). In addition, the Summer school provided the e-learning platform Moodle (http://www. moodle.org/) to manage the exchange of instructors' slides across all four workshops. This system was also intended to manage feedback to the Summer University as a whole and as a means to stay in contact.

Again, referring to Laurillard and her categorization of "media for learning and teaching,"[23] we came up with a blend of tools and media to cover all areas she suggests. We intended to employ *narrative media* for presentations; *interactive media* for demonstrations; and *communicative media* for discussions and documentation. The technical infrastructure

---

23  Laurillard, *Rethinking University Teaching*, 81ff.

we provided and used is an adaptive medium in the sense that it served the application of theoretical knowledge to practice and it is a productive medium as it also formed the platform the to-be-developed digital edition. This is discussed in greater detail in the following section.

## Technical Infrastructure

As mentioned earlier, one of the learning objectives was to teach the requirements for and the usage of infrastructure for digital editions. For the practical aspect of the course, we needed such technical infrastructure not only for publication (as a productive medium) but also to support the whole process as much as possible (as an adaptive medium). The system we were looking for should be easy to install, easy to use and its different components should be well coordinated so that the technical setup could be regarded as a black box instead of dealing with loosely coupled single components.

Key requirements from the production perspective are:

- Easy access to the infrastructure from the lab's computers and participants' laptops;
- Capacity for collaborative and synchronous work on the same project;
- Support for the creation of relevant models for metadata, text representation and visualization; and
- Transcription and encoding of texts.

Key requirements from the publication perspective are:

- To grant (online) access to the edition;
- To bridge automatically between data representation and data presentation, i.e. the facility to apply stylesheets to encoded texts and to display images; and
- To support basic browse and search functionality.

From a didactic perspective, another requirement arises:

- The impact that certain actions in the editorial process (e.g. changing metadata or encoding textual features) have on the final product should be conceived by the students immediately, i.e. made visible and transparent.

We finally decided to use the Scalable Architecture for Digital Editions or SADE (http://www.bbaw.de/telota/projekte/digitale-editionen/sade/) system developed by Alexander Czmiel (Figure 4).[24] As SADE is a prebuilt framework

---

24  See also Alexander Czmiel, "Editio ex machina: Digital Scholarly Editions out of the Box" (paper presented at Digital Humanities 2008, University of Oulu, Oulu, Finland,

containing substantial components for both creating and publishing a digital edition, it seemed a suitable instrument for our purposes as it provides:

- A native XML database to store the encoded documents;
- A web publishing framework;
- TEI-aware default transformation stylesheets;
- A customizable search interface; and
- An image viewer.

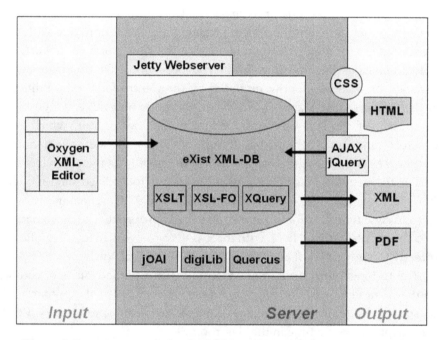

**Figure 4.** Components of the Scalable Architecture for Digital Editions (SADE) framework. Image sourced from the SADE project documentation.

The SADE framework addresses small-scale editions hence, the Ehrlich letter corpus fitted well into the system in terms of size. SADE is a bundle of software based on open standards. The main elements of SADE are a Jetty Webserver, which contains the native XML database eXist (http://exist. sourceforge.net/) and the digilib image server (http://digilib.berlios.de/). The database contains several TEI-aware XSLT stylesheets as default which transform TEI-conformant XML documents into a HTML presentation within the digital edition website or a PDF to download. All TEI stylesheets

June 25–28, 2008). The authors would like to thank Alexander Czmiel for his invaluable support in preparing and running the workshop.

are SADE customizations based on the stylesheets developed and maintained by the TEI Consortium.

This scalability of SADE can be understood in both directions. On the one hand, the editor is free to develop XML documents fulfilling the demands of each specific edition. On the other hand, the user has the possibility to generate transformation scenarios and to fulfill specific layout requirements.

The second major component of our infrastructure, the XML editor oXygen (http://www.oxygenxml.com/), was used for transcribing, encoding and CSS/XSLT modification. It provides a webDAV interface that we wanted to use for integration into the overall framework. Once connected with the eXist database of the SADE framework, it allows the students to work on the same data at the same time. For this purpose, the SADE framework was installed on a server (kindly provided by the Centre for Digital Editions at the Universität Würzburg) and made publically accessible. All desktop computers of the lab were equipped with the XML editor, which is a desktop- (and not a server-) based application, by the local assistants in advance. Nonetheless, the participants worked mainly on their own laptops.

For the generation and customization of our formalized data models (for metadata and text encoding) in the form of XML schemata, ROMA (http://www.tei-c.org/Roma/) appeared to be appropriate. The combination of components outlined here, with the SADE framework in its core, follows directly the principles of our model process for digital editing.

The technical infrastructure needed to be set up in advance, of course, so that it ran smoothly during the course. This included the preparation of source material, i.e. its image digitization and a preliminary OCR transcription to save time in the classroom.[25]

## Course Performance

While the previous sections dealt with the intention, planning and preparation of the course, we now turn to assess the practical outcomes and performance of the course. To do so, we highlight relevant modules from the overall course set-up (cf. Table 5) and focus on the practical parts that required students' interaction. This is done through the different didactic methods employed (Table 2). Overall, we can confirm the initial intention of spending 75% of the course on hands-on practice rather than on conveying theory.

---

25   We would like to thank the Digitization Centre of the Universitätsbibliothek Würzburg for doing this.

## Introduction

As planned, we started with "warm-up exercises" not only to get to know each other and to create a comfortable learning atmosphere but also to learn more about the technical skills of our students. Some icebreakers during the introductory session served this purpose well. In this way, we had a grasp of their prior knowledge, familiarity with the theme of the course and their literacy with regard to computer technology.

In the introductory session, we also decided to build small teams of two students each to perform the practical tasks together, especially transcribing and encoding. This had a pragmatic rationale: four of the ten participants were native German speakers and as the language of our material was German, we could fill most teams with one German and one non-German to overcome language limitations.

## Data Modeling

The most interesting sessions, with respect to didactics and in the context of the overall objective of bringing the material into a publishable form, were arguably those that encompassed data modeling—be it for modeling the requirements of the final product, metadata, text or visualization. In all modeling sessions, we built teams of three or four students, gave each team the same instructions, taken from our model editorial process, and let them work in teams for a certain amount of time (usually approx. 30 minutes). Each team was then asked to present their results, which were later documented on the wiki, and to discuss them with the whole group. The final discussion led to an agreement on one of the proposed (*mutatis mutandis*) models. To illustrate this approach, the instructions for one of the modeling sessions (modeling text, M6) were as follows:

I.   Conceptual model

    a.   Look at your document(s) and browse through the other material: What *could* be marked up?

    b.   Now consider the project's objectives (purpose of modeling): What *needs* to be marked up?

II.  Formal model

    a.   So far, we know what to encode, but only in a conceptual view. Now, design a TEI schema to formalize this and to prescribe in a formal way, how to encode.

Figure 5 illustrates the outcome of two modeling sessions: on the left, entity-relationship models developed by the students for metadata (formal model) and, on the right, the documentation of the model for encoding text (conceptual model). The following gives a brief overview of the achievements during the various analyzing and modeling sessions.

*Objectives of the digital edition:* These encompassed what the to-be-developed final product would feature. After creating an initial collection, the students were asked to prioritize these features (high, medium, low, nice to have) and eventually an agreement was found. The key aspects are to grant access to all letters as images and as transcribed and annotated texts; to allow full text search; to allow browsing by recipient, sender, date and address; and to provide an index of medical terms.

*Metadata:* All models proposed were sound in their intellectual content; their formalization in an ER-model understandable and useful for the following discussions. An agreement on a model (entities, attributes and relations) was reached within reasonable time (Figure 5).

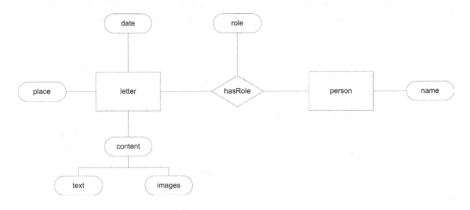

**Figure 5.** Metadata model developed during the course
(entity-relationship notation).

Discussions on how to encode the metadata took place within the group after a theoretical introduction into teiHeader but—due to time constraints—finally predetermined by the instructors.

*Text:* The agreement on the model (and hence the encoding rules) was based on the synopsis of the results presented by the teams. One should note that this analysis was performed after a basic introduction into TEI but before explaining chapters of the TEI guidelines in detail, let alone introducing particular elements. Features to be encoded were: page and line breaks;

text structure (paragraphs and lists); letter heads; address lines; greetings, signatures, openers and closures, occurrences of person names, place names, dates, numbers and technical terms; features of textual corrections (deletions, additions, substitutions).

## Transcription and Encoding

Since we had ten students in the class and paired them up for the practical work, only five letters could be transcribed and encoded. Therefore, it soon became clear that we needed to abandon the idea of bringing an edition of the whole corpus into publishable format. instead, we concentrated on a selection of letters.[26]

Transcribing the letters from the digital surrogate of their (typewritten) original was partly supported by OCR-software. This was primarily done to introduce the students to the different ways of transcribing (automated, keying) and secondly not to waste time in the classroom by repetitive tasks. However, the quality of the results from the OCR process was poor and often required manual intervention. A more careful preparation might have overcome this issue.

Encoding the letters raised—apart from the language constraints of the non-native German participants—anticipated problems in encoding lessons as well as in encoding projects. They encompass two areas: first, the question of how to decide on a certain feature of the text e.g. is "water" a medical term or not, and second, how to encode features not covered in the theoretical introduction. These challenges cost more time than expected and regularly needed to be discussed in the plenum. Overall, we have achieved less than we hoped in transcribing and encoding the letters.

## Publishing

Although we intended to pay high attention to quality assurance and devoted a whole session to at least crosscheck the work, the students mostly neglected it. An evaluation of the encoded texts after the completion of course hence revealed many flaws.

With regard to visualization, the students experimented a little bit with CSS and their impact on the display of the texts, for which the SADE infrastructure provided an intuitive tool. The visualization of textual

---

26  A major drawback from our original intention to let each participant work on two letters, i.e. to accomplish twenty letters overall.

features remained incomplete, however, and the layout of the digital edition as a whole rudimentary (Figure 6).

**Figure 6.** Screenshot of the edition at the end of the course.

The functionality for the edition was provided by the SADE infrastructure and customized by the instructors. As the course was dynamic in the sense that the results from one phase built the basis for the next phase of editorial work, it required nightly work by the instructors in order to prepare the system for the next day, e.g. to write XQuery scripts (required for database integration) to handle metadata in the format defined by the group during the day or to adopt stylesheets according to the encoding rules the group had agreed upon.

Regarding the infrastructure, we achieved our aims. The course appeared as collaborative work and the students could immediately follow the work of their peers. Even in the early stages of the project, one could grasp the edition holistically and see it growing and improving (new documents uploaded, encodings corrected, style sheets enhanced, etc) step-by-step.

Different style sheets were developed and uploaded and allowed the students to experience the relation between representation and presentation of data. Visualization of basic textual features, such as substitutions or highlighting of names, was accomplished. At the end of the Summer school, our edition allowed one to browse the corpus by date, place, sender and recipient.[27] A full-text search and an alphabetic index of

---

27   Browsing by sender and recipient was possible only in theory, as all the letters had the same sender and recipient.

medical terms were automatically created and linked the entries to their occurrences in the text as well as to Wikipedia.

However, it took a lot of time to get the system running. Setting up database connections (in oXygen), granting access and providing passwords may have been better prepared by the instructors. But it is generally a task that is time-consuming and risky in a classroom with a heterogeneous audience where one has to deal with different levels of computer literacy, various operating systems and so on.

**Figure 7.** Sample screenshot from the wiki made during the course, documenting the discussions on data models.

# Evaluation

In this final section we draw to a conclusion by critically assessing and didactically analyzing this summer school course. We do so by first looking at the feedback the students gave to us after the course, second by drawing our own lessons learned by evaluating course performance versus course objectives and third, we provide a possible explanation of mismatches.

## Participants' Feedback

At the end of this summer school, we asked the participants to give us their feedback on the course. This was collected in form of an open discussion, occasionally intervening by asking questions or insisting on issues that were of particular interest for the instructors.

In general, the combination of theory and practical experience was considered positive. Many students stated that the theory (especially of data modeling and text encoding) was difficult to understand at first, but became clear while practicing. This might be assessed as positive feedback with regard to the didactic success. From our point of view, it is natural (and has to do with different learning styles) that some students preferred more practical work and regard the theoretical parts—from their perspective—as too abstract, while others stated the opposite. On average, the ratio between conveying theory and practicing it was regarded as well balanced.

Simply including practical exercises was not the innovation of our teaching approach. Working continuously on the same object throughout a complete *value chain* in which the material was gradually enriched until it has reached its final output in a (more or less) nicely visible form ("actually seeing something on screen as part of a bigger story and not only markup"), accessible, searchable and browse-able, was regarded as rewarding and motivating. Another motivation was drawn from the collaborative approach in which all participants (or pairs) worked on the same material but had different tasks within the project, in our case by being responsible for different letters of the corpus.

While the theory we tried to convey in the lectures was generally assessed as being "too much" (and particularly as having "too much vocabulary"), the practical parts seemed to work well for most participants. The genre of letters and the corpus that we had chosen for this was regarded as appropriate. The shortness of the texts as well as the number of textual features to encode within the letters was appreciated: too few of them would not have allowed sufficient encoding practice; too many or too complicated features, however, would have led to frustration. It was also seen as useful that the corpus had texts of similar kinds so that the participants could help each other better. The students suggested working with texts in the English language, however.[28]

Regarding the digital editing infrastructure, the students grasped its role in the context of both creating and publishing a digital edition but their different components, let alone computational details, were considered too complex and, on a technical level, beyond the scope of this course.

It was commonly acknowledged by the participants that attending one summer school course can arguably only provide an outline of what digital editing involves and serves as a starting-point for further self-directed studies or learning-by-doing.[29]

## Lessons Learned

Changing the viewpoint to that of the instructors, we would like to discuss the achievement of the course (its "performance") in comparison with the learning objectives.

In general, what is realistically achievable in such a course? In particular, what is the best the balance between broadness (covering the whole editorial process) and depth (e.g. detailed knowledge of certain aspects)? It became clear that one cannot equally serve both objectives—the generalist as well as the specialist—in such a short time. In retrospect, the course achieved a generalist overview. For example, teaching the basic rules of entity-relationship modeling and using them in this phase of the project (modeling metadata) was useful as a means to make explicit what would otherwise be neglected. In this course, however, entity-relationship modeling was used more as a tool to force the students to think systematically and describe the

---

28 There were also a couple of minor issues addressed respectively by suggestions made by the students, which do not reflect on our approach as such. Suggestions that might be of general interest for teaching at summer schools encompass: providing a glossary of terms, handouts of slides and additional material (provided by us only on Moodle), charts and illustrations as references (e.g. of the process as a whole or the infrastructure).

29 Comparing the results of a recent study of TEI-based manuscript encoding, showing that it takes an average of 1.5 years from a first encounter with TEI until its first application in a project; see Marjorie Burghart and Malte Rehbein, "The Present and Future of the TEI Community for Manuscript Encoding," *Journal of the Text Encoding Initiative* 2 (2012), http://jtei.revues.org/372.

object of their study rather than claiming that entity-relationship modeling is necessary in any digital editing project and aiming to enable the students to use this technique perfectly.

To what extent is the course a starting point for the participants' own work? Although this had not been explicitly declared as a learning objective, it became clear in retrospect that it should be the overall objective or aim of the course. The students' feedback confirmed that the course enabled them to do further work and self-directed studies particularly through its generalist approach. Teaching students to use the TEI guidelines seems to serve this purpose better than thoroughly discussing single elements.

From these more general considerations, we would like to assess the achievement of the six major learning objectives as outlined in Table 1, compared with the actual course performance (Table 6).

| Learning Goal | Projected Learning Outcome | Actual Course Performance |
|---|---|---|
| 1 | To understand chances and challenges of the digital medium for scholarly editing. | Although difficult to assess, we believe that this objective could be achieved. What appeared to be really helpful was the fact that the course was embedded into the program of the summer university which allowed the students to learn about many other applications of the digital medium for the humanities. |
| 2 | To understand digital editing as a holistic process and to know typical phases in a digital editing project, methods and technologies applied and standards used in each phase. | This was certainly the main outcome and benefit of the course, although "know" could only be achieved on a generalist perspective (see above). |
| 3 | To know typical infrastructural requirements for a digital editing project and to use such an infrastructure. | This was part (and a requirement) of the "holistic process" of learning goal 2 and as such conveyed at least superficially. Deeper knowledge and understanding could not be conveyed (see above). |

| 4 | To know the definition and purpose of data modeling, to understand its importance in a project and to apply modeling techniques in simple editorial projects. | Although this was one of our focuses for the course, especially the last aspect of this objective—to apply modeling techniques—must be regarded as too ambitious. For the other two aspects (knowing and understanding), the same assessments apply as for learning goals 2 and 3. |
|---|---|---|
| 5 | To apply the Guidelines of the Text Encoding Initiative (TEI) to encode "easy" texts and to use the Guidelines for further self-study | This objective could be fully achieved. But naturally, in comparison with a weeklong course on text encoding only, the wording "easy texts" needs to be taken literally. |
| 6 | To be able to apply Cascading Style Sheets (CSS) for simple data representation. | Here, we intentionally achieved less than in learning goal 5 as the theoretical introduction into CSS was not systematic. A stronger emphasis on this aspect might be advisable for the future. |
| 7 | To experience collaborative work. | Although the wording of this objective does not really allow measuring its achievements, collaborative work was certainly facilitated during the course. |

**Table 6.** Achievement of (major) learning goals.

Our non-didactic objective to "bring [the edition of the corpus] to online publication" was clearly too ambitious. The result of one week's work was (naturally) quite far away from being publishable in both completeness and quality. What worked very well, however, was the succession of the various phases of our editorial process. Overall, our "final product" followed indeed the objectives the group had set in the beginning of the course, texts were encoded on the basis of rules defined by the group in the data modeling sessions, and the edition featured what was intended (browsing, etc).[30]

---

30   As an alternative, the instructors could have prepared a best practice solution for each phase of the workflow and use these as input for the next phase instead of using what the group agreed upon.

In the following, we would like to list some of the issues we encountered and suggest possible solutions that might help to prepare similar courses:

- With respect to organization, such a course requires extremely careful, anticipative and thorough preparation. In comparison to a "traditional" workshop with lectures and loosely (if at all) coupled exercises, the preparatory effort is higher and technical set-up takes longer.

- The "dynamics" of such an approach in combination with the heterogeneity of the group clearly requires two instructors respectively, one instructor and one tutor. In sessions in which the students are asked to reproduce something (e.g. set-up of a database connection) it is more helpful if one of the instructors explains and demonstrates while the other serves as a tutor and checks that everybody reaches the same level.

- The practical sessions require intensive coaching by the instructors.

- Concerning practicalities, minor details need to be taken into account or at least one should not be surprised. For example, oXygen installations can have different languages in the user interfaces. This makes explaining its usage a bit annoying; not everyone might be familiar with Moodle or a wiki or other tools you use, so introducing these tools takes additional time. The use of fewer systems than we did might be good general advice.

- It was very helpful that the SADE infrastructure we used covered most of our needs. This gave us the time to concentrate on digital editing as process performed as a humanist scholar rather than as "typesetters, printers, publishers, book designers, programmers, web-masters, or systems analysts," to reprise (and for the future hopefully refute) Shillingsburg's statement from the introduction of this chapter.

## Some Concluding Didactic Considerations

As we have already said, one of the main benefits of the course was a general overview of what is involved in digital editing and the basic principles of editing workflow and infrastructure. The learning objectives, however, were too ambitious and hence feedback like "too much" or "too much vocabulary" should be taken seriously.

Reviewing for a final time our learning objectives and regarding them in the light of the learning taxonomy suggested by Benjamin Bloom and revised by Lorin Anderson and David Krathwohl (Figure 8),[31] it is clear that the theoretical parts of the workshop emphasized *remembering* and *understanding* and the practical parts focused on *applying* and *creating*.

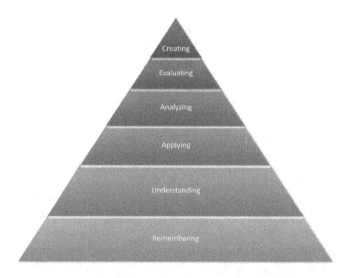

**Figure 8.** Taxonomy of learning objectives, according to Bloom (1956) and Anderson, Krathwohl, and Bloom (2001).

Analyzing the cognitive domain, on which learning goals 1-6 stressed, it becomes obvious (and had already been while planning the course) that we concentrated on the "higher level" categories: *understanding, applying, analyzing, evaluating* and *creating*.[32] The "low level" category *remembering*, which Anderson, Krathwohl, and Bloom define as "retriev[ing] [i.e. recognizing and recalling] relevant knowledge from long-term memory,"[33] was attempted but was not fully achievable. This was due to the time constraints of the workshop and especially the fact that in a comprehensive teaching approach as in summer schools (in comparison to a semester-long

---

31   Benjamin S. Bloom, *Taxonomy of Educational Objectives, Handbook I: The Cognitive Domain* (New York: David McKay, 1956), and Lorin W. Anderson, David R. Krathwohl, and Benjamin S. Bloom, *A Taxonomy for Learning, Teaching, and Assessing: A Revision of Bloom's Taxonomy of Educational Objectives* (New York: Longman, 2001).

32   For a definition of these categories, see Anderson, Krathwohl, and Bloom, *A Taxonomy for Learning, Teaching, and Assessing*, 67-68.

33   Anderson, Krathwohl, and Bloom, *A Taxonomy for Learning, Teaching, and Assessing*, 67.

course with lectures every week) it is hardly possible to affect the long-term memory. In such a schedule there was simply insufficient time for students' preparation, follow-ups and reflections in between sessions. As remembering also provides the basis for the "higher quality" objectives, this might also explain why the practical parts were so much slowed down in comparison to our plans and intention of accomplishing a completed project.

We believe that a "learning-by-project" approach as such is without doubt worth considering in teaching digital humanities. But one must be sensitive to the issues that might arise from the heterogeneity of the group and the fact that "higher" learning objectives, especially those in the category of creating, can only fully be achieved with a solid basis. A week-long course appears insufficient for a complex process that involves many different skills such as digital editing covering a wide range of learning objectives, as can be seen in the taxonomy by Bloom and by Anderson, Krathwohl, and Bloom.

Despite the digital edition of the corpus not being completed as intended, the aspiration and effort alone were beneficial. Students grasp a better sense of what digital editing as a holistic process involves, they learn at least how to conduct further self-directed studies and where to start their own projects and are definitely more motivated. We certainly would *mutatis mutandis* offer workshops and courses with the same aims again.

# 3. Teaching Digital Skills in an Archives and Public History Curriculum

*Peter J. Wosh, Cathy Moran Hajo and Esther Katz*

Digital technology has fundamentally altered the archival, public history and editing landscapes. New media have, in many ways, promoted a convergence of these various fields. Archivists, public historians and historical editors all face increasing demands to make analog resources available online, to manage and preserve born-digital materials and to incorporate social networking technologies into their products. Professionals within these fields also necessarily need to integrate new media and advanced technology into their daily work. Archivists, editors and public historians increasingly find themselves educating students and researchers remotely through their web sites, as well as helping to develop online curricular materials for use in secondary school and undergraduate classrooms. Each profession has struggled—too often independently and in isolation—with the need to provide better metadata and explanatory materials so that their users can access and understand digital collections. All three professions are confronting the challenges of mastering new media, working collaboratively and effectively with information technology staff without allowing such services to drive their programs, and ensuring the long-term preservation of born-digital materials.[1]

---

1   A growing body of archival literature, evident in such traditional professional journals as *The American Archivist* and *Archivaria,* as well in such newer e-publications as *D-LIB, Wired,* and *First Monday,* addresses these issues and concerns. The recent book by Daniel J. Cohen and Roy Rosenzweig, *Digital History* (Philadelphia: University of Pennsylvania

Preparing students for careers in archives, public history and historical editing has also become far more challenging. For generations, archivists learned to process and describe collections, public historians to create museum exhibits and film documentaries, historical editors to transcribe, annotate and publish primary source materials in print format. The products created by these scholars and professionals were aimed at a small and well-defined audience—the researchers consulting an archival collection, visiting a museum or scouring a print edition of documents. But as archives, museums and editing projects venture onto the World Wide Web, the tools of their trade are becoming more diverse, more challenging, and rapidly changing. Their audiences, previously a relatively known quantity, have expanded to the billions around the globe who have internet access. Preparing students to participate and thrive in a technologically complex and competitive world, as their products vie for attention alongside with those of enthusiastic, but untrained, amateurs has become a major challenge for educators as more and more cultural heritage and memory institutions seek to make their analog material available online.

Professional associations, grant agencies and employers recognize the need for greater emphasis on digital skills in professional education. The Society of American Archivists has, since 2002, required that "Digital Records and Access Systems" be a core contextual element of archival training, specifically noting that archival educators need to "include information on the development of new media formats and document genres, and changing information technologies for the creation, maintenance, and use of records and papers."[2] A 2007 survey of history-based archival education programs, however, found that most failed to adjust to these changing professional expectations.[3] In public history education, programs lag behind their information science colleagues when it comes to integrating digital technology with scholarship. A few exceptions, notably George Mason

---

Press, 2006), is addressed specifically to historians and offers an excellent overview of the salient issues. See also: Kate Theimer, *Web 2.0 Tools and Strategies for Archives and Local History Collections* (New York: Neal-Schuman, 2010).

2   "Guidelines for a Graduate Program in Archival Studies," Society of American Archivists (approved January 2002 and revised in 2005 and 2011), http://www.archivists. org/prof-education/ed_guidelines.asp.

3   Joseph M. Turrini, "The Historical Profession and Archival Education," *AHA Perspectives* 45, no. 5 (2007): 47–49.

University and the University of Nebraska at Lincoln, prove that it is possible to integrate new media, history, and technology, but the difference between these two leading edge programs and the typical history department is stark. Recent curricular surveys of the public history field contain virtually no discussion of technology or digital issues, despite the fact that such studies also document the fact that employers expect program graduates to possess precisely the blend of technological, collaborative, and administrative skills that immersion in digital history might provide.[4]

But students need more than a basic grounding in digital tools. They must still master their core professional skill sets: historiographical content, museological approaches and information theory. They also require practical immersion in such tasks as processing archival collections, curating museum exhibitions, and transcribing and annotating historical documents. They further need to engage with historical research and master some content area. In most graduate programs, this must be accomplished within the temporal constraints of a two-year masters program. If programs fail to provide real-world job skills, graduates will continue to face gloomy employment prospects. As educators need to carefully balance theoretical, practical and digital skills in their programs, program managers struggle with complex issues in trying to redesign curricula and keep programs current: Which skills do students really need? Should mastering a minimum set of digital skills constitute a graduation requirement? Should programs incorporate specific software programs and tools into their curriculum or should they focus primarily on underlying concepts? Should purely technical skills, such as learning HTML or programming be incorporated into history degrees? This chapter details the New York University archives and public history program's experiences in reconfiguring a long-standing program and integrating digital skills throughout its curriculum.

---

4  For example, see Philip M. Katz, *Retrieving the Master's Degree from the Dustbin of History* (report to the Members of the American Historical Association, 2005); Patricia Mooney-Melvin, "Characteristics of Public History Programs, Fall 2005" (report by the Curriculum Committee and Training Committee of the National Council on Public, 2006); and, Marla Miller, "Playing to Strength: Teaching Public History at the Turn of the 21st-Century," *American Studies International* 42 (2004): 174–212.

# New York University's Archives and Public History Program

New York University's History Department has offered programs in archival management and in public history since 1977 and 1981 respectively. Both programs emerged from the movements to professionalize archival training and advance the public history movement in the late 1970s, and each functioned as a highly successful advanced certificate program attached to the general MA degree within the Department of History. They shared faculty and curricula, and satisfied a common mission of providing students with a theoretically and methodologically sophisticated approach to the practice of history in such venues as historical societies, history museums, documentary film, historical editing projects, educational agencies, corporate and non-profit institutions and the public sector. Both programs were designed to prepare students for diverse careers, both in and outside of the academy. In 2007, the two programs were merged to create the archives and public history (APH) program, which offers a MA in Archives and Public History and allows students to concentrate on either discipline.[5] Included in its offerings is historical editing, taking advantage of the fact that New York University's History Department currently hosts two editing projects, the Jacob Leisler Papers (http://www.nyu.edu/leisler) and the Margaret Sanger Papers Project (http://www.nyu.edu/projects/sanger).

In 2008, the APH recognized the need to systematically review the curriculum. One significant gap in the course offerings involved digital skills. Program director Peter Wosh secured a grant from the Professional Development Grants Program of the National Historical Publications and Records Commission (NHPRC) to address this situation. The grant allowed the APH Program to hire a curriculum specialist who would consult with faculty and students, restructure the APH, integrate digital skills into existing courses, and develop new courses to meet student needs. Amanda French, with a PhD in English from the University of Virginia and demonstrated experience in digital humanities, was hired to fill the position. French focused first on constructing a definition of "digital competency"

---

5    For more on the history of the programs, see Peter J. Wosh, "Research and Reality Checks: Change and Continuity in NYU's Archival Management Program," *The American Archivist* 63, no. 2 (2000): 271–83; and, Rachel Bernstein and Paul Mattingly, "The Pedagogy of Public History," *Journal of American Ethnic History* 18, no. 1 (1998): 77–92.

and obtaining a sense of current students' skills and interests. Much popular literature claims that the new generation of "digital natives" possesses superior technological skills to their "digital immigrant" predecessors, but French's survey of APH students reflected a different reality.[6] Few appeared conversant with digitization methods and standards. Most proved unable to define so fundamental a term as metadata. Some had experimented with basic social networking tools, though even this was far from widespread. French established a series of six extra-curricular workshops, entitled "Digital Skills for Historians," that were intended to improve student skills. These included sessions concerning bibliographic research software, the use of HTML and CSS for web publishing, blogging with WordPress (http://www.wordpress.org/), using social networking tools, building an online archive/exhibit with Omeka (http://www.omeka.org/) and keeping up with technological trends.[7] The workshop series, which included students and faculty participants, provided a basic grounding in some of the digital skills that we hoped to integrate into coursework.

While workshops provided a short-term solution for students already enrolled in the program, more systemic changes were necessary. The APH faculty worked with French to develop a wish list of competencies and skills we hoped our students could master upon graduation. A close examination of syllabi and assignments revealed instructional gaps and overlap, as well as opportunities for incorporating new content into the program. Critical competencies were integrated into the program's required courses, while more specialized skills were included in the elective courses. This exercise allowed us to view the entire curriculum holistically, and to ensure that individual courses did not exist as isolated silos.

## Curriculum Revisions

The primary impetus for course reform was the need to incorporate digital technology across the entire curriculum. However, APH instructors, aside from Wosh, are adjunct professors, making collaboration with one another and discussion of the content and goals of their courses more difficult.

---

6   For example, see John Palfrey and Urs Gasser, *Born Digital: Understanding the First Generation of Digital Natives* (New York: Basic Books, 2008) for the conventional view of the "native/immigrant" divide.

7   For more on the workshops, see "Digital Skills Workshops," Archives and Public History Digital, http://aphdigital.org/more/digital-skills-workshops/.

Wosh reviewed all syllabi with French and worked with individual instructors to revise and develop new units with the goal of developing an integrated and coherent approach to digital and electronic issues. A course on Preservation and Reformatting, for example, not only needed to address the issues surrounding manuscripts and photographs, but also emphasized the use of digital technology as a preservation tool, the problems inherent with born-digital materials, the need for migration and maintenance, and sustainability issues. A course on The Historian and the Visual Record integrated the impact of digital technology in all its learning objectives. To be effective, this kind of programmatic approach requires continuous revision as software, tools, and best practices change. But restructuring had to begin with the program's core courses.

## Introductory/Required Courses

The APH offers a structured program with several required courses that form a solid base of both professional and digital competencies. Introduction to Archives and Introduction to Public History survey theoretical and methodological trends within each profession. Both courses have now been restructured to incorporate more content relating to digitization and new media. Students in the Introduction to Archives class, for example, are required to study and report on such projects as the Internet Archive (http://www.archive.org/), the Archives of American Art (http://www.aaa.si.edu/) at the Smithsonian Institution's approach to digital collections, the Library of Congress's National Digital Information Infrastructure and Preservation Program (http://www.digitalpreservation.gov/) and the Digital Lives Research Project in the United Kingdom (http://www.bl.uk/digital-lives/). They also receive exposure to such content management systems as the Archivists Toolkit (http://www.archiviststoolkit.org/) and Archon (http://www.archon.org/), study contemporary data structure and data content standards, consider remote reference and the use of social media in reconfiguring finding aids and gain some understanding of the ways in which archivists address born digital documentation. Students who enroll in the Introduction to Public History course systematically analyze and critique such projects as the September 11 Digital Archive (http://www.911digitalarchive.org/) and the Hurricane Digital Memory Bank (http://www.hurricanearchive.org/). They also learn about the ways in which historians have attempted to connect with local audiences through such collaborative ventures as the Historical Society of Philadelphia's

PhilaPlace (http://www.philaplace.org/) and the Maine Historical Society's Maine Memory Network (http://www.mainememory.net/). Finally, they explore historians' efforts to create online educational tools using primary sources for secondary schools and college courses.

Introductory courses, however, can only begin to suggest the transformative impact of digital technologies on historical practice. They also tend to rely more on describing and critiquing projects than examining the challenges inherent in creating digital projects. It therefore seemed necessary to supplement these introductions with an additional course devoted solely to digital practice. We created a new required course, Creating Digital History (http://www.aphdigital.org/courses/creating-digital-history/), which provides students with a basic grounding in the technological skills needed to conduct historical research and present the results of that research online. It addresses topics such as intellectual property, metadata, digitization and online exhibit curation. Wikis, collection and exhibit management software, maps and geolocation, timelines, and blogs have been incorporated into the class.[8] Creating Digital History has been taught twice now, in 2009 and 2010. In 2009 the course was team-taught by French and Wosh, and students created individual digital archives and exhibits based on their research interests.[9] Though this worked well for some students, it proved a frustrating exercise for others. Some encountered a scarcity of sources, others found it impossible to negotiate complex intellectual property issues in a single semester, and many of the projects failed to take full advantage of the collaborative possibilities involving public history and digital humanities work. In 2009, students purchased their own server space to house their work, but after completing the course many did not maintain these sites. In 2010 the course was taught by Cathy Moran Hajo, who decided to focus the class work on a single unifying theme, that of Greenwich Village

---

8   In the 2009 offering, students created Omeka archives and exhibits on self-selected topics and blogged about digital history (http://www.aphdigital.org/classes/G572033F09/). Students in 2010 blogged about Greenwich Village research (http://greenwichvillagehistory.wordpress.com/).

9   For some of the student's Omeka installations, see Samantha Gibson, "Double Consciousness in the Early Republic: Free Blacks in Philadelphia," http://www.samanthagibson.net/Project/; John Bence, "Major Battles of the Mexican War," http://www.johndbence.org/; Juliana Monjeau, "The Kosher Meat Boycott of 1902," http://www.somonjeau.net/project/exhibits/show/koshermeatboycott; and Brigid Harmon, "Affordable Eternity: The Lutheran Cemetery of Middle Village," http://www.brigidharmon.com/lutherancemetery/.

history.[10] Instead of building fifteen or twenty individual archives, the class produced one digital archive of almost 500 items and sixteen exhibits, the Greenwich Village History Digital Archive (http://www.aphdigital.org/ GVH/), mounted on the APH server. Future classes will contribute to this archive, which will allow discussions of issues arising from maintaining a collaborative archive, insuring quality, and consistent metadata. Hajo met with and established working relationships with archivists at repositories and with local history groups, such as the Greenwich Village Society for Historic Preservation, the New York Public Library Department of Rare Books and Manuscripts, the Tamiment Library, the Fales Rare Book Library, and the New York University Archives. Repositories allowed students to digitize appropriate material from their collections without charge, which eliminated many of the practical difficulties in obtaining digital objects to include in the archive.

Another new required course, Approaches to Public History (http:// www.aphdigital.org/courses/approaches-to-public-history/), was created for students in the Public History concentration. Building on the Introduction to Public History course, it focuses on the methodologies that public historians use in order to communicate and to collaborate with various publics. It includes segments on educational programming, oral history, documentary film and video production, and digital history. Each of these methodologies has been transformed profoundly by digital technology and introducing these topics into the course work has enriched the student experience. Ellen Noonan, who currently teaches the class, has extensive experience with the American Social History Project (http://ashp.cuny. edu/) and has worked on collaborative projects with the Center for History and New Media. She has incorporated several digital history units into the class and also explores such topics as electronic gaming, the Bracero Digital Archive (http://www.braceroarchive.org/) and new methods for digitizing and indexing oral history online.

Advanced Archival Description (http://www.aphdigital.org/courses/ advanced-archival-description/), taught by Thomas Frusciano, a required course for students in the archives concentration, was reconfigured to emphasize online representations of archival materials. It now stresses metadata standards for digital objects, the rise of content management

---

10   Students did have the option to work on independent projects if special circumstances permitted.

systems, institutional repositories, and the use of Web 2.0 techniques to create more collaborative interactive environments between archives and users.

# Elective Courses

By working additional digital competencies into the elective courses that make up the APH program, each student can personalize the curriculum, choosing the aspects of digital technologies that best meet their individual learning objectives. This requires considerable coordination between the APH faculty members, which can prove challenging when adjuncts comprise a significant portion of the instructors. One essential step has been to require prerequisites for many of the advanced electives, which guarantees that students have a baseline of digital skills and competencies.

The Historical Editing seminar (http://www.aphdigital.org/courses/historical-editing-seminar/), taught by Esther Katz, Director of the Margaret Sanger Papers Project, is an elective suitable for either concentration. The course now focuses largely on mastering the standards and techniques necessary to create online document archives and editions. By examining various online editions—including the Rotunda Projects (http://rotunda.upress.virginia.edu), Martha Ballard's Diary Online (http://www.dohistory.org/diary/), and the Einstein Archives Online (http://www.alberteinstein.info/), students are introduced to the new options available for selection, transcription and annotation, which are made possible by the fluidity and elasticity of digitization. Using XML authoring software (Oxygen) the course emphasizes manuscript encoding using the guidelines laid out by the Text Encoding Initiative (http://www.tei-c.org/), as well as using online collaboration tools (Google documents and wiki software) for transcription, research, writing and presenting manuscript materials on the web. Other software options such as A-Annotate (http://a.nnotate.com/) have also been introduced. Katz provides students with collections of manuscript material from the Sanger archive from which to prepare a mini digital edition. Students work in small groups to learn how to work collaboratively, assigning and dividing the tasks of transcribing, proofreading, annotating and tagging documents. They consult resources available in the Sanger Project offices, and make collective decisions on the structure and presentation of their online documents.

The Historian and the Visual Record class (http://www.aphdigital. org/courses/the-historian-and-the-visual-record/), an elective for either concentration, has been redesigned to include segments involving digital photography and representation, as well as contemporary theories involving new media and visualization. Students learn how to manipulate, curate, and describe complex digital objects, as well as master the techniques necessary for scanning, sharing and delivering access to digital materials.

History in the New Media (http://www.aphdigital.org/courses/history-in-the-new-media/), also taught by Hajo, is an elective follow-up to Creating Digital History that emphasizes designing and administering digital projects rather than creating them in class. Students design a digital project by selecting a set of historic documents, preparing a digitization plan, creating a project management blueprint and workflow and identifying staff and equipment needs. They plan a website that can include in addition to digitized documents, social networking technologies, added value and other appropriate tools. Their final product consists of a grant proposal, closely following the guidelines promulgated by the National Historical Publications and Records Commission (NHPRC), the National Endowment for the Humanities (NEH) or the Institute for Museum and Library Services (IMLS). Both the instructor and students use wiki software to draft and comment on student work.

Introduction to Preservation and Reformatting (http://www.aphdigital. org/courses/introduction-to-preservation-and-reformatting/), taught by Paula DeStefano, is an elective for the archives concentration that provides an overview of principles and practices of archives preservation. In this course, students examine the physical composition of archival materials in all formats, including digital ones, and learn about the causal agents that contribute to archival deterioration, the application of appropriate preservation and conservation methods, and various reformatting and re-housing techniques, including digitization.

Institutional Archives and Electronic Records (For more information, see http://www.aphdigital.org/courses/institutional-archives/), taught by Robert Sink, is an elective for the archives concentration. The changes made in this course include a greater emphasis on born digital content rather than a focus on paper-based resources. Students examine case studies adapted from real world situations. Making this shift to electronic records was difficult because of the lack of available online digital materials for students to examine. A potential solution to this issue may lie in a new Digital Archives and Curriculum Laboratory that is being developed by Simmons College under the auspices of NHPRC and IMLS funding (http://gslis.simmons.edu/dcl/lab). The laboratory will be an organized, open, non-proprietary space that provides integrated access to digital content, content management tools, standards, curriculum-based scenarios, and a workspace for learning modules that can be incorporated into classroom situations. The APH program will serve as a test site for the laboratory, and this free and web accessible resource has the potential to transform electronic records education. Our students will gain hands-on experience with archival processes and situations in virtual environments through a virtual sandbox in which to manipulate electronic records, experiment with metadata standards, and solve real-world electronic records problems.

In addition to such external partnerships, we have also collaborated with other NYU departments to enhance our elective offerings in the digital area. Courses now open to our students and approved as electives within the program include Museums and Interactive Technologies, Educational Design for Media Environments, Orality in the Electronic Age, Handling Complex Media and Digital Preservation and Restoration (http://www.aphdigital.org/courses/outside-courses/). We also have undertaken more multidisciplinary programming and joint course development with NYU's Museum Studies Program, the Department of Teaching and Learning and the Moving Image Archiving Program—and have created opportunities for students in various related programs to interact and share research interests.

## Internships and Capstone Projects

The APH program emphasizes both theory and practice, and these program elements typically meet in an internship, usually completed during the student's second semester. Our new technological emphasis meant that we needed to expand our network to develop internships that offered experience working on digital projects. These types of hands-on internships benefit the students greatly, but also serve to introduce some local institutions to best practices and academic trends in the field, providing an excellent synergy between academic training and local institutions and organizations.

We found that locating ongoing digital initiatives and existing projects to host interns proved more time-consuming than we had expected. There is no major digital humanities center in the New York City area, and many digital projects are scattered within individual university or library departments. They tend to employ very few students. The APH built a database of potential digital internships to provide students with a reasonably varied set of opportunities. However, this database needs to be constantly refreshed as projects are completed and new ones started, and the program director needs to be entrepreneurial in seeking out hosts and remaining in close contact with local projects. Because digital initiatives are often short-term, their needs change from year to year, far more so than do the offerings at traditional internship sponsors. We established positive working relationships with local institutions hosting long-term projects — for example, the New York Public Library and the International Coalition of Sites of Conscience (http://www.sitesofconscience.org/) — and have developed close partnerships with NYU's three repositories and its Bobst Library Digital Team. Without sustained efforts to locate a variety of new hosts for digital internships it will be difficult to match the specific needs of both the digital project and the student. Some successful digital internships have been incorporated into the program. One student worked with the New York Philharmonic Archives (http://archives.nyphil.org/) on its path-breaking project to digitize Leonard Bernstein's scores and provide online access to its collections for musicologists, historians, and general enthusiasts. Another student interned at the Darwin Manuscripts Project (http://darwin.amnh.org/), housed at the American Museum of Natural History, where she worked at establishing metadata standards and learned basic Text Encoding Initiative guidelines. A third intern worked on a data cleanup project with the Digital Experience Team at the New York Public Library. Though partnerships have proven more episodic and idiosyncratic than initially anticipated, we anticipate that as more digital work is done in the area and the Program gains a reputation for digital skills, we will be able to offer a broader range of opportunities.

## Capstone Projects

We also altered the capstone requirement for the program as part of our curriculum revision. Traditionally, we required a written thesis, thirty-five pages in length. We modified the requirements to allow for digital projects, as well as other forms of archives and public history activities, such as exhibition design, oral history projects, online documentary editions, and walking tours. Students have already begun to take advantage of these opportunities, and some have built extremely creative undertakings. An example is a historical blog, *First Hundred Days* (http://www.aphdigital.org/projects/firsthundreddays/), created by two students around the theme of the first hundred days of the Franklin Roosevelt administration. They invented several historical characters, embedded documents and media from the period into the site, and created lesson plans that secondary school teachers might use to incorporate the site into the classroom.[11]

In sum, the capstone project/internship component of the project has thus far worked very well, and we also have developed a good database of additional digital internships. One thing we have realized is that this is an ongoing project and will require regular refreshment. In any given semester there will be particular opportunities (the Leonard Levy-funded digital project at New York Philharmonic is a good example) and the landscape is constantly shifting.

## Challenges in Integrating New Technologies

New York University, like most universities, does not have a dedicated digital humanities center. This means that there is not a central place where all faculty and staff interested in the digital sphere can network. Instead we work in isolated silos, with minimal exposure to those running comparable programs at the university. One interesting side benefit of the curricular project is that we have made a concerted effort to locate kindred souls and similar projects in other humanities departments and in the Information Technology Service at NYU. After the NHPRC grant ended, NYU's Library began a humanities computing interest group that meets several times a semester to report on work, conferences and tools.

Due to security concerns, restrictions were imposed on the software that could be mounted on NYU's servers, thus hindering our early efforts to introduce technology into the curriculum. In order to install Omeka and

---

11  The site, created by Lindsay Dumas and Elizabeth Banks, was presented at the 2010 National Council for Public History meeting in Portland. They continue to develop the site after graduation.

WordPress, for example, the APH had to purchase its own commercial server space.[12] While there were advantages to running our own server, including the ability to have students work with servers and install and customize programs, as well as the flexibility to mount and test many open-source systems, a key disadvantage was that we could not use NYU's Information Technology Service to help us resolve problems and troubleshoot technical issues. Someone at the APH, initially French and later Wosh, had to be responsible for server operations such as updating software, adding and removing users and general maintenance.

In order to teach digital skills in the classroom, we also needed smarter facilities. The APH purchased a computer projector to use for its classes, orientation meetings and presentations. NYU's wireless network enabled students to follow along on their laptops during class demonstrations, and it was only rarely that we needed to use specialized digital classrooms. With only modest budgetary support for the digital curriculum revision, we found that most of our needs could be met by working with NYU's Library and Information Services Technology Department.

We recognize that the new emphasis on technology means that courses need to be constantly and sometimes substantially revised each year. Technology moves rapidly; new issues arise and new solutions appear at a fast pace. Faculty need to continually update their skills by taking courses, attending digital humanities conferences and workshops, and collaborating on new projects using different technologies. Lecturers need to rely far more on articles, blogs and websites than on textbooks, as the rapid pace of change quickly makes books obsolete, their website links broken, and references outdated.

Our faculty has realized that one of the general difficulties in teaching courses with a greater digital component is the varying levels of digital expertise that students bring to their work. Lecturers can become bogged down in explaining concepts that some students find difficult—while others grow impatient with the basic level of instruction. We have found that building some time in class for demonstrations of software or websites can make this process easier, though the most basic aspects of the course

---

12   In 2005, WordPress announced a hosted version of their software (http://www.wordpress. com). In 2010, Omeka introduced beta testing of a web hosting service that offers free and low-cost hosting for Omeka databases/exhibits (http://www.omeka.net/). These options will allow students to host their own projects and blogs and continue to use these programs once they are working without cost to their institutions.

often cause the greatest problems. In Creating Digital History, for example, there were more technical problems with the basics of finding an HTML editor and successfully mounting a bare bones website than with creating a digital exhibit. In the Historical Editing seminar, there was no readily available software that would enable students to mount their mini editions online.

Selecting appropriate software packages for classroom instruction also required considerable thought. Our goal in choosing particular software programs has been not to teach particular tools, but rather to engage students with the basic principles underlying the use of those packages. For example, it does not matter which software program you use to edit a scanned document—rather, students need to use those programs to focus on the principles of digitization and become familiar with available options. There are many content management systems that could work in classroom settings, but regardless of the one that is chosen, the important goal is to teach metadata standards for digital objects, as well as the advantages and disadvantages of particular systems. In order to teach a class effectively, however, instructors need to settle on software that the entire class will use. The APH consciously selected open-source software that was available free of charge. This type of software, as opposed to commercial programs that might be obtainable through NYU's site licenses, is something that students could easily continue using after graduation. As many of these packages have achieved widespread popularity within the archives and public history communities, graduates can also bring their knowledge concerning these packages to the smaller institutions that are most likely to implement them. Some of the software solutions we adopted are:

- Archives Toolkit (http://www.archiviststoolkit.org) is an open source content management system that provides broad integrated support for archival management. Since NYU participated in the initial development and implementation of the system, and since the NYU archives repositories have implemented it as part of their ongoing workflow, it seems natural to provide students with deep exposure to this tool. Further, the current discussions that involve merging the Archivists Toolkit with Archon suggest that the new product will become a standard package that will receive even more widespread adoption within the profession.

- Omeka (http://www.omeka.org) is an open source content management system, museum collections management and online exhibition system, and archival digital collection system, which was developed by the Center for History and New Media. Omeka enables the creation of large or small digital archives, as well as online exhibits using a number of different optional plugins. The Creating Digital History course uses Omeka to manage the Greenwich Village History site, as well as individual student exhibits. Students also often use Omeka for their capstone and internship projects. Using Omeka is relatively straightforward as long as one uses the handful of themes that can be installed. Program customization, however, requires some knowledge of PHP and CSS, something that few students have when beginning the program. It remains a challenge to introduce students to the capabilities of these scripting and web design languages in the short confines of a weekly class.

- WordPress (http://www.wordpress.org) is an open-source blogging and publishing platform that can be used to design websites, blogs and other web-based content. WordPress is used for the APH's own website, in the Creating Digital History course for the Researching Greenwich Village History blog, and frequently employed for capstone and internship projects.

- Wikidot (http://www.wikidot.com) is free wiki software that allows the creation of collaborative websites. The Creating Digital History, Historical Editing, and History and New Media courses use this software.

- Google Documents (http://docs.google.com) is an open source and free file sharing resource that enables students to work collaboratively on texts, spreadsheets, and presentations. The Creating Digital History course used one Google Documents spreadsheet to create a group timeline and another to record copyright permissions for its digital archive. The Digital Editing course uses Google Documents to share transcriptions and annotations.

- Google Maps (http://maps.google.com) is an open source mapping platform that enables students to create custom maps or walking tours. Students in Creating Digital History used Google Maps to create a themed map of Greenwich Village.

One of the benefits of using open source software is that there is a thriving community of users who are very responsive and helpful to faculty or students having problems.

# Feedback

Students and faculty have been overwhelmingly enthusiastic about the curriculum changes. Over 85% of those surveyed felt that digital competencies were either "very important" or "most important" in determining their career prospects. More that 92% "strongly agreed" or "somewhat agreed" with the revisions, and those with reservations wanted more not less technical training. By surveying students on each course, the APH will continue to revise the courses offered and balance the digital training offered in each course.

Interestingly, students demanded additional technical training but also worried that there might be an overemphasis on digital material and a shortage of historical content in the curriculum. Students want to make sure that digital techniques do not overwhelm other important aspects of archives and public history education: working creatively with local communities, engaging in sophisticated outreach activities and educational programming, and participating in significant historical debates. Maintaining an appropriate balance within the confines of a 32-credit curriculum is administratively challenging and requires a high level of coordination between the program director and the faculty.

A survey of our recent graduates confirmed that digital training increasingly constitutes a necessity in the job market. Web design especially emerged as an important skill for recent graduates, and we are exploring ways to expand our offerings by collaborating with NYU's Tisch School of Arts and Steinhardt School of Education.

Constant evaluation and adaptation is the only way to keep the APH's curriculum current and to provide its students with both the job skills and the theoretical and intellectual training that the professions demand. Most importantly, perhaps, we have seen a cultural change in the Program whereby students now expect, and are expected, to foster a deep intellectual and practical engagement with new media. This already has generated new types of capstone projects and research papers within individual courses, and has produced an extraordinary transformation in "tech literacy" among our graduate students.

The Archives and Public History program's curriculum was designed to be exportable, though this idea is not without problems. Every archives or public history program lives in its own unique institutional climate, facing particular challenges. Each program depends upon a peculiar ecology that includes institutional support, faculty networks and interests, student expectations and geography. To be sure, the philosophical principles that informed our effort could be adopted by other programs. But program curricula will remain dependent on particular academic contexts and the availability of local resources. So, while these changes have had a beneficial impact on New York University, it will be interesting to see whether other institutions facing the same challenges will make similar decisions.

# 4. Digital Humanities and the First-Year Writing Course

*Olin Bjork*

Stanley Fish's contention, in *Save the World on Your Own Time*, that "composition courses should teach grammar and rhetoric and nothing else" because "content is always the enemy of writing instruction" was provocation enough for a 2009 Modern Language Association (MLA) convention session on the relation between composition and the humanities.[1] The first two panelists, John Schilb and Arabella Lyon, argued that, *pace* Fish, composition courses should not focus on writing itself, but rather on humanistic topics like political theory or philosophy.[2] They agreed with Fish, however, that a first-year writing course—required at most American colleges and universities for students who do not "place out" through certain standardized tests—afforded little or no time to teach students to analyze the objects of digital culture, much less to use new media technologies.

This consensus flies in the face of a "Position Statement on Multimodal Literacies" approved by the National Council of Teachers of English (NCTE), which holds that "skills, approaches and attitudes toward media literacy, visual and aural rhetorics, and critical literacy should be taught in English/

---

1   Stanley Fish, *Save the World on Your Own Time* (Oxford: Oxford University Press, 2008), 44, 46.
2   John L. Schlib, "Turning Composition toward Sovereignty," and Arabella Lyon, "Composition and the Preservation of Rhetorical Traditions in a Global Context" (papers presented at the MLA Annual Convention, Philadelphia, Pennsylvania, December 29, 2009).

Language Arts classrooms."[3] More specifically, according to the "Outcomes Statement for First-Year Composition" adopted by the Council of Writing Program Administrators (WPA), students should "understand and exploit the differences in the rhetorical strategies and in the affordances available for both print and electronic composing processes and texts."[4] Indeed, the trend in college-level classrooms, especially in the United States, is to focus neither on "form" (i.e., basic writing and speaking strategies), nor on "content" from the traditional, material humanities, but rather on communication modes, new media and contemporary culture. Jeff Rice argues that the rise of the field of composition studies since the 1960s, traditionally attributed to increasing theoretical sophistication both in scholarship and in classroom practice, is also highly correlated with "technological, visual, and cultural studies movements paralleling the field's rebirth."[5]

These movements are associated with interdisciplinary fields such as technology studies, visual culture and cultural anthropology whose theories and methodologies have become increasingly vital to scholarship in rhetoric and composition. Yet when it comes to writing pedagogy, the primary influence of these movements has been to bring new objects of study into the classroom that are then analyzed through more traditional rhetorical frameworks such as assumptions, appeals and fallacies. Increasingly, not only elective and upper-level composition courses but also first-year writing courses consist of sections with different "cultural studies" themes such as Emo, zombies, baseball, popular feminism or Harry Potter. Within these topics, as well as weightier ones such as immigration or globalization, a range of cultural forms involving multiple modes of communication (aural, visual, written, non-verbal) and media (TV, film, Internet, video games, print) are considered fair game for analysis.

In this respect, it appears that composition is moving toward digital humanities even as it moves away from the material humanities, or that the humanities, in becoming digital, have moved toward composition. But this supposition is at best only half true. In "The Digital Humanities

3  Multimodal Literacies Issue Management Team of the NCTE Executive Committee, "Position Statement on Multimodal Literacies," National Council of Teachers of English (approved November, 2005), http://www.ncte.org/positions/statements/multimodalliteracies.

4  Council of Writing Program Administrators, "WPA Outcomes Statement for First-Year Composition" (adopted April, 2000; amended July, 2008), http://wpacouncil.org/positions/outcomes.html.

5  Jeff Rice, *The Rhetoric of Cool: Composition Studies and New Media* (Carbondale: Southern Illinois University Press, 2007), 17.

Manifesto 2.0," Todd Presner, Jeffrey Schnapp and numerous other contributors observe that digital humanities has been moving in two different directions: "The first wave of digital humanities work was quantitative, mobilizing the search and retrieval powers of the database, automating corpus linguistics, stacking hypercards into critical arrays. The second wave is qualitative, interpretive, experiential, emotive, generative in character."[6] N. Katherine Hayles astutely connects this "first wave" to a field that, from the mid- to late-twentieth century, was known as humanities computing.[7] Primarily based in traditional humanities departments or academic technology service units, humanities computing focused on scholarly activities such as text-based data entry and programming for stylistics, concordances and apparatuses. In the late 1990s, however, scholars at new humanities centers, institutes and offices formed in the blossoming of the internet opted to change the name of the evolving and expanding field to "digital humanities." The name change, however, did not signal the end of the first wave and the start of the second; in the first of four articles surveying the field for *Digital Humanities Quarterly*, Patrik Svensson finds that most of the work self-identifying as "digital humanities" remains in the humanities computing tradition.[8] This tradition, he argues, entails an instrumentalist view of technologies as "tools," a focus on texts as primary objects of study, and text encoding and text analysis as privileged methodologies.

The other major area within digital humanities is new media studies (alternatively named digital media studies). This field, broadly construed, views technologies as objects of study, not just tools. Instead of material culture and digitized objects, new media scholars focus on digital culture and "born-digital" objects such as blogs, computer games, email lists, interactive maps, machinima videos, text messages, user-generated content and virtual worlds. Their approach to the digital tends to be more theoretical than methodological, bearing the qualities that Manifesto 2.0 associates with the "second wave." Finally, whereas humanities computing

6  Todd Presner and Jeffrey Schnapp et al., "Digital Humanities Manifesto 2.0," University of California, Los Angeles, May 29, 2009, http://manifesto.humanities.ucla.edu/2009/05/29/the-digital-humanities-manifesto-20/.
7  N. Katherine Hayles, *How We Think: Digital Media and Contemporary Technogenesis* (Chicago: University of Chicago Press, 2012), 24–27.
8  Patrik Svensson, "Humanities Computing as Digital Humanities," *Digital Humanities Quarterly* 3, no. 3 (2009): paras. 1–62, http://digitalhumanities.org/dhq/vol/3/3/000065/000065.html

has traditionally been a research domain for faculty, librarians, and technologists, new media studies is a growing area of both undergraduate and graduate education. New media studies programs make their institutional homes in departments as diverse as Architecture, Mass Communication, Computer Science, English and Film, although many practitioners in the field are specialists who do not teach in such programs.

The divide between humanities computing and new media studies within digital humanities roughly aligns with the divide between literature and composition within English studies. Whereas a significant percentage of humanities computing projects, if not the majority, have involved literature faculty, the use of computers in the teaching of writing seems to have a separate history from that of humanities computing.[9] Today the subfield of composition studies known as computers and writing (or computers and composition) has more in common with new media studies. The fields share a more qualitative than quantitative research and teaching profile, a pedagogical orientation and a view of digital objects and culture as worthy of study in their own right, not merely for what they reveal about material objects and culture. Perhaps most significantly, instructors of computers and writing, like their counterparts in new media studies, now tend to incorporate into their pedagogies student *production* of multimodal digital objects.

The movement to teach students to be engaged producers and not merely informed consumers of digital culture reflects a shift in composition theory. In the 1990s, scholars such as Cynthia L. Selfe, Anne Frances Wysocki and Johndan Johnson-Eilola discussed new media under the rubric of literacy, arguing that digital forms challenge traditional notions of oral and print literacy and that we must now either discard the goal of literacy or accept the task of teaching multiliteracies, first articulated by the New London group.[10] More recently, a younger generation of

---

9   Gail E. Hawisher, Paul LeBlanc, Charles Moran, and Cynthia L. Selfe, *Computers and the Teaching of Writing in American Higher Education, 1979–1994: A History* (Norwood: Ablex, 1996).

10   See for example Cynthia L. Selfe, "Technology and Literacy: A Story about the Perils of Not Paying Attention," *College Composition and Communication* 50, no. 3 (1999): 411–36; Anne Frances Wysocki and Johndan Johnson-Eilola, "Blinded by the Letter: Why Are We Using Literacy as a Metaphor for Everything Else?" in *Passions, Pedagogies, and 21st Century Technologies*, ed. Gail E. Hawisher and Cynthia L. Selfe (Logan: Utah State University Press, 1999), 349–68; see also New London Group, "A Pedagogy of Multiliteracies: Designing Social Futures," *Harvard Educational Review* 66, no. 1 (1996): 60–92. The New London Group coined the term "multiliteracies" to describe

composition scholars, such as Collin Gifford Brooke and Jeff Rice, have sought to define a rhetoric of new media that would supplement or even replace the traditional canons of rhetoric, which they view as so firmly grounded in chirographic and print technologies as to have made that material base of communication invisible for centuries until it was revealed again by new media. The formulation of a rhetoric of new media distinct from that of older media not only justifies student digital projects but also entails a theoretical focus on contemporary high tech culture and a certain faddishness in computers and writing research and pedagogy. Brooke, for example, analyzes *Wikipedia* and the multiplayer online role-playing game *World of Warcraft*,[11] while Rice practices a "hip-hop pedagogy" in which students simulate in their hypertexts some of the writing and sampling practices of graffiti and rap artists.[12]

The scope of computers and writing projects, in contrast to those in the digital humanities, tends to be constrained by three factors: the technical proficiency of undergraduates and instructors, the timeframe of a single semester or quarter, and the availability of hardware and software. Especially in the first-year writing course—where the curriculum often specifies a minimum page requirement and where instructors are under pressure to teach basic reading, writing and argumentation strategies, fitting in multimodal literacies when and if they can—only small-scale projects are manageable. In the 1990s, a "hyper-essay" or thematic webpage, usually hosted on a private server, was the standard assignment. Since the last decade, however, a movement in web-based application design known as Web 2.0, which enables user-created content and online platforms, has inspired a new direction for computers and writing assignments. Students now contribute text and static images to blogs and wikis, build spaces within virtual worlds such as Second Life (http://www.secondlife.com), and make movies and podcasts to share online. Technical barriers are diminishing as free and open source software and the latest smartphones, which can record audio and/or video, make their way into the hands of the average college student. In addition to reservations about quality,

---

a pedagogical response to a changing, globalized communication landscape where literacies of sound, image, and electronic textuality would become equally important, if not more so, than traditional print and oral literacies.

11  Colin Gifford Brooke, *Lingua Fracta: Toward a Rhetoric of New Media* (Cresskill: Hampton Press, 2009).

12  Jeff Rice, "Writing about Cool: Teaching Hypertext as Juxtaposition," *Computers and Composition* 20 (2003): 221–36.

however, privacy or copyright issues often prevent or discourage the public sharing of student work on sites like YouTube or Flickr. Therefore, despite pedagogical rationales that emphasize the value of participatory media and interaction with a larger online community, many student Web 2.0 projects either remain protected within learning management systems or are hosted publicly for a limited time. Typically, however, such projects are not ends in themselves but lead to essays, presentations, or ePortfolios in which students defend their design choices in rhetorical terms.

## Humanities Computing for Computers and Writing

In the third and final paper at the 2009 MLA session on composition and the humanities, my colleague John Pedro Schwartz and I followed up professors Schilb and Lyon by stressing the largely untapped potential of humanities computing practices and technologies for computers and writing.[13] We sought to avoid promoting innovation for innovation sake and instead articulate a rationale that would appeal to the widest swath of composition scholars and instructors, even those determined never to engage in digital pedagogy. When considering the research orientation of humanities computing, it had occurred to us that among the seemingly limitless teaching outcomes of first year-writing courses is the inculcation of basic research skills. Composition textbooks draw a distinction between primary and secondary research and between qualitative and quantitative research. The first of these dichotomies tends to be well treated both in the textbooks and in the courses themselves, though the balance leans toward secondary research. To teach secondary research, instructors will typically assign at least one essay topic necessitating moderate to heavy citation, train students to document and evaluate sources, and take them to the library and/or have a librarian visit the class. Another course project may involve such primary research techniques as surveying students or interviewing administrators. In regard to the second binary, however, neither the textbooks nor the courses tend to apply it to student work. Although researchers in the field use quantitative methods, the bulk of the scholarship is qualitative, and in the interest of simplification and practicality this bias becomes magnified in the classroom to the point

---

13   Olin Bjork and John Pedro Schwartz, "What Composition Can Learn from the Digital Humanities" (paper presented at the MLA Annual Convention, Philadelphia, Pennsylvania, December 29, 2009).

that the distinction becomes academic. This state of affairs is problematic because the first-year writing class is supposed to prepare students for future writing experiences, and many of these students will major in highly quantitative, primary research fields.

Based on this diagnosis, we argued that importing primary and quantitative research methods from humanities computing would serve as a corrective for the first-year writing course. Of course, traditional categories are less viable in a digital context—is a digitized primary artifact a primary or secondary artifact? A weakness of digital humanities is that it under-theorizes the transformation of material objects into digital objects. As an example of the field's inattention to digital codes as opposed to material ones, Hayles points to the documentation of a flagship digital humanities project, the William Blake Archive (http://www.blakearchive.org):

> Of course the editors realize that they are simulating, not reproducing, print texts. One can imagine the countless editorial meetings they must have attended to create the site's sophisticated design and functionalities; surely they know better than anyone else the extensive differences between the print and electronic Blake. Nevertheless, they make the rhetorical choice to downplay these differences. For example, there is a section explaining that dynamic data arrays are used to generate the screen displays, but there is little or no theoretical exploration of what it means to read an electronic text produced in this fashion rather than the print original. [14]

It is debatable whether the Blake editors would consider their "rhetorical choice" to be a choice at all, for it would be difficult for them to underscore such differences and still assert, as they do, that the site is an archive of Blake's works. While humanities computing, as typified by the Blake Archive, tends to treat the digital surrogate as the material original, new media studies tends not to create digital surrogates. Composition studies, therefore, is well positioned to fill the gap by tracking how digitization modifies the rhetorical situation and properties of an artifact. As for the already somewhat tenuous and expedient distinction between quantitative and qualitative research, the two approaches may blend together in any particular digital humanities project. The Blake Archive, for example, offers both qualitative and quantitative applications and tools. Far from being an obstacle to pedagogy, these definitional quandaries can provoke productive class discussions.

---

14   N. Katherine Hayles, *My Mother Was a Computer: Digital Subjects and Literary Texts* (Chicago: University of Chicago Press, 2005), 91.

In our paper, we used the term "quantitative" to refer to research that uses computation to sort or process data and generate a list of hits, table of results, graphical representation, etc., and "qualitative" for research that uses computers primarily for their storage, linking and multimedia display capabilities, relying primarily on human processing of content. Humanities computing projects, unlike those in new media studies, tend not to be qualitative in the sense of delivering a rich multimedia experience to the user. This tendency is noted by Svensson, who ascribes it to the field's textual focus and lack of investment in human-computer interface design.[15] But the field also faces legal and ideological barriers on the path to multimodality. Since most artifacts created after 1922 are still under copyright, the great bulk of films and music are off-limits to those digital humanists who seek to digitize and publish cultural heritage materials, and consequently the texts and images contained in their electronic archives are often presented as pages that could (and often did) appear in a book or manuscript. Furthermore, the humanities computing community is philosophically committed to publishing with open web standards, such as CSS, HTML, and XML. This policy is quite feasible when the content is static text and images. However, when the content includes rich media such as animation, audio, and/or video, until recently there have been few reliable open source equivalents to proprietary technologies, such as Adobe Flash, which combine expensive development environments with free browser plug-in players.

The landscape is rapidly changing, however. Third party plug-ins are no longer necessary to display rich media in the latest browsers, and free and open source software for reading, writing, and publishing rich media is beginning to appear. One such product is Sophie (http://sophieproject. org), which is distributed by the Institute for Multimedia Literacy at USC. Sophie is designed for collaborative authoring and viewing of rich media "books" in a networked environment. Sophie books combine text with notes, images, audio, video and/or animation. Sophie offers server software for collaborative online authoring, an HTML5 format for multi-device publishing, and comment frames for discussion within the books.

Sophie has already been used in classroom projects. Sol Gaitán of the Dalton School in New York developed a Sophie book for her AP Spanish students so that they could explore the direct influence of

---

15    Svensson, "Humanities Computing as Digital Humanities," paras. 46, 51.

particular flamenco music styles on Federico García Lorca's poetry.[16] In an Introduction to Digital Media Studies class at Pomona College, Kathleen Fitzpatrick's students selected texts that they had read together for class and turned them into Sophie books.[17] In terms of goals, Gaitán's project shares with humanities computing the use of the electronic edition as a means of yielding insight into material objects and culture; in this case, Lorca's poetry. Conversely, Fitzpatrick's assignment uses the electronic edition in order to yield insights into digital objects and culture; in this case, Sophie books.

What might Sophie projects look like in a writing classroom? Schwartz and I contended that a qualitative humanities computing practice such as electronic editing could be adapted to achieve the traditional goals of composition pedagogy. Creating digital editions of speeches, books and essays from oral and print sources can reveal the rhetorical differences between digital and material culture. Students could select an argumentative text from the public domain, or for which rights have been waived—say, the Lincoln-Douglas debates—and use Sophie to create an electronic edition of the text annotated with notes, images, audio, video and/or animation. It might also include a rhetorical analysis of the text, either in the form of textual annotation or a separate section of the book. The comment feature would encourage fellow students to provide feedback on annotation and to debate points made in the rhetorical analysis. Upon completion of the edition, students might write an essay reflecting on their design decisions and the different mediatory and rhetorical properties and situations of the oral debates, the material records and their own digital edition. The first activity—design of an electronic edition of a canonical text—is typical of humanities computing. The second activity—rhetorical analysis and discussion of a text—is typical of computers and writing. The third activity—reflection on media and interface design—is typical of new media studies.

To complement such a qualitative research project, writing instructors can assign a quantitative research project to expand the analytical repertoire of their students from the rhetorical analysis of exempla to the

---

16  Gaitán's book, along with other examples of Sophie in action, are available for download from the "Demo Books" section of the Institute for the Future of the Book website, http://www.futureofthebook.org/sophie/download/demo_books/.

17  For Fitzpatrick's 2010 course syllabus, see http://machines.pomona.edu/51-2010/; for the Sophie assignment, see http://machines.pomona.edu/51-2010/04/02/project-4-sophie/.

computational analysis of corpora. Ideally, combining these two forms of analysis will allow students to become not only "close readers" but also "distant readers,"[18] no longer content with supporting their insights on culture and rhetoric solely with examples from individual texts. Students need not, as in humanities computing, study digitized material texts; they can turn instead to corpora of digital cultural production. In a text-mining project, students would use text-analysis tools to look for patterns and anomalies, and then report on their findings. This process would give students a new perspective on language and rhetoric as well as experience in using quantitative research methods and writing a technical report, activities that many of them will engage in later, both in college and in their careers.

In its most general application, the term text mining refers to the extraction of information from, and possibly the building of, a database of structured text. The term text analysis (or text analytics) is roughly synonymous with text mining but tends to be preferred in the case of natural language datasets with comprehensible content and well-defined parameters.[19] Many composition teachers have been exposed to text analysis through plagiarism detection tools like Turnitin (http://www.turnitin.com), which compares student submissions to previous submissions stored in databases as well as to online sources, or through pattern analysis tools that perform preliminary scoring of student or applicant essays. Search engines like Google, meanwhile, can be used to mine thematic subsets of the web. In a 2009 *Kairos* article, Jim Ridolfo and Dànielle Nicole DeVoss discuss a composition exercise informed by their theory of "rhetorical velocity," which in this instance means the extent, speed and manner in which keywords and content from government, military and corporate presses show up in news articles. Students select phrases from a recent press release and search for these phrases on the web as well as on the Google News (http://news.google.com) aggregator site. They then compare their results with the original release and discuss how the content was recomposed, quoted and/or attributed by the news media.[20]

---

18  This distinction between "distant" and "close" reading first appears in Franco Moretti, "Conjectures on World Literature," *New Left Review* 1 (2000): 54–68.

19  For a discussion of teaching text analysis in the humanities classroom, see Stéfan Sinclair and Geoffrey Rockwell's chapter, "Teaching Computer-Assisted Text Analysis: Approaches to Learning New Methodologies."

20  Jim Ridolfo and Dànielle Nicole DeVoss, "Composing for Recomposition: Rhetorical Velocity and Delivery," *Kairos* 13, no. 2 (2009), http://www.technorhetoric.net/13.2/topoi/ridolfo_devoss/.

A simple form of text analysis that some writing instructors employ is the tag or word cloud, which visualizes information based on the metaphor of a cloud. The cloud consists of words of different sizes, with the size of each word determined by the frequency of its appearance in a given text. On many blogs and photo-sharing sites, a script automatically generates a word cloud based on the blog entries or image tags. Wordle (http://www.wordle.net) is a free online tool that allows users to generate a word cloud from a text and edit its colors, orientations, and fonts. By making word clouds from their papers, writers can gain a new perspective on issues of diction (see Figure 1). The developers of Wordle describe it as a toy, and indeed word and tag clouds function more as artistic images than as sophisticated informational displays. In a *ProfHacker* blog entry, Julie Meloni calls Wordle "a gateway drug to textual analysis."[21]

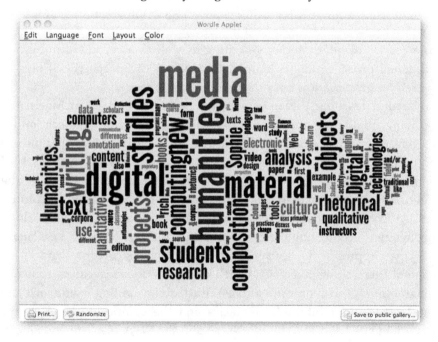

**Figure 1.** Wordle of Bjork and Schwartz's 2009 MLA Convention paper.

True textual analysis calls for a more powerful tool and a larger corpus. In a 2009 first-year writing course at Georgia Tech, David Brown

---

21   Julie Meloni, "Wordles, or The Gateway Drug to Textual Analysis," ProfHacker, *The Chronicle of Higher Education*, October 21, 2009, http://chronicle.com/blogs/profhacker/wordles-or-the-gateway-drug-to-textual-analysis/.

taught his students to use AntConc (http://www.antlab.sci.waseda.ac.jp/
antconc_index.html) and the Corpus of Contemporary American
English or COCA (http://corpus.byu.edu/coca/). AntConc is a freeware
concordance program named after its creator Laurence Anthony, a
professor of English language education at Waseda University in
Japan. The software is frequently used to assess or research corpora of
student writing.[22] Instructor Brown's students used AntConc to search
for linguistic features in the COCA corpus and wrote papers reporting
their findings. With over 425 million words drawn from American
magazines, newspapers and TV shows, COCA may be "the largest freely
available corpus of English," as its documentation claims. Some students
went beyond the call, comparing features of COCA to those of corpora
derived from Twitter, personal blogs and online reviews. In a follow up
assignment, each student assembled a corpus of his or her own academic
writing and used AntConc to compare linguistic features of this corpus
to a corpus of other students' writing as well as a corpus of published
academic prose. Students learned to use Part of Speech (POS) tags to
search for grammatical patterns within these corpora.

Beyond teaching research methods, Schwartz and I concluded that
bringing qualitative and quantitative digital humanities projects into a
first-year writing course would further several additional disciplinary
and curricular aims. First, the combination would entail both a focused
and a panoramic view of either humanistic content, such as the
politico-philosophical discourse that Schilb and Lyon advocate, or cultural
studies content, which is increasingly the predilection of composition
pedagogy. Second, linguistic text-analysis could potentially be a more
effective approach to learning about sentence structure than Fish's
content-free writing pedagogy, which involves language creation, sentence
diagramming and syntax imitation.[23] Third, digital editing would facilitate
the teaching of multimodal literacies and the composing in electronic
environments advocated by the NCTE and the WPA respectively. Finally,

---

22  At the 2012 Computers and Writing conference in Raleigh, North Carolina, a group from
the University of Michigan gave an AntConc workshop titled "Using Corpus Linguistics
to Assess Student Writing." For an example of a study using AntConc to research a
corpus of student text, see Ute Römer and Stefanie Wulff, "Applying Corpus Methods
to Writing Research: Explorations of MICUSP," *Journal of Writing Research* 2, no. 2 (2010):
99–127.

23  Fish, *Save the World on Your Own Time*, 41–49; see also Stanley Fish, *How to Write a Sentence
and How to Read One* (New York: Harper, 2011).

the assimilation of humanities computing practices by computers and writing, and vice versa, would help bridge the divide between literature and composition, adding coherence to the discipline of English studies.

## Teaching Digital Humanities in the Writing Classroom

The 2009 MLA session on composition and the humanities was well attended and there was much discussion following the papers. Scott Jaschik covered the session for the online daily *Inside Higher Ed* with an article titled "What Direction for Rhet-Comp?"[24] Among the comments posted below the article, a reader questioned by what right MLA served as the forum for this question as opposed to a rhetoric and composition conference like the Conference on College Composition and Communication (CCCC). Though a major conference, CCCC is more specialized than MLA, incrising the odds that some potential directions might not be considered there. The Computers and Writing conference, meanwhile, did not have a panel on their field's relation to digital humanities until 2011.[25] Having presented at the MLA five times since 2005 on topics related to computers and writing and/or digital humanities, I have found that it is one of the few venues where diverse humanities fields regularly cross-pollinate. The 2012 MLA convention bore the fruit of these transactions; there were almost twice as many sessions on digital approaches to literature, art, culture or rhetoric as there had been in any of the previous seven years. The spike prompted Stanley Fish to write three *New York Times* blog columns bemoaning the digital awakening of mainstream literary studies. In the second of these columns, Fish argues that non-linear, multimodal, and collaborative Web 2.0 textuality works against conventional notions of authorship and asks, "Does the digital humanities offer new and better ways to realize traditional humanities goals? Or does the digital humanities completely change our understanding of what a humanities goal (and work in the humanities) might be?"[26] In the third

---

24  Scott Jaschik, "What Direction for Rhet-Comp?" *Inside Higher Ed*, December 30, 2009.

25  Cheryl Ball, Douglas Eyman, Julie Klein, Alex Reid, Virginia Kuhn, Jentery Sayers, and N. Katherine Hayles, "Are You a Digital Humanist?" (Town Hall session of the 2011 Computers & Writing Conference in Ann Arbor, Michigan, May 21, 2011), http://vimeo.com/24388021.

26  Stanley Fish, "The Digital Humanities and the Transcending of Morality," Opinionator, *New York Times*, January 9, 2012, http://opinionator.blogs.nytimes.com/2012/01/09/the-digital-humanities-and-the-transcending-of-mortality.

column, Fish answers his own questions with regard to text mining, a method that he feels changes our understanding of literary analysis because it is not "interpretively directed," rather you "proceed randomly or on a whim, and see what turns up."[27]

As of the 2009 MLA convention, neither my co-presenter nor I had fully put into practice our theory that the methods of digital humanities could be used in the classroom to realize not only traditional humanities goals but also traditional composition goals. However, in the summer of 2010 at Georgia Tech, I had the opportunity to teach a first-year writing class on the theme of digital humanities to fresh high school graduates enrolling for an intensive six-week semester. The major projects in the class were a qualitative research project and a quantitative research project. For the qualitative project, students selected a single humanities text and turned it into a multimedia edition with annotations, images, and audio or video. For the quantitative project, students assembled a corpus of humanities texts, which they then mined with electronic text-analysis tools to find patterns or anomalies.

In these projects, students were confronted with challenges familiar to digital humanists engaged in similar endeavors. As editors and hypothetical publishers of their editions, students needed to learn about copyright and use only those texts, images and clips that had been released to the public for reproduction and redistribution. Some students chose texts from the public domain, while others excerpted from copyrighted texts or selected materials published under Creative Commons licenses. As quantitative researchers, meanwhile, they were tasked with constructing a valid research hypothesis, selecting representative data, extracting relevant results from this data and assessing their findings. In both projects, students had to employ open-source software: Sophie 2.0 and AntConc respectively.

Of the two projects, the qualitative was less successful from a technical standpoint due to the limitations of Sophie 2.0. Although I had tested this software on my own computer, the participating students had just

---

27   Stanley Fish, "Mind Your P's and B's: The Digital Humanities and Interpretation," *Opinionator*, *New York Times*, January 23, 2012, http://opinionator.blogs.nytimes.com/2012/01/23/mind-your-ps-and-bs-the-digital-humanities-and-interpretation.

purchased brand new laptops with the latest operating systems on which Sophie 2.0 was not verified to be compatible. On many of these machines, Sophie 2.0 was so bug-ridden and liable to crash that I had to lower the expectations for media and interactivity. Students struggling with the software also had less time to write annotations explaining and analyzing the text of their editions. Although I had intended the project to suggest the rhetorical possibilities unleashed through the interplay of different modes and media, it instead illustrated a problem plaguing free and open source software: the lack of a developer base extensive enough to adequately debug and update the software.

The qualitative project did, however, deliver on some of its pedagogical objectives. Students learned to apply the principles of intellectual property, the fair use doctrine, and the public domain. They also developed rough and ready distinctions between an edition, a text, and a work. If not all of the students were advanced enough to be insightful editors and annotators, most of them learned to appreciate the power that editing and annotation exert over a text. Some demonstrated awareness of the gulf between their multimedia presentation of the text and its original context. For example, the text that one student used in her edition of Patrick Henry's "Give Me Liberty or Give Me Death" speech to the 1775 Virginia Convention (see Figure 2) was reconstructed after the orator's death based on the accounts of audience members. Although the student did not acknowledge that the text is at best a close approximation of the speech's verbal content, she was appreciative of the different rhetorical situation of a speech versus a book. In her rhetorical analysis, she argued that the speech is light on evidence and narrative details but heavy on pathos and ethical appeals because Henry recited his address from memory and at any rate his audience was familiar with the facts of the case. To provide a sense of the original context, her edition includes clips from an audio reenactment on LibriVox and a contemporary illustration of Henry rousing the delegates. If the student had pursued the differences further, she might have noted that since the user of her edition can read the electronic text with or without the audio voiceover and open the annotations that supply the missing historical facts, the work has been completely transformed by the editor in order to accommodate an audience for which it was never intended.

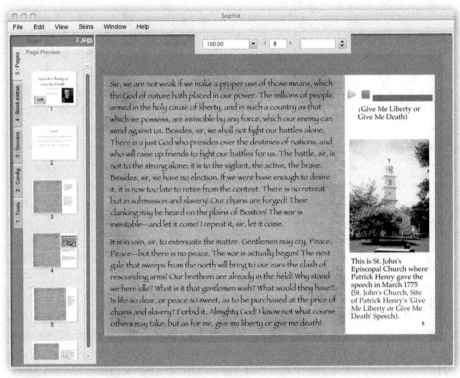

**Figure 2.** Student's Sophie Book example. This edition of Patrick Henry's "Give Me Liberty or Give Me Death," as displayed in the Sophie Reader application, includes a column for annotations to the right of the primary text. On this page, the student has provided an excerpt from an audio rendition of the speech as well as an image of the site where the speech was first given.

AntConc proved to be more reliable than Sophie 2.0. Although AntConc is relatively up-to-date and bug free, as of 2010 the documentation, consisting of a "readme" file and an "online help system," was not as accessible as the Sophie 2.0 website's combination of video screencasts and step-by-step textual instructions with screenshots (helpful video tutorials and a brief manual have since been added to the AntConc website). The AntConc readme, like most specimens of the genre, combines a text-only format with a matter-of-fact writing style. The online help system, meanwhile, reproduces the how-to portion of the readme while adding a few smallish screenshots. This documentation, though technically sound, assumes an audience familiar with the basics of corpus linguistics and therefore points up another problem plaguing free and open source software: the lack of documentation suitable for the uninitiated.

In order to use AntConc and other quantitative tools successfully, my students read Svenja Adolphs' *Introducing Electronic Text Analysis*.[28] This book was recommended to me, along with AntConc and the other resources used in the project, by David Brown, a colleague at Georgia Tech with a background in computational linguistics. Whereas Brown's first-year writing course projects, briefly described in the previous section, were spread out over most of a fifteen-week semester, I had just three weeks to spend on electronic text analysis. Consequently, I decided not to cover the more exact techniques such as chi-square, log likelihood, mutual information, and POS tagging, instead limiting coverage to more straightforward concepts such as collocates, frequency, keyness, n-grams, semantic prosody and type-token ratio. This more limited analytical framework proved difficult enough for the students to master, especially since Adolphs' book, while perhaps the most accessible introduction then available in print, is pitched to an advanced undergraduate or postgraduate audience with a basic knowledge of statistics.

For the quantitative assignment, students formulated a research question or hypothesis and then constructed a specialized corpus of plain text documents on which they could test their hypothesis. Unlike a general corpus, a specialized corpus is not representative of a language but rather of a certain type of discourse such as that of a particular profession, individual, generation, etc. Students used their specialized corpus as a target corpus to compare against a larger reference corpus. The most common choices for a reference corpus were COCA, which was described in the previous section, and the Corpus of Historical American English or COHA (http://corpus.byu.edu/coha), which contains 400 million words drawn from American fiction, magazine, newspaper, and non-fiction writing. Both of these resources were created by Mark Davies, a professor of corpus linguistics at Brigham Young University, and funded by the National Endowment for the Humanities. Although their frame-based interface has some usability issues, COCA and COHA are well documented with explanations and examples. At the time of this assignment, the Google Books Ngram Viewer (http://books.google.com/ngrams/), which fronts corpora drawn from books written in Chinese, English, French, German, Hebrew, Russian and Spanish, had not yet

---

28   Svenja Adolphs, *Introducing Electronic Text Analysis: A Practical Guide for Language and Literary Studies* (New York: Routledge, 2006).

been released. Davies argues that COHA, though many times smaller, is superior to Google's American English corpus for research because his site provides more versatile and robust searching techniques and more reliable and rigorously structured data.

I afforded the students broad leeway in constructing their corpora of humanities texts. Of the 23 students in the course, 13 worked with corpora drawn from rock and roll, hip-hop and other popular music genres. The majority of these students were not so much interested in identifying genre characteristics, which at any rate would have been difficult to accomplish experimentally, as they were in comparing artists or bands, so their target corpora were usually divided between two or more datasets each representing the music lyrics of a single artist or band. Of the remaining ten students, four focused on political speechmakers, four on novelists, one on the linguistic relation between Shel Silverstein's children's books and his writings for adults (including features in *Playboy*), one on the historical discourse surrounding marijuana, and one on a year of football sports-writing at the official athletics websites of Georgia Tech and the University of Georgia.

Although I was flexible about content, I prompted students to explain their selection criteria to show that their corpus was a representative dataset sufficient to their research question. Unfortunately, the criteria of representativeness, which I had internalized and therefore lacked the foresight to cover, proved slippery for many of the students. In some cases their incomprehension may have been feigned due to constraints on time or technical knowledge—some students were not able to assemble a corpus comprised of a prolific band's lyrical discography or a writer's oeuvre, let alone a representative sample of a musical or literary genre, and therefore claimed that they had chosen a random subset. A truly random subset is, of course, difficult to achieve and nearly impossible to verify, opening up the researcher to suspicion of selection bias. In these cases, I usually asked them to select a reproducible sample, such as singles or bestsellers, and modify their research questions accordingly. But in other cases students simply were not prepared, in a rushed context, to comprehend that a researcher could not draw valid conclusions about, for example, the difference between nineteenth and twentieth-century writing simply by comparing language differences between a few novels by Charles Dickens and John Buchan.

The students then tested their hypotheses through electronic text analysis. For most students, this analysis did not extend beyond comparisons of keyword frequency between and within their target and reference corpora. I was surprised to find that many of the students, all of whom were planning to major in science, technology, engineering and mathematics (STEM) disciplines, had difficulty with the concept of frequency; instead of statistical frequency, which is a rate, they would compare the absolute number of instances in one dataset to the absolute number of instances in another dataset even when these datasets were of unequal sizes. For some, the problem was solved by working in percentages instead of frequencies, but writing instructors should consider incorporating a primer on statistics when teaching quantitative analysis to humanities students or first-year STEM students.

The project was not entirely quantitative or objective—students often generated quantitative data based on qualitative premises and in any case they were to make highly subjective interpretations of their results. In one of the more successful studies, a student compared Sylvia Plath's juvenilia, a set of poems written before Plath's marriage to the poet Ted Hughes in 1956, to *Ariel*, the book of poems she wrote between her separation from Ted Hughes in 1962 and her suicide in 1963. Hypothesizing that Plath's language would be darker in *Ariel*, the student used AntConc's word list feature to identify words common to both datasets as well as those that had a high *keyness*, that is, those that were either unique or partial to one dataset. The student found that "negative" words such as *dead* or *black* were common in both datasets and surmised that Plath's life must have been bleak ever since her father's untimely death when the poet was just eight years of age. Yet the student unexpectedly discovered that "positive" words, such as *white* or *love*, tended to appear in negative contexts in *Ariel* but not in the juvenilia.

Such a qualitative judgment acquires an analytical foundation in the concept known as *semantic prosody*, which Adolphs defines as "the associations that arise from the collocates of a particular lexical item—if it tends to occur with a negative co-text then the item will have negative shading and if it tends to occur with a positive co-text than it will have positive shading."[29] A text-analysis tool like AntConc can generate, filter, and sort a list of collocates, which are words that appear

---

29  *Ibid.*, 139.

within a given span (or word count) to the left and right of one or more instances of a user-defined keyword or phrase. These instances, when presented in a column flanked on each side by their respective co-text, or span of collocates, form a Key Word in Context (KWIC) concordance. In her book, Adolphs offers an extended example of how to perform electronic analysis of a literary text using this technique and the concept of semantic prosody.[30] She begins by displaying a random sample from a KWIC concordance of the word *happen* in the spoken-word Cambridge and Nottingham Corpus of Discourse in English. She then observes that the word tends to be collocated with words that convey uncertainty or negativity, such as *something* or *accident*. She then moves to a KWIC concordance of the verbal phrase *had happened* from Virginia Woolf's novel *To The Lighthouse* and shows that this form of *happen* has a strongly negative shading and occurs more often when the narrative reflects the mindset of Mrs. Ramsay rather than that of one of the more confident male characters.

Following up on Adolphs' example, one of my students expanded Adolph's investigation of the verb *happen* to a corpus of all nine of Woolf's novels, hypothesizing that instances would increase as the publishing history drew nearer to the date of her suicide in 1941. This hypothesis rests, of course, on the premise that the degree of negative and/or uncertain points of view in Woolf's novels can serve as a barometer of the author's own state of mind. The student found that instances of the four different tenses she examined actually decreased in Woolf's last three novels (see Table 1). She then compared the collocates of the verb in Woolf's novels to those in COHA, her reference corpus, using the time range 1910–1940, and found that Woolf's are proportionally more likely to convey uncertainty as opposed to negative or positive events. The student cleverly concluded that if the decrease in the use of the verb means that Woolf was assuming greater control of her life, or becoming resigned to her fate, then a follow-up researcher should find that the collocates in her later novels express less uncertainty.

---

30   *Ibid.*, 69-73.

| | Novels (1915–1941) | | | | | | | | |
|---|---|---|---|---|---|---|---|---|---|
| | *The Voyage Out* | *Night and Day* | *Jacob's Room* | *To the Light-house* | *Orlando* | *Mrs Dalloway* | *The Waves* | *The Years* | *Between the Acts* |
| happen | 27 | 13 | 4 | 9 | 3 | 8 | 8 | 5 | 1 |
| happens | 7 | 7 | 1 | 3 | 4 | 2 | 1 | 1 | 0 |
| happened | 42 | 29 | 6 | 24 | 12 | 18 | 4 | 13 | 6 |
| had happened | 10 | 11 | 1 | 10 | 2 | 6 | 1 | 1 | 0 |
| Total hits | 86 | 60 | 12 | 46 | 21 | 34 | 14 | 20 | 7 |

**Table 1.** Student's table of four different tenses of the word *happen*. Not taken into account in this table is the relative length of these nine novels, the last three containing less than half as many words on average as the first three. This difference in word count, however, does not quite flatten out the trend suggested here.

Since the two student projects described above involved traditional humanities materials, a writing instructor who leans more toward cultural studies might find greater inspiration in a third project that tracked historical change in the collocates of the word *marijuana* and a few of its many and sundry synonyms. This student speculated that since the 1960s, attitudes toward the drug have become increasingly more positive. His study, though flawed, seemed to support this hypothesis, and could be taken as a first-year student's version of an emerging form of scholarly inquiry that the authors of a 2010 *Science* article term *culturomics*, or the "quantitative analysis of culture."[31]

After obtaining and interpreting their results, students proceeded to the final step in the assignment: writing up their research. Whereas the qualitative Sophie editions were accompanied by an analysis, in a standard essay format, of the rhetorical and mediatory aspects of the edited text, their quantitative visualizations called for a technical report format. This genre is rarely taught in high school science courses, let alone in English, so I prepared the students by showing them examples of college-level literature essays, lab reports, and social science papers. We discussed the general differences in content, writing style, and document design and

---

31   Google Books Team et al., "Quantitative Analysis of Culture Using Millions of Digitized Books," *Science* 331, no. 6014 (2011): 176–82.

came to the conclusion that a digital humanities report should probably be an amalgam divided into sections corresponding to each of these types in varying degrees. The format would consist of four sections: introduction, methods and results, discussion, and conclusion. While the first and last of these sections could be interpretive, the numerical data in the methods and results section had to be presented in as empirical a fashion as possible and the specifics of these results objectively analyzed in the discussion section. This procedure emulates some of the best practices of writing in STEM and social science disciplines. Digital humanities thus provides a rationale and opportunity for composition instructors to expose their students to aspects of technical writing processes alongside the argumentative and expository writing processes practiced in the discipline of English studies.

Although some students were unsettled by what they saw as the technical and open-ended nature of these assignments, most were pleasantly surprised to be learning, in an English class, how to conduct quantitative research and report on their findings. As a composition teacher and a digital humanist, I was surprised by how much time had to be devoted to preparing students for these projects yet pleased by the unexpected insights they gained, through editing and linguistic analysis, not only into matters of language and rhetoric but also into humanities content. As for Stanley Fish, he might be taken aback to discover that even first-year students are capable of using text mining to pursue a hypothesis, not merely to dig one up.

In the two years since I taught the course, the affinity between computers and writing and new media studies has grown. Increasingly, software and even search engines are seen as sites of "procedural" or "algorithmic" rhetorics.[32] More akin to humanities computing is student tagging of digitized primary materials, such as those in the Library of Congress Flickr Pilot Project.[33] Text analysis, meanwhile, is appearing more frequently on

---

32  "Procedural rhetoric" is the title of the first chapter of Ian Bogost's *Persuasive Games: The Expressive Power of Videogames* (Cambridge: MIT Press, 2007), a new media studies book that helped inspire a software studies movement in computers and writing. John M. Jones gave a paper on "Algorithmic Rhetoric and Search Literacy" at the 2011 Humanities, Arts, Science, and Technology Advanced Collaboratory Conference in Ann Arbor (Michigan, December 13, 2011)—his slides and notes are available at http://www.slideshare.net/johnmjones/algorithmic-rhetoric-and-search-literacy-hastac2011.

33  See Matthew W. Wilson, Curtis Hisayasu, Jentery Sayers, and J. James Bono, "Standards in the Making: Composing with Metadata in Mind," in *The New Work of Composing*, ed., Debra Journet, Cheryl E. Ball, and Ryan Trauman (Computers and Composition Digital Press/Utah State University Press, in press), http://ccdigitalpress.org/; see also "Library

lesson plans.[34] Although rhetoric and composition scholars are beginning to receive NEH digital humanities start-up grants, most of their proposals describe archiving or publishing projects that seem to fall within familiar humanities computing territory.[35] The 2012 grant guidelines, however, call for "scholarship that focuses on the history, criticism, and philosophy of digital culture and its impact on society."[36] This change is promising for both computers and writing and new media studies, but until that glorious day when the word *pedagogy* appears in the guidelines, college teachers should advocate that at least some of the projects benefit students, even those in a first-year writing course.

---

of Congress Flickr pilot project," http://www.flickr.com/photos/library_of_congress/collections/.

34  For an example of an assignment using the Voyeur text analysis tools, see Michael Widner, "Essay Revision with Automated Textual Analysis," *Digital Writing and Research Lab's Lesson Plans*, http://lessonplans.dwrl.utexas.edu/content/essay-revision-automated-textual-analysis.

35  See, for example, Cheryl E. Ball, "Building a Better Back-End: Editor, Author, & Reader Tools for Scholarly Multimedia," https://securegrants.neh.gov/PublicQuery/main.aspx?g=1&gn=HD-51088-10; Shannon Carter, "Remixing Rural Texas: Local Texts, Global Context," https://securegrants.neh.gov/PublicQuery/main.aspx?g=1&gn=HD-51398-11.

36  NEH Office of Digital Humanities, "Digital Humanities Start-Up Grants," http://www.neh.gov/grants/odh/digital-humanities-start-grants/.

# 5. Teaching Digital Humanities through Digital Cultural Mapping

*Chris Johanson and Elaine Sullivan, with Janice Reiff, Diane Favro, Todd Presner and Willeke Wendrich*

"The Emerald Buddha: Politics, Religion and Buddhist Imagery in Southeast Asia;" "High Line New York City: An Economical and Cultural Revival;" "Mapping Mami Wata: The African Water Goddess;" "Mapping the Bilbao Effect" —all of these were final project proposals by undergraduate students in UCLA's three-year Digital Culture Mapping Program sponsored by the W. M. Keck Foundation (http://www.keckdcmp.ucla.edu/). These projects showcase how students envision harnessing digital technologies to address a broad range of questions in the arts, humanities and social sciences. While the range of student interests in digital projects was exciting, it revealed an underlying tension: should the digital or the humanities win out? To wit, our areas of domain-specific expertise include Egyptian archaeology, the history of Los Angeles and Chicago, Roman culture and literature and the city of Berlin, but we had only superficial familiarity with, for example, African water spirits. How does one teach students the digital tools to address such a wide variety of projects without neglecting traditional discipline-specific issues of research formulation and data collection? How can one honestly and effectively evaluate student projects for content that lies outside one's domain expertise? While fully acknowledging that teaching a technological skill set can lead students to ask new and original questions of cultural data, when and in what instances must we nonetheless start with a domain-specific research question, and then move to teaching the digital?

This chapter will outline the process we employed to address these questions as we developed a multi-track program centered on digital humanities at the University of California, Los Angeles (UCLA). Driving our curriculum is the belief that informatics, spatial modeling, time-space visualizations and the like should be utilized not only as ends in themselves, but also as tools and methods that contribute, at least in part, to current scholarly conversations in more established disciplines. We are humanists, after all.

First, we describe what we have already accomplished by examining the different ways we have collectively and individually approached the question of teaching digital tools, methodologies and theories in our classrooms—both in the multi-quarter series of digital mapping classes team-taught in 2009–2011 at UCLA, as well as in classes developed over the last decade and offered within our own subject disciplines. Second, we explore how this introductory program has formed the foundation for subsequent phases in digital humanities pedagogy at UCLA. Rather than begin a degree-granting program at the undergraduate and graduate levels, we have first introduced curricular offerings that mirror our own varied, individual paths through digital humanities. Building on traditionally-defined humanities-based training, we have each identified a specific area of research, attempting not only to ground emerging digital technologies in traditional fields of humanistic inquiry, but also to combine the critical-thinking skills and intellectual openness characteristic of the humanities with the team-based problem solving and collaborative, hugely social nature of digital platforms. After reaching the end of our three-year digital mapping curriculum, we see the successful expansion of the program into an undergraduate minor in digital humanities as a way to foreground the *humanities* in the development of the evolving definition of the *digital humanities*.

# The Keck Digital Cultural Mapping Program: Goals and Curricula

UCLA's Digital Cultural Mapping Program (DCMP) emerged from a desire to introduce undergraduate students to the potential for using new technologies and theoretical approaches in research and knowledge acquisition. Three- and four- dimensional digital modeling, Geographic Information Systems (GIS), virtual globes and a host of newly conceived and rapidly developing mapping tools—all traditionally used by those outside the humanities—are now being harnessed to investigate questions relating to these disciplines.[1] We believe that the ability to understand, analyze, critique and create these technologies is essential for twenty-first century students, who will be increasingly asked to evaluate materials produced and presented through these digital media.

The project focuses on three main pedagogical goals:

1.   To teach students how to understand, utilize and critique the tools and technologies related to the geospatial/geotemporal web, that is, to equip them with a form of geospatial, digital literacy;

2.   To provide students with the technological tools to evaluate and to contribute to digital mapping projects in the humanities; and

3.   To teach professional vision, that is, to develop students' critical thinking skills and visual sophistication as they relate to material presented in a spatial and/or temporal format.[2]

In order to achieve these aims, we introduced a set of "core" skills we deemed necessary for fluency in the geospatial humanities. Core Course A, the first in the three-quarter series, lays down the intellectual foundations for the program, introducing students to the history and development of the visual presentation of data. The course centers on data representation through mapping, reasoning and critique, asking students to create and analyze data presented in a spatial format.[3]

---

1   For a historical review of "the spatial turn," as it has developed in a number of disciplines, see Joanna Guldi, "What is the Spatial Turn?" *Spatial Humanities*, Institute for Enabling Geospatial Scholarship, n.d., http://spatial.scholarslab.org/spatial-turn/. For evidence of projects on the ground, see the print-based, circa 2010 state-of-the-art survey by David J. Bodenhamer in *The Spatial Humanities: GIS and the Future of Humanities Scholarship* (Bloomington: Indiana University Press, 2010). For a cautionary note on "borrowing" technologies from other disciplines and a call-to-arms to focus on humanistic visualizations, see Johanna Drucker, "Humanities Approaches to Graphical Display," *Digital Humanities Quarterly* 5, no. 1 (2011): paras. 1–52.

2   We have only begun to teach how to interrogate multi-dimensional maps in a way that approaches that articulated in Charles Goodwin, "Professional Vision," *American Anthropologist* 96 (1994): 606–33.

3   Assigned texts range from the rudimentary but still extraordinarily compelling Mark

Core Course B, designed as a lab, offers students direct instruction on a number of mapping platforms. Existing scholarly projects that use two-dimensional online mapping, virtual globes, three-dimensional modeling and GIS are introduced and analyzed, acquainting students with the variety of research questions currently being addressed by these technologies. Students are then asked to use these programs creatively and to design their own projects based on datasets from their area of academic interest. Each project builds on the skill set learned in the previous week, with the course culminating in a final GIS project designed by each student. In order to address a specific question within their discipline, students gather a dataset, input the information into a GIS, and create an argument about their results. Past projects include: investigating the impact of New York City's High Line project on the surrounding community, the correlation between school failure and location in modern Los Angeles, and the democratization of funerary literature in ancient Egypt. By utilizing these new techniques in digital mapping, our humanities and social science students are grappling with how spatial and temporal factors are crucial to understanding place.

The final core class, Core Course C, offers a small-group, research "capstone" experience for undergraduates, in which students work closely with faculty members on an ongoing research project, utilizing the critical thinking and technological skills learned in the Core A and B classroom.

The strength of the Keck Digital Cultural Mapping Program lies not in the "core" courses, however, but in the integration of spatial concepts and mapping technologies into new and existing classes at UCLA. The Keck faculty is committed to adding new digital mapping elements to its current classes to transform these traditional humanities and social science classes into collaborative and interactive learning spaces. Additionally, by recruiting a group of associated faculty and offering them instruction and ongoing classroom support for the use of these technology programs, the Keck DCMP has expanded incrementally.

---

Monmonier, *How to Lie with Maps*, 2nd edn (Chicago: University of Chicago Press, 1996) to David Rumsey and Meredith Williams, "Historical Maps in GIS," in *Past Time, Past Place: GIS for History*, ed. Anne Kelly Knowles (San Diego: ESRI Press, 2002), 1–18, and Edward R. Tufte, *Visual Explanations: Images and Quantities, Evidence and Narrative* (Cheshire: Graphics Press, 1997).

# Challenges Integrating Digital Toolsets in Humanities Instruction

Integrating the teaching of robust and sophisticated digital tools into a modern undergraduate program will never be straightforward. Contrary to glib, but seemingly intuitive assessments of our twenty-first century students, those born in a post-Internet world are certainly sophisticated consumers of well-designed, commercial technology, but their march through the primary and secondary school systems has not prepared them to develop and analyze complex digital arguments.[4]

The university system exacerbates the problem. If students have not received a rudimentary technical introduction in secondary school, remedial training is clearly warranted. The curricular demands of a research university such as UCLA—and the same doubtless holds true for small liberal arts colleges—do not easily allow for a seminar or a lecture course to focus solely on technological approaches. A quick scan through course offerings at any major research institution illustrates the issue: there is only a scattering of lab courses devoted to purely technical training. Even in the computational sciences, it is difficult to find a course entitled, "An Introduction to X Language." Instead, one finds "An Introduction to Computer Science" or "Software Construction Laboratory," and only by browsing the current syllabus will the case-study language be apparent. To belabor an obvious point: there was an art and science to using a complicated scientific calculator, but understanding the math and the potential problems to be solved is the only way to even begin to understand how to get work done. Even when teaching a fairly robust tool, one must focus primarily on the theory underlying it. Teaching the tool alone can lead to a tool-specific, rather than a theoretical approach to problem solving.[5]

Practical demands of tool acquisition cannot simply be brushed aside, however. Modern software, which should be conceived in its broadest forms, ranging from cloud-based (or whatever the next decade's terminology will call it) to systems installed on a local machine, can be deceptively easy to use, but its capabilities require a theoretically complex

---

4  For an overview on the technological savvy of the so-called millennials, see Sue Bennett, Karl Maton, and Lisa Kervin, "The 'Digital Natives' Debate: A Critical Review of the Evidence," *British Journal of Educational Technology* 39, no. 5 (2008): 775–86, and Neil Selwyn, "The Digital Native: Myth and Reality," *Aslib Proceedings* 61, no. 4 (2009): 364–79.

5  For a discussion of these issues, see Simon Mahony and Elena Pierazzo's chapter "Teaching Skills or Teaching Methodology?"

understanding to exploit. Every software package has a learning curve, and some—especially in the realm of geographic information systems or statistical analysis—are well known for being almost user-unfriendly. Students cannot be expected to apply even rudimentary GIS-based theory within the confines of such an extraordinarily counter-intuitive program as any of the current GIS solutions, regardless of whether they use open source, free, or for-pay software. Such a tool cannot easily be taught, nor can it easily be mastered.

In walks the digital humanist. The following brief thought experiment illustrates the unfortunate ramifications of a tool-based course in the humanities, with no better place to start than an introductory programming class. One might offer a class on "mapping for archaeologists," or "programming for humanists,"[6] but if one were to offer a course entitled "Java for humanists" what might be the result? What is the result of offering a course such as Latin for medical students, or an introduction to the German language for students of intellectual history? The courses are indeed useful, but learning outcomes are in no way comparable to those of introductory language courses. If we were to devote a humanities class to similar training on a tool, we could produce students who use GIS, but who do not understand its full capabilities. Better to learn GIS through a formalized structure run outside the humanities curriculum, and focus the precious time allotted to the humanities on issues humanists can do best. If the effort were simply to teach an army of semi-competent programmers, then the digital humanities would be an abject failure.

If, however, the definition of the digital humanist includes a deeper understanding of the present set of software affordances—in order to suggest, first the right theoretical approach, then the right tool for demonstrating and practicing a theoretical concept applicable to the humanities—then, in our view, progress has been made. We are not so much concerned that the student intimately knows specific software—rather we want him or her to understand the conceptual framework of, for example, the geospatial or even the geotemporal web. We wish to avoid teaching the specific details surrounding which key is pressed to draw a point or a polygon in a software program, or, even worse, accidentally conveying that one software company's approach to geospatial material is the only

6   For a discussion of such a course as successfully offered at the University of Nebraska–Lincoln, see Stephen Ramsay's chapter "Programming with Humanists: Reflections on Raising an Army of Hacker-Scholars in the Digital Humanities."

way, so that the limitations of one software package do not constrain the intellectual research agenda.

Critical to these endeavors at the undergraduate level is the construction and intelligent use of a suite of examples. A new field does not so easily yield exemplary material in sufficient quantity. While it is exciting to imagine that our students, an extraordinarily creative lot, will push the limits within their digital projects, when given an assignment to create a thematic map of their local neighborhood that changes over time, many will struggle without clear examples. Students have been trained to write, and though we often complain that they do not seem to have benefited from such training, nonetheless, the time they have spent writing journal entries, essays, blogs and research papers dwarfs the time they have spent producing analytic, digital investigations. Though students are steeped in a digital, media-driven culture, they have not been trained to interpret and critically evaluate it. Therefore, modeling is critical.[7]

The tools have changed over the years, but the focus of the courses remains the same: we teach core concepts of analysis and research method. The independent scholar working alone is no longer the only model, however. Digital projects invite a team-oriented, collaborative approach; similarly, the work on specific tools fosters a collaborative spirit and a team-oriented research methodology.

## Integrating Digital Tools into Historical Narrative: The LA Cluster

Touring LA, one of a suite of courses designed for the Keck DCMP and now offered as a digital humanities minor elective, is also part of another innovative UCLA instructional initiative: the freshmen clusters. These cluster classes provide first-year students with an opportunity to take a yearlong course sequence on a focused topic delivered from an interdisciplinary perspective. In the first two quarters, cluster courses rely on the lecture/discussion section format familiar to many introductory courses. What is most distinctive about them is that they are team-taught by faculty from up to four different disciplines who approach the topic— ranging from the cosmos, to sexuality, to myth, to the 1960s—from their

---

7   This echoes the findings of Mahony and Pierazzo, "Teaching Skills or Teaching Methodology?"

own perspectives while engaging in interdisciplinary conversations with their colleagues. In the third quarter, students have the opportunity to select a topical seminar taught by one of the teaching team members (made up of lecturers and teaching fellows) from the previous two quarters. These seminars allow most students to choose a topic and methodology of some particular interest to them as well as create a substantial piece of scholarship that rests on the background knowledge gained in the first two quarters. Touring LA was part of GE66: LA—The Cluster, a class designed to introduce students to the complexities of urban environments through the prism of Los Angeles, the students' home for (at least) the next four years.

Throughout the first two quarters, students engaged with the spaces of Los Angeles from a variety of perspectives. Lectures and readings challenged students to consider them from historical, literary, sociological and legal perspectives. They were introduced to the imagined spaces of city boosters, realtors and novelists, and they researched particular geographic communities for their writing assignments. In the first of these assignments, they wrote a history of a neighborhood or community in Los Angeles County. For the second, they conducted an ethnographic interview of someone who lived or worked in that community and subsequently wrote up their findings. Their last assignment took the form of a letter written to the appropriate government official, in which they documented a problem currently facing that community and suggested a solution. Students began their spring quarter seminar, Touring LA, having surveyed the city of Los Angeles and having developed a rudimentary range of tools for performing city-based research.

Students also received a brief introduction to the importance of tourism for Los Angeles—for bringing prospective residents to Southern California and for bringing tourist dollars and jobs into the economy. These themes were more fully developed throughout the seminar. They read about urban and heritage tourism. They debated whether a tourist bubble really existed in Los Angeles and then unintentionally proved that it did when they began plotting places they wanted to visit on a class-created online map. They were even more surprised when their sites corresponded with the places German and French guidebooks suggested visitors see in Los Angeles. By the quarter's end, class members had a good sense of the importance of tourism for cities more generally and for Los Angeles in particular.

The largest part of their effort during the quarter—and of particular interest for this chapter—was to prepare their own interpretive tour of

Los Angeles. The requirements for creating the individual tours were fairly simple, although the challenge for the students was substantial. First, the tour had to introduce its proposed audience to Los Angeles from a perspective it would not have had otherwise. Second, the tour itself had to include at least ten physical locations in Los Angeles and vicinity. Third, it had to be presented in two formats: a written document equivalent to a tour guide and a digital version, done either in a commercial online mapping program or in the HyperCities platform (http://www.hypercities.com/). The tour itself could be historical or contemporary. In the digital environment, it could be richly illustrated with images, sound or video. What ultimately would determine the success of their individual tours would be the interpretive argument they were making about Los Angeles as they led their tourists through their introductions, the individual sites, and the descriptions that accompanied them.

The assignment was not as simple as it might seem. Students had to do substantial research in order to construct their narratives and to find locations that best reflected and sustained it. The first two quarters' research had provided them with many potential ideas for tours, but not all of them were well suited for a geographic presentation. Nor did all of those possibilities have what the tourism-savvy students recognized as tourist appeal. That was of some concern to them because their classmates served as critics of their tours at three different times during the quarter: when they first proposed the topic of the tour, after they identified the first five locations, and when the tour was completed. Being freshmen, few had access to cars, making it difficult to visit many of their sites (while enhancing the practical value of the "street view" function in digital mapping platforms).

In the two years this course has been offered (and taught by Janice Reiff, a historian), the students have designed a wide range of fascinating and diverse tours on topics that have shed interesting perspectives on Los Angeles (see Figure 1). One student created an "insider's guide" to ethnic restaurants in Los Angeles, documenting eateries frequented by neighborhood residents but unknown to trendy Angelenos. Along with good eating tips, her "tourists" also learned about many of the city's newest immigrants and the neighborhoods in which they lived. Another student provided a surfer's guide to LA: starting out as simple list of where to surf, the final tour—displayed atop satellite imagery so the visitor could actually see the waves—offered a history of Southern California surfing and surf sites, emphasizing their own distinctive characteristics and characters. Still another investigated and mapped institutional continuities and changes in South Los Angeles as neighborhoods changed from being predominantly African American to Latino.

**Figure 1.** Tours created by students in the 2008 offering of Touring LA.

Although more deserve highlighting, three stand out. One student had, before she enrolled in the class, developed an interest in Howard Hughes after watching the film, *The Aviator* (2004). Reading his biography, she decided that Hughes' life story could reveal much about the city so she created her Howard Hughes Tour of LA (Figure 2). It began as Hughes moved, like many Angelenos, from Texas to Los Angeles to seek his fortune. It explored the film, oil, and aerospace industries as well as the spaces Hughes frequented before becoming a recluse in Las Vegas, a site she also pulled into her LA story.

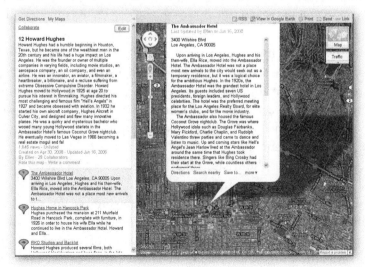

**Figure 2.** Howard Hughes Tour of LA.

Another began life as a shopper's guide to Los Angeles but ended as a fascinating presentation on the garment industry. The tour, naturally, ended on Rodeo Drive and Melrose Avenue, but it began in the sweatshops and factories of a very different Los Angeles and moved through union halls and the fashion district before arriving at the high-end retail and resale shops. The act of following the tour documented one of Los Angeles' largest industries. The single most ambitious project used the tour/map format to engage with the contention of the LA School of urban scholars that their theories about Los Angeles—the archetype for the post-modern American city—had also supplanted the old models of urban theory developed by the Chicago School some seven decades earlier when Chicago seemed to be the archetypal city. Spanning the vast spaces of the Los Angeles metropolitan region, the tour showed that Los Angeles with its historical layers reflected elements of both.

As they completed their projects, the students easily mastered the basics of online mapping and, by necessity, developed basic skills in markup languages, and in transferring their digital maps into social mapping platforms where they could take advantage of historical map overlays to illustrate their points about change over time.[8] They struggled with many of the issues cartographers must address when creating maps that are analytical and narrative as well as simply representational. They mined the photo collections at UCLA, the Los Angeles Public Library, the California Digital Library's Calisphere (http://www.calisphere.universityofcalifornia. edu/), the University of Southern California Library, the Library of Congress, and other places to make their virtual tours richer.

The final learning experience for both classes came on the last day of the quarter. On that day, the students climbed on a bus for a live tour of the sites they, as a group, decided were the most interesting to visit. Both classes had ambitious agendas: a 57-mile trip that took them from Watts Towers to Hollywood, from Leimert Park to Silver Lake, from Angel's Flight to Pink's Hotdogs. The second tour was affected by what at least two students had built into their virtual tours—LA traffic. The rain that day cut the planned tour almost in half and introduced students to new, uncharted neighborhoods as the bus driver sought alternatives to the

---

8   Many developed skills in HTML and KML, and the process required students to geo-reference imagery and add it to platforms such as HyperCities. An undercurrent of our program's focus is to balance the use of experimental projects with that of software and standards supported by academia and industry. As evidenced by the use of KML for geospatial markup, we sometimes use the more widely adopted standard in preference to the more robust.

clogged freeways. Fortunately, they also retained the virtual versions to visit the sites at their leisure during their remaining years at UCLA.

## Devising Humanistic Experiments: Roman Architecture and Urbanism

Another Keck-related course examined Roman architectural history (taught by Diane Favro, an architectural historian). Based in the Department of Architecture and Urban Design, the class attracted students from such solidly humanistic fields as classics, near eastern languages and cultures, art history and critical studies in architecture, as well as those working to become practicing architects. As a result, the participants displayed not only widely divergent knowledge of history and design, but also widely divergent graphic and spatial literacy. Some students were familiar with historical research, but had no graphic experience; those in architecture had extensive experience with three-dimensional modeling, but none with archaeological analysis; others were experts at dissecting texts, but could not easily read maps. The course adopted a science-based model, emphasizing experimentation based on specific problems. Working in groups, the students selected an issue and developed an experiment to either test a defined hypothesis, or evaluate an alternative solution to architectural challenges relating to the Roman era. As much as possible, the groups were composed of students with different backgrounds and skill sets who worked in concert. The research was formed and presented collaboratively on the geotemporal HyperCities platform, allowing the exploitation of diverse digital media and strategies while maintaining the scholarly apparatus of a research paper.

The incorporation of new technologies compels instructors to ask new questions and reframe old ones, reinvigorating both traditional and digitally based research and pedagogy. For example, ancient architectural historians frequently use architectural reconstructions, but rarely interrogate their accuracy or discuss the context in which they were created. Lectures using multiple digital as well as pictorial reconstructions resulted in conversations about the role of each in knowledge production and their varied applications by researchers, teachers, and the general public. A discussion centered on reconstructions of the Villa of the Papyri in Pompeii compared a physical "rebuilding" at the Getty Villa in Malibu with two digital simulations, one for digital heritage and one for scholarly analysis. In effect, these architectural representations paralleled the comparison of differing outcomes from the same dataset undertaken in the LA cluster. The interrogation of media and sensory experiences also prompted the class to challenge the dominance of vision in traditional architectural history, and argue for more polysensory analysis.

Courses incorporating digital technologies require a rethinking of pedagogical choreography. Lectures remained central to the Roman Architecture course, but included extensive multimedia and presentation types, as well as increased discussion. Several lectures were given in the Visualization Portal (Figure 3), an immersive environment allowing the instructor and students to move in real time through digital reconstruction models of ancient Roman cities and buildings created by the UCLA Experiential Technologies Center (http://www.etc.ucla.edu/). In the Roman Forum model, sound is localized. For example, a speech by Cicero from atop the Rostra becomes louder as the class approached and recedes as it moved away. This multimodal experience provoked a rich discussion on urban acoustics, rhetorical gesturing, view-sheds and other factors. Another lecture featuring the digital simulation of crowds in the ancient Forum at Pompeii stimulated discussions about variations in urban use by different social groups and the efficacy of procedural modeling.

**Figure 3.** Students experiencing the Flavian Amphitheater in UCLA's immersive Visualization Portal.

For this digital humanities course, lectures on Roman architecture were interspersed with exercises and workshops that relied heavily on peer-to-peer learning. Short class activities (dubbed "mind raves") challenged students to develop a position in relation to an issue covered in class lecture and propose an appropriate digital means to convey the argument; the results were peer reviewed. These debates drew upon the students' rich and varied collective knowledge of digital media and its capabilities for inquiry, analysis and presentation. For example, in one case, urban design students argued for the use of animated programming diagrams to show the sequence through a Roman bath. Those from an art history background felt a three-dimensional model would better convey the immersive experience, while classics students recommended pop-up windows of texts to integrate ancient voices with spaces.

An initial lab-based workshop demonstrated the capabilities of HyperCities, but most learning was through doing. Instructor and peer evaluations were made throughout the term, which greatly helped to hone issue definition and the appropriate implementation of digital strategies. Students drew upon diverse methods. Some exploited the tenets of "experimental archaeology," which advocates controllable, imitative experiments to replicate past phenomena. For the most part, early experimental archaeology testing was small in scale, primarily recreating known, portable objects; digital tools now facilitate the creation of large architectural and urban simulations. One student group studied the construction process for the Pont du Gard aqueduct (Figure 4), testing several different types of scaffolding based on the archaeological remains, ancient images, Roman architectural handbooks, and post-antique examples of formwork.

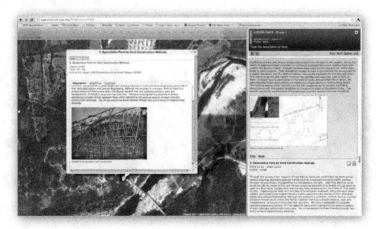

**Figure 4.** Screenshot of interactive HyperCities platform showing a student project analyzing alternative structural scaffolding solutions for a Roman aqueduct.

The technical sophistication of digital technologies inspired the adoption of scientific models, in particular hypothesis testing. In effect, HyperCities became a laboratory for historical humanistic inquiry. Two creative experiments demonstrated the value of such interdisciplinarity. One group explored how theater design might have evolved in the Roman world without the influence of Greek models. After identifying and isolating Greek architectural features, students analyzed religious, social, political and construction techniques on the Italian peninsula. Their final project featured all the supporting materials, written analysis and a hypothetical design for a "born-Roman" theater presented in the three-dimensional model and animation (Figure 5).

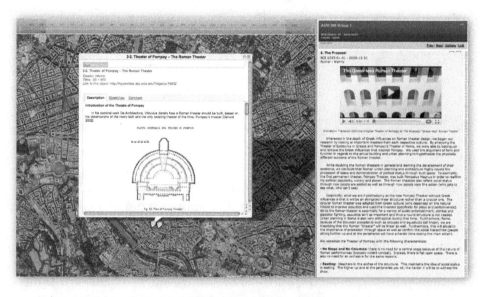

**Figure 5.** Screenshot of interactive HyperCities platform showing a group project which used images, lines of association, text and an animation to explore the hypothetical appearance of a Roman theater devoid of Greek influences.

Another group explored why the Claudian port at Ostia failed not long after its construction; drawing upon analyses of tidal movement, ship types, use patterns, artistic representations, mole design and available ancient technologies, the students proposed an alternative site and design for the harbor of Rome (Figure 6).

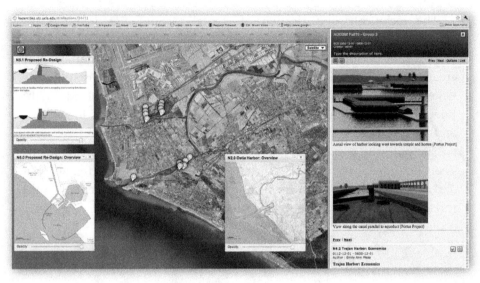

**Figure 6.** Screenshot of interactive HyperCities platform showing a group project demonstrating possible redesign solutions to improve the port of ancient Rome.

The direct confrontation of geography and mapping in HyperCities significantly enriched the work produced by the class. All the student projects were multidimensional in every sense of the word. The platform's geographic emphasis showcased spatiality and the vertical (Z) dimension in analyses. In addition, the collaborative approach did more than foster interdisciplinarity—it made it a necessity. Every project drew upon materials and methods from numerous academic fields. Examining the motivations for locating a major highway under a temple platform, one group created a three-dimensional model of the site that underscored the site's logistical advantages; analysis of religious, economic, geographic, and architectural issues demonstrated that the tunnel was utilized to monitor and tax livestock to Rome during the Republic, as well as meet cult needs. Another group examined how extensive rebuilding at Pompeii after the earthquake of 62 CE resulted in municipal adjustments to traffic flow including such creative solutions as a proscribed circular route for vehicles carrying construction materials and debris (Figure 7), a study that combined urban planning, technology, demography, and archaeology.

**Figure 7.** Screenshot of interactive HyperCities platform showing a group project analyzing traffic densities and construction routes in Pompeii.

Certainly, such approaches could have been undertaken before the advent of digital humanities, and without the aid of an externally funded program. Nonetheless, they were never tried. Digital technologies stimulate spatial and chronological thinking and collaborative, multidisciplinary engagement. The geotemporal HyperCities platform obliged students to engage constantly and simultaneously with time and space, text, and multimedia. Students developed and articulated their ideas in written arguments, models, graphs, images, films and other media directly situated within the geo-browser. Non-verbal components thus gained equality with words in the process of argumentation. Overall, the perceived need to justify the new technologies led to the assessment of means as well as results. Students perceptively discussed the enduring predominance of the visual in digital humanities projects and critiqued the challenges of selecting the most appropriate digital tool, platform and software. Most productive of all was the interrogation of humanistic research in general in the last class session; students and instructor together debated the definition of humanistic inquiry and the application of digital tools to facilitate the analytical, critical and speculative methods to study the human condition.

# Visual Argumentation in a Digital Laboratory: Roman Spectacle

A third "affiliated" course was adapted from an advanced undergraduate lecture on Roman spectacular entertainments (offered by Christopher Johanson, a classicist). Rather than integrate digital production throughout the course, the first seven weeks focused instead on detailed historical and chronological study of Roman spectacle. Opening with a clear theoretical approach to the Roman notion of *spectacula*—events that offered opportunities to see and be seen—the course began with an examination of the aristocratic funeral of the Roman republic, which amassed many of the key components of early spectacular stagecraft, and progressed to the apex of Roman imperial shows, staged in purpose-built complexes, attended by thousands. Lectures surveyed *ad hoc*, ephemeral spectacle of the city of Rome, power dynamics on display during planned events, the visual competition of symbolic capital, the role of the gladiator and the martyr in Roman society, and practical matters of staging such significant, spectacular entertainments.

The first segment of the course followed a fairly traditional, lecture and discussion program, save that born-digital material served as the foundation for presentations. Each week's readings were framed within digital "tinker-toy models"[9] representing monumental spaces of the urban environment of ancient Rome (Figure 8). Rather than receive an unmediated presentation of these reconstructed spaces, students were first given a short critical introduction to epistemological issues related to studying hypothetical—and often controversial—representations of an ancient city and its historical events.[10] Students examined different experimental attempts to describe daily life in the city, which ranged from standard encyclopedic entries to historical-fictional attempts to study the experience of Roman daily life. They interrogated digital reconstructions, not as attempts to reproduce a past reality, but as hermeneutical tools and

---

9   On "tinker-toy models," see Willard McCarty, "Modeling: A Study in Words and Meanings," in *A Companion to Digital Humanities,* ed. Susan Schreibman, Ray Siemens, and John Unsworth (Malden: Blackwell, 2004), 254–70. As applied to historical reconstructions, see Christopher Johanson, "Visualizing History: Modeling in the Eternal City," *Visual Resources: An International Journal of Documentation* 25, no. 4 (2009): 403-18.

10   Diane Favro, "In the Eye of the Beholder: Virtual Reality Re-Creations and Academia," *Journal of Roman Archaeology,* Supplementary Series 61 (2006): 321–34.

experimental laboratories. Each subsequent week's lecture was steeped in representations of ancient spectacle. Each study built on the last, laying the foundation in the Roman Forum, the heart of large-scale public spectacle, then moving through the narrow surrounding arteries to examine Roman street theater, and then fast-forwarding through time to situate discussions within digital representations of the Flavian Amphitheater and Circus Maximus coupled with filmic depictions of the two. The midterm exam asked students to demonstrate their broad command of the overall historical development of spectacle, discuss the definition of spectacle at Rome, and show specific knowledge of core concepts and key technical terminology.

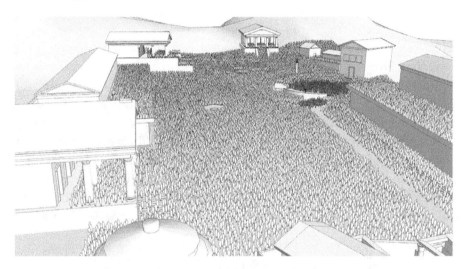

**Figure 8.** A digital "tinker-toy" model of the Roman Forum of the Middle Republic.

The students' role in the course shifted dramatically from that of content consumers to producers after week seven, when the parameters of the final project were fully revealed. Asked to synthesize work from the first section of the course, they would develop a narrative that discussed the transformation of spectacular entertainment and stagecraft in the Roman world by examining three distinct time periods. Their digital project—a fusion of two-dimensional mapping and three-dimensional world building—illustrated, augmented and enhanced a paper-based narrative. They were, on the one hand, tasked with illustrating their own work with their own digital creations, but also, more importantly, encouraged to develop arguments that could only be made by using space-based argumentation.

Though some students were motivated to become three-dimensional modelers, many had little experience working with three-dimensional content. Rather than start from scratch, students were given pre-built content to develop the three-dimensional lab. By using digital reconstructions developed in earlier projects at the UCLA Cultural VR Lab (http://www. cvrlab.org/) and the UCLA Experiential Technologies Center, students had a pre-built set of three-dimensional iconography to be used in their mapping exercises. Of course, they could (and did) manipulate the pieces and populate them with their own representations of crowds or performers.

Nearly half the twenty-four students in the class presented arguments that had equally compelling visual and textual components. One project interrogated large-scale entertainment venues to contend that imperial power manifest itself through an overt control of the spectacular spaces (Figure 9). Another traced the lineage of funerary image manipulation, situating the use of the bloody clothes of Caesar at his funeral within the larger context of visual storytelling at the Roman funeral (Figure 10). Another focused on the transformation of monumental billboards, beginning with the political sponsorship of Roman games, transitioning to the permanent, named spaces that would honor their dedicator during the staging of each event, and culminating with the development of pure propaganda such as that illustrated in the Imperial, triumphal arch. A final example compared the changing nature of audience participation at the theater in Rome to that of the nineteenth-century United States (Figure 11).

**Figure 9.** An experimental representation of the natural depression where early circus games might have been held in Rome.

**Figure 10.** Caesar's bloody clothing used as a prop during the eulogy said on his behalf.

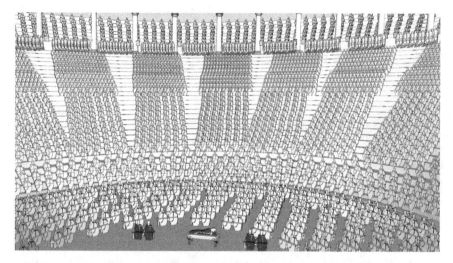

**Figure 11.** The cavea of the Theater of Marcellus filled with spectators whose clothing clearly indicate a seating system defined by social class.

The evaluation process was critical to the success of the course. The raw digital material was not evaluated for craft or technique. Instead, students were asked to transform their visual, interactive argument into a short six-minute performance given during finals week. Therefore, preparation and ideas could be evaluated independently of the digital ability of the student, and each successful presentation focused first on the humanistic problem rather than digital fireworks.

# A "Core" Curriculum in Digital Mapping at UCLA

While most of the courses associated with the Keck DCMP, including those discussed above, are firmly grounded within specific academic departments, the "core" courses by design are intended to teach students across many disciplines. This approach has its advantages, but it also results in a number of methodological hurdles. For example, the Core B Course, centered on lab-style digital technology instruction, is designed to engage students actively in creating individual projects using digital mapping software such as GIS, virtual globes, and three-dimensional modeling. Students enrolled in the first year of the program came from seven different majors, with interests that ranged across the globe and spanned ancient to modern times. While it would likely be easier to teach this course simply as a series of technological tutorials, it is vital to our mission that students grapple with the technological and Humanistic questions simultaneously. How does one evaluate projects with such a diverse focus successfully?

In this class, we found a solution in the fundamentals of humanistic inquiry, which essentially do not change across department or disciplines. Be it history, archaeology, cultural studies or English, we follow similar rules for research problem design, demand the same rigor in data collection, and expect the same critical analysis of our results. With this in mind, we asked students to learn and experiment with the capabilities of the various technologies taught in class, focusing on what each platform could and could not do well, and how the visualization of the data differed from one to the other. As the course progressed, and students began to distinguish strengths and weaknesses of the different platforms, they were asked to create a series of projects on a topic within their own major field of interest. Each project's design was required to take advantage of the strengths of each platform, capitalizing on the platform's organizational and visualization capabilities to address a research question (Figures 12 and 13). Datasets must be appropriate for answering the desired question, and visualized in a clear and well-designed manner for expressing one's argument. Students presented their digital projects in class or posted them to the class website, and fellow students were asked to critique each other's projects for design, clarity and strength of conclusions.

**Figure 12.** Screenshot of a student project investigating the cultural and economic impact of New York City's High Line Park.

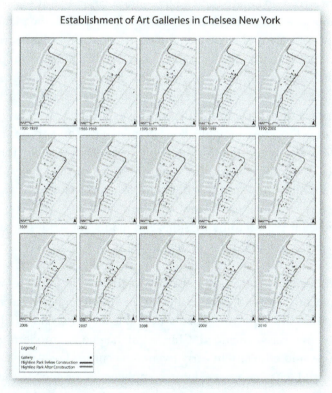

**Figure 13.** Iterative GIS maps of the growth of art galleries related to the opening of the High Line Park show its cultural influence; a three-dimensional model examines its relationship with the neighborhood.

Essentially, we discovered that the constant focus on digital design in practice—such as color, size and location for objects and lines added to a two-dimensional web-based mapping project, or the folder organization in a virtual globe project allowing different groups of objects/lines/polygons to be turned "on" or "off" collectively—led to added focus on the initial research design of the project. By thinking through how the project would be organized and appear in the digital environment, students had to think critically about the individual and collective meaning of each piece of information brought into the project: What is its meaning as entered? Could it be interpreted or represented in a different way? How would changing its representation affect results? How does it relate to other types of data in the project? Here, then, lies an opportunity to integrate our study of the humanities and social sciences with the digital toolbox, and our means to evaluate such a wide-range of student research projects. By assessing whether research design is (1) appropriate to the platform used, and (2) appropriate to the research question asked, both the instructor and fellow students can provide a broad critique of work outside our own areas of interest. This cuts to the heart of what it means to teach digital literacy and, in effect, offered a practical approach to teaching critical cartography.

In the case of this class, the platform was a digital one, but the skills honed to develop a research question and match it to an appropriate means of analysis and presentation of data apply to research in many formats and disciplines. By continually addressing questions of how research design and presentation influence the outcome of a project—both within their own projects and in their review of fellow students' projects—students sharpened their critical thinking skills and made real strides in identifying problems in argumentation or visualization.

A more difficult area for critique lay in the evaluation of a student's dataset. Indeed, it is impossible for any instructor (in the case of the first offering of Core Course B, Elaine Sullivan, an Egyptologist) to have in-depth knowledge of the types of sources available in a myriad of disciplines, which, in one class, included Chinese archaeology, modern American architecture, and ethnicity in early twentieth century Los Angeles. Student projects could not be assessed for completeness of the dataset, as the bibliography of source material used in most cases could not be fully evaluated by a non-specialist. The spatial aspect of each of the datasets gave both students and instructor a set of similar points on which to begin a critique. Initial questions spurred by the visualization of the dataset included issues of change over time, techniques of data collection, gaps in the datasets, size and completeness of the dataset, and reliability of data. In some cases the collaborative nature of the projects, which underwent a series of reviews by fellow students in class and on the online forums, provided even more substantive analysis. Students with majors or minors in the same fields gave subject-specific critiques and recommendations on sources used for their peers' projects. The varied nature of the data also meant that students (and the instructor) encountered dataset issues unfamiliar to them from their own fields. Class participants had to try to solve data collection issues creatively, often leading to inventive and insightful strategies that may not have occurred to those within the same discipline.

On the whole, we approached this skills class as a testing ground for incorporating digital methodologies into traditional humanistic questions. We hoped that students would take the technological and critical-thinking skills back into their departmental coursework, where future projects could and would be evaluated by subject specialists. Thus, while questions of dataset conceptualization and visualization are of utmost importance, for this approach we left the assessment of the accuracy and fullness of the dataset itself to another time. In fact, a number of our students mapped out projects for which the gathering of a complete dataset would take more than the few weeks available in UCLA's ten-week quarter system. They saw their final projects as only preliminary results, providing examples of how more data-rich projects could appear. What is vital for this course is not the gathering of such rich sets of data, but the articulation of what should be in the dataset, how this information should be organized and visualized, what cannot or should not be included (e.g., due to the quality and nature of the original data, the definition of the problem to be solved, or the level of representational granularity stated in the project design), and a demonstration of what these preliminary results would look like.

The final step in each mapping project asked students to evaluate the results of their data visualization. Early in the quarter, the entire class was provided with a large dataset of published archaeological finds from an ancient city. Each student mapped a section of the dataset in order to investigate a specific question about the possible function of different sections of the city. They then drew conclusions based on their digital map. When presented to their peers, the students were amazed by how many different conclusions about neighborhood function emerge from the same set of data (Figures 14, 15, and 16). This exercise was specifically designed to spur their thinking about how data is interpreted.

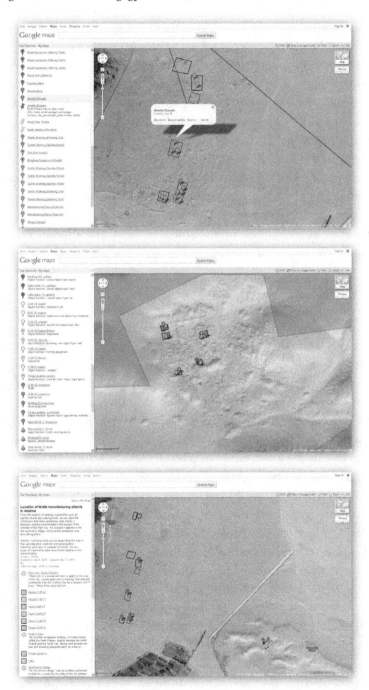

**Figures 14, 15, and 16.** Screenshots of three student projects mapping the same dataset. One student chose to map the full dataset by function, a second by material, the third mapped out only selective data related to a specific topic.

A large part of the evaluation of each student project rests on how they have created and supported their argument with the data. In digital projects, this often means including screenshots of one's GIS maps or views of one's virtual globe as figures within a traditional written paper. In other cases, students add their thesis directly to the digital platform and create an argument their viewers must follow within the digital space. In both cases, projects are critiqued on the basic premise of good scholarship: has the author successfully argued that the data supports their conclusions? Ultimately, the visual nature of these digital platforms leads students to engage with the data in a more sophisticated way, encouraging better analysis and more thoughtful conclusions, more interesting papers and projects, and what we hope to be real, "immersive" learning that transfers to other aspects of their academic lives.[11]

## The Program in Digital Humanities at UCLA

The collective institutional experience at UCLA in digital tool development, as well as the advanced study of theoretical approaches in digital cultural mapping, enabled through the in-class digital laboratory, supplied ample foundation upon which to build not only an exciting experimental and highly-focused program, but also a fully-fledged, more broadly conceived, curriculum for undergraduate and graduate education. We saw the natural outcome of this three-year program in digital cultural mapping as the creation of a more far-reaching program in Digital Humanities, one that would remain project-specific but would expand to comprise corpora analysis, text and data visualization, and social research on a significantly larger scale. We modeled our expanded curriculum on the specific research profiles of practicing digital humanists. Our own variegated paths to the production of digitally enabled scholarship and digital humanities research had each started in a traditionally defined — albeit extraordinarily progressive — humanities program. We self-identified as Egyptologists, architectural historians, classicists, urban historians, archaeologists and the like, while we also increasingly began to immerse ourselves in the literature that had coalesced over time around the

---

11  Such project-based approaches to curriculum are hardly new, but it is clear that recent focus on immersive learning, such as the immersive learning initiative at Ball State University, is directly enabled by digital technology; see "What is Immersive Learning," *Strategic Plan 2007–2012*, Ball State University, October 5, 2011, http://cms.bsu.edu/About/StrategicPlan/WhatisImmersiveLearning.aspx.

idea that has now become the digital humanities. We hoped to record those paths, generalize them where appropriate, and turn them into a program in which our students would be equipped to participate in current scholarly conversations in humanities-based disciplines. A scholar's contribution to Roman studies, for example, is handicapped if he or she does not have a firm grounding in the discipline's theoretical approaches, its canonical literature, its current research themes, the tone of the present scholarly conversation and the directions of the hottest topics. Our time with students is extraordinarily limited, and though we might wish to teach critical approaches to map-based visualization, for example, digital humanities courses necessarily must connect to the roots of the humanities. Otherwise should they not instead be called digital studies, media studies or information studies? When the focus is on geospatial digital research design for the humanities, developed in discipline-specific environments, then those roots are firmly grounded.

The paradox inherent in a digitally-centered program is that undergraduates are actually much better prepared to make significant contributions to traditional research areas through their digital experience than through their undergraduate training in traditionally defined disciplines. A sophomore majoring in near eastern languages and cultures has received a minimal introduction to the field. A senior majoring in classics can, in all but the rarest exceptions, claim to have received only a broad introduction to texts, material evidence, the research methodologies, tools and approaches to scholarship. In general, we cannot expect an undergraduate major in architectural theory to participate in an undergraduate seminar as an expert architectural historian. We can, however, expect to see a budding digital humanist, with broad training in his or her domain-specific discipline, approach a traditional problem in a radically new way, or conceive of an entirely fresh approach to the traditionally defined field.

We created a program intended to highlight our specific institutional strengths in digital humanities project development and our internal focus on training students in domain-specific areas, while at the same time engaging in the current digital humanities conversation. The Keck Digital Cultural Mapping Program offered us a rare luxury in academia: we were able to experiment with a radical alteration of a curriculum and traditional teaching methodologies, which resulted both in valuable teaching and learning experience and in the creation of an official course of study for those interested in combining the digital with the humanistic.

In the winter of 2011, we successfully launched an undergraduate minor and graduate certificate program at UCLA,[12] both of which are project-based, humanities-focused, but tailored to give students the flexibility to explore serious humanities questions in ways hitherto impossible to imagine.

---

12   The University of California system does not offer a minor at the graduate level, but instead provides a "graduate certificate" program. The terminology is confusing, especially considering that industry-sponsored certifications run rampant in the digital world. For a compelling discussion of a digital humanities certificate program endorsed by the digital humanities community at large, see Lisa Spiro's chapter, "Opening Up Digital Humanities Education."

# 6. Looking for Whitman: A Multi-Campus Experiment in Digital Pedagogy

*Matthew K. Gold*

Perhaps the greatest of all pedagogical fallacies is the notion that a person learns only the particular thing he is studying at the time. Collateral learning in the way of formation of enduring attitudes, of likes and dislikes, may be and often is much more important than the spelling lesson or lesson in geography or history that is learned. For these attitudes are fundamentally what count in the future. The most important attitude that can be formed is that of desire to go on learning.

—John Dewey, *Experience and Education* (1938)

Cut the hawsers—haul out—shake every sail!
Have we not stood here like trees in the ground long enough?
—Walt Whitman, "Passage to India" (1871–72)

Walt Whitman was a terrible teacher, at least when judged according to the pedagogical standards of his day. During the two teenaged years he spent teaching in rural Long Island schoolhouses (1836–38), Whitman violated most of the educational conventions of his era. Unlike the schoolmaster described as a "brisk wielder of the birch and rule" in John Greenleaf Whittier's poem "Snowbound," Whitman refused to discipline his pupils with physical force.[1] He opposed the kinds of rote, drill-based learning strategies popular among

---

1   John Greenleaf Whittier, "Snow-Bound: A Winter Idyl" (Boston: Knor and Fields, 1866), 34.

many teachers of the period, choosing instead to engage his students through a series of progressive educational techniques: open-ended conversations, question-and-answer sessions, and social games of baseball and tag.[2] This pedagogical inventiveness earned him the enmity of his peers; one colleague remarked sarcastically that Whitman's "pupils had not gained a 'whit' of learning" in his classes.[3] Whitman, in turn, grew depressed about his lot as a teacher, writing to a friend that "Never before have I entertained so low an idea of the beauty and perfection of man's nature, never have I seen humanity in so degraded a shape, as here. Ignorance, vulgarity, rudeness, conceit and dullness are the reigning gods of this deuced sink of despair."[4] Even so, the years that Whitman spent as a schoolteacher shaped his work—most notably *Leaves of Grass*, the collection he published and republished in successive editions over the course of his lifetime.

Over a hundred and fifty years after the first appearance of that text, Whitman's work inspired a series of pedagogical experiments that transposed his experimental teaching philosophy and his poetry into the era of networked learning through a project entitled "Looking for Whitman: The Poetry of Place in the Life and Work of Walt Whitman". Sponsored by two Digital Humanities Start-Up Grants from the United States National Endowment for the Humanities (NEH), the project brought together classes from four academic institutions in a collaborative digital environment that emphasized place-based learning and progressive educational techniques. The project set forth a new model for aggregated, collaborative and open learning practices that mirrored Whitman's own poetic ideals and that has served as an important example of digital pedagogy for the digital humanities community.[5] Like Whitman's own

---

2    Justin Kaplan, *Walt Whitman: A Life* (New York: Simon and Schuster, 1980), 82–83; Ed Folsom and Kenneth M. Price, *Re-Scripting Walt Whitman: An Introduction to His Life and Work* (Malden: Blackwell, 2005), 7.

3    David S. Reynolds, *Walt Whitman* (Oxford: Oxford University Press, 2004), 7.

4    Quoted in Folsom and Price, *Re-Scripting Walt Whitman*, 7.

5    *Looking for Whitman* was highlighted as an example of open content projects in the 2010 *Horizon Report*; see: Larry Johnson, Alan Levine, Rachel S. Smith, and Sonja Stone, *The 2010 Horizon Report* (Austin: The New Media Consortium, 2010), 14. Lisa Spiro has also repeatedly cited the project as a compelling example of Digital Humanities pedagogy; see: Lisa Spiro, "Emerging Technologies That Hold Promise for Education" (paper presented at the E-Learning Symposium, Lone Star College, Houston, Texas, November 12, 2009); and "Opening Up Digital Humanities Education," *Digital Scholarship in the Humanities*, September 8, 2010, http://digitalscholarship.wordpress.com/2010/09/08/opening-up-digital-humanities-education/. More recently, Rebecca Frost Davis included the project in "Case Studies of Digital Humanities Pedagogy," *Rebecca Frost Davis*, August 3, 2012 http://rebeccafrostdavis.wordpress.com/2012/08/03/case-studies-of-digital-humanities-pedagogy/.

checkered career as a teacher, however, the project's successes and its failures point towards future developments along related lines. As I discuss the project and describe some of the ways in which others might extend its work, I hope to articulate some of the reasons why the digital humanities, as a field, would benefit from a more direct engagement with issues of teaching and learning than it has exhibited thus far.

## Project Design and Background

I am with you, you men and women of a generation, or ever so many generations hence,
I project myself, also I return—I am with you, and know how it is.
Just as you feel when you look on the river and sky, so I felt,
Just as any of you is one of a living crowd, I was one of a crowd,
Just as you are refreshed by the gladness of the river and the bright flow, I was refreshed,
Just as you stand and lean on the rail, yet hurry with the swift current, I stood, yet was hurried,
Just as you look on the numberless masts of ships, and the thick-stemmed pipes of steamboats, I looked.

—Walt Whitman, "Sun-Down Poem" (1856)

At the conclusion of the 1855 edition of the poem that he later titled "Song of Myself," Walt Whitman advised his readers to "look for me under your bootsoles,"[6] suggesting that the dilated, celebratory poetic presence they encountered on the printed page would continue to flower in the landscape around them. "Looking for Whitman" was designed to help students and faculty members trace the lingering imprints of Whitman's footsteps in the local soil. Utilizing open-source tools to connect classrooms in multiple institutions, the project asked students to research Whitman's connections to their individual locations and share that research with one another in a dynamic, social, web-based learning environment.

As originally designed, the project would engage classes at four academic institutions (New York City College of Technology [City Tech], New York University, University of Mary Washington and Rutgers University-Camden) located in Whitman's three principal areas of residence (New York, Washington DC and Camden) in a concurrent, connected,

---

6  Walt Whitman, *Leaves of Grass*, 1st edn (Brooklyn: Andrew H. Rome, 1855), 56.

semester-long inquiry into the relationship of Whitman's poetry to local geography and history. In the New York location, students from a class at CUNY taught by Matthew K. Gold and a class at NYU taught by Karen Karbiener would explore Whitman's connections to the Brooklyn Waterfront, Lower Manhattan, and Long Island, and would focus particularly on the texts he wrote during the years he lived there, including his journalism, his early temperance novel *Franklin Evans*, and the landmark 1855 first edition of *Leaves of Grass*. At the University of Mary Washington in Fredericksburg, Virginia, students in a class team-taught by Mara Scanlon and Brady Earnhart would consider Whitman's mid-career experiences as a nurse in the Civil War, focusing on his later editions of *Leaves of Grass* and his war-related writing of the 1860s. Students in two classes taught separately at Rutgers University-Camden by Tyler Hoffman and Carol Singley would explore Whitman's late career as they investigated the city in which Whitman spent the final decade of his life. Faculty members, working with historical societies, museums and archives such as The Library of Congress, the Brooklyn Historical Society and the Walt Whitman House, would identify and make available site-specific Whitman-related resources and research opportunities.

A year of planning work began in 2008 after the project received a $25,000 Level 1 Digital Humanities Start-Up Grant from the NEH Office of Digital Humanities. During the planning phase, the project team, which included faculty members, instructional technologists and consulting Whitman scholars, held a series of in-person and online meetings with the goal of bringing together faculty members to create shared assignments and connections. An important secondary goal involved training faculty members on project technologies, a task made crucial by the fact that faculty members had been chosen for the project more on the basis of their expertise in Whitman's work and their physical location than their expertise with digital technology. During this initial planning year, a team of technologists and web designers constructed the project website (http://lookingforwhitman.org) and began to create support materials that students and faculty members would later use.

The project received a second round of funding in 2009 in the form of a $35,000 Level 2 Digital Humanities Start-Up Grant. This new grant helped fund additional technical support, curriculum development, project meetings and a student conference that would bring student and faculty participants together to meet one another in person after a semester of shared online learning. An important variation from the neat symmetry of the initial project design emerged when NYU faculty member

Karen Karbiener received a Fulbright Fellowship to Serbia (a country Whitman never visited) for the 2009–2010 academic year. Because of her importance to the development of the project during the previous planning year, it was decided that Karbiener's graduate-level American Studies class on Whitman at the University of Novi Sad would take part in the project in place of her class at NYU. While this disrupted the alignment of project locations and Whitman residences, it added an international angle of collaboration that resonated with recent trends in Whitman scholarship and American Studies that have set the poet's work within global contexts.[7]

## Technologies Behind the Project

Utilizing popular open-source platforms, the project website consisted of a multisite installation of WordPress (http://www.wordpress.org), an open-source blogging platform that allows multiple blogs to be created from a single installation. A plug-in system called BuddyPress (http://www.buddypress.org/) helped transform the blogging platform into a customized social network, adding features such as profiles, friends, groups and forums. The nexus of the entire project was a central page on the website that aggregated blog posts, digital images, videos, news feeds, wiki entries and post tags from each of the classes, so that students from one location were able to follow the progress of students in other locations.

Indeed, the project made extensive use of aggregation to draw together student work into fluid and agile communal spaces. Building upon the model of the "personal learning environment" and a "domain of one's own,"[8] the project asked each student to create a personal blog for the course and to post all coursework in it. Once work was published in those individual spaces, course hubs pulled student posts together and republished them together on the course homepage (see, for example, the course homepage for the UMW "Digital Whitman" course: http://marywash.lookingforwhitman. org/). When student blog posts were tagged with specific terms, they were also pulled together into project-wide spaces. For instance, if a student from

---

7   See, for example: Gay Wilson Allen and Ed Folsom ed. *Walt Whitman and the World* (Iowa City: University of Iowa Press, 1995); and, Walter Grünzweig, "Whitman and the Cold War: The Centenary Celebration of *Leaves of Grass* in Eastern Europe," in *Leaves of Grass: The Sesquicentennial Essays*, ed. Susan Belasco, Ed Folsom, and Kenneth M. Price (Lincoln: University of Nebraska Press, 2007), 343–60.

8   Jim Groom, "A Domain of One's Own," *Bavatuesdays*, November 29, 2008, http://bavatuesdays.com/a-domain-of-ones-own/.

UMW posted about a special event such as a field trip, the student could add the tag "fieldtrip" to her post. The tagged blog post would then appear not just on her own blog and on the UMW class blog, but also on a third site that aggregated posts from across the entire project that had also been tagged "fieldtrip." In that collective space, work from students in every class and every city would appear together, so that posts describing a University of Mary Washington field trip to the Library of Congress in Washington, DC would appear next to posts describing a Rutgers class trip to the Walt Whitman House in Camden and a CUNY trip to the Fulton Ferry landing in Brooklyn. For the student, all that was required was a single post on a single blog that was completely under her control, but that post was then repurposed and republished into various other parts of the site through tags, RSS feeds, and aggregation.

## Enabling Multi-Campus Connections: Assignments and Activities

In addition to creating the site in which the project would take place, a central goal of the planning year of the grant involved the creation of assignments that could be shared among all classes involved in the project. These shared assignments formed the basis of connection among classes and fostered the creation of a project-wide community.

### Frontispiece Project

In the landmark first edition of Whitman's *Leaves of Grass*, first published in 1855 in Brooklyn, Whitman famously left his name off the title page, choosing instead to use an engraved frontispiece image as an introduction to his readers. In the "Looking for Whitman" project, all classes began their semesters by reading the 1855 edition, even though they would all focus on different periods of the poet's career in later weeks. As a way of having students introduce themselves to their classmates and to other project participants during the first week, students were asked to create a frontispiece of their own—an image of themselves, along with a few lines of from Whitman's poem that they found meaningful. These posts were aggregated into a central course blog (http://frontispiece. lookingforwhitman.org/), the home page of which showed images of the students. When readers "moused over" those images, the text chosen by the student would appear as an overlay. Clicking on the image would lead visitors to the blog post on the student's personal blog. In this way, the frontispiece project became a kind of larger frontispiece mosaic for the project itself, introducing its participants to the open web.

## Image Gloss Project

In this assignment, which was due in the second week of the course, students chose a specific image or reference from the 1855 *Leaves of Grass* that seemed unfamiliar, intriguing or historically distant to them. They were asked to write a blog post that would explain that image or reference and to contextualize it within mid-nineteenth century American history. Each blog post was required to include an image, an audio file, or a video related to the subject. The resulting blog posts appeared on individual student blogs and were aggregated into a project blog (http://imagegloss. lookingforwhitman.org/). Sample topics covered included "scrofula,"[9] "embouchure,"[10] "dray,"[11] and "accoucheur."[12]

## Material Culture Museum

In an effort to encourage students to focus their research on material culture and to understand how history could be viewed through specific material artifacts, they were asked to collectively build a Material Culture Museum by writing posts that focused on a specific material and local context of a course reading.[13] Students posted their work on their own individual blogs, and those posts were then aggregated into a site that formed the virtual museum (http://digitalmuseum.lookingforwhitman. org/). Sample objects presented in the museum included "enfield rifles,"[14]

---

9   Adam B., "Image Gloss—Scrofula," *Looking for Whitman*, September 28, 2009, http:// adamb.lookingforwhitman.org/2009/09/28/image-gloss-scrofula/.

10  Emily M., "Image Gloss: Embouchure," *Looking for Whitman*, September 16, 2009, http:// emilym.lookingforwhitman.org/2009/09/16/image-gloss-embouchure/.

11  Joseph Dooley, "Image Gloss of 'Dray,'" *Looking for Whitman*, September 15, 2009, http:// imageglossjoelemagne.lookingforwhitman.org/2009/09/15/hello-world/.

12  Meghan Edwards, "Meghan's Image Gloss," *Looking for Whitman*, September 8, 2009, http://meghanedwards.lookingforwhitman.org/2009/09/08/meghans-image-gloss/.

13  This assignment was adapted from Jeffrey McClurken of The University of Mary Washington, who had created a similar museum in his *American History and Technology* course (http://historyoftech.umwblogs.org/).

14  "Enfield Rifes," *The Material Culture Museum*, October 20, 2009, http://digitalmuseum. lookingforwhitman.org/2009/10/20/enfield-rifles/.

"surgical saws in the Civil War,"[15] "hardtack,"[16] "wool"[17] and "Lincoln lecture ticket."[18]

## Annotations Project

Each course involved in the project examined a set of texts that Whitman had composed while living in that particular project location. In order to strengthen student skills in performing close readings of literary texts, and as a way of creating resources that future students could build on, each course created an annotated version of one of Whitman's texts. The annotated texts were set up using digress.it (http://www.digress.it/), a WordPress theme forked from CommentPress (http://www.futureofthebook.org/commentpress/), which had been developed by The Institute for the Future of the book and used by a number of high-profile digital humanities projects.[19] Both CommentPress and digress.it allow comments to be linked to specific paragraphs of text in a sidebar, thus creating a hybrid document that combines text and marginalia in a single space. For the "Looking for Whitman" project, digress.it presented a few difficulties, since it was originally designed for prose rather than poetry. We configured it in such a way that comments could be attached to individual lines of poetry, thus allowing for very specific and targeted commentary on Whitman's work. Examples of annotated texts included The University of Mary Washington's version of *Drum Taps* (http://annotations.lookingforwhitman.org/), a selection of Camden-era poems annotated by graduate students at Rutgers-Camden (http://notes.lookingforwhitman.org/), an annotated version of *Sands at Seventy* and *Goodbye My Fancy* from Rutgers-Camden (http://camdenannotation.lookingforwhitman.org/), and selected passages

---

15  "Surgical Saws in the Civil War," *The Material Culture Museum*, October 20, 2009, http://digitalmuseum.lookingforwhitman.org/2009/10/20/surgical-saws-in-the-civil-war/.

16  "Hardtack and Other Indelicacies," *The Material Culture Museum*, October 20, 2009, http://digitalmuseum.lookingforwhitman.org/2009/10/20/hardtack-and-other-indelicacies/.

17  "Wool," *The Material Culture Museum*, November 18, 2009, http://digitalmuseum.lookingforwhitman.org/2009/11/18/wool/.

18  "Lincoln Lecture Ticket," *The Material Culture Museum*, October 20, 2009, http://digitalmuseum.lookingforwhitman.org/2009/10/20/lincoln-lecture-ticket/.

19  See, for example, the following set of academic texts that used CommentPress during the peer-review process: McKenzie Wark's *GAM3R 7H30RY*, http://www.futureofthebook.org/gamertheory/; Noah Wardrip-Fruin's *Expressive Processing*, http://grandtextauto.org/2008/01/22/expressive-processing-an-experiment-in-blog-based-peer-review/; and Kathleen Fitzpatrick's *Planned Obsolescence*, http://mediacommons.futureofthebook.org/mcpress/plannedobsolescence/.

from Whitman's early temperance novel *Franklin Evans* annotated by students from City Tech (http://franklinevans.lookingforwhitman.org/). All of these annotated poems remain open to commentary by future students of Whitman's work.

## Field Trips

In each project location, classes partnered with prominent cultural institutions in their region to arrange for walking tours and hands-on student experiences with archival materials. Students from City Tech took a guided tour of Whitman's Brooklyn Heights led by Jesse Merandy, creator of the online critical edition of "Crossing Brooklyn Ferry,"[20] and also toured Whitman's Fort Greene with Greg Trupiano, Director of the Walt Whitman Project. The University of Mary Washington took tours of the Fredericksburg battlefield and Chatham Manor under the guidance of the National Parks Service, and then had a tour of Whitman's Civil-War era Washington DC, with tour guide Kim Roberts. Students then visited the Special Collections Manuscripts Division at the Library of Congress, where they saw a range of Whitman artifacts including the haversack that Whitman carried with him as he visited injured soldiers in a Civil War hospital,[21] a pair of Whitman's eyeglasses, and a cane, as well as manuscripts of his poetry and letters.[22] The Camden classes visited the Walt Whitman House on Mickle Street and the mausoleum in Harleigh Cemetery, where Whitman is buried. As with other projects, posts describing these visits first appeared on individual student blogs, and then were aggregated into both class blogs and project blogs (http://fieldtrips.lookingforwhitman.org).

---

20  *Crossing Brooklyn Ferry: An Online Critical Edition*, ed. Jesse Merandy, n.d., http://micklestreet.rutgers.edu/CBF/index.html.

21  For a student's report on the experience, see: Mara Scanlon, "Free tickets to Ford's Theater for 19 people through Ticketmaster plus $2.00 access fee? $49.50. Thirteen hours of parking for three vehicles? $30.00. Bodily presence? Priceless," *Looking for Whitman*, October 28, 2009, http://mscanlon.lookingforwhitman.org/2009/10/28/free-tickets-to-fords-theater-for-19-people-through-ticketmaster-plus-2-00-access-fee-49-50-thirteen-hours-of-parking-for-three-vehicles-30-00-bodily-presence-priceless/.

22  Mara Scanlon posted a "Favorite Manuscript Moment" to her blog about the field trip, October 28, 2009, http://mscanlon.lookingforwhitman.org/2009/10/28/favorite-manuscript-moment/.

## Finding Whitman Videos

At the end of a semester in which students had simultaneously explored Whitman's texts and his roots in the surrounding region, one of the final shared assignments of the project asked students to create a video of themselves reading a passage of Whitman's work in a local space that seemed to embody, or to be connected to, his oeuvre. These videos were collected and placed on a shared Google Map (http://videomap.lookingforwhitman. org/) that eventually encompassed entries from Fredericksburg to Camden to New York City to Novi Sad. Students filmed themselves reading Whitman's words in locations that included Times Square, Grand Central Station, Civil-War battlefields in Fredericksburg, Virginia Beach and Friends Street in Camden.

## Final Project Videos

For their final projects, students in classes at the University of Mary Washington and Rutgers-Camden created a series of mashups and cinepoems that mixed Whitman's words with images and music or, in some cases, created entirely new narratives around his work. Standout videos included a creative short film titled "In Search of Wendall Slickman" (a mockumentary that purported to follow Wendall Slickman, a figure conceived of as a mashup of Walt Whitman and Elvis Presley);[23] a moving mediation on Whitman's work titled "Whitman, Commercialism, and the Digital Age. Will Whitman Survive?"[24] and a cinepoem titled "City of Ships,"[25] among many others (http://cinepoem.lookingforwhitman.org/).

## The Vault

In an effort to stimulate greater communication between students in "Looking for Whitman" courses and the larger public community of Whitman scholars, a new blog called "The Vault" debuted late in the fall semester (http://vault.lookingforwhitman.org/). Although it became active

---

23  Sam P., "In Search of Wendell Slickman," *Looking for Whitman*, April 8, 2009, http://swords. lookingforwhitman.org/2010/04/08/sam-p-s-final-project-in-search-of-wendell-slickman/.

24  Virginia Scott, "Whitman, Commercialism, and the Digital Age. Will Whitman Survive?" *Looking for Whitman*, December 15, 2009, http://lookingforwhitman.org/2009/12/15/ whitman-commercialism-and-the-digital-age-will-whitman-survive/.

25  Tara Wood, "City of Ships," *Looking for Whitman*, December 8, 2009, http://twood. lookingforwhitman.org/2009/12/08/t-woods-final-project-cinepoem-city-of-ships/.

too late in the semester to make a strong impact on the project, it did host one important public discussion about the use of Whitman's work in a Levi's commercial that drew responses from students, faculty members in the project, Whitman scholars and the wider public.[26]

# Campus-Specific Projects

In addition to the above projects that were shared across courses, several classes embarked upon projects specific to their location.

## The Address Project (City Tech/Brooklyn)

Between 1823, when Whitman was four years old, and 1859, when he was forty, the poet and his family moved through a series of Brooklyn residences and boarding houses. Whitman's correspondence had given us the addresses of twenty-two of these homes, but biographers of Whitman had been able to provide only scant historical details about these locations. Students from City Tech each chose an address and then visited the Brooklyn Historical Society, where they received guidance on doing historic house research from a BHS librarian and began to explore archival materials, such as historical atlases and fire-insurance maps, land conveyances, and directories of Brooklyn residences in an effort to find out more about the address they had been assigned. When students were unable to piece together material related to the period of Whitman's stay at a particular address, they compiled a "place history" of the address in an effort to track its development in subsequent years. This was the first experience that many of these students had had in an archive of any kind; as they ran into dead ends and made new connections, they learned the value (and the frustrations) of exploring history through primary documents. Among the unexpected results of this project was a guide to researching historical locations that one student made to help his classmates with their research — a nice example of student-led peer-to-peer learning.[27] Sample projects include "Johnson Street, North of Adams" (http://1824waltwhitmanshouse.lookingforwhitman.org/),

26  Matthew K. Gold, "Walt Whitman and the Levi's Ad Campaign: A Provocation, A Challenge, and An Invitation," *The Vault*, November 11, 2009, http://vault. lookingforwhitman.org/2009/11/11/walt-whitman-and-the-levis-ad-campaign-a-provocation-a-challenge-and-an-invitation/.
27  Techwhit, "Some tips on working with your location," *Looking for Whitman*, November 19, 2009, http://techwhit.lookingforwhitman.org/2009/11/19/some-tips-on-working-with-your-location/.

"91½ Classon Avenue" (http://classonavenuebrooklynnewyorkwhitman. lookingforwhitman.org/), and "99 Ryerson Street" (http://99ryersonst. lookingforwhitman.org/).

## Visitor's Center Scripts (Rutgers-Camden/Camden)

The house that Whitman bought on Mickle Street in 1884 — the only house he ever owned — and lived in for the last years of his life is now a national historic landmark. In concert with a planned expansion of the house that will include the construction of a new Visitor's Center on a lot next to the home, students in Professor Tyler Hoffman's course on Whitman at Rutgers-Camden worked with curator Leo Blake to create research materials that will later be adapted for exhibits in the Center (http:// visitorscripts.lookingforwhitman.org/). Sample topics included "Whitman and the Beats,"[28] "Whitman and Socialism"[29] and "Whitman's 'disciples.'"[30]

## Translations (University of Novi Sad/Novi Sad)

As a Fulbright Fellow at the University of Novi Sad, Karen Karbiener taught a graduate course titled "Walt Whitman: A Global Perspective". Discovering that many of Whitman's poems had never been translated into Serbian, Professor Karbiener asked her students to create translations of some of Whitman's most racy and homoerotic poems from the "Calamus" section of *Leaves of Grass*. Students then created visual cinepoems that mixed readings of Whitman's work in English and Serbian. Among the powerful creations to emerge from this course was Whitman's "To a Stranger," a short film by a student named Indira that consists of a series of lines of Whitman's poems being read by a cross-section of Serbian residents,[31] and

---

28  Lizmoser, "Visitors Center Script: Whitman and the Beats," *Looking for Whitman*, December 3, 2009, http://drumtaps.lookingforwhitman.org/2009/12/03/whitman-beats/.
29  Adam L., "Adam L's Visitor Center Script," *Looking for Whitman*. December 10, 2009, http://adaml.lookingforwhitman.org/2009/12/10/adam-ls-visitor-center-script/.
30  Emily M., "Visitors' Center Script: Whitman's Disciplines, part three," *Looking for Whitman*, December 3, 2009, http://emilym.lookingforwhitman.org/2009/12/03/ visitors-center-script-whitmans-disciples-part-three/; and, Adam B., "Adam's visitors center script — Whitman disciples — Sadakichi Hartmann," *Looking for Whitman*, December 3, 2009, http://adamb.lookingforwhitman.org/2009/12/03/ adams-visitors-center-script-whitman-disciples-sadakichi-hartmann/.
31  Indira J., "To A Stranger," *YouTube*, December 30, 2009, http://www.youtube.com/ watch?v=oZ56zonpOKA.

"Walt Whitman, Calamus 9,"[32] a meditation by candlelight on Whitman's words.

## Conference

Despite the immense amount of work produced by students in the "Looking for Whitman" courses, the experiment was designed to last only one semester—the Fall of 2009. But in the Spring of 2010, a project-wide student conference was held at the campus of Rutgers-Camden that brought together students from Fredericksburg, New York and Camden. Students had a chance to meet one another after a semester spent reading each other's work, and the group visited both the Walt Whitman House on Mickle Street and the Whitman gravesite.

# A New Model for Networked Pedagogy and Online Learning

"Looking for Whitman" is part of a growing trend towards what has been called, variously, "open education" or "edupunk" pedagogy.[33] In contrast to models of online learning that involve proprietary or open-source Learning Management Systems (LMS) such as Blackboard, Moodle, Desire2Learn or Sakai, this project followed a "small pieces loosely joined" approach as it brought together a number of different platforms and social networking applications into a confederated learning environment. The loose connections between tools allowed students to take more control over their online learning environments and to mold those environments to their particular learning styles.[34] Because students took part in projects that were shared openly with the public, they joined their professors in contributing scholarly energy and

---

32  Elma Porobic, "Walt Whitman, Calamus 9," *YouTube*, December 27, 2009, http://www.youtube.com/watch?v=fNG5MEiOv84.

33  Jim Groom, "The Glass Bees," *Bavatuesdays*, May 25, 2008, http://bavatuesdays.com/the-glass-bees/.

34  For example, the site was based on WordPress and used WordPress as a blogging platform. WordPress blogs allow for far greater visual and functional customization than the blogging feature of traditional LMS systems such as Blackboard, Moodle, and Sakai, or CMS systems such as Drupal. For discussions of various LMS models, see: Lisa M. Lane, "Insidious Pedagogy: How Course Management Systems Affect Teaching," *First Monday* 14, no. 10 (2009), http://firstmonday.org/htbin/cgiwrap/bin/ojs/index.php/fm/article/view/2530/2303; and, Jon Mott and David Wiley, "Open for Learning: The CMS and the Open Learning Network," *In Education* 15, no. 2 (2009), http://ineducation.ca/article/openlearning-cms-and-open-learning-network.

knowledge towards public dialogue in ways that closed learning systems, with their emphasis on privacy, often preclude.

"Looking for Whitman" drew upon a few kinds of open-education projects:

- Open Courseware Sites: Examples of such sites include those created by M.I.T. (http://ocw.mit.edu), Yale (http://oyc.yale.edu/), Notre Dame (http://ocw.nd.edu/), and Utah State (http://ocw.usu. edu/). All of these examples work within existing institutions and open up courses offered on particular campuses. They convert face-to-face classes into material that can be presented online, via the lecture model, to students. Recently, the Open Scholar project (http://www.openstudy.com/) has enabled the creation of social, peer-to-peer study groups around these static courses.

- Online and Partially Online Courses: Examples of these kinds of courses are too numerous to mention, but recent movements towards courses engaging social media platforms such as YouTube, Twitter, Facebook, Flickr, Del.icio.us, and MediaWiki were influential upon the design of "Looking for Whitman". Such courses usually retain the structure and schedule of traditional academic courses, but move them into online formats and environments.

- University-Wide Academic Commons and Blogging Projects: Experiments such as UMWBlogs (http://umwblogs.org/), The CUNY Academic Commons (http://commons.gc.cuny.edu), Blogs@Baruch (http://blsciblogs.baruch.cuny.edu/), UBC Blogs (http://blogs.ubc. ca/), and the Georgetown Digital Commons (https://digitalcommons. georgetown.edu/) have all created online communities in institutional settings. Each of them has employed some aspects of social networking to foster communities in virtual spaces.

- Massive Online Open Courses (MOOCs): MOOCs, courses offered online that are open and free to as many participants as desire to register, have become increasingly popular in the years since "Looking for Whitman" began. While many MOOCs operate entirely outside of the system of college credit, new models have begun to emerge. Jim Groom's Digital Storytelling class at UMW (popularly known by its course number and hashtag, #DS106, http://ds106.us/) offers credit to students taking the class at the University of Mary Washington, but also allows participants from across the globe to participate in a simultaneous open version of the course.

"Looking for Whitman" was unique among these projects in that it worked within discrete institutional settings to create a shared online learning experience that bridged institutional divides. Like open courseware sites, it followed the principles of "open access" by making pedagogical materials available for free on the web, but it did so in a way that engaged students in active learning experiences that enacted the principles of constructivist pedagogy. Like many online and partially online courses, the project used popular Web 2.0 programs to make digital humanities learning experiences engaging, creative and fun, but it structured these activities in such a way that materials created in one section of the project responded to materials created in other parts of the project. Like many MOOCs, the project crossed institutional lines, but it did so in a way that encouraged open-ended, creative-critical engagement rather than lecture-driven pedagogical models. Like university-wide academic commons or blogging projects, "Looking for Whitman" created an online community, but it did so in the interstitial space between universities. The online community created through the project thus became a shared landscape rather than a walled garden.

## Hacking Together Egalitarian Communities

"Looking for Whitman" operated within the existing curricula of participating institutions by running classes in traditional, credit-bearing disciplinary and institutional frameworks, but it also subverted codified elements of those structures. Perhaps the most radical element of the project was the way in which it brought participants from very different types of schools into linked virtual learning spaces. The colleges chosen for participation in "Looking for Whitman"—New York City College of Technology (CUNY), New York University, University of Mary Washington and Rutgers University-Camden—represented a wide swath of institutional profiles: an open-admissions public college of technology, a highly selective and private research-intensive university, a public liberal arts college and a public research university, each with very different types of students. Beyond that, the courses explicitly engaged different learners with very different types of backgrounds and knowledge-bases. The class at University of Mary Washington included senior English majors who were taking the course as a capstone experience, the summation of their undergraduate work in literary studies. There were two classes at Rutgers; one contained a mix of undergraduate English majors and master's-level students; the other consisted entirely of graduate students who were taking a methods course that served as an introduction to graduate English studies. At City Tech, meanwhile, undergraduate students with little training in literary studies were taking a third-year course on Whitman as part of their general education requirements. As noted above, the roster of schools involved in the project expanded further when NYU professor Karen Karbiener received a Fulbright Fellowship to Serbia and decided to include her class at the University of Novi Sad in the project.

It was this mix of diverse institutions that instructional technologist Jim Groom, who served as the project's Director of Technology, highlighted in a blog post about the project:

From the University of Mary Washington to Rutgers-Camden to CUNY's City Tech to Serbia's University of Novi Sad, the project represents a rather compelling spectrum of courses from a variety of universities that provide a unique network of students from a wide array of experiences. This is not a "country club for the wealthy," but a re-imagining of a distributed, public education that is premised on an approach/architecture that is affordable and scales with the individual. It's a grand, aggregated experiment that will hopefully demonstrate the possibilities of the new web for re-imagining the boundaries of our institutions, while at the same time empowering students and faculty through a focused and personalized learning network of peers, both local and afar.[35]

As Groom points out, mixing a heterogeneous set of students together in a single online space—especially one that places a great deal of emphasis on social interaction—might seem to some observers to be at best a bad idea, and at worst a dangerous one. What could graduate students studying literature learn from undergraduate students taking general-education courses at an urban school of technology? Would undergrads be intimidated by the work of more advanced students who were working within their fields of specialization? Would undergrads engage in flame wars on the course site?

In a significant way, the act of bringing together students from selective and open-admission colleges, undergraduate and graduate departments, struck at the heart of the systems of privilege and exclusivity that gird the power and prestige of many elite educational institutions. Promotional

---

35  Jim Groom, "Looking for Whitman: A Grand, Aggregated Experiment," *Bavatuesdays*, September 1, 2009, http://bavatuesdays.com/looking-for-whitman-a-grand-aggregated-experiment/.

materials from such schools typically laud the expertise of faculty members and the elite attributes of the student body, promising prospective students sheltered learning experiences that will put them shoulder-to-shoulder with the best and brightest of their peers. And nowhere is the exclusive intellectual spectrum of a college's culture more closely guarded than the classroom. But, just as Walter Benjamin described the way that the urban street "assembles people who are not defined along class lines,"[36] and as Whitman's own vast poetic catalogues of scenes of New York City streets leveled differences between citizens, so too did "Looking for Whitman" puncture the boundaries of selectivity that educational institutions have erected around themselves. In the spirit of Whitman's own democratic beliefs, it offered the possibility that a radically diverse mix of students could enrich one another's learning, particularly when the place-based orientation of each course ensured that even the least-advanced students would be able to contribute unique material from their own project location that would be valuable to students in other venues. Place-based learning thus becomes a great leveler, one that buttresses the ability of all types of students to contribute to the larger conversation. Of course, the act of creating a single space in which a broad spectrum of students and institutions might learn together is not enough to ensure the creation of a more egalitarian learning environment. For that, we will turn to comments from the students themselves, who discussed the successes and failures of the project.

## Evaluating the Project

At the end of the Fall 2009 semester, students were asked to participate in a voluntary student survey that sought to canvas their opinions on the course, the project, and the technological tools that had brought their classes together. Participation rates were relatively low—roughly a third of all students answered the survey—in part because the necessity of acquiring institutional review board approval at all participating schools delayed the distribution of surveys until the Spring 2010 semester. But the 29 students who did respond to the extensive survey included representatives of each school involved in the project, and they provided a great deal of useful detail about the class.

---

36  Walter Benjamin, *Charles Baudelaire: A Lyric Poet in the Era of High Capitalism*, trans. Harry Zohn (London: Verso, 1983), 62.

Questions in the survey focused on a range of issues: how much experience had students had with Web 2.0 tools before the course, and how did they feel about them afterwards? Did their usage of blogs make them feel more or less confident in their writing and research skills? To what extent did they utilize the privacy options available to them for their blog posts? Which parts of the course website did they find most and least useful? To what extent did they benefit from each of the shared project assignments?

Respondents to the survey gave us much to feel good about: 63% of respondents felt more confident as writers after taking the course; 85% felt more confident as researchers after the course. Although 57% of respondents had never studied Whitman's work before the class and 92% of them indicated that they began the semester with little or no knowledge of Whitman's work, 70% of respondents felt that they had expert or close-to-expert level knowledge of Whitman and of literature more generally after the course. 78% of respondents agreed or strongly agreed with the statement, "This course made me want to learn more about Whitman and/or nineteenth-century American literature." Though 56% of respondents had never blogged before the class, 48% of them felt that they had a great deal of "ownership and control" over their blog. One respondent remarked that "I pretty much viewed it as an extension of my intellectual being" and many indicated their pleasure at discovering that they could customize their learning environments to suit their preferences.

Of all the questions we asked of our students, perhaps the most salient for the project as a whole and for further prospects for digital humanities pedagogy involved the degree to which the project helped students in different locations learn from one another. The grant proposal originally submitted to the NEH suggested that there would be interaction between classes simply because all student posts would appear in the same space. In one section of the proposal, a specific form of interaction was envisioned:

In the course of this project, students and faculty members will be encouraged to follow Whitman's call, in *Leaves of Grass*, to "Unscrew the locks from the doors!/ Unscrew the doors themselves from their jambs!" as they move their learning outside of the four walls of the traditional classroom and into the geographical locations in which Whitman lived and worked. For example, students in the New York/Brooklyn location will travel to the Fulton Ferry Landing at the base of the old Fulton Street. As they gaze across the East River and read aloud the words of "Crossing Brooklyn

Ferry," which have been etched into the railing encasing the landing, they will experience a scene much like the one Whitman experienced when he imagined future readers standing at the same spot. Students will take digital photographs of this location, add them to the image-sharing service Flickr, and geo-tag them so that they can be located on a map. They will then write blog posts that describe this experience and incorporate photos from it. Meanwhile, students at other project locations will notice a stream of posts and images related to "Crossing Brooklyn Ferry" roll through the central site aggregator. A student studying Whitman's *Specimen Days* in Camden, who has just puzzled over Whitman's ruminations upon the "soothing, silent, wondrous hours" he spent aboard the Camden Ferry, will make an immediate connection to Whitman's earlier experience at the Fulton Street Ferry. [...] In this way, the explorations of each class will inform and enrich the learning of the other classes. Site-wide tag clouds will provide an ongoing barometer of the issues, themes, and discoveries that students make during the course of the project.[37]

The degree to which the types of student interactions imagined in the grant proposal actually came to fruition can be seen in student responses to the survey. 69% of respondents agreed or strongly agreed with the statement, "Shared projects created collaboration among students in the same course"; by contrast, 46% of respondents agreed or strongly agreed with the statement, "Shared projects created collaboration among students in different courses" (31% of respondents neither agreed nor disagreed). In answer to the question, "How often did you read material from other people in your class?" 74% of survey respondents answered "often," while 26% answered "sometimes" and none answered "never." When it came to other classes, results again were mixed: 11% of students said that they "often" read the work of students in other classes, while 81% answered "sometimes" and 7% answered "never."

Several questions in the survey asked for comments on the types of interactions respondents had with other students in the project. In answer to the question, "To what extent and in what ways did you communicate with and learn from other students in the project," students offered the following observations:

---

37  Matthew K. Gold, "Looking for Whitman: The Poetry of Place in the Life and Work of Walt Whitman" (proposal submitted to the Digital Humanities Start-Up Grant Program, the National Endowment for the Humanities, May 2008).

- "Honestly, I did not learn much from the other classes. Partially because their projects were either earlier or later than ours—if they had been timed simultaneously, then I might have had more interest."
- "Perused some of their blogs to check out what kinds of things they were studying/how their focus differed from ours."
- "Not much, just through reading their posts. [It] was hard to connect posts written on literature we weren't studying and that I didn't know."
- "Some people, after reading my posts, sent me links that they felt [would interest me]. I read other people's posts and commented on them. I had my posts commented on too."
- "My interaction with other students mostly consisted of commenting on their blogs, adding salient points where appropriate complementing their respective posts, or noting when their research benefited my own."
- "I thought the level of scholarship from other courses was pretty low. I quickly lost interest and quit reading their material."
- "Aside from the occasional comment on someone's posting, I did not really communicate with other students involved in the project. I felt that I did not have time to properly immerse myself in other students' work. On one occasion, a student from another university reacted strongly to a posting of mine and I enjoyed the opportunity to respond to the student's criticism of my work."
- "I communicated with them in person, via email, Facebook and blogs. I learned from their insights, feedback and input."
- "I communicated with a few colleagues from my course, commented their posts and sent messages. Also, I read posts from other courses, and I got ideas from all of these people for my work."

Such comments reveal a range of attitudes, both positive and negative, towards students from other courses. While some students clearly enjoyed the ability to read the work of students very much unlike themselves, studying related but different texts than those being read in their own classes, others clearly found themselves unable to connect meaningfully with students in other project locations.

The survey asked students to "describe some important or memorable exchanges with students from other courses." Here, responses were more positive:

- "I enjoyed writing and reading the students work in Novi Sad. It was interesting to see their translations and how some of Whitman's work was different in their language."

- "It was fun meeting new people and seeing their work online. I loved the idea that it wasn't just our school, but others as well [overseas even] who took part in this project. And the fact that everyone was a point and click away was awesome!"

- "Helping other students with their work was a rewarding experience. I also liked helping students with the technology issues they had all semester. The best part is when they become self-proficient and more confident because they have the skills to work on their own. This course promotes teamwork because we can help each other actively with the work. Reading and discussing other students' posts give me additional insight. Having the students teach other was a wonderful idea."

- "I think that some students who I interacted with during this course helped, encouraged and gave advice on things that I was unsure of. It was fun getting to know how other bloggers felt during their Whitman experience."

- "I found [it] interesting that other students in other universities were commenting on my blog and sharing information to what/where to find different materials."

- "The other classes' comments on our posts (UMW) seemed quite condescending. One person commented on a blog saying, 'Interesting post and well written!' That really bothered us, it was such a back handed comment and it may have not been meant that way. However, when you are not connected face-to-face with the other courses, tones of responses have to be interpreted, sometimes incorrectly."

- "The best exchange I had was with students who were debating about the Levi's commercials; before it had gone up on the Vault, a student had posted about the commercials, and I really enjoyed going back and forth about the differing opinions on Whitman's views, whether the commercials were well done or not, etc."

- "I also got to communicate with students from Novi Sad on my final project, which was working on modern global perceptions of Whitman. The fact that I got to speak with students from another continent (when I've never left the East Coast) was incredible. I also got to connect with someone from Qatar."

- "Exchange with students from other courses was not really a big part of the course for me. They did not seem to take the work done by my class seriously."
- "I can't say that I had an exchange, but some of my posts found an audience in other classes. I was very pleased to read comments on my posts."

Perhaps because the question itself invited more positive reflections on interactions between students in different project locations, the responses to this question reflect more serious engagement between classes than the previous question discussed above—though examples of disconnection still exist. While some tensions are evident ("[students in other classes] did not seem to take the work done by my class seriously"), learning within a networked environment seems to have been strengthened the course experience.

In answer to a survey question that asked students to reflect on the reasons why it was easy or hard to interact with students from other classes and what might be done to improve such interactions, respondents shared a desire to make face-to-face connections before engaging in extended online interactions. Sample comments included:

- "It was hard at first because I wasn't quite sure what to say or how to respond to their posts. But over time, you get familiar with faces and it gets easier."
- "It was hard to interact because I thought they were English majors and I felt a little timid."
- "You're not sure how to reply or how others might interpret your comment, you don't know the person your responding to so there is no personal connection. Try having a conversation first to get to know people in other classes."
- "When someone compared our writing to 'text message level discourse' I got hugely offended. Being the only undergrad program in the grant and feeling like we blew the other schools out of the water with our research, projects and blogs... to hear that was like a smack in the face and clearly affected my views of their projects. If we could Skype as a class to each other, it would help IMMENSELY!!!! Some sort of face-to-face or even voice-to-voice contact would seriously help create relationships through the courses."
- "It was really easy to interact with students from other classes who used humor in their blogs; the humor lightened the mood and made it easy to comment or message without a sense of stiffness and formality."

These responses indicate that the many divides between classes and schools involved in the study were not easily bridged, and that students sometimes felt apprehensive about crossing boundaries between classes. Though the project included a conference at the end of the project in an effort to bring students together, it might have been beneficial to have some kind of gathering at the beginning of the semester, either in person or through a video-conferencing tool, to allow students to get to know one another personally. These comments also suggest that community is not something that can be expected to develop on its own within a structured academic setting; it must be intentionally fostered and sustained through the duration of a project such as this.

In answer to questions about their overall feelings about the project and the way in which it had affected their future career plans, survey respondents expressed a great deal of enthusiasm:

- "It was probably the most influential class I've ever taken and I loved it!"
- "I took this course because I heard that we were going to the Library of Congress and I thought Whitman was all right. Now, I am nearly literally in love with Whitman, and I feel incredibly close to my professors and classmates who went through this course with me. [...] I'm incredibly happy to have participated in this project and connected with both students and teachers who I might never have gotten to collaborate with otherwise."
- "I found this to be a really interesting experience. I sometimes felt as though our class was participating to a limited extent with the blogging; we'd often do our projects and then post on the blogs later. I think it might have been a nice forum in which to share works-in-progress (as opposed to only final products) and receive some feedback."
- "I will never forget it."
- "This was the class that ultimately pushed me to decide that I wanted to be a professor; I was inspired by the discourse and teaching methods in this course, and although there is still a chance that I will change my path, I am fairly confident that lessons I have learned and the conversations that I have had in this course are ones that I will carry with me always. Furthermore, it has made me a Whitman fanatic. My parents consider him my second boyfriend."
- "I decided that I want to focus on the interdisciplinary approach to literature. The course introduced me to various possibilities for exploring literature."

- "I want to pursue more study of nineteenth-century US literature."
- "It just made me even more sure that I would like to continue researching. I learned a lot of new things and a lot of new ways and tools to help me researching and it also made me more comfortable with sharing the results with others."
- "I am interested in a career in library science and this course has solidified my belief in the usefulness of technology in academic work."

Overall, the course appears to have had a very positive effect on the students who participated in it, though aspects of it could certainly be improved in future iterations of the project.

## Future Directions: "Looking for Whitman" as a Model for Linked Courses Across Campuses

"Looking for Whitman" was framed as a multi-campus experiment in digital pedagogy, but the experiment was relatively short-lived: the courses that were part of the project ran only for a single semester. The long-term value of the project is that it can serve as a demonstration of the possibility of connected courses across institutions and as a model for linked courses. Certainly, other single-author/multi-campus projects that emphasize place-based learning might be easily imagined: paired courses on the work of T.S. Eliot with one course offered in St. Louis and the other in London; courses on the literature of the Harlem Renaissance that paired classes in Harlem with classes in Paris; and classes on Hemingway and Stein that paired courses in the US and Europe. And of course, such classes need not be single-author projects; many classroom projects would benefit from such inter-institutional connections.

As future projects based on this model of interconnected courses across institutions are planned, some of the lessons learned through "Looking for Whitman" might be useful:

1.  As shown by student respondents to our survey, connecting students across institutions is difficult. Real barriers to connection—socio-economic differences between institutions and students, level of academic preparedness in the shared subject matter and willingness to share material—must be dealt with openly. Students indicated that more active face-to-face social engagement with students from other classes, especially at the beginning of the semester, would have made them feel more at ease with one another.

2.  The disruptive power of institutional scheduling should not be underestimated. In "Looking for Whitman," for example, one school began its semester a week earlier than other schools involved in the project, which meant that it completed some project-wide assignments, such as the Frontispiece Assignment, before others. Students cited the resulting lack of coordination between classes as a difficulty in connecting to other students.

3.  Finding faculty members within constrained geographic regions who are both trained in the specialized subject matter of content-specific classes and who possess the requisite technical expertise to lead their classes through a semester of heavy technology use is no easy matter. In "Looking for Whitman," we wound up prioritizing content expertise and location, which forced us to spend time and resources training faculty members in technology usage during our planning year.

4.  Given the difficulty of securing funding for digital humanities projects like "Looking for Whitman," future experimenters hoping to foster cross-campus projects should consider a number of options to reduce costs. These include the implementation of shorter periods of cross-campus collaboration and connection (week-long projects as opposed to semester-long ones), working with faculty members who are already proficient in the technologies to be used in the project, and building on the platforms for collaboration and shared learning activities that have already been developed for existing projects, such as "Looking for Whitman."

    •   Ultimately, the kinds of learning experiences that can be fostered through cross-campus collaborations are too powerful to be ignored. Consider the answers that students gave to the Looking for Whitman survey question, "How did you describe this class when you were talking to family and friends?" "I described this class to my family as an amazing learning experience. It was a lot of work but the discovery of the work and the unknown was great."

    •   "I am taking an English class unlike any other English class I have ever taken."

    •   "This was my bridge to the poet and place that I love, and the people and place I hoped to connect with."

- "That I was totally blown away by the content and how the teachers presented the material, being pretty uncomfortable/ inexperienced with poetry I felt accepted and learned a lot. It was great using the blog, but I did not connect with students from the other classes."
- "The most nourishing, inspiring, incredible educational experience I've ever had."
- "It was an amazing creative, innovative experience! It was an unforgettable experience collaborating with other universities across the globe—a perfect ending to my graduate school coursework."
- "I was thrilled. I told them I have never taken a course where I could so freely express my own opinions."
- "Innovative, interesting, dynamic, creative."

In all of these responses, one sees the results of a kind of pedagogy that was articulated by Whitman himself in *Leaves of Grass*:

> I am the teacher of athletes,
> He that by me spreads a wider breast than my own proves the width of my own,
> He most honors my style who learns under it to destroy the teacher.[38]

While no teachers were harmed during the making of "Looking for Whitman," they were certainly displaced from the center of the classroom by a network of students engaged in peer-to-peer learning. That these students, like the residents of Whitman's beloved New York City, came from a diverse set of backgrounds and mingled successfully in a shared communal space, speaks to some of the ways in which students spending a semester looking for Whitman found his spirit embodied in their own collaborative efforts.

---

38   Walt Whitman, "Song of Myself," *Leaves of Grass*, 7th edn (Boston: James R. Osgood and Company, 1881–82), 74.

# 7. Acculturation and the Digital Humanities Community

*Geoffrey Rockwell and Stéfan Sinclair*

What graduate students want […] is simply answered at the present time: they want a job.

—John Guillory[1]

One can think through a digital humanities curriculum in three ways. One can ask what should be the intellectual content of a program and parse it up into courses; one can imagine the skills taught in a program and ensure that they are covered; or one can ensure that the acculturation and professionalization that takes place in the learning community is relevant to the students. This chapter will focus mainly on the third approach, but use that to touch on issues of content and skills.

Professionalization involves the development of skills, identities, norms and values associated with becoming part of a professional group.[2]

Acculturation, or as it is often called, professionalization, is the process of preparing students to fit into the culture of the professional community.[3]

---

1  John Guillory, "Professionalism: What Graduate Students Want," *Profession* (1996): 91–99 (91). It should be noted that Guillory is critical of pre-professionalization. We will return to him in our conclusion.
2  Felice J. Levine, "Professionalization, Certification, Labor Force: United States," in *International Encyclopedia of the Social and Behavioral Sciences*, ed. Neil J. Smelser and Paul B. Bates (Oxford: Elsevier, 2001), 12146.
3  We prefer acculturation, as it will become clear that we have in mind something broader than just preparing students for jobs. Acculturation is preparing students so they fit in the culture of a field that may span many different types of jobs. Nonetheless, we find

It is an often-neglected part of the curriculum that is tacked on at the end with a few workshops or an industry speaker's series. Good students should be able to figure out the professional culture by observing their supervisor or acquire it during the first months in a new job. Sometimes a gracious supervisor will mentor their students, but this mentoring is rarely planned.

Despite the historical lack of attention to acculturation, most undergraduate and graduate programs have begun to address it because of students' anxieties about getting a job after graduation, and because it is increasingly clear that the jobs available to them are outside academia. For these reasons we need to do more than model academic professionalization.[4]

How then is professionalization introduced into the humanities curriculum? Professionalization, and more generally acculturation, is—given its ambiguous place in the humanities—rarely introduced as explicit content. More often it is introduced through non-credit activities, reflecting a curricular bias toward concepts over applications:

1.    Professionalization is woven into a course as a discussion topic in the final year like a Senior Thesis course.
2.    It is delivered through workshops about specific issues.
3.    Some universities provide internship opportunities that place students in professional contexts.
4.    Professionals are invited to present their work and work culture.
5.    University career centers often have general services including services to connect students to professionals for mentoring.

It should be noted, however, that the core curriculum does familiarize students to some professional activities—namely the narrow range of activities that are typical of academia. Professors in the humanities are expected to read widely in their field so we assign regular readings that familiarize the student to reading. Professors in the humanities are expected

---

ourselves using the word professionalization interchangeably.
4   There was a flurry of articles in *The Chronicle of Higher Education* in April 2010 that dealt with the lack of jobs for PhDs in the humanities: Peter Conn set out the dismal data and proposed recommendations including programmes being more open to alternative jobs; Diane Auer Jones suggested preparing students for a broader spectrum of jobs, and Katharine Polack called for ideas. See Peter Conn, "We Need to Acknowledge the Realities of Employment in the Humanities," *The Chronicle of Higher Education,* April 4, 2010, http://chronicle.com/article/We-Need-to-Acknowledge-the/64885/; Diane Auer Jones, "Are the Humanities Dead, or Are Academic Programs Just Too Narrow?" *The Chronicle of Higher Education,* April 9, 2010, http://chronicle.com/blogs/brainstorm/are-the-humanities-dead-or-are-academic-programs-just-too-narrow/22454;andKatharine Polack, "A Letter from a Graduate Student in the Humanities," *The Chronicle of Higher Education,* April 4, 2010, http://chronicle.com/article/A-Letter-From-a-Graduate/64889/.

to publish monographs and journal articles (or perish) so we assign the writing of academic papers and theses. Professors are expected to give conference papers so we ask students to practice giving papers in seminars and student conferences. In short, professionalization happens even in the core of what we ask of students, but for only one type of profession—ours.

We basically prepare students at both the undergraduate and (even more so) at the graduate level to become like us and do what we do.[5] And that is the crux of the problem with this sort of curricular acculturation: it only prepares students for academic careers in their field of study, in which there are fewer and fewer jobs.[6] It is no surprise that, as the number of academic jobs dries up, people are asking whether it is worth doing a traditional doctorate aimed at an academic job or whether we should be preparing students exclusively for academic positions. As Peter Conn puts it,

> At a minimum, even if graduate faculty members themselves refuse to engage in training or advising students toward alternatives, they should destigmatize such decisions on the part of students and should support those who choose to explore careers outside the academy. Information about nonacademic careers should be included on placement websites. Among other outcomes, broadening postdoctoral career opportunities would serve the interest of departments eager to maintain higher rather than lower levels of graduate-student enrollments.[7]

This is why acculturation is so important and why it is important to think beyond academic professions. This is also one of the virtues of the digital humanities, as it is an intersectoral field that brings together researchers, librarians, computing staff and even industry practitioners.[8] In other words digital humanities is a field that is potentially broader than the academy. The jobs available to graduates already include non-academic jobs or *#alt-ac*

---

5  Frank Donoghue goes further and suggests that there is something self-serving in the number of students admitted into graduate programs; that we need them to "provide teachers for their lower-division courses (particularly first-year writing sections) as cheaply as possible" ("An Open Letter from a Director of Graduate Admissions," *The Chronicle of Higher Education*, April 4, 2010, http://chronicle.com/article/An-Open-Letter-From-a-Director/64882/). One could add that this explains what professionalization we do provide—we train them to do the work we don't want to do, like teaching undergraduates.

6  See Conn, "We Need to Acknowledge," and Jones, "Are the Humanities Dead."

7  Conn, "We Need to Acknowledge."

8  If you want a sense of the breadth of digital humanists, you can look at the list of contributors to *#alt-academy: Alternate Academic Careers*, ed., Bethany Nowviskie, MediaCommons, http://mediacommons.futureofthebook.org/alt-ac/. Alternatively, you can look at the contributors to the Day of Digital Humanities over the last three years at http://tapor.ualberta.ca/taporwiki/index.php/Day_in_the_Life_of_the_Digital_Humanities.

(or alternative academic) jobs.[9] The question is how digital humanities programs can prepare students for a breadth of careers including academic careers. Having introduced the case for acculturation, now we will look at its purported goal—what are the objectives of digital humanities acculturation?

# What Do We Do, Really?

One way to think about acculturation is to ask what professional digital humanists do and don't do and then ask how those activities are encouraged in the design of curriculum and community. It is useful to start with what digital humanists do not do, though we need to be clear that we are talking about what they don't *necessarily* do as part of being a digital humanist. We want to know what they do and don't do *qua* being a digital humanist. Some of the things digital humanists don't necessarily do are write books, teach credit courses and get academic jobs.

## Don't Have to Write Books

Digital humanists don't necessarily write books. It isn't part of the job the way it is for English professors, even if many DH-ers do it. One of the ironies of graduate programs in digital humanities is that they are often modeled on traditional humanities programs that highly value the writing of sustained works of research like books, even though digital humanists typically don't write books and a number of digital humanists have received tenure without having written one. One might wonder if we should even insist on a written thesis or whether, like art programs, we shouldn't be open to capstone works in different media. Can one do sustained research that doesn't result in a book? Presumably the digital humanities is committed to the idea that digital work can be considered research.

## Don't Have to Theorize New Media

Though arguably regrettable, many digital humanists are not

---

9   Bethany Nowviskie defines #alt-ac jobs as "a broad set of hybrid, humanities-oriented professions centered in and around the academy, in which there are rich opportunities to put deep—often doctoral-level—training in scholarly disciplines to use" ("The #alt-ac Track: Negotiating Your 'Alternative Academic' Appointment," ProfHacker, *The Chronicle of Higher Education*, August 31, 2010, http://chronicle.com/blogs/profhacker/ the-alt-ac-track-negotiating-your-alternative-academic-appointment-2/26539).

theorizing new media in recognizable ways. That is what new media studies, game studies, communications studies, philosophy of science and even English do well. The digital humanities is about developing things and it is experimental, though we would like to think that we experiment in a theoretically informed fashion.[10] The challenge in the digital humanities is to avoid a split between theory and practice and find ways that building can be theorizing and vice versa. Thus many are experimenting in the digital humanities with new ways to develop theory and therefore our work does not always resemble the theoretical outcomes of other traditions in the humanities. In other words we do not necessarily write theoretical works that encourage others to think through new media. Instead we try to develop new ways of engaging theory and practice. This is not to say that new media theory is unnecessary, it is just to say that many digital humanists are trying alternatives and therefore don't have to be trained in traditional theoretical practices.

## Don't Have to Teach Credit Courses

Digital humanists do not necessarily teach university credit courses. Many digital humanists are not instructional staff and therefore are not required to teach as part of their professional responsibilities. That said, it is important to be able to explain technology and many digital humanists have to run workshops to train people whether in a library or for a project, but they don't need to be trained to be undergraduate instructors (in fact, very few professors are formally trained to teach anyway.) There is a difference between the commitment to education of a professional pedagogue, which is what teaching professors should be, and the commitment of someone who occasionally needs to train others.

## Don't Have to Become Professors

In short, many digital humanists do not get faculty jobs, though they may work in learning institutions in other capacities. Many work in libraries or electronic text centers or computing services. This explains why much of the acculturation of graduate programs (and, to a lesser degree, undergraduate programs) are missing the mark.

---

10   For a discussion of the digital humanities as building, see Stephen Ramsay's blog entry "On Building," *Stephen Ramsay*, January 11, 2011, http://lenz.unl.edu/papers/2011/01/11/on-building.html, and the comments to the post.

So what do digital humanists do? The short answer is *projects in community*.[11] Digital humanists work on projects in interdisciplinary teams whose goal is to create rich digital works that make artistic, cultural and historical content available using computing. This is what acculturation in the digital humanities should prepare students to do. Meaningful experience working on digital projects is what makes digital humanities graduates (even when their degree is in another field, as most are) so attractive and this is what employers are looking for. This is professionalization that does not run the risk of being narrowly focused on a particular job category. This is professionalization that prepares students for academic and para-academic positions.

What then are the characteristics of digital projects for which we need to prepare students? Some of the things digital humanists typically do is work in interdisciplinary teams, apply digital practices to the humanities, manage projects or collaborate in the management, explain technology and build community.

## Work in Interdisciplinary Teams

Typically digital humanists have to work with others in teams that will include content experts, librarians, computer scientists, software engineers, programmers, designers, videographers, GIS specialists and project managers. To thrive in projects students need to learn about these roles, the discourse of these roles and their traditions of formation. It is especially important to be able to work with people with a technical or scientific formation who may have little experience with the arts and humanities.

## Apply Digital Practices

Creating digital works is a craft that requires the appropriate use of different media, technical skills, artistic and rhetorical competencies, and an awareness of the intended audiences and uses; each of these can be developed through a combination of teaching, apprenticeship and autonomous project work.

---

11   Geoffrey Rockwell presented a short version of this argument for acculturation at a conference on "A Vision for Digital Humanities in Ireland" organized by the Digital Humanities Observatory of the Royal Irish Academy (Dublin, March 31, 2011). For more details, see his report, "Conference Report on the DHO conference A Vision for Digital Humanities in Ireland," *philosophi.ca*, April 20, 2011, http://www.philosophi.ca/pmwiki.php/Main/DHOAVisionOfDigitalHumanitiesInIreland.

For some kinds of computing practices, familiarity with development strategies is also useful, such as agile programming.[12] Digital humanists are typically expected to have a sense of the breadth of digital technologies and associated methods that can be applied to challenges in the humanities. They are at the interface between humanists and technologists advising on what should be done and then implementing technology-rich solutions.

## Manage Projects

Digital humanities projects that are developed by a team over time must be managed. Students, therefore, should be introduced to project management. They should know how to use the tools of management and communication from wikis to issue tracking tools to conferencing tools.[13] More importantly, they should have been exposed to project management strategies and the discourse around project management, so that they can fit into teams and think critically about how projects are managed and about their role in its management. This is not to say that all projects need explicit management, just that students should be prepared for complex projects in which they have to reflect on management.

## Explain Technology

While we argued above that digital humanities students will not necessarily have to teach university credit courses on information technology, they probably will have to explain technology to people— from team members to potential users. DH students often have to write documentation, train people to use a system, track bugs, interface between content specialists and programmers and give public presentations about projects. They should therefore understand the technologies they use critically, learn to use technical language accurately, be able to patiently explain technical concepts to those who do not have a digital humanities background and be able to present technical projects effectively.

---

12  Agile programming is essentially a methodology that emphasizes short, iterative cycles of development in close collaboration with a client.

13  There are many tools out there and many lists of project management tools. A good place to start is Cameron Chapman's "15 Useful Project Management Tools," *Smashing Magazine*, November 13, 2008, http://www.smashingmagazine.com/2008/11/13/15-useful-project-management-tools/.

One could argue that we are brazenly trying to define the discipline in this discussion of what digital humanists do; that is not the case, at least in the traditional sense of defining a canon. We are arguing that the training students receive should reflect what they will have to do as professionals, instead of unthinkingly mimicking traditional graduate training in the humanities. A new field in the early stages of developing its academic practices should take advantage of the opportunity to question graduate training and experiment with alternative models. To the extent that disciplines are about self-replication, (the formation of disciple students) we admit to trying to model the discipline. We propose that we should aim to train students to be able to participate as professionals rather than grafting old habits onto the digital. To do this we have to think about how we plan, maintain and audit programs, which is what the rest of this chapter will focus on — ways of thinking through programs and the acculturation they facilitate.

## Case Study 1: Multimedia at McMaster University

At this point we will illustrate how acculturation can be woven holistically into curriculum at both the undergraduate and graduate level with two case studies. The first case is the undergraduate multimedia program at McMaster University and the second is the graduate MA program at the University of Alberta. Both authors have worked at both institutions and have been involved with the design and delivery of both cases.[14]

The undergraduate program in multimedia at McMaster was developed in 1998 in response to a call from the Province of Ontario for expanded programs that would prepare students for careers in advanced technology. Rockwell led the preparation of a proposal to the Province from the Faculty of Humanities for a Combined Honors in Multimedia (and another subject).[15] The proposal, which was funded, built on humanities computing courses that Rockwell had developed from 1995.[16] Thanks to the generous new base funding that

---

14  Stéfan Sinclair helped start the Humanities Computing MA at the University of Alberta and was then recruited to McMaster where he teaches in the Multimedia program. Geoffrey Rockwell developed the Multimedia undergraduate program at McMaster and was later recruited to the University of Alberta where he taught in the Humanities Computing MA and has been the graduate coordinator. We continue to work well together, especially at this distance.

15  Originally, students could only take Multimedia in a double major combination with another subject; now they can do a single honors. For more on the current program, see http://www.humanities.mcmaster.ca/undergraduate/multimedia.html.

16  For more on the development, rationale and naming of the program, see Geoffrey Rockwell, "Is Humanities Computing an Academic Discipline?" (paper presented at the

came with Province of Ontario's Access to Opportunities Program (ATOP), the program was not developed out of cross-listed courses across the humanities as many programs are. (We recognize that this was a luxury not shared by all as administrations are pressed to invest more meaningfully in new digital humanities programs without having the base funding to create a program from all new courses). This allowed us to develop the project logically, to build proper multimedia facilities for the students, to hire faculty *specifically* for this program and to have a core of hands-on studio courses that are taught in sections small enough for students to be able to learn skills in the context of meaningful assignments.

Rockwell designed the multimedia program based on the definition of a multimedia work: "A computer-based rhetorical artifact in which multiple media are integrated into an interactive artistic whole."[17] There was thus a core of mandatory courses that dealt with the creation of multimedia works through "integration" of multiple media and then courses on individual digital media like electronic texts, digital images, digital video, animation, electronic music and so on. Since then courses on subjects like Web Programming have been introduced, while others like Writing in the Electronic Age have been dropped, but the logic of a studio program that focuses on the creation of multimedia works remains.

**Figure 1.** Core courses in the multimedia program at McMaster University.

University of Virginia, Charlottesville, November 1999), http://jefferson.village.virginia. edu/hcs/rockwell.html, and "Multimedia, is it a Discipline? The Liberal and Servile Arts in Humanities Computing," *Jarhbuch für Computerphilologie* 4 (2002): 59–70. We deliberately decided not to call it a Humanities Computing program, as we did not think that would communicate appropriately to prospective undergraduate students.

17   The way this definition plays out is explained in Rockwell, "Is Humanities Computing an Academic Discipline." For more reflections on multimedia and its teaching, see also Geoffrey Rockwell and Andrew Mactavish, "Multimedia," in *A Companion to Digital Humanities*, ed. Susan Schreibman, Ray Siemens, and John Unsworth (Malden: Blackwell, 2004), 108–20, and Andrew Mactavish and Geoffrey Rockwell, "Multimedia Education in the Arts and Humanities," in *Mind Technologies: Humanities Computing and the Canadian Academic Community*, ed. Raymond G. Siemens and David Moorman (Calgary: University of Calgary Press, 2006), 225–43.

This logic can be seen in the mandatory core courses. In the chart of these courses (Figure 1), the bolded courses have assignments where students create projects that integrate multiple media. The others deal with individual media or some important related topic. To get into the multimedia program, students had to take two of the three first-year courses and show facility with the creation of multimedia. (Entry into the program is limited to cohorts of the best first-year applicants, as we have limited space in studio classes and limited space in the labs.) These first year courses also serve as general digital arts and humanities courses for students across the faculty—indeed, they have proven to be very popular with senior students looking for an elective that prepares them digitally, which has required us to develop strategies to ensure that prospective program students aren't denied seats in the first year courses.

The Introduction to Humanities Computing (now Introduction to Digital Media), for example, is a course that can handle hundreds of students with a large lecture every week and a tutorial in smaller groups of twenty in a lab where students build website essays. The tutorial labs are taught primarily by fourth-year multimedia students as well as, more recently, some graduate students with a multimedia background, which gives them paid work experience explaining the skills they have learned, in addition to reinforcing or expanding basic skills. (It's amazing how easy it is to forget how to create a sophisticated web page, but technologies—like CSS—evolve so quickly, that refreshing one's technical competencies is valuable.) In our experience, being a teaching assistant in their fourth year is a great way to take responsibility for learning and managing learning. This paid work experience professionalizes the fourth years by preparing them to be able to talk about technology and train people.

Given the focus on the creation of multimedia at McMaster, it will not come as a surprise that there is a strong project focus to the program, with most classes culminating in some sort of collaborative project.[18] While project skills are developed throughout the program, project work is dealt with explicitly in the capstone experience in the fourth year where students must take a Management of Multimedia course in the fall term followed by a Senior Thesis

---

18   One constant challenge is to ensure that all students working collaboratively develop a core set of competencies—it can be too easy for students to specialize and continue honing acquired skills, rather than investing the time and effort in developing new ones. We have found that mixed evaluation methods (individual and group work) can be effective for this.

Project course in the winter term. These two courses are coordinated. In Management of Multimedia, they plan their thesis project dealing with project management issues like intellectual property, budgets, timelines, writing proposals, presenting ideas, building teams, working with clients, working in teams and documenting projects. The Senior Thesis Project is run differently, as students are let loose to do the project with minimal supervision and no required class meetings. While Management of Multimedia is a class with weekly meetings and the usual structure of assignments, the Senior Thesis Project is run like an independent study or thesis project. Each of the supervising professors has (credited) hours set aside to meet the project individuals or teams, but the students have to choose to come in and consult with their supervisor. The idea is to encourage students at the end of the program to first plan their project and then to actually manage the planned project through to implementation without the usual academic pacing of class meetings. The effect for most students is empowering, though a few get lost and leave the completing of the thesis until the last moment with predictable results. All this culminates in three or four days of presentations open to all, which highlight and celebrate the creativity of the cohort.

## Competencies and Curriculum

While a definition of multimedia may have provided the logic for the types and deployment of courses, we also used another technique to help us design and then audit the program—to think through the *competencies* we wanted to teach. In the curricular literature, "competencies" are usually associated with vocational skills. The idea is that when designing a curriculum you start by identifying what you want graduating students to be competent at. This encourages curricular designers to describe in concrete terms what graduates should be capable of doing so you know that they had the competency. Competencies, in curricular planning, have the following features:

- They are used to describe *what students can do*, not what you are going to teach, thus focusing planning on student achievement. It is too easy to plan curriculum in terms of abstract subject components.
- They can be used to *complement other ways of planning* curriculum. Most of us begin with a list of courses that cover the important content. Competencies allow you to track important components that cross courses—especially skills that have to be carefully staged and reinforced across multiple courses.

- They should describe things that students can demonstrate. This makes it easier to imagine assessment techniques. When describing competencies the idea is to *describe outcomes as behaviors* that would indicate successful learning.[19] Once you have a description of student successful behavior you can imagine authentic assessment activities. This then connects the planning of curriculum to the planning of individual courses. In effect, you can reverse engineer individual course outcomes from what you want the successful graduating student to be able to do. Teaching is thus not an end in itself, but the creating of a context for student achievement.

- They should be *comprehensible to students* so that they can take the measure of what they are learning and compare the curriculum to their expectations. If they are articulated in accessible language then they can be used to communicate what the program is about to prospective students and to incoming program students. Ideally students should get to the point of being able to negotiate (and critique) their education in terms of the competencies developed. They should be allowed to contribute to the ongoing curricular planning and auditing; competencies enable them to think about their education. It allows them to say to you, "I thought I would be able to do X by the end." Competency planning, if negotiated with students, also gives them tools for reflecting and managing their own learning after graduation, a general goal of student-centered education and an important competency in itself; students are in a better position to articulate their strengths to prospective employers.

- Many government, educational and industry organizations describe the *competencies expected of people in industry* and the world, which allows program participants, both students and instructional staff, to compare how students are prepared to what is expected or recommended by

---

19   This has led this approach to be described as "reconstituted behaviorism" in a critical article by Terry Hyland, "Competency, Knowledge and Education," *Journal of Philosophy of Education* 27, no. 1 (1993): 57–68. He concludes, "Competence-based approaches to education have a weak and confused conceptual base, are founded on dubious and largely discredited behaviorist principles, and display systematic ambiguity in their treatment of knowledge and understanding" (66). The problem with Hyland is that ambiguity and conceptual differences are true of any principles used in curricular design. "Knowledge" and "understanding" are notoriously ambiguous and contested concepts. Ultimately we have to use the concepts at hand with their weaknesses and traditions of use while being willing to critique the very tools we use.

practitioners.[20] This is not to say that curriculum should be designed to fit industry or government mandates, it is to say that if university programs are to prepare students for a breadth of careers you need to have a vocabulary for comparing student preparation to expectations in professions. Competencies are one way to do that.

- *Job ads are often articulated in terms of competencies* desired in applicants. Students and instructors who are comfortable discussing competencies thus have a way of assessing job prospects and suitability of different types of jobs. Whether we like it or not, students are justifiably concerned at the end of their program with their career options and job prospects. To wave our hands and try the old platitudes about the value of a liberal arts education doesn't help them with the real stress of finding their way after university. Without narrowcasting a program for specific job types, the discussion of competencies can give students a way of thinking about what they can do.

In our case, we didn't think of competencies in the limited sense of technical skills, but we used it as a general rubric to gather all the knowledge, skills and abilities that we felt were important. This allowed us to develop one rubric of what we wanted students to know, understand and be able to do technically in one place. This included what we called intellectual competencies like "know about the history of computing so as to be able to discuss the history of computing and better understand the contemporary context" with technical competencies like "have the skills to be able to create sophisticated web pages" and social competencies like "be able to play both leadership and contributor roles in groups." The list of competencies were then negotiated, simplified and grouped into *core technical* competencies (that all graduating students should have), *core intellectual* and *others* which included social competencies and elective competencies (that students should have if they wanted and took the requisite course). For a list of the competencies we were using, see Appendix 1.

Finally these competencies were mapped against the courses (see Table 1). We started the mapping with the assumption that any competency that we care about should be introduced early on and then explicitly

---

20 See, for example, the "New Media Competencies" of the Cultural Human Resources Council of Canada, http://www.culturalhrc.ca/minisites/New_Media/e/01-02-01.asp, or "The New Media Literacies" of the New Media Literacies project, http://www.newmedialiteracies.org/the-literacies.php.

developed in a second or third year course (by which we mean that the competency should be taught in a module and there should be an assignment aimed at testing competency), and subsequently reinforced in one or more additional courses. To test this we assigned to a course a [1] for competencies introduced, a [2] for those explicitly taught, and [3] for those reinforced. These assignments were placed in a spreadsheet with all our courses down the side and all the competencies across the top. The results were instructive. Some competencies were often introduced but were never dealt with explicitly at any length. Some competencies were not reinforced. Some courses were overloaded with [2]s so that they had to carry too much of the load. And some competencies that we thought were important were only dealt with in elective courses. This gave us a way of balancing the curriculum and arguing for resources from the administration.

| Core Courses | | | Core Technical Competencies | |
|---|---|---|---|---|
| | | | HTML | Graphics |
| 1st Year | 1A03 | Introduction to Humanities Computing | 1 | 1 |
| | 1B03 | The Digital Image | 1 | 1.5 |
| | 1C03 | Writing in the Electronic Age | 1 | – |
| 2nd Year | 2A03 | Introduction to Multimedia | 2 | 2 |
| | 2B03 | Digital Media (Audio/Video) | – | 3 |
| | 2C03 | Computer Architecture & Networks | – | – |

**Table 1.** Portion of an early competency chart.

Not only were the competencies used to design the program; they were also used to audit the program as we changed courses (this is akin to unit tests in programming).[21] They also helped us introduce new instructors to the way courses they were hired to teach fit in the curriculum. It allowed us to show sessional instructors what competencies they were responsible for introducing, teaching explicitly or reinforcing. This becomes especially important in the case of technical skills that build on each other. A student can be expected to use digital video in a third year course if the instructor of

---

21   They were used, for example, in a five-year retreat when, with a full faculty complement, we reviewed the curriculum.

the second year Digital Media course has taught the expected competencies. Last of all, and to return to the subject of this chapter, this competency approach let us plan a curriculum in an integrated fashion, during which we took into account content (intellectual competencies), technical skills and acculturation in one planning/auditing matrix.

## Case Study 2: MA in Humanities Computing at the University of Alberta

The MA in Humanities Computing was launched in September 2001, following two to three years of planning and development.[22] In a similar fashion to the multimedia program at McMaster, a one-time funding opportunity (ACCESS, a government of Alberta funding agency) had a catalyzing effect: the additional funding allowed for a proper investment in infrastructure and personnel, but also meant that funds were not being begrudgingly siphoned from other areas. Susan Hockey and Patricia Clements led the initial planning, though consultation was broad across the Faculty of Arts, the University of Alberta and beyond (Ian Lancashire and Harold Short were consulted, for example.) It is worth noting that several graduate students contributed significantly to the initial planning of the program—this involvement is also a form of academic acculturation.

The MA in Humanities Computing, which was created before the term "digital humanities" was coined and widely adopted,[23] confronted many of the same challenges that similar programs might face today (though at the time with few precedents from which to learn). For instance, we recognized that the MA program would include students from across the humanities, social sciences and fine arts, so we wanted to ensure a broad representation of intellectual perspectives, while also allowing students to develop deeper expertise in specific domains. By and large, this balance was accomplished by incorporating a wide range of issues into the seminar discussions and

---

22   See the Humanities Computing website, http://humanities computing.ualberta.ca, for information about the program. For a fuller account of the development of the MA in Humanities Computing at Alberta, including additional details on the curriculum, see Stéfan Sinclair and Sean Gouglas, "Theory into Practice: A Case Study of the Humanities Computing Master of Arts Programme at the University of Alberta," *Arts and Humanities in Higher Education* 1, no. 2 (2002): 167–83.

23   Matthew Kirschenbaum explains how the term "digital humanities" originated in 2001 during discussions with Blackwell Publishing about what would become the *Companion to Digital Humanities*. See "What Is Digital Humanities and What's It Doing in English Departments?," *ADE Bulletin* 150 (2010): 55–61.

allowing students to create more narrowly focused projects. This transfer and adaptation of skills from the general to the specific is clearly relevant for a range of professional contexts.

Another common challenge in developing a digital humanities curriculum is in striking an appropriate balance between theoretical and practical components.[24] We strive to train students to get up to speed as quickly as possible with technical skills that will allow them to engage effectively with tools, and—in some cases—adapt those tools or even create new ones. At the same time, we are wary of limiting ourselves to specific software packages and methodologies. For instance, we may want students to understand the fundamental techniques and broader implications of digital image manipulation; this could involve becoming familiar with Adobe Photoshop, even though competency in Photoshop would be a secondary objective. Likewise, we encourage students to understand and critique the limitations of existing text analysis tools;[25] this can help them to recognize how a small amount of programming knowledge can empower them to accomplish idiosyncratic but extremely useful tasks.[26]

The Humanities Computing MA is a two-year program that ends with a thesis as a capstone experience. Over the two years, students take four mandatory humanities computing courses and five electives, two of which have to be humanities computing courses. Students can choose to study humanities Computing alone or do a specialization in another subject like English, philosophy, art and design, or in any of the Faculty of Arts departments that offer a specialization with humanities computing. This interdepartmental option gives students the ability to apply digital humanities practices to problems in their specialization so that they could continue on to a PhD program in their area of specialization. If they choose a specialization, they then have to apply to both units (i.e., humanities computing and the department of specialization), take at least two of their electives in the area of specialization, and have their thesis co-supervised by someone from each unit. In addition, we have a special three-year joint MA/MLIS that

24  For a discussion on this relationship, see Simon Mahony and Elena Pierazzo's chapter, "Teaching Skills or Teaching Methodology?"

25  On teaching text analysis, see our chapter, "Teaching Computer-Assisted Text Analysis: Approaches to Learning New Methodologies."

26  For a discussion on teaching programming in the humanities, see Stephen Ramsay, "Programming with Humanists: Reflections on Raising an Army of Hacker-Scholars in the Digital Humanities," another chapter in this collection.

gives students both the professional library and information science degree and the academic arts degree.

Ultimately, the two-year timeframe of the MA in Humanities Computing is extremely short for building a foundation in digital humanities, while also providing core skills training. This is especially true since humanities computing is typically an entirely new discipline for incoming students—it is not, as with most other graduate offerings, an extension of an undergraduate degree. We have explored several solutions to this dilemma, including a skills boot camp when students first arrive, as well as offering a separate stream of workshops (intended for first year students and offered by second year students). One of the dominant guiding principles for us has been to try to anticipate what balance of theoretical and practical skills would be most valuable to students after they leave the program, whether they stay in academia or not.[27] Currently, the program has the following two formal components that help acculturate new students to the digital humanities.

## Intensity Experience

In 2009 we introduced an "intensity" experience at the start of the academic year. The first week of classes is cancelled and all new students are formed into teams with returning students and students from other programs that volunteer. These teams are given a week to make progress on a challenge that is typical of a professional project. For the first two iterations the challenge was to develop an Augmented Reality Game (ARG). The teams are given a tour of the resources that are available (from labs to the library) and let loose to figure out how they would develop an ARG that, for example, can be used for health education. They are expected to present what they developed a week later. Needless to say, they do not complete the project, but in the spirit of problem-based learning the idea is that they should start their program with a real challenge; typical of what they should be able to do by the end of the program.[28]

---

27  For more details on our efforts to balance technical and theoretical skills, see Sean Gouglas, Stéfan Sinclair, and Aimée Morrison, "Coding Theory: Balancing Technical and Theoretical Requirements in a Graduate-Level Humanities Computing Programme," in *Mind Technologies: Humanities Computing and the Canadian Academic Community*, ed. Raymond G. Siemens and David Moorman (Calgary: University of Calgary Press, 2006), 245–56.

28  For an introduction to problem-based learning, see James Rhem, "Problem-Based Learning: An Introduction," *National Teaching & Learning Forum* 8, no. 1 (1998): 1–4.

We call this an "intensity" experience because the idea is to ask students to focus intensely on one challenge at the beginning, rather than dividing their time among different classes. This is partly designed to orient students to the field by giving them an initial experience that is more typical of the field, rather than giving them more classes like those they had as undergraduates. We ask them to work in a team on a project that will require different skills, many of which they do not possess: to think about how they organize their team, how they break the project down, what they can achieve and how to present it back. While the intensity experience is a non-credit activity, they respond enthusiastically. In informal conversations afterwards, we have been told that the intensity experience dramatically changed students' views of what they were getting into—for the better.

# Technical Approaches and Project Management

Our four mandatory first year courses can be broken into two streams with a fall and winter course. The first stream is composed of more traditional courses, namely, Survey of Humanities Computing in the fall followed by Theoretical Issues in Humanities Computing in the winter. The second stream includes Technical Concepts and Approaches in the fall and Project Management and Design in the winter term. Students are first introduced to the encoding and programming that they need to build a database-driven website in these courses, before practicing their technical skills in the context of a community project. Technical Concepts and Approaches covers HTML and CSS (with attention to XML), PHP (as a first programming language) and mySQL (as an introduction to databases.) In Project Management and Design, students are divided into teams of two to work on a project organized by the University of Alberta's Community Service-Learning (CSL) unit (http://www.csl.ualberta.ca/).[29] CSL works with community organizations that want digital projects done. Proposals are presented to the students who then complete them over the term. The projects can range from developing a database for materials in an activist organization office to a needs-analysis for a website for an organization. These projects rarely call on all the skills taught in Technical Concepts and Approaches; in fact, the projects often call for skills that the

---

29  It should be noted that this is the way Rockwell has organized the course. Other instructors, depending on the number of students in the class, will have all the students work on one project for CSL or have them develop their own projects. Regardless of the organization, we believe the learning is similar.

students did not learn in the course, such as when a community organization wants a new component to a website already developed in another framework. Nonetheless, the course gives them a real-world experience in which they have to adapt the skills they learned to a real need for an organization outside of the university. As part of completing the project they have to:

1. Identify and negotiate what can be done in the time available;
2. Agree on tasks and a timeline;
3. Work with the client organization learning to communicate effectively;
4. Develop a digital deliverable, document it and deliver it so that it can be used; and,
5. Finish a project, present it and identify next steps.

Class time in this course is shared between working on the projects and discussing challenges. While any one team may not have the skills needed for the project they have undertaken, there are almost always other students with ideas or relevant experience. This way, all sorts of techniques are introduced as needed by teams. If a team needs to develop an interface to a web tool, for example, this is brought to the class for discussion.

## Apprenticeship through Research Projects

There is, however, another less formal way that students at the University of Alberta are brought into the field of digital humanities and that is through their research assistantships. These research assistantships are the primary way that we currently fund graduate students, as we don't have an associated undergraduate program that needs teaching assistants. While these research assistantships are limited by funding, we have been able to offer them to all incoming students in recent years, though not all students take advantage of them because of other commitments.[30] Research assistantships have the advantage that they involve students in real research projects that call for the skills they are learning, such as digital research and development.[31] In the Project Management and

---

30  Approximately one in ten students already has a job and has negotiated flex-time to complete the MA part-time. These students are typically mature students, already integrated into a profession.

31  Not all of the research assistantships are in digital humanities projects. In some cases they are brought into larger teams working on projects in the humanities that have a

Design course, they are applying their learning to projects that typically are not academic and which do not involve research in the digital humanities. In research assistantships, students apprentice in teams using digital research practices.

The challenge, as with all research assistantships, is how to involve students new to the field in a meaningful way, giving them tasks they can accomplish when they are still learning the skills needed by the project. As anyone who has employed a new MA student as a research assistant knows, there can be a conflict between the needs of the project and the skills of the assistant. Research projects often have to develop digital solutions quickly (e.g. in a year) so that researchers can use them. Managers of such projects often don't want to take on a student who, having just started, has to learn on the job. Pragmatically, it is often cheaper and faster to hire a programmer, experienced encoder or trained graphic designer. We have addressed this tension by assigning assistantships strategically—so that no project has only new research assistants—and by supporting colleagues taking on MA students new to the digital humanities. We have developed a rough series of tasks that incoming students can tackle, as both a benefit to the project and as a way of learning professional skills. If you pace students properly and challenge them incrementally, they can learn the skills they need in order to participate, while helping the project concretely. This pacing of tasks is, in effect, an apprenticeship in which students learn through a series of gradually more complex challenges. The series of challenges involves the following tasks, though the order varies from project to project: an environmental scan, maintaining an open research site, a literature review, reporting to the team, interface design, and preparing conference proposals and papers.

## Environmental Scan

Students new to a project are asked to conduct a scan of all the projects in the environment that have similar goals to theirs. They typically start with the grant proposal, which will have identified similar projects, and are then asked to broaden the list and to document what they find so that they can present it back to the team.

---

digital dimension. Thus, they might be working with other English research assistants on a digital edition or with philosophy research assistants on the web site for an ethics project.

## Maintain an Open Research Site

Most of our projects follow an open research model in which all of our documents are shared both within the team and with anyone interested through wikis, blogs and other project management tools like Basecamp (http://basecamphq.com/). An incoming research assistant can be asked to take over the management and updating of the project's documentation. To do this, they will have to learn whichever collaborative documentation tool is being used and they will have to read what is already there—both useful activities. We find the difficult part is training the graduate student to maintain the site; this is about habits of careful documentation of activity. Every time a new project is found that relates to our project a useful summary with links should be added to the environmental scan wiki page.

## Literature Review

A task that someone with a good humanities degree should be prepared to do it is review the relevant literature. Incoming students should have the skills to find relevant literature and summarize it. By and large, incoming students are able to do this, which is why it makes a useful sub-project for them at the start of their research assistantship. We generally ask them first to find reports, articles and other documents reporting on the projects found in the environmental scan, and then to move on to the more open-ended task of searching the broader literature for interesting materials. Often students find the open-ended search daunting, as they don't know what others in the team might find interesting. A tactic we use is to have students first gather lists of anything that might be relevant without reading the items. We then go over the list, discussing what we are looking for, eliminating items, and prioritizing items that seem promising. We then ask the students to skim the items and report back to the team. Students are asked to identify the key ideas gleaned and arguments put forth, which leads to a further prioritization. In the last pass, students are asked to read the items prioritized carefully, to write a précis for each, and to create a bibliographic entry in our shared bibliography with the précis. The shared bibliography is itself another form of documentation that they take responsibility for. Nowadays we tend to use Zotero (http://zotero.org/) and form a Zotero Group (http://zotero.org/groups/) for each project. Students thus have to learn, in this context, another technology that is useful in the field.

## Report to the Team

An important activity associated with both the environmental scan and the literature review is ongoing reporting. We tend to have weekly "lab" meetings in a space where we can project from our laptops. At these meetings, students report back their progress, issues are discussed (such as exactly what are we looking for in the literature?) and research assistants make presentations. It is tempting to save time and not meet until there is some final outcome, but it is in these weekly meetings that a lot of informal acculturation and guidance takes place. Meetings pace students and keep them on track. Most importantly, students learn when you care about what they are doing. They can tell if the research assistantship is a make-work project because in these cases, one is not interested in the results. We tend to ask students to report often, and use the reports to train them so that we can trust them to do vital tasks like the environmental scan and the literature review. For this reason, at weekly labs we give immediate feedback when the tasks are not done in a timely fashion or when they aren't done in a way that the team can trust to use in their research. Nothing motivates a student to be careful with details in compiling a bibliography more than when we find obvious errors of transcription in the report during our discussion of it.[32]

Reporting to the team also builds student confidence in presenting research and the discourse of research. By the time students are asked to present at conferences they should have presented short reports and drafts of things over and over to a friendly (but critical) team. Finally, the usefulness of reporting lies in what we learn from the students. At some magical point in the year, we find ourselves learning something new and exciting from the students. When they get to the point of bringing these contributions to us and motivating others is the time when you enjoy the benefits of the apprenticeship—when a research assistant contributes rather than distracts from research. Lab meetings that are completely sidetracked by some original idea from the research assistant are, we believe, one of the rewards of research—to learn something new in community.

---

32   A separate issue is how to gracefully correct and encourage quality in graduate student work. This sort of apprenticeship is a very different relationship than marking an assignment that has no real purpose beyond assessment. We believe it is important to the spirit of collaborative work that problems in the work be addressed immediately, and the student then asked what help they need to meet a standard of quality suitable for publishable research. The key is that you need to get to the point where you trust their work enough to use it—then you are collaborators, and that is an important transition.

# Interface Design

So far the tasks we have described are not central to the creation of digital works. Because many students don't have programming skills, one way to involve them in development is to have them manage the interface design of a digital work. We favor a Personas/Scenarios/Wireframes/Designs approach, in which the student is first asked to develop "personas" or archetypal users and then generate usage scenarios that can be used to plan the software and audit the interface.[33] From the scenarios they can develop wireframes that communicate the functionality of the system being developed, and then produce graphic designs for the finished interface. They can then work closely with the programmer to implement the system testing the iterations against the prioritized scenarios. Finally, they can write the "about" text for the system, the online help text and user manuals, as well as other forms of documentation.

The point of this approach is that research assistants are given responsibility for a staged process — they are not being asked to go away and come back with a polished design. At each stage they have to work with the stakeholders to develop a consensus. Thus, when developing personas, they might start by interviewing stakeholders and potential users. From the interviews they might develop five possible personas and return them to the research team and content experts for refinement and prioritization. This managing of a negotiation is important for projects in which the digital humanities group is developing a digital presence for a larger research team. Negotiating personas is a way of making sure the digital humanities group is serving the larger research needs of, and is in communication with, the larger group. The research assistant becomes a vital conduit for this communication. Further, the research assistant serves as a vital communications link to stakeholders outside the digital humanities team.

One advantage of this approach is that it also stages the learning the research assistant has to do in order to usefully lead the process. They don't really have to learn any technologies until creating wireframes, and there are easy-to-learn tools for that.[34] The trickiest part is if you ask the

---

33  For an introduction to this method, see Jared M. Spool, "The Essence of a Successful Persona Project," *User Interface Engineering*, February 17, 2010, http://www.uie.com/articles/essence_personas/, and then look at Alan Cooper, *The Inmates Are Running the Asylum* (Indianapolis: Sams Publishing, 2004).

34  See Paul Andrew, "10 Completely Free Wireframe and Mockup Applications," *Speckyboy Design Magazine*, January 11, 2010, http://speckyboy.com/2010/01/11/10-completely-free-wireframe-and-mockup-applications/.

research assistant to go from functional wireframes (which just shows functionality with little color, font, layout and art) to actual graphic designs. In a wireframe you don't want any touchy design ideas creeping in, as they tend to distract stakeholders with strong views about design.[35] A crude wireframe that is well annotated is an advantage. The moment you move to graphic designs the research assistant has to have a sense of web design. In many projects, this is where a professional designer might be brought in to create Photoshop mockups that the research assistant can use for negotiating final designs. Where a research assistant can learn is in translating the mockups into HTML and graphics for the programmer. This presents an opportunity to deepen their knowledge of HTML and CSS, and learn how to create web-efficient logos using graphics tools like Photoshop.

## Conference Proposals and Papers

A last task that inexperienced research assistants can help with is developing conference proposals, writing draft conference papers/slides and delivering the papers. This process starts in the fall, when the calls-for-papers come out. In the group we will discuss the calls and what we will have to present. A research assistant will be assigned to write a one-page draft proposal with an outline of what will be presented. We go over this in the lab meetings to refine it. We often find that we have to rewrite the opening paragraphs, as conference proposals are a genre of writing that students are not typically familiar with. Iteratively discussing a proposal and occasionally rewriting it is a very different way of training students to write for the field than assigning papers and marking them. They know the proposal will not go out until it is acceptable to the team, so there is more at stake in the writing. They are also told that if the proposal is accepted they will get to write the full paper and deliver it, which means a trip to a conference (for which we budget in grant proposals). This also provides a context for discussing research credit.

If the proposal is accepted, research assistants then work on drafts of the paper. Even if it isn't accepted by a national or international conference, we will ask the research assistants to draft full papers for local presentation

---

35    Another advantage of this process is that you secure consensus among stakeholders at each step, so you are not forced to redevelop the interface because someone objects to an interface at the last moment. It can be hard to negotiate interface when stakeholders are presented with finished designs and have no stake in the process that generated the final design.

(partly so that we have drafts of papers for the next round.) They have already done much of the legwork putting together the environmental scan and literature review. Often we first ask them to put together slides and present the paper informally. Only once we have refined what will be presented do they write a draft, which again they present in a lab. This helps train them to read papers and gives the team a chance to give detailed feedback. We usually end up editing the final version of the paper and the research assistant presents it. If the conference paper is of a high enough standard, we then discuss how it should be edited for submission to a journal—but that usually takes place in the second year of their research assistantship as the conferences are mostly in the early summer.

We cannot overemphasize the amount of learning or the sense of accomplishment that comes from managing the interface design of a system that, by the end of the academic year, is working and has real users. Likewise, we can't overemphasize the sense of participating in the larger research community that comes from presenting at a national (that is, Canadian) conference like that of the Canadian Society for Digital Humanities / *Société canadienne des humanités numériques* (CSDH/SCHN). Students are motivated by the opportunity to actually contribute publically to the field and learn by doing for others. The acculturation of this sort of apprenticeship is not a simulation of professional activity; when they present and take questions from active professionals at a conference, they are no longer acting at being a professional the way they might do in the simulacra of a seminar—they are being professionals, thereby acquiring the confidence that comes from presenting research to our peers.

Some of the sense of accomplishment comes from learning on their own, as they need to in order to accomplish useful research tasks. When we ask a student to create wireframes for a design we don't give them much guidance and we don't teach them any tools. The student has to figure out what a wireframe is supposed to do for us, figure out what tool they want to use and figure out how to present it back to us. Often students come to the next lab meeting lost or with inappropriate reports. They then have to learn to ask for help, where to get help and how to take criticism. When we rewrite a conference proposal from scratch because it was entirely unsuited for the venue, there is an implied criticism that they have to handle and learn from if they want to be tasked with the next proposal. We can characterize this apprenticeship approach as a reversal of the way students are taught in training courses, in which they are usually trained in a tool and shown successful models before they try their hand. In an apprenticeship, they are asked to do something the way a professional would be asked, and then helped as needed. It is a form of learning to swim by being thrown into the pool—or at least being asked to jump into the shallow end. When, after a year of successively more complex tasks, they see that they have contributed to real outcomes they realize that they have learned *how to achieve such outcomes on their own*, or at least *how to learn how to achieve on their own*. This is what training professionals in the digital humanities is about—preparing students to be able to do digital research on their own, where they continually have to learn new skills as needs be.

Needless to say, this is an ideal set of apprenticeship tasks. The tasks are not sequential (i.e., interface design has to start immediately and the literature review is iterative.) No grant-funded projects need the same tasks, and many projects that students are brought into are ongoing, so that some of these tasks were completed before. Each graduate student research assistant is also an individual, with his or her own strengths, weaknesses, and desires. We try to match research assistants with tasks for which they are prepared, tasks they want to do, or tasks that will help them with their own research, but often the tight timelines of grants mean that they have to do tasks they are unprepared are. We try to stagger the tasks so that they can learn incrementally, but sometimes the project needs things done in a different order. Sometimes the timelines of the grant conflict with the academic schedule of a student and they are afraid to say "no" to a request for a report just when a paper is due. Some students do such good work they get loaded with more and more tasks until they work beyond the hours contracted whereas others seem to never finish anything so they get marginalized in a project that has to meet deadlines. Some students thrive on the stress of learning new things quickly and seeing their work implemented, while others get anxious and are reluctant to ask for help because they see successful peers thriving and worry that they should know basic things. Caring supervisors and students thinking about such relationships can manage these difficulties. Supervising graduate students is a human art, which all thesis supervisors should learn and graduate students should consider. It is an art on which much has been written and at which we get better with experience.[36] It is beyond the scope of this chapter to discuss how to handle these inevitable tensions other than to say that more

---

36   A starting point is the Graduate Studies office of your university. They have to deal with dysfunctional supervision in all its forms and will typically have resources, workshops, and advice for both supervisors and students. If your university does not have anything of this sort, we suggest consulting Heather Latimer's *Literature Review on Graduate Student Supervision* (prepared for the Dean of Graduate Studies Task Force on Graduate Student Supervision at Simon Fraser University, 2005), http://www.sfu.ca/uploads/page/06/lit_review_.pdf.

experienced research assistants can help. We are, however, convinced that students who apprentice in the field are better prepared, feel better integrated into the profession and are more likely to complete their program.

In conclusion, with regard to growth, graduate education appears now to be a kind of pyramid scheme. The prospect of its collapse has revealed something extraordinary, that the growth of literary study consists largely in the growth of graduate programs and in the transformation of graduate students into a public for literary criticism. Professors of literature now write and teach for graduate students; graduate students have become their constituency and collectively now exert a considerable pressure on the profession, moving it in certain directions, along the cutting edge of criticism. Hence the most symptomatic professional desire one can harbor today is expressed in the desire to teach graduate students in preference to undergraduates.[37]

A critic might object to the focus on acculturation in this chapter as premature. Faculty members hired before there was a job crisis may remember being able to concentrate only on their intellectual development without having to worry about learning how to teach, how to present conference papers, or how to now manage the design of a research interface. There is a feeling that we should create a safe space free of professional and cultural concerns in which students can develop their research thinking and that acculturation should take place only after intellectual development. Such views assume one can isolate the intellectual from the cultural. Jennifer Wicke describes "an institutionalized reluctance to admit that undertaking a PhD in the field [that is, English] constitutes entering a professional arena with rules, guidelines and protocols that may remain unarticulated."[38] The Modern Languages Association Ad Hoc Committee on the Professionalization of PhDs summarized the debate and made some safe recommendations in their 2002 report, *Professionalization in Perspective.*[39] They asked, "Given the intensity and elaborateness of the public discussions on this topic in recent years, how can we explain the continuing resistance to professionalization in general and to professional training of graduate students in particular that we have witnessed so often in our consultations?" They concluded that departments have to take responsibility for "the difficulties faced by the graduates they produce" and they should at the very least provide career counseling comparable to what undergraduates get.

---

37   Guillory, "Professionalism," 97.
38   Jennifer Wicke, "I Profess: Another View of Professionalism," *Profession* (2001): 52.
39   The report is freely available on the MLA website, http://www.mla.org/professionalization.

In the paper quoted at the beginning of both this chapter and the conclusion, however, John Guillory makes a more nuanced point about the dangers of professionalization. He argues that professionalization can encode in a program the desires and politics of the stakeholders. He ends by accusing the system of becoming a pyramid scheme, in which the professional desire is to do research and teach graduate students, so that is what graduate students are trained to do, which then creates the need for more graduate students than are needed as professionals.

It would be easy to say that the approaches outlined in this chapter avoid the recursive danger of such a pyramid scheme. We could argue that the acculturation approaches discussed here aim not at producing more students who only want to become professors like us. We could and have argued that the digital humanities has an opportunity to prepare students for a breadth of careers, thereby avoiding the worst of a doctoral job crisis where there are too many graduates prepared only for the few new positions—and we would be right. But that shouldn't blind us to the danger of self-reproduction inherent in professional preparation. When we design programs, even ones that are designed to prepare for a breadth of careers, we are designing for the careers we know and the types of jobs we value or desire. In a fast moving field like the digital humanities, such preparation is usually tailored to what is past or current, not what may be in the future. Students who apprentice on text encoding projects will know little about areas like crowd-sourcing, serious games and physical computing. We can only hope that students begin to anticipate what will be innovative when they are looking for professional positions; that they will have learned how to learn new technologies and that they may even redirect the field with their enthusiasm and fresh views. In Appendix 2, we offer some advice and linked resources for students who want to think about professionalization and for curricular developers wishing to integrate professionalization into their digital humanities curriculum.

The paradox of designing programs that replicate our ideas about the profession is that most of us now designing the programs were not formally prepared in digital graduate programs. Most of those senior enough to design programs were trained in the digital humanities outside the programs they were awarded degrees in, and they were trained often in the face of discouragement. This has led to a romantic view of acculturation as a heroic overcoming of tradition-bound disciplinary values. As much as it may motivate students to think they are joining the revolution, as humanists we should be skeptical of our own fantasies of creation. Vico concluded that institutions were born in crimes (against the institutions they pushed out of the way.) What crime was committed against whom in the creation of graduate programs in digital humanities? What are we losing as we redesign the graduate experience? Are we perhaps encoding into the new culture our desires for revenge on the disciplines that couldn't fit us? One ideal of the humanities that we should remain committed to is that of self-reflection or knowing ourselves, not only individually, but also professionally. As Guillory concludes,

> What I call preprofessionalism is nothing other than the realm in which the profession's fantasies, both professional and political, are acted out. The kind of sociological analysis I have in mind will demand that we suspend some of our investments in specific agendas of professionalization and politicization in order to clarify what is merely phantasmic in those investments. The decline of the job market is a reality check, then, and perhaps an opportunity.[40]

---

40  Guillory, "Professionalism," 98.

# Appendix 1: Multimedia Competencies (2001)

## Core Technical Competencies

- Build a sophisticated WWW site
- Create bit-map and vector graphics
- Create an interactive CD-ROM
- Create time-dependent media (audio and video)
- Set up and network a PC or Mac
- Use a WWW server
- Create interactive works

## Elective Technical Competencies

- Create and study an electronic text
- Create electronic music and compose on the computer
- Design a typeface and design a publication
- Create an animation
- Create a virtual space
- Create instructional materials
- Create an electronic presentation

## Core Academic Competencies

- Be able to discuss the design of a multimedia work
- Be able create rhetorically effective multimedia works
- Be able to read critically, write effectively, analyze problems and solve them
- Be conversant with the history of multimedia design and information technology
- Be aware of the social, political and ethical issues related to multimedia technology

## Other Competencies

- Be able to work in groups and understand the management of multimedia projects
- Use computing tools and techniques in other disciplines and understand the effects of this integration for further academic study
- Be prepared to proceed to graduate level work in multimedia and related disciplines or enter a technology-rich work environment
- Be aware of intellectual property issues as they apply to multimedia

# Appendix 2: Resources and Advice

## Know the Job Situation

Figure out the job situation in your field and be honest about your chances. This doesn't mean you shouldn't continue if there are few jobs; it just means you should know what you will be facing. Peter Conn's *Chronicle of Higher Education* piece "We Need to Acknowledge the Realities of Employment in the Humanities" is a good place to start, as are Bethany Nowviskie's "The #alt-ac Track" and the Media*Commons* project she edits, *#Alt-Academy*.

## Know the Expectations in the Field You Want to Pursue

As mentioned in the chapter, many government, educational and industry groups have developed descriptions of the skills, literacies and competencies they expect or hope for. Read those and ask whether you have the skills and how you demonstrate competency in your CV. Some examples of competencies are:

- New Media Competencies
  http://www.culturalhrc.ca/minisites/New_Media/e/01-02-01.asp
- The New Media Literacies
  http://www.newmedialiteracies.org/the-literacies.php
- Researcher Development Framework
  http://www.vitae.ac.uk/policy-practice/234301/Researcher-Development-Framework.html
- Key Leadership Competencies
  http://www.tbs-sct.gc.ca/tal/kcl/intro-eng.asp

## Read the Job Ads Long Before

Look for advertisements for the types of jobs you would like and pay careful attention to the competencies and requirements they list. Do this before the moment that you desperately need a job. Job ads inform you about the field and the expectations of employers. Ask yourself how you can get to the point where your CV would show that you are suitable for the jobs you would like. Here is an example of a job ad posted to *Humanist* in 1997 (*Humanist Discussion Group* 10.752) that helpfully describes the competencies the organization is looking for:

**Project Manager**

The Getty Information Institute is a leader in promoting innovative and effective uses of information technology in the arts and humanities.

The Institute is looking for a full-time professional with strategic skills to develop and manage projects that promote worldwide access to cultural heritage information. The successful candidate will have creative, administrative and financial responsibility for a range of activities involving digital imaging, interoperability, data standards, intellectual property rights, information policy and training. Typically will lead several simultaneous projects, act as an in-house advisor in the area of digital imaging and conduct or supervise research. Will oversee any special conferences, symposia, workshops, and/or publications related to project activities.

Requirements include a graduate degree in the arts, humanities, or information science, or equivalent; 8–10 years experience, including management of complex projects with technology components; digital imaging expertise; excellent oral and written communications skills. International experience and a foreign language are highly desirable.

## Follow Sites about Professionalization and Project Management

There are a number of curated web sites where you can get advice about becoming a professor or managing projects. The *Chronicle of Higher Education* has an edited and multi-authored blog with lots of advice called *ProfHacker* (http://chronicle.com/blogs/profhacker/). The Association for Computing in the Humanities (ACH) runs a *Digital Humanities Questions & Answers* site where you can post questions or just read the discussion around those of others. They have a section on project management and digital humanities professions (http://digitalhumanities.org/answers/forum/project-management).

## Get Advice from Others at the Start

There is good advice out there for new graduate students, but that advice can make the most difference if you pay attention early on. It is much easier to weave activities in that enhance your portfolio if you think about it early and can opportunistically add activities as you go. It is much harder to try to jam all the professionalization in at the last moment. A great place to start if you are a new graduate student in the humanities is Brian Croxall's "An Open Letter to New Graduate Students," *Chronicle of Higher Education*, August 19, 2010, http://chronicle.com/blogs/profhacker/an-open-letter-to-new-graduate-students/26326.

Your professors, fellow students and supervisor are also good sources of advice. Career counseling centers are full of advice, most of it too sensible to stand.

Remember, however, not to trust any one source of advice. If your supervisor tells you not to worry about professionalization and just concentrate on the thesis you need to ask whether that is the right path for you (and it may be.)

## Get Experience in Digital Humanities Projects

Seek out digital projects that you can contribute to. Few digital humanists graduated from programs that prepared them in computing in the humanities. Most fell into it or sought out project work that provided them an apprenticeship in the field. If you want to get experience and if you want to be able to demonstrate experience then find and volunteer to work on such projects. If there aren't curricular opportunities then try the following:

- See if the library is digitizing materials and if you can participate in that.
- See if your university has undergraduate or graduate research opportunities where you could propose your own project and be paid to pursue it. Alternatively, you could propose an independent study.
- Introduce yourself to faculty and staff who seem to have projects and see if they need someone with your skills. If they have regular meetings ask if you can sit in to see if there is a fit. To figure out who has projects, check out the website or news feed of your faculty.
- See if you can get a job in the computer store or computing services and learn from the job.

## Learn How to Program

One of the skills in greatest demand is programming as it makes digital things work. If you think you would like to program then try to learn one or more languages. Learning to program is a great thing to do in school because you have access to courses, there are lots of people to help you and you have time. Your first language will take you six months to learn to the point where you can build stuff easily. As for which language to learn, choose the one that attracts you and for which you can get friendly help. The Association for Computing Machinery (ACM) has a magazine for students called *XRDS Crossroads* (http://xrds.acm.org) that has advice, including an article by Ben Deverett on "How to Learn Programming Languages" (http://xrds.acm.org/resources/how-to-learn-programming-languages.cfm).

## Acquire Other Technical Skills

There are a number of other technical skills that are in demand. The ability to solve computing and networking hardware problems is always in demand. The ability to run server systems is in great demand as more and more of our projects go onto servers. Good graphic design skills combined with an understanding of web technologies are always needed by web projects. Many digital humanities projects need people who can edit XML or work with GIS tools.

## Join a Community of Inquiry or Create One

A great way to get involved in the field is to join a community whether it is a mailing list like *Humanist* (http://digitalhumanities.org/humanist/), a local working group or an international association like the Association for Computing in the Humanities (http://ach.org/). Most organizations are looking for keen volunteers and through volunteering you can meet people and informally learn the tacit knowledge of the field.

Some organizations organize events that bring us together in face-to-face meetings like seminars and conferences. Go to the meetings you can, because much of the breaking research is reported at conferences and not in publications. Much of the scholarship in this field is digital, which is shown before being written up. Conference presentations are where you can find out about how digital works were made and ask questions. One annual conference that is graduate student friendly is that of the Canadian Society for Digital Humanities or CSDH-SCHN (http://csdh-schn.org/), which has meetings each year somewhere in Canada as part of the Congress of the Humanities and Social Sciences. If you don't have many local community resources, access to conferences, or a community to learn from, you should try to kick-start your own community by organizing events. One type of event that builds community is an "unconference." An unconference is one where the participants decide the agenda and teach each other. An unconference is not your typically collection of expert talking-heads who lecture you from the pulpit; rather, it is designed to encourage participants to share what they know. An unconference can be organized by students for students. The point is that you don't need anyone authorizing you to start doing stuff. For a tested model of an unconference, see the THATcamp web site (http://thatcamp.org/).

An alternative approach is to join an industry association, especially if you know the industry you want to be part of. For example, if you want to work in technical writing and communication and you are in British Columbia, the Society for Technical Communication–Canada West Coast (http://stcwestcoast.ca/) have volunteer opportunities, job seeking events, meet-ups and guides. Such associations typically have student membership rates and their meetings can be a good way to network with potential employers.

Above all, enjoy what you do.

# II. Principles

# 8. Teaching Skills or Teaching Methodology?

*Simon Mahony and Elena Pierazzo*

While there have been a number of publications exploring the research possibilities opened up by digital humanities and arguing for its place in the higher education curriculum,[1] it is not our purpose in the present chapter to contribute to this ongoing critical conversation. Instead, we wish to explore precisely *what* we should be teaching under the banner of "digital humanities". In the case studies that follow, we argue that this curriculum should focus on teaching students new approaches and new ways of thinking about the humanities and—in order to accomplish this with different groups of learners at disparate levels—that there is a need for teaching methodological approaches and not simply technological skills.

## Critical Background

In addition to acquiring key research methodologies and skills, students need to develop their collaborative and interdisciplinary skills—skills that are increasingly required within and outside the academy. Thus there is a real need for training students in collaborative methods and reflective practices in order to build a community of learning that will lead to a community of practice.[2] A starting point may be a "fundamental information literacy" module able to

---

1  See Martyn Jessop, "Teaching, Learning, and Research in Final Year Humanities Computing Student Projects," *Literary and Linguistic Computing* 20, no. 3 (2005): 295–311.
2  Simon Mahony, "Using Digital Resources in Building and Sustaining Learning Communities," *Body, Space & Technology Journal* 7, no. 2 (2007), http://people.brunel.ac.uk/bst/vol0702/simonmahony/.

address some of the issues that educators have been aware of for some time but have now been qualified and quantified in a recently report on "Higher Education in a Web 2.0 World."[3] This report makes explicit many of the issues of concern to higher-education lecturers for which previously there was little other than anecdotal evidence. For instance, in recent years it has become apparent that the increasing familiarity with the web amongst the so-called "digital natives" (i.e. those who have grown up with the web) has developed alongside a dependency upon, and an uncritical acceptance of, whatever is provided at the top of the list of results returned by their favorite search engine. The investigations of the CIBER group at University College London into the so-called "Google Generation," confirm the existence of such a trend and counter the common assumption that those born or brought up in the Internet age are the most adept at using the web.[4] Just because we in the academic (and digital humanities) community have access to, and an understanding of, the wide range of resources that we take for granted, we must not assume that our students do too. The so-called "digital divide," the division between the digital "haves" and "have-nots," has not been entirely overcome and persists in several dimensions: in access to, and engagement with, technology; an understanding of the capability of the technology; and in individual competence.[5] An important finding of the "Higher Education in a Web 2.0 World" report is that there is a significant and growing deficiency in students' "information literacies, including searching, retrieving, critically evaluating information from a range of appropriate sources and also attributing it."[6] The report similarly highlighted the importance of teaching staff and the need to keep their skills current with regard to web-based materials and techniques.[7]

A major problem for incoming students is that they do not know what is available and, more importantly, what it is that they need to know to

---

3  David Melville, Cliff Allan, Julian Crampton, and John Fothergill et al., "Higher Education in a Web 2.0 World" (report of the Committee of Inquiry into the Changing Learner Experience to the Joint Information Systems Committee, May 12, 2009), http://www.jisc.ac.uk/media/documents/publications/heweb20rptv1.pdf.

4  David Nicholas, Ian Rowlands, and Paul Huntington et al., "Information Behavior of the Researcher of the Future," University College London CIBER Group briefing (paper prepared for the Joint Information Systems Committee (JISC) and the British Library, January 11, 2008). The full reports and findings are available from the JISC website for the project, http://www.jisc.ac.uk/whatwedo/programmes/resurcediscovery/googlegen.aspx.

5  Melville et al., "Higher Education in a Web 2.0 World," 33–34.

6  *Ibid.*, 6.

7  *Ibid.*, 10–11.

become successful learners. This is where their familiarity with online social networking can be used to advantage and something that educators can build on to scaffold appropriate learning activities using a new media approach. Many of those coming to Higher Education already have an online lifestyle in which they use social networking sites, and this familiarity can be built on to support teaching and learning through group interaction and collaboration. However, it is important to remember that to be effective teaching, interaction needs to be at a level removed from the students' online social activities, which should be considered private and entered into "by invitation only," if at all. It is one thing for the students to set up a Facebook group to work together, but it is quite another for their tutor to set one up in what is after all a "closed" space. To many students, their online social networks are a diversion used to escape from learning rather than a mechanism to support it: "Hence their discomfort with staff-initiated discussion groups in social networking space when they are at ease with those they set up themselves for study-related purposes."[8] Indeed, these are often places where students feel free to criticize their tutors and their study programs and so would feel inhibited if tutors were able to view their comments. What is needed is the development of a group space that exists somewhere between study and social areas. Using the social web develops a sense of community that reduces the possibility of the sense of isolation,[9] and so can be employed to create a sense of cohesion within the group, particularly if they meet infrequently in person. Through the use of these interactive web technologies, we have the tools to develop systems that promote learning with and through the use of technology, to develop best practice in the use of social networking tools in a pedagogical framework, to bring about a culture of participation and collaboration, and "to sustain a learning society."[10]

Students who have grown up not knowing life without the web (the so-called "digital natives") have little, if any, understanding of the way in which it works. For them, the internet and the web has become one and the same thing. They know how to "point and click" and, as the above reports have shown, rely too heavily on the first five results given to them by their favorite search engine. They expect Google to give them the answer when their tutor does not, since the latter, of course, wants them to critically evaluate their primary and secondary material and come to reasoned

---

8   *Ibid.*, 24.

9   See Mahony, "Using Digital Resources."

10   Ron Dearing et al., *Higher Education in the Learning Society: The Report of the National Committee of Inquiry into Higher Education* (London: Her Majesty's Stationary Office, 1997), 13.

conclusions based on that.[11] For many students, the Google search has become "research." A pertinent example of this in practice is the increase in student references—particularly amongst undergraduates—to journal articles held in JSTOR (http://www.jstor.org/) since it opened up to indexing by Google. While using an institutional network, provided that institution subscribes to JSTOR, clicking on that Google link will return the full article.[12]

At UK institutions of higher education, IT services often offer courses to support students as well as staff. For students, the topics of these courses typically range from word processing, spreadsheets, and databases, through to multimedia applications, aimed at developing students' technical skills and teaching them which buttons to press and how to manage their files. This, however, is not research training, which is necessary for students to progress their learning and, in the case of research students, to satisfy research committees and funders. Graduate schools often have individual sessions to support students, although these often focus on areas such as professional development and self-management. Again, these courses do not advance the research capabilities of the students and do not have pedagogical underpinning. By contrast, the case studies introduced here address both these areas and stimulate and support student learning.

## Case Studies

The Department of Digital Humanities (formerly the Centre for Computing in the Humanities), King's College London, delivers a number of courses on the "world of angle brackets" (XML, TEI, XSLT, HTML, and so on) in several forms and at different levels, ranging from one-day full-immersion focused training to a full twenty-credit academic master's module, as well as a

---

11  This was clearly demonstrated in a module run by one of the authors in which graduate students were asked to source quotes. Many searched Google using the quote surrounded by double quotation marks and then read off the source from the links returned without clicking that link and investigating further, that is, without moving beyond the Google results page. The notion of finding the printed source in the library to validate their references always seemed beyond most, if not all, of them.

12  This behavior explains why so many students refer only to JSTOR in their referencing rather than the journal in which the article was published. Moreover, this behavior also explains why so many students are completely unaware that the articles they are accessing are often digitized from back-issues of print journals, that the most recent issues are often unavailable from JSTOR, and that these materials are being accessed via a subscription-only service.

week-long PhD training course.[13] Most incoming students are genuinely concerned to some degree that the content that we deliver will be too complicated for them, and most initially do not have a very strong motivation to attend the classes. Even those students with strong motivation and commitment often struggle in an unfamiliar environment, as formal languages (such as markup) force the liberal humanist to think in a different, perhaps more structured, way. All of these considerations pose serious problems and limitations to the way students might learn, requiring teachers to adopt creative strategies to help them with both the contextual understanding of the content being delivered, as well as with long-term learning skills. Before we examine the methods implemented in our teaching, let us first briefly survey the types of courses and their respective audiences:

- **A one-day training in XML and TEI.** This type of training is targeted to academics involved in collaborative research projects with the Department of Digital Humanities, covering the basics of XML and an introduction to the principles of the Text Encoding Initiative (TEI). These training days are fairly generic and tend to take place when we have collected a sufficient number of interested participants to be instructed across several projects. In some cases, such as when the research project involves deeply specialized XML marking of a corpus of documents, a series of individual follow-ups takes place oriented at the specific needs of the researcher/s. Some of the participants in these training days are genuinely curious and interested in learning about these new technologies, but many attend only because XML is the technology that has been chosen for the project they work in.

- **A one-week intensive training course on Medieval Manuscripts.** This is a five-day training course for PhD students in the United Kingdom, Medieval Manuscript Studies in the Digital Age, supported by the Arts and Humanities Research Council under their Collaborative Research Training Scheme.[14] It includes theoretical

---

13  Many people are involved at various level in teaching these classes: Eleonora Litta Modignani Picozzi; Charlotte Tupman; Gabriel Bodard; Paul Spence; and Raffaele Viglianti in 2011; and previously John Lavagnino; John Bradley; Arianna Ciula; Juan Gracés; and Zaneta Au. The authors wish to thank their colleagues for their fundamental contribution in the development of the teaching strategies discussed in this article.

14  The course is based at the Institute of English Studies, which is one of the Schools of Advanced Study in the University of London. Other collaborating institutions

classes on codicology, palaeography, editing and art history, as well as visit to libraries.[15] Half of the week is devoted to digital contents—in particular learning XML and the use of TEI for editing and cataloguing, and in general, digital publication. Attendance is vocational and positively sought by the participants—most students apply because they think that the technologies taught in the course will help them with their research; others because they think they will learn reusable skills that will help them find a job once they complete their PhDs; while others are simply curious.

- **An undergraduate course: Introduction to the Digital Humanities.** From 2010–11, this course includes introductory classes on XML, HTML and TEI, as well as on text analysis and databases. Students in the course typically come from a variety of disciplinary backgrounds, such as engineering, business and finance, education and humanities. The students have generally very little motivation (with some bright exceptions) for technologies involving the use of angle brackets and in some cases they have simply been directed to the course in order to fill credit requirements.

- **An undergraduate module on Texts in the Digital Humanities.** This is a second year module for students that have already taken the Introduction to the Digital Humanities in their first year or otherwise with previous knowledge of the digital humanities. The course focuses strongly on analysis and modeling, and covers XML and TEI, Relax NG Schemas (previously DTDs) and XSLT. Most students choose the module out of a genuine interest in digital technologies, either because they think that it will give their degree a more "modern" flavor, or because they simply like computing.

- **A postgraduate module on Advanced Text Technologies.** This module is part of the MA in Digital Humanities offered by the Department of Digital Humanities, but it is also taken by students of the MA in Digital Culture and Society (formerly Digital Culture and Technology), again offered by the Department of Digital

---

include the Department of Anglo-Saxon, Norse and Celtic at Cambridge University, the Department of Digital Humanities at King's College London, and the Warburg Institute, which is also part of the Schools of Advanced Study.

15    For more on this course, see Peter A. Stokes, "Teaching Manuscripts in the Digital Age," in *Kodikologie & Paläographie im Digitalen Zeitalter 2 / Codicology & Palaeography in the Digital Age 2*, ed. Franz Fischer, Christiane Fritze, and Georg Vogeler (Norderstedt: Books on Demand, 2011), 231–47.

Humanities, and seldom taken by students from other departments in the School of Humanities. In terms of content, the course shares most of the topics taught at the undergraduate level, but with a greater emphasis on analysis and modeling with a specific focus on cultural heritage material. Several PhD students wishing to learn skills that may be of use for their own research often also audit the module. Most students are highly motivated; most are enrolled in a vocational MA program in which the taught technologies are a core component, while others see the course as offering the key set of competencies necessary to their own research projects.

As the brief outlines above make clear, most students share a strong research interest: either they are researchers (e.g. PhD students, research faculty, or research associates within a research project) or they have a research task to accomplish (e.g. a dissertation). Most students clearly see the use of "angle bracket technologies" within their own research profile, and this also constitutes the principal motivation for taking a course on such topics. These considerations are at the base of the teaching approach we have adopted with this group of students. We have built all of our teaching practices by taking into account that most of our students want to learn *how to do better or new research*. The teaching strategy we have developed includes:

- The use of relevant examples, with the selection coming from the domain of the course participants;
- The use of exercises that are relevant for the participants, again by selecting material from the students' domains; and,
- Presentations of specific resources and supports that will be available to the participants after completion of the courses in order to allow students to accomplish their research on their own.

This approach is best exemplified by the work done for Medieval Manuscript Studies in the Digital Age course. The training course simulates the life cycle of a typical research project (a dissertation, a publication, a project) in the field of medieval manuscripts involving some sort of digital component. In the first three days of training the students are taught about scripts, binding, parchment, gatherings and decoration, before being taken into several libraries (Parker Library at Corpus Christi College, Trinity College Library and St John's College Library in Cambridge, Lambeth Palace and the Wellcome Institute in London) to see the same features with their own eyes in selected manuscripts. In the last three days they learn how to transcribe, edit, annotate and catalogue in a digital environment the very manuscripts they have studied in theory and handled in practice, with the help of digital surrogates.

In previous offerings of the course, we have chosen one manuscript in particular to be used as a continuous exercise, namely CCCC 422 (the "Red Book of Darley") preserved at the Parker Library in Corpus Christi College, Cambridge. This manuscript is used first as an example for theoretical lectures on scripts and decorations; it is then shown *in situ* at the Library, where the students have the opportunity of inspecting it; it is then described and catalogued using the TEI manuscript description module before it is transcribed and edited; and finally, the digital images of selected pages are annotated for descriptive and editorial purposes.

The results with the PhD students have been outstanding—even the more digital-skeptic participants displayed a level of commitment and enjoyment in doing the exercises and attending the classes that was beyond our expectation. Feedback from the students has subsequently confirmed the impressions we made from the classroom, with repeated reports that "it all fitted" and "it all made sense". Most students declared that by using such digital technologies they had seen things in a way they had never previously thought about. By applying these unfamiliar technologies to a familiar and interesting object (the medieval manuscript), students recognized how such techniques could form the basis of a methodological approach to learn something new and exciting about the objects of their research.

This passage from skill to methodology is conceptually more difficult for undergraduate students who in their first year lack strong motivation to attend their module: in most cases it represents yet another module "to pass" on their way to the final degree. Second year students, by contrast, show a good level of awareness and motivation. Some students think they will learn something useful for their final year independent project;[16] others take the modules with future vocations in mind. The key to reaching all types of students, regardless of the levels of motivation and fear, is to stimulate their sense of natural curiosity. In our courses, one method of accomplishing this has been to present students with finished products (research project websites, for example) and to challenge them to find out how these were achieved. One frequently used example, because of its clear encoding and

---

16   See Jessop, "Teaching, Learning, and Research."

outputs, is The Language of the Landscape: Reading the Anglo-Saxon Countryside project or LangScape for short (http://www.langscape.org.uk/). For this project some 1,500 Anglo-Saxon bounds extracted from the corpus of the Anglo-Saxon charters have been deeply annotated in XML-TEI with linguistic and editorial tags.[17] The project website presents the short texts in three different versions—semi-diplomatic, edited and glossed—and by using a simplified dataset it is often not too difficult for students to map each element/attribute of the source files with what they see on the live site, and then to question the methodology used to transform from one to another. Another method of stimulating student motivation we have found is to appeal to their sense of competiveness. To this end, a weekly challenge is included in the homework for the following class, in which the first to email the teacher with the right answer receives a public award.

Of course, the weekly challenge and the top-down approaches outlined above are not enough to help students understand the methodological implications of the contents they are learning—these are only "tricks," able at best to keep their interest awake. However, to some extent, the same can be said about the use of relevant examples and exercises for research students and researchers. Ultimately, teaching methodological understanding is the result of the time devoted to encoding and analyzing texts and discussing specific modeling issues—only the active demonstration that encoding is an intellectual activity, and not merely the mechanical application of angle brackets, can stimulate real engagement from the students with the possibility of their reusing the skills taught for their own purposes. It is this approach that makes students declare that XML makes them "think," and in particular "think about the text," in a different way.

Modeling is a process that is implicit in the act of encoding—one cannot apply markup without having first analyzed the material and planned the goals and purpose of the encoded text. Indeed, as Willard McCarty has observed, modeling is the one activity necessary to enable any computational application.[18] It is therefore essential to cover analysis and modeling while teaching XML, especially when engaging with students not familiar with computers or for whom such an approach may be new. No matter how intensive and short the training session may be, it is fundamental to find

---

17   For more on this project, see Peter A. Stokes and Elena Pierazzo, "Encoding the Language of Landscape: XML and Databases at the Service of Anglo-Saxon Lexicography," in *Perspectives on Lexicography in Italy and Europe*, ed. Silvia Bruti, Roberta Cella, and Marina Foschi Albert (Newcastle-upon-Tyne: Cambridge Scholars Publishing, 2009), 203–38.

18   Willard McCarty, *Humanities Computing* (New York: Palgrave Macmillan, 2005), 20–72.

some space to discuss modeling and analysis: this will not only ensure that the teaching will make a deeper impact on the students, but will also ultimately mark the difference between teaching and learning skills (that are easy to forget) and teaching and learning methodologies, which have the potential to radically change a student's research and professional life.

# Conclusion

What becomes apparent from these case studies is the fundamental need to teach research methodologies. Skills training is not research training: the knowledge gained is transient because, like a language, it requires constant practice and repetition to be retained in memory. By contrast, thinking skills are the most important because they are the most deeply embedded and the most transferable. As educators, how do we develop our students' ability to think? The case studies discussed above suggest that this may be accomplished by building upon students' existing familiarities: students accustomed to the web are challenged by the incorporation of new ideas and novel methods with which to undertake traditional humanities pursuits, while all students are encouraged to reflect upon and think through new processes and principles as they work with materials (such as medieval manuscripts) already familiar to them. Both strategies rely upon the students' desire to improve their research as a lever to engage their interest.

Our experience has shown that digital humanities teaching needs to be relevant to the students' studies or research interests. It is imperative that students are prompted to think in a new and different way, even when dealing with familiar topics or objects of study. What we should be teaching under the umbrella of the "digital humanities" are not skills—although they too play their part—but new methodologies and new ways of thinking.

There are still some institutional barriers to overcome. The case studies above exemplify the critical and methodological approaches to teaching and learning that reflect the fundamental difference between teaching digital humanities and the institutional support courses designed for professional advancement. As teachers, the struggle we face is that our colleagues within many humanities departments consider the teaching of digital humanities to consist solely of the instruction of techniques deprived of any critical thinking and, as a result, are skeptical of its merits and do not recommend it to their students. The chapters in this volume prove otherwise. One way forward may be to engage with other academic departments and to share courses, perhaps by embedding an introductory digital humanities module as a core component of undergraduate degree programs.[19] Once colleagues across the arts and humanities see how their students benefit from the digital humanities approach, they will better understand our work and support the training of future digital humanities researchers.

---

19   At the time of writing, this approach is being promoted at University College London, where a digital humanities module is offered as core curriculum as part of a new Bachelor of Arts and Sciences (BASc) program.

# 9. Programming with Humanists: Reflections on Raising an Army of Hacker-Scholars in the Digital Humanities

*Stephen Ramsay*

---

> Let us change our traditional attitude to the construction of programs:
> Instead of imagining that our main task is to instruct a computer what
> to do, let us concentrate rather on explaining to human beings what we
> want a computer to do.
>
> —Donald E. Knuth, *Literate Programming* (1992)

"Program or be programmed." That is the strong claim made by Douglas
Rushkoff in a recent book that eloquently—at times, movingly—articulates
an argument often made by those who teach programming:

> In the emerging, highly programmed landscape ahead, you will either
> create the software or you will be the software. It's really that simple:
> Program, or be programmed. Choose the former, and you gain access to
> the control panel of civilization. Choose the latter, and it could be the last
> real choice you get to make. [...] Computers and networks finally offer
> us the ability to write. And we do write with them on our websites, blogs
> and social networks. But the underlying capability of the computer era is
> actually programming—which almost none of us know how to do. We simply
> use the programs that have been made for us, and enter our text in the
> appropriate box on the screen. We teach kids how to use software to

write, but not how to write software. This means they have access to the capabilities given to them by others, but not the power to determine the value-creating capabilities of these technologies.[1]

Such language is powerful and attractive (especially for those who already possess the requisite skills), but its highly utilitarian vision of education tends to weaken claims to relevance within the humanities. Anyone teaching a skill or a method—however abstractly we may define such matters—has recourse to arguments that are essentially based on fear and shame. "Learn calculus or be calculated!" is the underlying message of many first-day lectures in that subject, and the argument works equally well in chemistry ("Everything you see is a chemical!"), foreign language classes ("In our increasingly global world..."), and even history ("Those who cannot remember the past are condemned to repeat it"). All such statements presuppose usefulness as the criterion for relevance; the humanities, as our declining budgets make clear, have a harder time making such claims. It is difficult to say what one becomes if left without knowledge of, say, European oil painting or Derek Walcott's poetry—difficult, because the traditional answers are also unavoidably the most elitist. Santayana's profound and memorable dictum, when re-presented as a reason to take a course, is reduced to being yet another habit of highly effective people.

It must be frankly admitted, however, that if an English or a history student finds his or her way into a class on programming, it is not because of some perceived continuity between the study of Shakespeare or the French Revolution and the study of for-loops and conditionals. Most students see programming—and not without justice—as a mostly practical subject. Many students, over the years, have freely admitted to me that their primary motivation for studying the subject was linked to their job prospects after graduation. If Rushkoff's argument is persuasive, it is because the students have already arrived at some less strident version of it independently.

The emphasis on usefulness is deeply encoded in the terminology—or better, the analogy—of "software engineering." As Pete McBreen reminds us, the term was invented in the late sixties to describe a type of project that rarely appears in contemporary development: extremely large systems

---

1    Douglas Rushkoff, *Program or Be Programmed: Ten Commands for the Digital Age* (New York: O/R Books, 2010), 7, 3.

that require the fabrication of specialized hardware.[2] Engineering has undoubtedly persisted as the term of art because of a desire—only partially revised by the so-called "agile methods" that emerged in the 1990s—to have the development of software behave according to the far more predictable principles of specification and testing used to fabricate things like bridges and automobiles. "Engineering" is a term that allows programming to join with other activities long recognized within the university as being mostly ordered toward building useful things, and for which there are processes and methods that are repeatable and well understood. Many programmers (myself included) entertain a certain skepticism toward the engineering analogy as a practical matter, but the analogy is particularly weak when used as a framework for thinking about computing in the humanities. The suggestion I would like to offer (and the one I regularly offer to my students) is that programming is most of all like writing.

Writing, it should be noted, is one of the areas of education for which strongly utilitarian justifications are most obviously appropriate. "Write or be written" is a true, if overly poetic way of stating the relationship between the skills associated with print literacy and issues of social justice and mobility. Yet writing is also—and for some scholars of rhetoric and composition, even more so—a tool for *thinking through* a subject. Undergraduate courses regularly assign writing projects to students without any expectation that those essays will be useful to anyone other than the person writing. The task of writing is a part of the normal pedagogy of education in the humanities, because we think of the writing process as the methodology by which the artifacts of the human record are understood, critiqued, problematized and placed into dialogue with one another.

It is possible to make the case for teaching programming in the humanities on utilitarian grounds. In a set of disciplines still primarily concerned with artifacts of communication—both as objects of study and as internally useful discursive media—the ability to participate in the design and creation of new media is at least relevant if not exactly incumbent upon all. But the analogy with writing is, for me, the deeper and more necessary one. Like writing, programming provides a way to think in and through a subject. Alan J. Perlis's description of programming

2   Pete McBreen, *Software Craftsmanship: The New Imperative* (Boston: Addison, 2002). McBreen traces the term to a NATO conference in 1968 and offers, as a typical example of the sort of thing being described, the SAFEGUARD Ballistic Missile Defense System developed between 1969 and 1975, which took "5,407 staff-years" to build (1–3).

in his foreword to *Structure and Interpretation of Computer Programs* could, with only minor modification, describe the writing process:

> Every computer program is a model, hatched in the mind, of a real or mental process. These processes, arising from human experience and thought, are huge in number, intricate in detail, and at any time only partially understood. They are modeled to our permanent satisfaction rarely by our computer programs. Thus even though our programs are carefully handcrafted discrete collections of symbols, mosaics of interlocking functions, they continually evolve: we change them as our perception of the model deepens, enlarges, generalizes until the model ultimately attains a metastable place within still another model with which we struggle. The source of the exhilaration associated with computer programming is the continual unfolding within the mind and on the computer of the mechanisms expressed as programs and the explosion of perception they generate.[3]

Such thoughts lead inexorably to the sort of insight expressed by Knuth in the epigraph to this essay and echoed by Harold Abelson and Gerald Jay Sussman in their preface to *Structure and Interpretation of Computer Programs* itself; namely, that "programs must be written for people to read, and only incidentally for machines to execute."[4] Communication of that idea has been one of the few constants in my teaching of this subject.

I have taught a class on programming and software design to graduate students and advanced undergraduates in the humanities every year—and sometimes twice a year—since 2002. The idea for the course first arose in a faculty seminar I attended at the University of Virginia (UVA) in 2000–2001. At the time, there was a felt need for a course that could provide concrete technical training to undergraduate students in a prospective media studies program at UVA. The hoped-for synergy between technical and more conventional humanistic study seemed particularly appropriate at the time, since UVA had faculty both in digital humanities (a designation that had only just begun to replace "humanities computing") and media studies. Yet the subject tended to provoke concern and anxiety. How much technical training was appropriate? Who would teach such classes? Which skills were necessary?

---

3    Alan J. Perlis, "Foreword," in Harold Abelson and Gerald Jay Sussman, *Structure and Interpretation of Computer Programs*, 2nd edn (Cambridge: MIT Press, 1996), xii.
4    Abelson and Sussman, *Structure and Interpretation of Computer Programs*, xvii.

I left UVA (where I had been working as a programmer for the Institute for Advanced Technology in the Humanities) for a professorship at the University of Georgia (UGA) while these debates were still going on, but I was deeply affected by these conversations. And since we were given the specific task of creating a curriculum, I eventually tried to outline what some of the relevant technologies would be for a digital humanist in 2002. I began, therefore, with a list that included XML (and related technologies), UNIX, web design, relational database development and programming. As soon as I arrived at UGA, I encountered graduate students involved with digital humanities who also felt the need for these kinds of competencies. Some had taken classes in the Computer Science Department, but found the choice of examples frustrating (one student told me that after a few weeks of C++, she timidly asked the professor if the class would ever do anything involving words).

All of this set the scene for the creation of a two-semester course, the first semester of which taught UNIX, web design, XML and database design, with the second semester devoted almost exclusively to programming—a pattern that persisted until two years ago, when I decided to reverse the sequence. Today, I teach the programming course first and offer a second, workshop-style course in which I introduce other technologies as needed in the context of particular projects. Since 2006, I have taught these courses at the University of Nebraska-Lincoln (UNL), where I am an associate professor of English. This year, for the first time, I am teaching the material in a one-semester course (cross-listed with various humanities programs) within the Department of Computer Science and Engineering, where it is called CS 1: Humanities. Though it is focused on programming for the humanities, it counts as one of the required entry-level courses for the computer science major.

I offer this brief history to illustrate the way in which the course has contracted its subject matter over the years. During that time, I had had cause (in my own research) to write software in at least a half-a-dozen languages (and as many domain-specific languages), work with three or four different database platforms, and manipulate several different modulations and additions to the ecology of XML. As any programmer knows, the ability to shift easily from one technology to another is made possible by firm knowledge of the mostly invariant concepts that underlie all of these technologies. Eventually, I came to realize that all of these underlying concepts could be had through study of programming alone.

This is not to deny that technologies like relational databases and XSLT have instructional value. Indeed, both of those technologies have the additional feature of having endured where other technologies (including many programming languages) have not. But time being of the essence, it is, I think, better to introduce students to things like declarative programming, constraint logic and regular expressions with the idea that they can apply those concepts to particular technologies later. Today, the course has three main components: UNIX, Ruby programming and seminar-style discussion of articles relevant to the creation and use of technologies within the digital humanities.

I continue to introduce students to the UNIX operating system and its command-line interface as an ordinary part of the course. One rationale for this is simply to give students some familiarity with the server upon which the vast majority of web-based projects run. From the beginning, however, the idea has been to start by estranging students from the normal sense of what a computer is and what sort of interface it has. UNIX (in practice, some version of Linux) allows us to "start again" in an environment in which there is no mouse, no icons, no notion of a desktop and no windows, but in which metaphors still abound (for example, the file system "tree," the notion of a pipeline, the idea that a process "forks" and then returns).

The first couple of weeks are therefore devoted to the survival commands and underlying principles of UNIX from a user's standpoint. In practical terms, this means teaching students about file system navigation, redirection, file permissions and basic editing. Throughout, however, the emphasis is placed on what some have called "the philosophy of UNIX".[5] I tell students that for many UNIX developers, the goal is to write software that conforms to Doug McIlroy's injunction: "Write programs that do one thing and do it well. Write programs to work together. Write programs to handle text streams, because that is a universal interface."[6] I return to these ideas again and again over the course of the semester, as I ask students whether their own programs are behaving according to the usual expectations of UNIX software. My purpose, though, is less to turn

---

5   See M. D. McIlroy, E. N. Pinson, and B. A. Tague, "Unix Time-Sharing System: Forward," *The Bell System Technical Journal* 57, no. 6 (1978): 1899–904; Mike Gancarz, *Linux and the Unix Philosophy* (Amsterdam: Elsevier-Digital, 2003); and Eric S. Raymond, *The Art of UNIX Programming* (Boston: Addison, 2003).

6   Quoted in Peter H. Salus, *A Quarter Century of UNIX* (Reading: Addison-Wesley, 1994), 52–53. McIlroy was the inventor of the UNIX pipeline; see Gancarz, *Linux and the Unix Philosophy*.

them into UNIX developers than it is to ask what the "philosophy" of the computers, cell phones and gaming devices they generally use might be, and what it means to conform to a philosophy as a user and as a developer.

The second component of the course—and the one we spend the most time on—involves learning to write software in the Ruby programming language. Language choice is always a contentious subject, and many good choices are possible. From the beginning, however, I felt that a few criteria had to be met:

- **It had to be a "scripting language."** This is an imprecise and ultimately self-refuting designation, but as a matter of common usage, this term has tended to include languages like Perl, Python, PHP, Ruby, Tcl and Lua, while excluding languages like C, C++, Java, Lisp and Haskell. Without giving the term undue attention, we can say that the former usually offer a relatively low barrier to entry, do not require (or even allow) low-level manipulation of memory, have a small number of sophisticated built-in data structures and have large, practically-oriented APIs and third-party libraries.

- **It had to support multiple programming paradigms.** When I started, that meant (at the most basic level) support for both procedural and object-oriented programming. Today, I would add functional programming facilities to those requirements. In general, however, I feel that the language should support a number of different programming styles, and should make it easy to talk about programming paradigms in general terms.

- **The language had to have a consistent syntax.** This is perhaps even more vague a term than "scripting language," but I will say that while consistent syntax is not automatically a virtue in a language, it is a great help to students learning to program. Ideally, the language would have almost "no syntax" (in the sense that a language like Scheme has no syntax), but at the very least, it should have a small number of syntactic constructs that are repeated over and over. It should also be reasonably forgiving, since students can very often waste hours debugging a program that is missing a terminal semicolon.

I would not say that Ruby is the perfect language for teaching, but it meets these requirements. It supports a number of features usually associated with Lisp-like languages (including closures, continuations and anonymous functions) that make it easy to teach concepts like functional programming, recursion and meta-programming. It is also a rigidly object-oriented language that can at the same time masquerade as a procedural programming language.[7] Most of all, it allows students to start writing useful programs right away, and remains useful for quite sophisticated projects later on. Many graduates of the course have gone on to proficiency in Java, PHP and Haskell (among others).

The course proceeds, as most courses in programming do, through the major constructs and concepts germane to any programming language: statements and variables, loops and conditionals, arrays, hashes, iterators, classes and objects, basic algorithms and elementary data structures. There are, however, a few key differences between the material taught in a standard introduction to programming (as it usually appears in computer science departments) and the humanities-focused version. For one thing, there is a marked emphasis on the manipulation of text data. Computing is not possible without at least basic mathematics, but computing the Fibonacci sequence or the factorial of n is simply not the sort of thing likely to seem pertinent to a humanities student. Mathematical examples have undoubtedly persisted in computer science education, because they allow one to introduce concepts — including some quite advanced ones — while using only primitive, scalar objects (integers). Strings, for all their familiarity, are far more complex, and necessarily compound data types. But this, again, is a strong reason for using the so-called scripting languages, which tend to treat strings as if they were simple, uncomplicated primitives.

It is increasingly possible to treat XML as a built-in data structure. XML facilities are part of the standard library of Ruby (as they are in most scripting languages), and recent trends suggest that XML is becoming a native data-type in more-and-more new languages (for example, Clojure and Scala). The popularity of XML as a data representation within the digital humanities community would be enough to recommend it for inclusion, but it has the additional feature of allowing for straightforward explanations of basic tree structures (and, should the need arise in a succeeding course, the basics of parsing). I also spend quite a bit of time, several weeks into the course, on regular expressions. This, again, is a matter of practical utility; few technologies are more useful to people

---

7   It is rigidly object-oriented in the sense that everything in the language — including the elements of the symbol table — is an object. It lacks some of the OO features found in other class-based languages like Java, C++, and Scala, but can be made to emulate the prototypal inheritance of languages like JavaScript and Lua.

working with text. But along the way, it allows me to talk a bit about state machines (thus introducing another layer to the idea of what a computer might be). Clearly, there is not enough time to introduce formal language theory (let alone the mathematics of finite state automata), but it is possible to gesture toward these subjects in a way that can solicit interest in more advanced subjects and courses.

As I tell students at the beginning of the semester, this class has no papers, no presentations, no quizzes, no midterm and no final exam. When I first started the course, I did have some of these, but they all gave way in the end to the one assignment type that consistently helped students (as reported, again and again, on student evaluations)—namely, the problem sets. Problem sets (which are only occasionally sets of problems) give students about five days to write a small program or to enhance a previously written one. We start out simply, though I make sure that students write a complete, working program (usually a "mad libs" program) after the very first lecture on Ruby. Other assignments include writing "poetry deformers", word frequency generators, text-based games, and, eventually, tools for analyzing text corpora (tf-idf analyzers, basic document classifiers, sentence complexity tools and so forth). In direct violation of my university's syllabus policies, I also try to avoid giving the students a rigid schedule in advance. Some groups simply move at a different pace than others, and I try to follow student interest when I can. I have also had varying cohorts over the years. One year I had a class made up almost exclusively of graduate students in linguistics; another year I had students who were studying composition and rhetoric. The goal, in every case, is to get away from "toy programs" as quickly as possible and into projects that are relevant to the students' actual interests: for linguistics students, that meant an emphasis on natural language processing; for composition teachers, that (at the time, at least) meant greater emphasis on web-based pedagogical applications. I even tell students that they can get out of having to do problem sets entirely if they can present me with a substantial idea for a project. I then tailor the sequence of development for that individual project according to the sequence of subjects we're covering in class. In practice, the students who pursue this option are highly motivated and able to work independently.

One unusual aspect of the class is the complete "open book" policy with regard to problem sets. I explicitly tell students that they are allowed to use any source of information in pursuit of the solution to a problem set: the books for the course, information available online and (most especially) each other. Such a policy would appear to invite plagiarism, but I am careful to explain that plagiarism is primarily about misrepresenting the nature of one's use, and not a prohibition against using outside sources. The purpose of this policy is simply to recreate the conditions under which software is actually written. A few students have abused what is in essence an honor system over the years; the overwhelming majority has not.

The third component of this class is the "Friday seminar" (held every third day of a course that meets three times a week). These class meeting involve free-ranging discussions of important articles in the history of computing, theory of new media, digital humanities and sometimes popular works on cyber culture. There can be no question that devoting a third of the course to such material reduces the time available for teaching programming, but I regard these class meetings as completely essential to the course. Originally, this aspect of the course had perhaps more to do with my own insecurities about teaching a highly technical course in an English department than with any organized pedagogy. Over time, however, it began to have the unanticipated effect of putting people at ease. Teaching programming involves complicated, demanding lectures, difficult assignments and the persistent feeling on the part of the student that they're not quite getting it. I tell them (with as much good humor as I can summon) that this feeling never entirely disappears (since to be a technologist is very often to dwell in unknown territory) and that it is more important that we grow accustomed to that state by learning to ask questions, get help, work in groups and try different solutions. But all of this requires that the students feel comfortable with each other and with the professor. The fact that humanities students are accustomed to seminar-style discussions helps with this, but I think it is even more important that students see themselves as becoming the people they read about—programmers, designers, developers and digital humanists.

Every third day, therefore, we have a general discussion on material that they will never be tested on and for which they do not have to produce any kind of written response. These conversations have, for ten years, been among the liveliest and most interesting discussions I have participated in as a teacher. Without the pressure of having to do anything but talk, they nearly always develop an easy rapport with one another, which carries over into the parts of the class where they often have to risk seeming "stupid" in front of one another. When they are comfortable enough to risk that, it allows me to assure them that they are where they need to be. This further allows me to help them to imagine themselves as becoming programmers at the end of the class—a motivational technique identified by Duane Shell as key to students' sense of control and self-regulation within classroom learning environments.[8]

I am often asked what texts I use in these classes (aside from various technical manuals). I tend to draw on a large pool of articles and book chapters, customizing the reading list in accordance with students' interests. I try to focus, however, on readings that raise issues for people building and designing software systems. I would say that in some cases, I have a bias toward older works, especially those in which a now familiar technology is being presented (or commented upon) for the first time. A typical sequence might start with Neal Stephenson's *In the Beginning Was the Command Line*,[9] an essay which, despite its focus on the Microsoft anti-trust case over a decade ago, provides an interesting focus for meditation on interfaces in general (particularly in relationship to identity). We might then move on to early definitions of work on human-computer interaction in the work of Vannevar Bush, J. C. R. Licklider and Douglas Engelbart. As our discussions of this subject grow more philosophical, I might turn them toward Walter Benjamin's "The Work of Art in the Age of Mechanical Reproduction" (1936)[10] and a few essays by Marshall McLuhan (usually "The Medium is the Message," "Media Hot and Cold" and "The Gadget Lover: Narcissus as Narcosis") from *Understanding Media*.[11] Questions about the limits of computation invariably arise during our discussions,

---

8    I am paraphrasing extensive and detailed research undertaken by Duane F. Shell and Jenefer Husman, "Control, Motivation, Affect, and Strategic Self-Regulation in the College Classroom: A Multidimensional Phenomenon," *Journal of Educational Psychology* 100, no. 2 (2008): 443-59. This work has been a part of the "Renaissance Computing" initiative at UNL (sponsored by the U.S. National Science Foundation), which tries to imagine versions of introductory computer science classes specifically designed for students in the humanities, music, art and the life sciences. On this initiative, see Leen-Kiat Soh, Ashok Samal, Stephen Scott, Stephen Ramsay, Etsuko Moriyama, George Meyer, Brian Moore, William G. Thomas, and Duane F. Shell, "Renaissance Computing: An Initiative for Promoting Student Participation in Computing," in *Proceedings of the 40th ACM Technical Symposium on Computer Science Education, SIGCSE 2009, Chatanooga, 4–7 March 2009*, ed. Sue Fitzgerald, Mark Guzdial, Gary Lewandowski, and Steven A. Wolfman (New York: ACM, 2009), 59–63.

9    Neal Stephenson, *In the Beginning Was the Command Line* (New York: Avon, 1999).

10   Walter Benjamin, "The Work of Art in the Age of Mechanical Reproduction," in *Illuminations: Essays and Reflections*, ed. Hannah Arendt, trans. Harry Zohn (New York: Schocken Books, 1969), 217–51.

11   Marshall McLuhan, *Understanding Media: The Extensions of Man* (London: Routledge & Kegan Paul, 1964).

and so I nearly always add Alan Turing's "Computing Machinery and Intelligence" (1950),[12] and perhaps John R. Searle's "Minds, Brains, and Programs" (1980).[13] Discussions of gender, the body, and online identity might prompt examinations of essays by Sherry Turkle, Karen Franck, Mark Dery, N. Katherine Hayles and Donna Haraway. I have been known to assign Martin Heidegger's "The Question Concerning Technology" (1954) and excerpts from Deleuze and Guattari's *A Thousand Plateaus* to groups of more advanced students.[14] I almost always draw essays from two edited collections specifically focused on digital humanities: *A Companion to Digital Humanities* (2004) and *A Companion to Digital Literary Studies* (2007).[15] Despite this considerable range of subjects and themes, there is always a central question to which I try to return as often as possible: What might computation mean in the context of humanistic inquiry?

Though I retired the explicit two-course sequence a few years ago, I do offer a sequel to interested students from time to time. This course is invariably a workshop, in which students plan, design, develop, document and test a complete software system. These courses can suffer from some of the usual problems associated with group-based learning (uneven participation and hard-to-define grading criteria, for example), but at their best, these courses work well at exposing students to the complexities of project management and application design. In our own program, it is more likely that exposure to such matters will now occur through focused internships and independent study projects. However, the work that has come out of these classes in recent years is of a very high standard. One group, for example, developed an application that allowed the user to submit a poem that the program then pairs with an appropriate image drawn, using basic machine-learning techniques, from Flickr (http://www.flickr.com/). A more recent group wrote a program that generated graph visualizations of sentence complexity metrics over a 250-volume corpus of Victorian novels. It is in the context of such work

---

12   Alan Turing, "Computing Machinery and Intelligence," *Mind* 59, no. 236 (1950): 433–60.
13   John R. Searle, "Minds, Brains, and Programs," *Behavioral and Brain Sciences* 3, no. 3 (1980): 417–57.
14   Martin Heidegger, "The Question Concerning Technology," in *The Question Concerning Technology and Other Essays*, trans. William Lovitt (New York: Harper & Row, 1977), 3–35; Gilles Deleuze and Félix Guattari, *A Thousand Plateaus: Capitalism and Schizophrenia*, trans. Brian Massumi (Minneapolis: University of Minnesota Press, 1987).
15   Susan Schreibman, Ray Siemens, and John Unsworth, ed. *A Companion to Digital Humanities* (Malden: Blackwell, 2004); Ray Siemens and Susan Schreibman, ed. *A Companion to Digital Literary Studies* (Malden: Blackwell, 2007).

that I am usually able to introduce matters such as relational database design, web services and web application frameworks (as well as software development tools like profilers, debuggers and revision control systems). In many cases, however, I encourage the students themselves to discover which technologies might be relevant to their project, and to assign team members the task of developing particular expertise on a given subject. Here again, the focus is on emulating the ways in which software projects are actually developed among researchers and project teams in digital humanities.

In recent years, there have been various attempts to redefine the knowledge gained from the study of computer science to something like "computational thinking".[16] This is an attractive term in many ways, since it expands the range of subjects through which that knowledge might be gained. It seems to me entirely possible to give students an experience of computational thinking using only a relational database system, a domain-specific language like Processing or XSLT, or even the UNIX shell. But I continue to think that what is gained when humanities students learn to think in the context of sophisticated computational tools is not only computational thinking, but also "humanistic thinking." The center of digital humanities, after all, is not the technology, but the particular form of engagement that characterizes the act of building tools, models, frameworks and representations for the traditional objects of humanistic study. "The emerging, highly programmed landscape ahead," so often the object of fear and anxiety, can become a new instrument for contemplation if we can help our students to learn to think in and through what Rushkoff rightly calls "the underlying capability of the computer era."[17]

---

16  See Peter J. Denning, "Beyond Computational Thinking," *Communications of the ACM* 52, no. 6 (2009): 28-30; Mark Guzdial, "Paving the Way for Computational Thinking," *Communications of the ACM* 51, no. 8 (2008): 25-27; Committee for the Workshops on Computational Thinking, *Report of a Workshop on The Scope and Nature of Computational Thinking* (Washington: National Academies Press, 2010).

17  Rushkoff, *Program or Be Programmed*, 13.

# 10. Teaching Computer-Assisted Text Analysis: Approaches to Learning New Methodologies

*Stéfan Sinclair and Geoffrey Rockwell*

Using a computer to analyze a text intimidates many humanities students, but the reality is that text analysis is becoming a fundamental and naturalized part of how we operate in a digital society. Text analysis is what enables Google to compile and index tens of billions of web pages so that our search terms produce results; it is fundamental to building IBM's Watson, a computer-system that was able to beat two of the top human *Jeopardy!* players of all time; it allows smartphone developers to build predictive texting capabilities; it also enables a humanist to study the relationship between Agatha Christie's dementia and the richness of her vocabulary over the course of her writing career.[1] Significant transformations of

---

1  Watson is a DeepQA system developed by IBM to answer questions posed in a natural language. In February 2011, Watson successfully competed in three episodes of *Jeopardy!* For more about Watson, see the IBM Watson page, February 21, 2001,http://www-03.ibm. com/innovation/us/watson/. Ian Lancashire and Graeme Hirst conducted the research into Agatha Christie's Alzheimer's and her vocabulary, which the *New York Times* selected as one of the notable ideas for 2009. Ian Lancashire, "Vocabulary Changes in Agatha Christie's Mysteries as an Indication of Dementia: A Case Study," in *Forgetful Muses: Reading the Author in the Text* (Toronto: University of Toronto Press, 2010), 207–19.

how we handle the written record are occurring as more and more of it is digitized and made available for computer analysis. Analytics are no longer an exotic preoccupation of digital humanists and computational linguists: humanities students need to understand automated methods if only because we are surrounded by their use—in everything from our email to the news.[2] This chapter will therefore:

- Briefly describe what text analysis is;
- Make the case that analytics should be taught;
- Discuss how it can be integrated into humanities courses;
- Discuss recipes as a way of introducing students to text analysis; and
- Introduce the idea of notebooks for advanced students.

Our goal is to start by making the case for teaching text analysis, then to provide ideas as to how it might be taught, and to end with reflections on advanced support in the form of notebooks—where the analysis becomes a form of research writing.[3]

# What is Text Analysis?

Computer-assisted text analysis or text analysis for short, is the use of computers as an aide in the interpretation of electronic texts. A concording tool, for example, can help an interpreter find all the passages in a text where a certain word appears and act as an index to help the interpreter find passages. It can also go further and present these passages with in a Keyword-in-Context (KWIC) display, where one line of context for each occurrence is presented in a new gathered text for the convenience of

---

2  The company Cataphora (http://www.cataphora.com/), for example, provides investigative services using their analytics. The company's website describes their services as follows: "For over nine years, we have pieced together the digital footprints left by individuals and organizations going about their daily lives. We have used these footprints to help clients understand the actions of their employees, and to mitigate the sometimes dangerous consequences".

3  Our research and development of tools was made possible with grants from the Social Science and Humanities Research Council of Canada and the Canada Foundation for Innovation.

the author. Thus we can say that text analysis actually consists of two processes:

- **Analysis**, in which the computer breaks apart the text into basic units like words; and,
- **Synthesis**, in which the computer counts these units, manipulates them and reassembles a new text.

The counting and synthesis can become quite sophisticated and go beyond finding. For example, statistical techniques can generate clusters of words for visualization to help you figure out for what to search.

Why bother with text analysis tools? After all, most word processors and web browsers can search texts quickly. In the section of the Text Analysis Developer's Alliance (http://tada.mcmaster.ca/) wiki on "What is text analysis?" we describe what text analysis systems do thus:

- **Text analysis systems can search large texts quickly**. They do this by preparing electronic indexes to the text so that the computer does not have to read through the entire text. When finding words can be done so quickly that it is "interactive," it changes how you can work with the text—you can simultaneously and serendipitously explore without being frustrated by the slowness of the search process.
- **Text analysis systems can conduct complex searches**. Text analysis systems will often allow you to search for lists of words or for complex patterns of words. For example, you can search for the co-occurrence of two words.
- **Text analysis systems can present the results in ways that suit the study of texts**. Text analysis systems can display the results in a number of ways; for example, a Keyword In Context display shows you all the occurrences of the found word with one line of context.[4]

---

4  Geoffrey Rockwell, "What is Text Analysis? A Very Short Answer," *WikiTADA*, Text Analysis Developers Alliance, April 30, 2005, http://tada.mcmaster.ca/Main/WhatTA. This wiki is generally a good resource for text analysis links, documents, and tutorials. Some are suitable for students, however, as a wiki the content is raw and parts are unfinished.

The issue of scale is important to text analysis. Computers allow us to interpret texts that are so large that we couldn't study them with traditional reading practices. With Google Books (http://books.google.com/) we can search across a million books, more than we could ever read and digest. Thus we can imagine interpreting new collections of texts that we wouldn't before have imagined or dared to interpret. We can bring interpretative questions to these new texts, formalize them for the computer and get results back that we can interpret instead of reading the whole. Franco Moretti, for example, talks about using computers to perform "distant reading,"[5] being able to consider textual evidence inclusively — perhaps even exhaustively — rather than our close reading practice that tends to be exclusive. Stéfan Sinclair's innovative text analysis tool HyperPo (http://www.hyperpo.org/), which led to Voyant Tools (http://www.voyant-tools.org/), was designed to provide an interactive reading environment that does not pretend to answer questions so much as extend the users' ability to read and proliferate representations of texts.

## Why Teach Text Analysis?

Until recently, text analysis tools looked like an obscure research area for those interested in programming and statistical techniques. Analytics have, however, become common on the web, and the scale of information available makes the need to teach students about computer-aided interpretation more urgent. Word clouds and Wordles have, for example, become popular on blogs and web pages. Some news sites, including that of the *New York Times*, have started building custom interfaces to help readers analyze transcripts of events, such as the Republican presidential candidate's debate on October 21, 2007. This analytical toy (Figure 1) lets users search for words and see which candidate's used the word(s) and when in the debate.

---

5   Franco Moretti, "Conjectures on World Literature," *New Left Review* 1 (2000): 54–68; "Graphs, Maps, Trees: Abstract Models for Literary History—1," *New Left Review* 24 (2003): 67–93; "Graphs, Maps, Trees: Abstract Models for Literary History—2," *New Left Review* 26 (2004): 79–103; and, "Graphs, Maps, Trees: Abstract Models for Literary History—3," *New Left Review* 28, (2004): 43–63.

**Republican Debate: Analyzing the Details**
Watch the interactive video from the Oct. 21 debate and analyze the transcript.

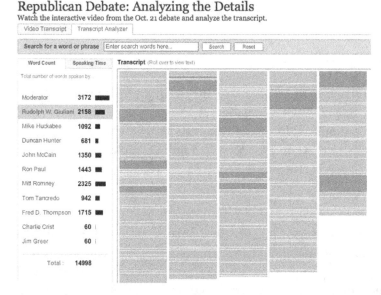

**Figure 1.** Transcript Analyzer, "Republican Debate: Analyzing the Details," *New York Times*, October 21, 2007, developed by Shan Carter, Gabriel Dance, Matt Ericson, Tom Jackson, Sarah Wheaton and Jonathan Ellis.[6]

As such analytical toys proliferate and as users embed simple analytics in their own web texts students will need to be taught basic analytical literacy so that they can interpret these visualizations just as we (should) teach students to read basic graphs in the news.[7] A further reason is that students need to understand how others are using analytics to study them. Companies and other organizations use analytic techniques to mine the data we freely share on social sites, like Facebook.[8] By trying text

---

6   You can still experiment with this Analyzer tool on the *New York Times* site, October 21, 2007, http://www.nytimes.com/interactive/2007/10/21/us/politics/20071021_DEBATE_GRAPHIC.html#video.

7   On embedding analytics, see Geoffrey Rockwell, Stéfan Sinclair, Stan Ruecker, and Peter Organisciak, "Ubiquitous Text Analysis," *The Poetess Archive Journal* 2, no. 1 (2010), http://paj.muohio.edu/paj/index.php/paj/article/view/13/.

8   For an accessible article on how social media data is being used, see Jeffrey Rosen, "The Web Means the End of Forgetting," *The New York Times Magazine*, July 21, 2010, http://www.nytimes.com/2010/07/25/magazine/25privacy-t2.html. There is also some evidence that the FBI in the United States developed large-scale analytical tools for surveillance purposes. See the Electronic Privacy Information Centre's documentation on the Carnivore and Omnivore systems reported in 2000, January 19, 2005, http://epic.org/privacy/carnivore/. It is not clear, however, how effective such tools are, even if we can clearly see that they are pervasive.

analysis, students should learn not only about literature, but also about the potential—and the limits—of surveillance analytics.

# Integrating Text Analysis into a Course

Once convinced that it is useful to integrate text analysis learning into courses, one must then consider how to do it. Here are three models that go from a simple and short text analysis assignment—that asks the student to provide the text and the tool, to a more complex model—that requires students to create their own text.

## Using an Analytical Tool

The easiest way to integrate text analysis into teaching is to provide access to a pre-populated text analysis tool, by which we mean a tool for interactive reading that already has an indexed text loaded. This way, students do not need to worry about finding an electronic text, preparing it for analysis and loading it. Instead, they can concentrate on thinking through how to use the tool to analyze the text. It is also easier to support a text/tool combination with which you are familiar. The unfortunate reality of these text analysis tools (in the humanities) is that they are research tools developed by academics, and therefore not as robust as commercial tools. If students are to focus on the text, a combination of text and tool which is known to work (and that can be shown and taught) is needed.

One way to create such an assignment is to use an existing online resource like Mark Davies' Time Corpus (http://corpus.byu.edu/time/), which comes with analytical tools with a linguistic bent. Another way to do this would be to prepare a text yourself (making sure you have the necessary permissions), load it in Voyant Tools, and then ask Voyant to export a stable URL for the tool and text combination.[9] Generally speaking, if you can find a URL for the text you want—on Project Gutenberg (http://www.gutenberg.org/), for example—you can create a Voyant tool/corpus combination for your students. This allows you to provide an analytical environment customized to the text that you are teaching, rather than having to adapt your course to whatever existing text/tool combination is out there.

---

9   When you load a text in Voyant Tools, you can ask for a URL to be able to access the corpus again by clicking on the floppy disk icon in the upper-right corner. It will give you a URL or the option to go to a layout manager where you can create a "skin" with exactly the tools in the Voyant portfolio that you want your students to use.

Once you have a tool/text combination available for students, you need a suitable assignment to encourage students to use the tool. Some ideas for assignments include:

- Provide students with specific patterns of words to search for and to follow through the text in preparation for a tutorial in which you want to discuss the themes associated with those words. This assignment also allows you to discuss the broader issue of whether patterns of words accurately track subtler themes.

- Provide students with a theme or themes and ask them to prepare a short written summary of how the theme unfolds in the text. They may require help imagining how to follow a theme through a text. You can point them to a thesaurus, where they can generate words to search for, count and follow. Encourage students to look also for words indicative of contrasting themes—for example, if they are looking at how women are portrayed in a text, they might also look at how the men are discussed in order to construct an argument by comparison. Simple comparisons of word counts can be interesting and provoke hermeneutical questions—for example, 'what does it mean if, in a corpus of videogame reviews, the words "man," "princess," and "alien" occur far more often than "woman"'?

- Related to thematic analysis, students may be asked to look at the structure of themes by using a distribution graph to see where certain themes are dealt with in the text. Does a theme appear to frame the work appearing at the beginning and end? Are there themes that co-occur or repel each other? This only works with a coherent text, in which there is some logic to the order of the parts of a corpus—for example, a collection of short stories that are not in any order will not show structure, but a collection in diachronic order might. Students can be asked to present a distribution graph in a tutorial to other students, using that visualization to make a point about the text.[10]

---

10  John B. Smith's article, "Image and Imagery in Joyce's *Portrait*: A Computer-Assisted Analysis," in *Directions in Literary Criticism: Contemporary Approaches to Literature*, ed. Stanley Weintraub and Philip Young (University Park: Pennsylvania State University Press, 1973), 220–27, is a nice early example of this type of analysis if you want an exemplar for students to read. Smith was a pioneer in the development of text analysis tools, with one of the first interactive text analysis tools called ARRAS. He also experimented with visualizing texts before we even called it visualization.

When asking students to write from text analysis, one of the challenges is helping them frame an argument that draws on analytic results. This, of course, creates an opportunity to discuss the rhetoric of using computers to demonstrate arguments and claims about a text. Do computer results change the character of the interpretation? Can you prove things with computing in ways that you cannot with human practices? One way to help students to write about results is to ask them to find a visualization that they believe is interesting and to base a short paper on it—including a discussion of how it was generated and what it means. TAPoRware (http://taporware.ualberta.ca) and Voyant Tools have visualization tools, but there are also other collections of tools, such as Many Eyes by IBM (http://www-958.ibm.com/). Many Eyes has the added virtue of a gallery of visualizations produced by others with their texts. Students can look at different types of visualizations and different uses across the same or different texts, helping them to form ideas about what they might generate themselves.

## Building a Corpus to Study

The limitation of having students use prepared text/tool combinations is that they don't learn to find texts and build their own corpus. If there is time, students can be asked to develop their own research questions using their own texts. This works particularly well when students are encouraged to gather texts from non-literary sources that often exhibit less subtle uses of language, which means that simple analytical techniques are more likely to generate interesting results. Here is a suggested order of steps for teaching:

1.   Ask students to identify a phenomenon they wish to study using text techniques. You could discuss appropriate phenomena in class after having read an introduction or example essay. Encourage students to choose a popular cultural phenomenon for which they might be able to find a variety of texts online.

2.   Have students use Google (http://www.google.com/) to find a representative sample of 50 to 100 texts that deal with the phenomenon. They should not use the first 100 hits from Google, but make defensible choices. They should cut and paste the relevant text into a text editor and keep track of the URL where they found each fragment. They should clean up the text and

edit out the HTML or XHTML. Most text analysis tools work well with plain text files, so students should be encouraged to save each individual fragment of their corpus as a text file with a ".txt" extension for use in these tools.

3. Students should then run the text through various tools, starting with tools that might suggest themes or anomalies to follow more carefully. We often start with a word cloud (such as the Cirrus Word Cloud included in the Voyant Tools, http:// voyant-tools.org/tool/Cirrus/) or Wordle (http://www.wordle. net/), which presents the high-frequency words in the text graphically (Figure 2). The juxtapositions often suggest themes to follow through. A frequency-sorted word list is another tool that you can use to see lots of words. For students, looking for patterns in the high-frequency words can be a way into the text.

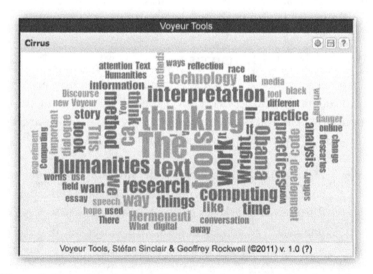

**Figure 2.** Cirrus Word Cloud, Voyant Tools, developed by the authors.

4. With words or themes of words that students want to follow carefully, they might look at the distribution of the word, at the words that co-occur with the target word and at concordances of words. Encourage students to take careful notes as they go along so they can recreate a result later. Students might keep a running journal of what they did and their results. This will help them when writing up a paper or presentation for the project.

5.    Alternatively, you could have a discussion about what hermeneutical questions we can bring to a text and how text analysis tools can help us formalize a question. Students could be encouraged to have a set of questions and hypotheses before they even touch the computer, since this forces them to look for the tools that might help them answer their questions.

6.    You can ask students to look at the Recipes we have developed (discussed below) to get ideas and to see examples.

The goal should be a paper or presentation about the phenomenon, not about text analysis, in which students describe the choices made in creating their corpus, discuss the questions asked through computing, discuss the results and how they were arrived at and present an original reading of popular culture through its texts online. We have found that, given time and support, students can gather surprising results about phenomena they are interested in.

## Introducing Text Analysis

However you choose to weave text analysis into your teaching, it is worth introducing the subject explicitly, especially if you want students to think about how computers can be used to analyze data. Here are some ideas for introducing the topic that we have found useful:

- Have the students read a short **introduction** to text analysis. You could use materials on the Text Analysis Developers Alliance site (http://tada.mcmaster.ca/), such as the entry for "What is text analysis?" or more substantial discussions, like the collection of articles on the subject in the 2003 special issue of the journal *Literary and Linguistic Computing* (volume 8, number 2).

- Have students work through an online **workbook**, like the TACTweb Workbook,[11] which walks students through the subject with interactive panels that students can experiment with. Given the

---

11    TACTweb was developed in the mid 1990s and is now a bit dated, but it is still online at a number of universities. For example, an installation of the workbook can be found at http://khnt.hit.uib.no/tactweb/doc/TWIntro.htm. For more on TACTweb and its use as a teaching tool, see Geoffrey Rockwell, Graham Passmore and John Bradley, "TACTweb: The Intersection of Text-Analysis and Hypertext," *Journal of Educational Computing Research* 17, no. 3 (1997): 217-30.

flexibility of the web you can even create your own tutorials and workbooks with text analysis tools woven in.[12]

- Have students look at **example essays** that present the interpretative results of text analysis. We have written such an essay, "Now Analyze That," which uses our tools to compare speeches on race by Barack Obama and his mentor Jeremiah A. Wright, Jr.[13] The essay has live Voyant panels embedded right into the essay where we try to make points from the analysis.

## Recipes

For students who want to go deeper into text analysis and master it for research purposes, we have developed a collection of "Recipes."[14] The idea of Recipes is to describe text analysis in terms of interpretative tasks that humanities researchers may want to do. Rather than starting with the technologies of analytics and their jargon, Recipes start with something a humanist may want to do, like identifying themes in a text. This allows students to start with the interpretative tasks they should understand.

We chose the name "Recipes" for these abstract tutorials because we wanted to understate the technological and use the metaphor of a cooking recipe to organize what users needed to know. The term was actually suggested by Stan Ruecker at the 2005 Canadian Symposium on Text Analysis, "The Face of Text," during a discussion about how tool rhetoric might be alienating. Like a recipe in a cookbook, each "Recipe" has **Ingredients** and **Utensils** (a list of what you need to compete the task), **Steps** (a sequence of interactions with the computer that will generate results relevant to the task), a **Discussion** of issues that may arise or opportunities for further exploration, a **Glossary** with definitions

---

12  The Text Analysis Developers Alliance site maintains a list of other text analysis tutorials. See "Tutorials and Documentation," *WikiTADA*, Text Analysis Developers Alliance, May 6, 2005, http://tada.mcmaster.ca/Main/TATuts.

13  Stéfan Sinclair and Geoffrey Rockwell, "Now Analyze That: Comparing the Discourse on Race," *The Rhetoric of Text Analysis*, April 2, 2009, http://hermeneuti.ca/rhetoric/now-analyze-that.

14  These Recipes were developed by Shawn Day, under our supervision, as part of the CFI-funded TAPoR project (http://portal.tapor.ca/). While they point to specific tools in the TAPoR project, the Recipes were written in such a way to allow others to substitute different tools. We are currently in the early phase of developing a Methods Commons (http://hermeneuti.ca/methods), where people can post and comment on such methodological recipes.

of text analysis jargon, a section for **Next Steps** or **Further Information** offering suggestions for other Recipes that might follow and a concrete **Application Example** of the entire process on a specific text with specific questions (Figure 3).

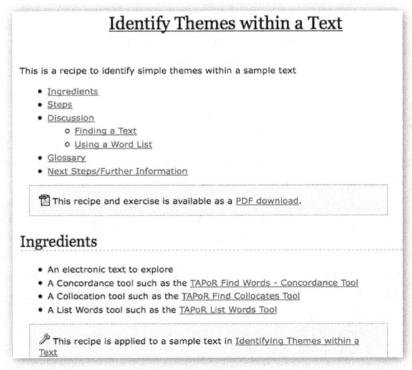

**Figure 3.** Example "Recipe" Page.

There are currently 29 Recipes on the site (http://tada.mcmaster.ca/Main/ TaporRecipes), though some cover pragmatics such as how to handle French texts. We found that we needed some utility Recipes so that the others could be written concisely. These Recipes are all freely available online and may be printed or saved in PDF. Instructions on how to contribute your own "Recipes" to the site are also available.[15]

With all these tools, Recipes and tutorials, the central issue when teaching text analysis is to get students to think methodically and to be able to explain how they developed their interpretations. This issue is not

---

15  Shawn Day, "Contributing Your Own TAPoR Portal Recipes and Exercises," *WikiTADA,* Text Analysis Developers Alliance, April 18, 2007, http://tada.mcmaster.ca/Main/ RecipeStructure.

unique to text analysis—students will often have insights into a text that could be brilliant, but they are unable to explain how they arrived at that insight or explain how others might see it the same way. In other words, students often don't know how to convince us of a perspective verbally/ they don't know how to express their perspective convincingly. When using text analysis tools, especially those that are interactive, students can likewise arrive at some display or result that they cannot recapitulate and, therefore, they don't really understand. As we outlined above, one possible solution is to teach students to record their analysis carefully and to keep a running commentary of results for later use. Alas, this is like asking students to keep a record of their code when they are more likely to leap ahead and neglect to document their methodical work. With this problem in mind, the next section will deal with a way of thinking about text analysis tools that offers a new perspective on the recording process, encouraging students to document what they do.

# Literate Programming

We will now switch to a more theoretical discussion of where we are going with Voyant Tools. Specifically, we will introduce an idea—literate programming—from one of the key figures of computer science, Donald E. Knuth, which has always struck us as useful for thinking and documenting intellectual processes, including those of analytical research.

Literate programming is essentially a paradigm for writing a highly blended mix of computer code and documentation. Although computer code is almost always accompanied by some documentation, literate programming tends to favor documentation that is more prosaic and exegetical. The objective is not only to describe what the specific lines of code do, but also to provide some narrative context. In a seminal article, Knuth suggests that, "Instead of imagining that our main task is to instruct a *computer* what to do, let us concentrate rather on explaining to *human beings* what we want a computer to do."[16] For Knuth, it is not only the documentation style, but also the coding style that changes, which develops more symbiotically with the narrative. The discursive reasoning embodied in the documentation leads to better code.

---

16  Donald E. Knuth, "Literate Programming," *The Computer Journal* 27, no. 2 (1984): 97, emphasis original.

A useful analogy is the way that mathematical proofs (or formal logic in philosophy) are expressed. There are equations, but these tend to be illustrations (and interruptions) of the narrative flow. It would be easier to understand the mathematical proof if one took away the equations than if one took away the prose and, as such, we might assert that the equations are there to help better understand the text. With computer programming, documentation is typically included to help better understand the code, but with literate programming the relationship is somewhat inverted in that the human reader is better served by reading the documentation than the code. The code is still crucial, but it is primarily intended for the computer to read. A brief example will help to illustrate the difference, even if the specifics here are contrived:

*// CONVENTIONAL CODE*

*// send message to standard output*

print("Hello World!");

*[LITERATE PROGRAMMING]*

*[I'm trying to learn a new programming language and I'll start by writing a very simple program. It's been a tradition since the 1970s to output the text "Hello World!" as a simple program when first learning a language. This language has a "print" method that takes as an argument, between parentheses, the quoted string "Hello World!", which will appear on the output console.]*

print("Hello World!");

Not only is the literate programming version more verbose, it also makes the program more self-explanatory—it tells a story. The story may not be of interest to more advanced programmers but, just as this story may be of interest to other novice programmers, the stories told by more advanced programmers may be more enlightening to other advanced programmers. The verbose and explanatory style has the potential to serve an important pedagogical purpose.

Crucially, this pedagogical purpose is not only related to how literate programs can teach others, but also how the literate programming style can help programmers teach themselves. Encouraging novice users to explain explicitly how the language structures work in the documentation helps them understand the structures for themselves. Explaining why one is doing something in a specific way may lead to reflection about other ways of doing it, some of which may be preferable. Indeed, part of the documentation may include an explanation of various approaches considered and attempted, as well as a justification of the approach chosen—typical documentation loses any trace of that intellectual work and focuses only on the code that remains.

The focus on expression and rhetoric in literate programming will be very familiar to most humanists: the value of what is expressed is calibrated by how it is expressed (the functional value of the program—whether or not it works—may be distinguished from the rhetorical value of the code). Knuth captures this succinctly in stating that the "practitioner of literate programming can be regarded as an essayist, whose main concern is with exposition and excellence of style."[17]

Literate programming is a good fit for the humanities since the first priority is prosaic expression (something familiar to all humanities students) and the actual code (which is foreign to most humanists) is secondary. One might even imagine an introduction to programming course in which students begin by writing a procedural essay and learn to backfill the essay with snippets of actual code as the course proceeds. Such an approach would help to ensure that the programming component does not hijack the overarching humanistic impetus.

The primary challenge for humanities students is probably not learning a new programming language. The syntax can be time-consuming to learn and the formalism of a programming language can be frustrating at first—a missed semi-colon can invalidate several hundred characters of otherwise perfectly valid code (depending on the programming language used), whilst such details do not have such drastic effects in essay writing. The real intellectual challenge is learning to think algorithmically about texts: 'the digital texts are there, now what operations can I perform on them (and why would I want to)?'

For many humanists, the text essentially represents an analogue object, one that is continuous from start to end. Though readers are aware of various structural breaks such as paragraphs and chapters in prose, the text is still considered a singular object. The digital transforms that model by allowing the text to be divided into tiny bits and reconfigured in infinite ways. Common reconfiguration tasks in text analysis include filtering, counting and comparing. However, using computers to perform formal operations on texts does not require humanists to approach texts from a positivistic perspective: we can ask formal questions of texts in service of speculative or hermeneutic

17   Knuth, "Literate Programming," 1.

objectives. Stephen Ramsay calls this approach *algorithmic criticism*, and explains, "one would not ask how the ends of interpretation were or were not justified by means of the algorithms imposed, but rather, how successful the algorithms were in provoking thought and allowing insight".[18]

The most effective way of helping students think algorithmically about texts is to provide templates and examples. Recipes are a form of template: they describe steps to follow in relatively generic terms. The texts may be different, but the principles and methodologies can have commonalities across applications. Though enormously useful, Recipes can present two major disadvantages for students learning text analysis. First, a lot of technique and knowledge are implicit. Just as most cookbooks would not bother explaining the mechanics of how to, say, whisk eggs, text analysis Recipes should not be expected to explain the purpose and techniques involved in every step along the way. Second, and more importantly, Recipes tend to be teleological, focusing on a singular end-point rather than a process. Algorithmic criticism is not about monolithic breakthroughs made possible by computational methods, but rather about incremental and iterative explorations. Moreover, the intellectual wanderings tend to be idiosyncratic and thus resist any formalization into reusable Recipes.

Whereas Recipes provide conceptual templates with some instructions for achieving an objective, literate programming can be used as a model for providing specific examples of following an intellectual process. Exposing this process is unusual in the humanities, since scholarly articles tend to be heavily synthesized and reorganized knowledge (which is why it is difficult to teach humanistic methodology based on scholarly articles). Literate programming, on the other hand, inverts the model and allows insights into the process that was followed.

It is worth noting that, despite its conceptual strengths, literate programming has remained relatively marginal in computer science and software engineering. Kurt Nørmark, who states, "it is probably fair to say that the ideas have not had any significant impact on 'the state of the art of software development,'" outlines several factors that have prevented a wider adoption of literate programming.[19] One pragmatic consideration is that most programmers do not have ambitions to write literary code;

---

18    Stephen Ramsay, "Toward an Algorithmic Criticism," *Literary and Linguistic Computing* 18, no. 2 (2003): 173.

19    Kurt Nørmark, "Literate Programming: Issues and Problems," Department of Computer Science, Aalborg University, August 13, 1998, http://www.cs.aau.dk/~normark/litpro/issues-and-problems.html.

writing code that works is more valued than writing documentation that explains. In any case, the literate programming model may actually work better in the humanities because the point is not to run a program (the functional concern) but to read the documentation (the code snippets are merely arguments). For the same reasons, literate programming has had more of an impact in mathematics, where capturing reproducible process and reasoning are essential.

There exist several development tools for those wishing to write works of literate programming. The original system developed by Knuth was called WEB (named in the 1980s before the advent of the World Wide Web) as it was an interweaving of documentation and code in the Pascal language. Other language-specific environments exist (such as CWEB for the C++ language and FWEB for the Fortran language), as well as tools that support any programming language (such as noweb, FennelWeb and nuweb). The documentation in these latter systems can be expressed in a variety of formats, including LaTex, HTML and troff. Similarly, just about any text editor can be used depending on one's preferences (for syntax highlighting, code completion, etc.) Arguably, the most common use of literate programming is in mathematics and statistics. Sweave, for instance, allows developers to write literate programming in LaTeX and have code executed by R, a widely used open source software environment for statistical computing and graphics. Maple and MATLAB have similar mechanisms available. However, while these tools are not typically difficult to use, the technical barrier for a humanist just starting is significant: programmers are now required to learn two syntaxes (the programming language and the documentation format), and the compilation of documentation and executable code requires additional steps (a tool has to be run to generate the documentation and to extract the code).

A more promising solution is offered by Mathematica, in which documentation is written using a styled editor (similar to writing in Microsoft Word) and code is clearly demarcated in separate blocks. As such, there is no need to learn a separate syntax for the documentation. Also, critically, code blocks can be executed directly within the environment—removing the need to extract, compile and run them in separate steps. Mathematica notebooks (Figure 4) provide a very compelling model for literate programming: writing documentation is like working in a word processor, which strips away several technical barriers, allowing the new user to focus on learning the programming syntax. Though originally designed for mathematics and currently used in a wide range of scientific disciplines, Mathematica offers some powerful functionality for text analysis in the humanities. Its WordData function, for instance, enables a wide range of operations for English texts, such as looking up synonyms, phonetic transcription, part of speech, and base form (for example, larger and largest becomes large). These specialized text-processing functions, combined with extensive statistical calculations and graphic options, make Mathematica a convincing candidate for literate programming in the humanities. However, Mathematica's major obstacle is its price tag: Mathematica Professional costs upwards of $1,000 USD, though a student license for the Standard Edition is listed at $139 USD. The price tag is arguably justifiable, but probably prohibitive for most humanities programs.

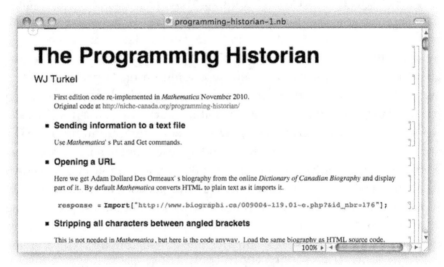

**Figure 4.** A snapshot of a literate programming notebook in Mathematica. The author of the notebook, William Turkel, is explaining steps to fetch content and analyse it. Only one line of code is visible here, beginning with "response =".

This situation has led us to start developing our own literate programming interface within the Voyant Tools framework.[20]

---

20   We had earlier developed for the TAPoR Portal a notebook-like feature, in which you had a blog to journal what you were doing and could save results. Though promising, its performance was often slow.

# Voyant Notebooks

Voyant Tools (http://www.voyant-tools.org/) is an online text analysis environment specially designed for humanists who wish to spend more time exploring their corpus than learning complicated statistical and analytical software. It allows researchers to quickly and easily create their own corpus of texts in various file formats (such as HTML, XML, plain text, Microsoft Word, PDF, RTF and so forth) and begin using an extensive collection of tools to examine interactively and visualize characteristics of the texts. Though the interface strives to have a low technical bar of entry, it also enables more advanced operations. There are currently about 20 analytic tools available, ranging from a simple word cloud visualization to a graph of term distributions, from term frequencies tables to correspondence analysis graphs (Figure 5). Most importantly, these tools are designed modularly, which allows them to be used in different combinations and configurations and to interact in useful ways.

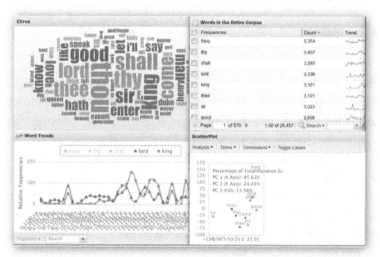

**Figure 5.** A sampling of visualization and analysis tools available in Voyant Tools.

One of the most innovative features of Voyant Tools is the ability to export tool results from the main site and embed live tool widgets—similar to YouTube clips—into remote digital content, such as blog posts or scholarly essays (Figure 6).[21] This may be considered a type of visual literate

---

21  See also "Viral Analytics: Embedding Voyant in Other Sites," Voyant Tools, October 19, 2010, http://hermeneuti.ca/Voyant/embed.

programming in that tool results—instead of code—are interspersed with essay argumentation.

**Figure 6.** An example of a live Voyant Tools widget embedded in a web essay.

Voyant Tools has proven useful in a variety of contexts, including courses in the digital humanities. An example is the historians studying the Old Bailey corpus of 200,000 trial accounts from London. However, its primary limitation is that users are constrained to the existing tools and methodologies that they impose.

Voyant Notebooks, in contrast, allows a much more flexible mode of interaction: the environment exposes the powerful backend system in Voyant Tools and enables users to write custom code to assist in exploring a corpus. User feedback of Voyant has indicated that humanists appreciate standard functionality, but very often wish to pursue a specialized process that would require custom tools.

Just like Voyant Tools, Voyant Notebooks is web-based, which makes it very easy to visit and start using—no downloads or configurations are required. The interface is essentially a web page with editable sections: the documentation sections use a styled editor (where no special syntax is required) and the code sections use a custom code editor (that supports syntax coloring, among other features).

Voyant Script, the programming language, is essentially Javascript enhanced by a library that facilitates communication with Voyant Tools.

Voyant Tools is a mixture of interface panels for displaying tables, graphs and other output, as well as a back-end system that executes analytic operations. Many operations would be too slow and too memory-intensive to execute within the browser without making calls to the server. However, this distinction is hidden from the developer in Voyant Notebooks, client-side and server-side operations interact seamlessly. Although still in prototype stage—it is currently not publicly available—an example of Voyant Notebooks will help illustrate the system (Figure 7).

**Figure 7.** A screenshot from the prototype Voyant Notebooks interface. This shows styled documentation, code blocks and results blocks.

From a programming perspective, the real strength of Voyant Notebooks is that it not only allows all of the operations made possible by the core Javascript language, but also adds convenience methods and interface functionality from Voyant Tools (such as embedding a Cirrus visualization).

Given that Voyant Notebooks is web-based, the intent is to make it as easy as possible for users to find, share, rate, comment and create variations of notebooks. Each notebook will have a unique and persistent

URL that allows a user to bookmark and distribute their work. Popular notebooks will be showcased in the hope they provide useful or exemplary examples of what is possible within Voyant Notebooks—the site will have its own social ecology. Above all, notebooks offer a form for sharing text analysis experiments that can both explain an insight and allow someone to recapitulate an experiment. This has potential for teaching students to think and explain what they are trying to do.

## Text Analysis Tools and Resources

**CATM** or **Computer Aided Textual Markup & Analysis** (http://www. catma.de/) is a client-side tool developed by Jan-Christoph Meister. It lets you markup a text and use the markup in analysis, which encourages very close reading and interpretation.

**DiRT** or **Digital Research Tools Wiki** (https://digitalresearchtools.pbworks. com) is a wiki with links relevant for digital research, maintained by Lisa Spiro. A section of the wiki is devoted to "Text Analysis Tools," which includes links to many of the tools available.

*Literary and Linguistic Computing* (http://llc.oxfordjournals.org) is the journal of a number of digital humanities associations and published by Oxford University Press. A special issue on text analysis was published in 2003 (volume 8, no. 2), but there are articles on the subject in other issues.

**TACT** or **Text Analysis Computing Tools** (http://projects.chass.utoronto. ca/tact/) is a DOS-based text analysis and retrieval system developed at the University of Toronto by John Bradley and Ian Lancashire. **TACTweb** (http://tactweb.humanities.mcmaster.ca/) is a version of TACT that runs on the web.

**Text Analysis Developers Alliance** or **TADA** (http://tada.mcmaster.ca) runs a wiki full of resources and links relevant to text analysis. As a wiki it has some rough parts, but you can obtain a user account and edit it to suit your teaching purposes.

**TAPoR** or the **Text Analysis Portal for Research** (http://portal.tapor.ca/) is an advanced portal for text analysis tools that has links to web based tools and other resources.

**TAPoR Recipes** (http://tada.mcmaster.ca/Main/TaporRecipes) are the Recipes discussed in this chapter, which can be adapted to many tools and help students understand how they might use computing to tackle interpretative tasks.

**TAPoRware Tools** (http://taporware.ualberta.ca) are a set of "primitive" tools that can be used with smaller texts on the web. These tools emphasize individual processes, as opposed to the interactive reading philosophy of Voyant.

**TextSTAT** (http://www.niederlandistik.fu-berlin.de/textstat/software-en.html) is a simple text analysis tool.

**TokenX** (http://tokenx.unl.edu) is a web-based tool developed by Brian Pytlik Zillig that presents different views of a text. It has sample texts and can take XML texts.

**Using TACT with Electronic Texts** is a book by Ian Lancashire in collaboration with John Bradley, Willard McCarty, Michael Stairs and T. R. Wooldridge, originally published in 1996 by the MLA and now freely available in PDF (http://www.mla.org/store/CID7/PID236). The book has chapters that serve as a manual for **TACT**, as well as chapters that can serve as a general discussion of text analysis or examples of analysis at work.

**Voyant Tools** (http://www.voyant-tools.org/) is a web-based tool that can handle large texts, developed by the authors Stéfan Sinclair and Geoffrey Rockwell.

**Wordle** (http://wordle.net/) is a tool for generating word clouds developed by IBM Many Eyes.

# 11. Pedagogical Principles of Digital Historiography

*Joshua Sternfeld*

"What is metadata?" The question was raised by a student in my graduate seminar, History, Media and Technology. The course was open to both history and information studies graduate students, and this query came from a history student with no background in archival or information theory. It halted my rapid introduction to the ten-week course during which I had been rattling off terms such as "Dublin Core," "context," "historiography," "digital archive" and "preservation." Instead, we launched into an impromptu discussion about metadata that touched upon areas beyond its basic definition and utility. The information studies students discussed ways in which metadata influences search and discoverability, while the history students shared their own experiences in archives that revealed a fresh perspective on user access and research behavior.

The question and ensuing discussion reflect the pedagogical challenge for digital history, specifically how to accommodate its interdisciplinarity. Scholars and practitioners must familiarize themselves with new terminology, theories, practices and disciplines. The field extends beyond historians to include archivists, librarians, information specialists, computer scientists, engineers, scientists and linguists. Until now, pedagogical efforts have focused on advancing digital literacy—understood here as skills such as web design, database building, web blogging and other similar activities—within a history curriculum context. Digital literacy, however, marks just the starting point for higher order skills necessary in the production and use of innovative history works. Digital history has the capacity to reshape our conception of History, to generate new lines of inquiry, challenge entrenched theories using vast sets of data and materials, or draw comparisons that span wide geographic and chronological landscapes. In short, digital history holds the potential to raise complex questions of representation, epistemology and narrative.

Given its collaborative nature, digital history requires a common language and set of theoretical principles that will allow disparate groups to talk effectively with one another. This chapter discusses the conceptualization, implementation and anecdotal assessment of an original graduate-level course taught twice at the University of California, Los Angeles (UCLA), from 2008–2009 titled History, Media and Technology.[1] The course was listed jointly with the UCLA History and Graduate School of Education and Information Studies programs, and open to other programs as well, including the Moving Image Archive Studies program. It was designed to address the following question: How do we develop a theoretical and methodological framework to evaluate effectively and comprehensively digital historical works? The solution demanded a theory capable of handling multiple media formats, technical processes and historical content. That theory is called *digital historiography*, which is defined as the "interdisciplinary study of the interaction of digital technology with historical practice."[2]

The History, Media and Technology course represents the pedagogical manifestation of digital historiography. The first section of this chapter will discuss how digital historiography was expressed in the structure and pedagogical approach to the course. Three principles of digital historiography guided its conceptualization:

1.    Digital history works are *representations*, the product of subjective decisions that humanists characterize as interpretation.

2.    Digital historical representations include both academic works, as well as non-academic productions that traverse media genres and audience groups; their unifying trait is their use of historical evidence.

The thoughts and ideas expressed in this paper are entirely my own and do not reflect those of the U.S. National Endowment for the Humanities or any other federal agency.

1    I would like to note that my course was taught just prior to the establishment of the UCLA Digital Humanities undergraduate minor and graduate certificate by the Center for Digital Humanities. The ongoing and tireless work to develop this program, led by Todd Presner, Johanna Drucker, Diane Favro, Janice Reiff, Chris Johanson, Lisa Snyder, and others has been tremendous. Had it been in place, I am sure I would have adjusted my course to follow programmatic requirements. I am grateful for the many informal, yet enlightening discussions that we had over the years.

2    For a complete definition of "digital historiography," see Joshua Sternfeld, "Archival Theory and Digital Historiography: Selection, Search, and Metadata as Archival Processes for Assessing Historical Contextualization," *The American Archivist* 74 (2011): 544–75.

3. Regardless of a representation's scholarly or non-scholarly intent, evaluation requires a working grasp of relevant historiographical knowledge.

The next section will discuss the execution of the course, including a discussion of the course syllabus, readings, assignments and examples of exemplary student work. The overall course objective was for students to learn how to analyze contemporary historical representations including documentary film, educational websites, online museum exhibitions, graphic novels, and databases. Select secondary readings guided students to consider how historiographical, informational, technical and media elements did or did not coalesce to communicate a coherent, logically sound and engaging representation. Two periods—the Holocaust and the Cold War—framed the selection and discussion of historical representations.

The concluding section will explore briefly how to apply digital historiographical principles developed in History, Media and Technology in three areas: history and information studies graduate curriculum; undergraduate history curriculum, including courses designed to teach practical skills creating digital history; and, trans-disciplinary academic programs. In all three areas, we find opportunities to merge traditional, established theories and practices with new media studies and the digital humanities. It is my hope that the ideas sketched here will spark more programmatic, cross-disciplinary dialogue at all academic and administrative levels.

# Pedagogical Principles

Digital history has spurred an explosion of innovative work. As humanities scholars interact with larger datasets, construct complex relational databases and conduct research across digital collections and archives, they must apply standards and best practices to ensure the reliability of their analysis. Similarly, archivists, librarians, museum curators, and information specialists employ technology that has expanded and reshaped access to cultural heritage content. The creation of metadata schema, digital interfaces, and the aggregation of materials that span virtual and physical repositories affects historical context in new and sometimes unexpected ways. Digital history pedagogy, thus, should provide students with the methodological means to interrogate digital historical works, build complex questions and arguments and evaluate scholarship.

The following are a preliminary set of pedagogical principles that apply to digital historiography at all educational levels. First, digital historiography can direct students to approach digital historical works critically, to perceive them as the product of a series of design, technical and content decisions. This perhaps may be the most difficult realization for students to make. Consider the difficulty educators face trying to teach students not to accept textbooks on face value, and then consider what it would take to teach students to do the same for a database or a three-dimensional virtual reconstruction. Digital historiography challenges students to question the aura of objectivity that surrounds digital works. Students must recognize that every decision—from formal design elements to the selection of historical information—also marks an act of interpretation. Once they become aware of this, they can begin to analyze digital works for their subjectivity, just as they would primary and secondary historical texts. In short, digital historiography helps students become aware of digital historical works as *representations*.

This brings us to the second principle, specifically how to define digital historical representations. Educators are welcome to adapt their definition of a digital historical representation according to the parameters of their course. With History, Media and Technology, I took an inclusive approach that included representations from all media types, which intentionally co-mingled scholarly with non-scholarly works. Digital and new media have diversified and fragmented our reception of non-textual historical information. What began with film and television documentaries has now expanded to include digital libraries, online collections, graphic novels, videogames, blogs, social media and geospatial visualizations. Trying to examine any one of these genres in isolation would be counterproductive, as many of them have borrowed traits from one another. For example, three-dimensional reconstructions appropriate navigational mechanisms from videogames, digital collections resemble documentaries and museum exhibits, while documentaries employ digital visualizations in dramatizing the past. Digital historiography encourages a flexible approach to reviewing a representation's properties, which in the process can expose the epistemological boundaries between fictional and non-fictional narrative constructs. The media format determines the analytical approach. In History, Media and Technology, students discover that they may need to apply a combination of theoretical approaches including film, media, information, archival or game theory. Digital historiography, therefore, lays emphasis on selecting the methodological approaches most appropriate to discuss the representation.

Critics of this approach may wonder whether popular culture formats such as graphic novels or videogames do in fact convey historical information worthy of analysis. The fact of the matter is that these genres are appropriating in greater degrees actual historical evidence. Whether we like it or not, they are becoming the *de facto* sites for shaping historical perception for an entire generation. For example, videogames such as *Assassin's Creed* or *Call of Duty 4* have included professional historians in their production team in an attempt to enhance historical realism. Many young adults likely spend more free time playing these games than reading a high school history textbook, which means that they are actively internalizing the past through these new media in ways that we perhaps do not yet fully recognize or understand. The popular graphic novel *Maus*, one of the representations covered in History, Media and Technology, synthesizes oral history interviews conducted between the author, Art Spiegelman, and his father, a Holocaust survivor, with a distinct visual aesthetic.[3] History and English teachers now teach *Maus* in high school classrooms. In History, Media and Technology, I encouraged students to acknowledge the fragmentation of historical reception through new media, with an objective to discern ways in which these genres represent—and at times distort—historical information.

Recognizing a representation's enhancement or distortion of historical information brings us to the third and perhaps most important principle: Analysis of a digital historical representation requires working historiographic knowledge. Historiography is understood in this context as the culmination of knowledge for any given historical subject, whether we are considering a specific geographic region (e.g. East Asian history), event (e.g. the U.S. Civil War), time period (e.g. the Industrial Revolution), or figure (e.g. Albert Einstein). Historiography provides the means to conduct logical inquiry and construct coherent narratives. It also recognizes that historical knowledge is not absolute, but always under revision through the application of new theories, practices and methodologies.

---

3   Art Spiegelman, *Maus: A Survivor's Tale,* vol. 1, "My Father Bleeds History" (New York: Pantheon Books, 1986), and *Maus: A Survivor's Tale,* vol. 2, "And Here My Troubles Began" (New York: Pantheon Books, 1991).

Of course, this principle is not unique to digital historiography, but it may be harder to delineate than with traditional textual media. In the case of a scholarly monograph, we train students to identify the thesis, scour footnotes to compare how authors use evidence, deconstruct a table of contents to understand the work's overall argumentative structure and ultimately place the work within the context of other relevant scholarship. Digital historical representations often fail to provide us with the same structural conveniences. They may lack sufficient documentation, references may be poorly cited, and quite often, one may be challenged to locate a "thesis statement." This should not deter us from placing the representation within a historiographical context; rather, it may require constructing context based upon historical perceptions, assumptions, and beliefs that reside outside scholarly discourse.

These three principles constitute a working framework with which to teach digital history. Digital and new media works, like their analog counterparts, are representations that communicate a subjective interpretation of the past. We should, therefore, not overlook the fact that digital historiography is very much a product of the humanities, with a capacity to raise difficult epistemological questions that often do not have a definitive answer. Teaching digital historiography, therefore, should mirror the strengths of the humanities by promoting ongoing dialogue among peers, examining an issue from different perspectives, considering wider socio-cultural contexts and engaging in broadly defined scholarly discourse.

## History, Media and Technology

The above principles of digital historiography guided the development of the graduate seminar. The objective was not to have students construct new works of digital history (this would be addressed in a follow-up course called Design of a History Website), but to discuss issues of historical representation through evaluation of available resources. I modeled History, Media and Technology after a traditional history reading seminar that included weekly readings, in-class open-ended discussion, and a final research paper that analyzed a digital historical representation of the student's choosing. A copy of the original Fall 2008 syllabus is included as an appendix to this chapter (Appendix A).

The challenge was to accommodate the different disciplinary backgrounds of the students. One solution was to limit the historical thematic material, a decision that carried with it some advantages. First, it avoided a situation in which the class analyzed a Civil War website one week and a classics database the next. Selecting a "best of" collection of digital works would have highlighted the formal merits of each work, but it would also have prevented students from connecting with the broader historiographic issues at play. Second, it added a cumulative dimension to the course readings. Information studies students, many of whom had not taken a graduate-level history course, became conversant in historiography after spending several weeks on a single topic. Conversely, history students picked up terminology and concepts related to archival, film and new media theory that broadened their perspective of historical representation.

All representations considered in the class were narrowed to two historical periods, the Holocaust and the Cold War. It should be noted that one could adapt the framework for this course to any historical period or geographic region that possesses an ample body of digital or new media work. For my course, I selected Holocaust and Cold War secondary literature that addressed meta-historiographical areas. Since the public exchange between Saul Friedländer and Martin Broszat in the late 1980s over the historicization of National Socialism, Holocaust studies has interrogated the limits of historical epistemology. Recent scholarship has addressed issues of representation, narrative, trauma and experience through a variety of media, in particular film and documentary, which fed nicely into the objectives of the course.[4] Historians, of course, spend entire semesters teaching the intricacies of Holocaust historiography. For the purpose of this course, the modest goal was to convey in a matter of a few weeks that the Holocaust has engendered numerous models

---

4   The Broszat-Friedländer exchange appeared in Martin Broszat and Saul Friedländer, "A Controversy About the Historicization of National Socialism," *New German Critique* 44 (1988): 85–126. As mentioned, one could generate an extensive bibliography on the topic of Holocaust representation in scholarship and the media. Besides the readings listed in the syllabus, the following works provide a useful starting point: Saul Friedländer, ed., *Probing the Limits of Representation: Nazism and the "Final Solution"* (Cambridge: Harvard University Press, 1992); "Historical Representation and Historical Truth," the special Theme Issue of the journal *History and Theory* 48, no. 2 (2009) (in particular essays by Wulf Kansteiner, "Success, Truth, and Modernism in Holocaust Historiography: Reading Saul Friedländer Thirty-Five Years After the Publication of Metahistory": 25–53, Judith Keilbach, "Photographs, Symbolic Images, and the Holocaust: On the (Im) Possibility of Depicting Historical Truth": 54–76, Claudio Fogu, "Digitalizing Historical Consciousness": 103–21, and Christoph Classen, "Balanced Truth: Steven Spielberg's *Schindler's List* Among History, Memory, and Popular Culture": 77–102); and Daniel Levy and Natan Sznaider, *The Holocaust and Memory in the Global Age*, trans. Assenka Oksiloff (Philadelphia: Temple University Press, 2006), among many others.

of explanation, narrative techniques and theories about memory and historical experience.

Similarly, the Cold War was selected both for its chronological proximity to the Holocaust, and for the fact that within its era we see the blossoming or spawning of a host of media formats. One week was spent on CNN's documentary series *The Cold War* (1998), which raised interesting questions about how to use archival news footage as evidence. The Cold War, unlike some earlier historical periods, arguably marks an occasion where too much, as opposed to too little, archival— and especially multimedia—evidence is available.

Each week, students analyzed one digital or new media historical representation, accompanied by supplemental academic readings. Selecting a set of representations involved a delicate balance that considered a representation's media format, historical coverage, intended audience and availability of secondary literature. Ideally, the reading set provided students with some historiographical background, media-specific theory and if available, expert analysis of the representation itself. The key to a successful pairing of a representation and supplemental readings depended on drawing connections between broader historiographic issues or problems, as expressed by the scope of the representation's content, with the representation's formal and design properties. At first, most students did not discover a clear correlation. For many, a search interface seemed like nothing more than a search interface. It was my responsibility to lead a guided discussion that considered how a search interface impacts user experience and consequently the user's interaction with historical information. Once students discovered that a search interface could indeed guide the user towards forming conclusions from the representation's content, they could hold up those conclusions against other historiographic perspectives of the topic. Students ultimately considered whether a representation reaffirmed established historiographic theories, raised possible new conclusions worthy of further investigation or perhaps reinforced long discredited postulations.

To give a couple of examples of course readings and assignments, Week Four showcased Claude Lanzmann's documentary *Shoah* (1985). This film, considered one of the most acclaimed works about the Holocaust, has inspired a rich body of academic work by historians, intellectuals and film scholars that is perfect for seminar discussion. For example, *Shoah* raises interesting questions about archival and historical representation. The film's deliberate exclusion of period photographs and reliance on extended shots of the contemporary landscape, coupled with eyewitness testimony, challenged preconceptions of archival evidence and its use in documenting historical events.

A selection of essays from an anthology about the film directed students to consider these issues.[5] Well-known intellectuals, including Elie Wiesel, Dominick LaCapra and Simone de Beauvoir, contributed essays. An essay by Leon Wieseltier discusses how the absence of archival video or photographic evidence heightens the experience of remembering.[6] He proposes that the term "documentary" insufficiently describes the film and that we should instead call it a "documemory," which triggered class discussion about the work's narrative form.[7] Other essays discuss the film's spatialization of the Holocaust as expressed through the long shots of camp locations. Even though Lanzmann may not have relied upon sophisticated digital geospatial visualizations, the discussion of the *sites* of the Holocaust complemented later discussions in the course. Students returned week after week to issues such as geographic representation that traversed traditional media formats (that is, film and documentary) and digital formats (such as GIS applications).

*Shoah* and the questions it raised about archival evidence, memory and representation transitioned well into the following week's examination of digital exhibits produced by the U.S. Holocaust Memorial Museum. The background reading assignment, *Preserving Memory: The Struggle to Create America's Holocaust Museum* by Edward T. Linenthal,[8] provides a history of the physical museum from its contentious founding to the development of its permanent exhibit. This work, coupled with additional articles, considered the historiographic issue of the memorialization— and consequently politicization—of the Holocaust. Linenthal's work discusses the shifting place of the Holocaust in American memory, and how political forces expanded the Museum's mission from documenting the Holocaust to its broader mission of documenting genocide.

---

5  Stuart Liebman, ed., *Claude Lanzmann's Shoah: Key Essays* (Oxford: Oxford University Press, 2007).

6  Leon Wieseltier, "Shoah," in *Claude Lanzmann's Shoah: Key Essays*, ed. Stuart Liebman (Oxford: Oxford University Press, 2007), 89–93.

7  Wieseltier, "Shoah," 92.

8  Edward T. Linenthal, *Preserving Memory: The Struggle to Create America's Holocaust Museum* (New York: Viking, 1995).

The Week Five assignment asked students to consider the issues associated with the brick and mortar museum in the context of online exhibitions produced by the museum (http://www.ushmm.org/museum/ exhibit/online/). Several students selected the exhibit "Auschwitz through the lens of the SS: Photos of Nazi leadership at the camp," which featured an individual officer's photo album that documented the everyday and leisure activities of the SS at Auschwitz. Students who chose this exhibit reflected upon the museum's selection of the photo album from amidst its vast photograph and artifact holdings. Further, the site presents a digital facsimile of the physical photo album, which led students to explore concepts of evidential authenticity and provenance.

The seminar's final project mirrored the weekly reading and discussion assignments. Students selected a digital or new media historical representation related to the Holocaust or Cold War and composed a twenty-page research paper evaluating that work. The only limitation was that the representation needed to demonstrate the use of archival historical evidence, which excluded many filmic and literary works of historical fiction. The decision here was that works of pure fiction, while perhaps tapping into an historical *Zeitgeist*, strayed too far from the course objective to analyze the interaction between historical evidence and media formats. That being said, countless works of fictional or popular genres openly use historical evidence to great effect, which made them eligible for analysis. One student convincingly petitioned to analyze a videogame that took place during the height of the Cold War in the 1960s because of its use of archival video news footage of John F. Kennedy and Nikita Khrushchev in its cut scenes. Another student working towards a master's in children's librarianship selected a children's book that merges autobiographical testimony with illustrative depictions of historic newsworthy events. One of the most rewarding aspects of teaching the course was to see the variety of final projects that included documentaries, geospatial visualizations, virtual museum exhibitions, children's literature, board games, and film. Indeed, some of these examples did not explicitly incorporate digital technology, but students nonetheless found it useful to borrow concepts and theories derived from new media studies to discuss their representation.

Through a series of formative assignments that culminated with the final paper, students also developed important research and writing skills. For the preliminary assignment (listed in the syllabus as Assignment #1), students were required to present their representation by Week Three in a written proposal that defended their selection and indicated any preliminary research that they may have conducted. Besides getting students to map out their project early in the semester, this assignment also provided me an opportunity to accept or amend their selection. For a follow-up assignment (Assignment #3), students submitted an annotated bibliography, with strict requirements for source types. The syllabus explained that students "are expected to become fluent in three [...] areas: [their] historical representation, the specific historical period or question that it addresses and the design or form elements that contribute to the representation's composition (for example, a [...] documentary filmmaking technique or a technology or program such as Google Earth)." The students' bibliographies needed to include a minimum of four historiographic works and four works associated with relevant media, technology or information theory. This assignment enabled me to assess the progress of each student's research. For example, I could identify and redirect students who initially cited weak secondary historical literature. If a student selected a representation about the Auschwitz camp experience but opted to use only general surveys of the Holocaust, then I would recommend more relevant works about Auschwitz for them to evaluate and consider integrating into their analysis. Furthermore, the bibliography assignment allowed students to apply evaluative skills acquired through the course to defend their selections. Students quickly discovered that the challenge was not to reach the minimum number of sources, but to apply self-imposed criteria to limit an overabundance of available sources.

Successful papers demonstrated a close analysis of the work at both the historiographic and representational levels. Two standout papers by students in the information studies master's program, Steven Bingo and Kristen Chamberland, featured, by coincidence, the same online site, *Surviving Auschwitz: Five Personal Journeys* (http://dornsife.usc.edu/vhi/survivingauschwitz/), produced by the Survivors of the Shoah Visual History Foundation (now the USC Shoah Foundation Institute for Visual History and Education) in 2005.[9] *Surviving Auschwitz*, according to the site, "follows the lives of five Holocaust survivors before, during and after their deportation to Auschwitz and other concentration camps." The site presents these five journeys—two by men and three by women that span multiple continents—using various representational formats and types

---

9    I would like to thank Steven Bingo and Kristen Chamberland for granting me permission to discuss and cite passages from their student work.

of historical evidence, including video oral testimony, interactive digital maps, text and photographs.

Although Steven and Kristen arrived at similar overall conclusions, they employed entirely different analytic approaches. Steven focused on the geospatial dimension of the site by analyzing the interactive map as a representation of Jewish diaspora. In his work titled "Exploring Diaspora in *Surviving Auschwitz*," he probed the site's decision to select five survivor testimonies that terminated on five different continents, concluding that the site produced a problematic homogenization of the survivor experience. Drawing upon scholarly literature on 20th-century Jewish diaspora, he writes,

> Jewish communities in Britain and Australia have a unique internal dynamic and relationship with the broader national population. Unfortunately, the exhibit does little to test these observations by paying little attention to comparative experiences of diaspora according to differences in local Jewish communities.

Steven's research also coincided with scholarly concerns that geospatial visualizations sometimes have trouble representing change over time. He acutely observed, for example, that the 1938 political map underlying the survivors' journeys remains static as each journey unfolds over several decades, which belies significant geopolitical changes that likely affected their travel.

Similarly, Kristen, in her paper "Seeking Gendered Meaning in Holocaust Testimony: A Look at the *Surviving Auschwitz* Online Exhibition," identified the site's homogenizing effect on the survivors' narratives, but she employed an altogether different analytic framework. She applied a feminist critique to the site's use of oral testimony, and questioned whether the site contributed to a suppressing of gender-specific camp experiences. Like Steven, she concluded that the site's creators "struggled" to fit the testimonies into a coherent space-time framework. The video editing, which segments each survivor's testimony into bite-size anecdotes, de-contextualizes their experience and therefore presents a predominantly gender-neutral survivor story. She wrote:

> *Surviving Auschwitz* is not intended to be an all-inclusive in-depth resource for mature scholars. It is an online tool for high school students, built in the way lesson plans are built, with a simple objective that is easy to convey and digest. But this explanation also says something interesting about how easy it is to neglect gendered experiences, either intentionally or unintentionally. If "feminine" experiences are still considered deviations from the norm, then they will continue to be easily overlooked or ignored for the sake of universality.

Kristen was not only interested in the oral history methods applied in the video testimony, but also how the testimony was edited and presented on the web. The merging of the testimony with "points on a map," she argued, creates a "disjointed," "erratic" sense of narrative. She concluded that, "while it is possible to trace the [interview] subject's journey geographically, it is difficult to match it truly to the narrative."

Both papers perceptively and persuasively critiqued the fragmented narrative conveyed in *Surviving Auschwitz* by exploring the interplay of historiographic, media and digital components. Through their probing of this intersection, they explained the site's historical contextual deficiencies. Their selection of contested historiographic topics—Holocaust oral history testimony and Jewish diaspora—allowed both studies to examine how audiences interact with new media representations. What set the two papers apart was how the authors qualified their conclusions according to the site's educational objective. *Surviving Auschwitz* was created for a high school audience. Nonetheless, Steven and Kristen argued, the creators have a responsibility to consider the consequences of how they contextualize the survivors' narratives, or they run the risk of perpetuating one-dimensional, hackneyed and potentially distorting narratives.

## Applying Digital Historiography Principles to Curriculum and Programmatic Development

History, Media and Technology was conceived and executed as an experiment in applying digital historiography in the classroom. My goal was never to develop a course that could be replicated week-for-week; rather, it was to develop a pedagogical framework that could be adapted for a variety of educational settings. If nothing else, digital historiography embodies the spirit of the digital humanities, that is, its adaptability and willingness to experiment. No one can anticipate precisely the latest research tool or representational mode that will ignite a wave of research. Nonetheless, digital historiography reminds us that, no matter how experimental or radical a method may appear, it must nevertheless satisfy evolving epistemological standards and expectations.

I will conclude with a brief overview of how to consider applying the principles of digital historiography more broadly in three areas: graduate history and information studies curriculum, undergraduate history curriculum and trans-disciplinary academic programs. The following remarks are meant to serve not as a fixed guide but as a blueprint for fostering additional interdisciplinary discussion. Please note that my remarks shift back and forth between an ideal vision of digital history pedagogy and the current reality. I hope that digital history will one day become integrated with traditional curriculum to the point that the "digital" qualifier simply disappears. The reality is that we must first train a new cohort of educators at all levels to be equally proficient in both digital technologies and history.

## Graduate Curriculum

As mentioned earlier, the principles developed through History, Media and Technology could apply to any historical period or topic. It could also apply to information, library science and archival programs. The main objective would be the same regardless of the subject matter: to pair historiographical with information and media-related principles contingent to a given representation in order to analyze the representation's contextualization. In the future, courses may shift away from generic titles such as History, Media and Technology towards subject-specific titles. For example, History, Media, and Technology might be called Holocaust Studies in Contemporary Media, or simply Cold War Studies.

Digital history pedagogy at the primary and undergraduate levels will never take off unless we consider applying digital historiography principles at the graduate level. We must first train a cohort of future history educators to be conversant in both historical and digital theory and practice. Educators must develop the language and skills with which to assess student progress in non-traditional forms of historical work, including documentaries, websites or databases. Although more historians are adopting new media technologies in their daily practices,[10] many still find it difficult to explain to students why a particular website is inappropriate to cite in a paper or project, or how to recognize subjectivity in a digital work.

---

10  For a recent study on the extent to which the historical profession has adopted new media technologies, see Robert B. Townsend, "How Is New Media Reshaping the Work of Historians?" *Perspectives on History* 48, no. 8 (2010): 36–39, also available on *Perspectives on History Online*, November 1, 2010, http://www.historians.org/perspectives/issues/2010/1011/1011pro2.cfm.

Advanced digital historical analysis can only move forward with sufficient resources, support, and access to historical data. Digital access to the historical record is dependent upon numerous factors ranging from digitization costs to copyright permissions that influence the capacity to conduct research. Consequently, the state of access influences the computational work that can be conducted using humanities collections. Ideally, history graduate curriculum will evolve so that historical inquiry drives technological developments, rather than the other way around. Currently, many digital history projects are conceived and executed based on showcasing the potential of a digital tool or methodology. In these cases the historical question that should be the driving force of the work is often overlooked.

Similarly, as information programs move increasingly towards professionalization, students are discovering that they are frequently at a disadvantage without some fluency in humanities methodology and vocabulary. Construction of digital information systems, either in a library, archive or museum setting requires deep subject knowledge in order to preserve or create contextual layers. While obtaining advanced subject knowledge in a graduate program may prove too impracticable, we can nonetheless train students in basic historical practices and terminology.

The question, however, is who would teach such a course or set of courses now? The number of instructors conversant in historical, new media and information theory remains extremely limited. For the moment, courses might best function with co-instructors: one from the history department, and the other from an outside department or program. Such collaboration may help persuade departments reluctant to support a full digital program to at least support cross-departmental partnerships that could lead to more concerted curriculum development.

## Undergraduate History Curriculum

The reality and the ideal for integrating digital methods in undergraduate curriculum are already merging as more instructors abandon the essay format. Students produce YouTube mashups that combine commentary with multimedia archival footage, write Wikipedia articles, work on a local history web project or participate in generating data for an instructor's research study, all of which are exciting and potentially rewarding endeavors. Digital historiography teaches students to approach every digital historical artifact or work of scholarship critically, not unlike current history curriculum that deals primarily with textual materials. The key to develop effective curriculum is not to discard previous methods, but to consider ways of translating the most successful elements of those methods with available technologies. While students already have developed habits to consult digital media for information, we must do a better job at guiding them to use the tools responsibly, including how to conduct online searches, retrieve items from a digital library, add persuasive contextualization to their multimedia presentations and evaluate both primary and secondary born-digital resources.

Already we find a number of digital history courses that teach practical skills, such as best practices for developing a blog or for constructing a history website. Such curriculum prioritizes a proactive approach to *doing* history rather than a passive approach to consuming it, and for this reason alone, they serve as valuable pedagogical models.[11] Nonetheless, in the process of having students obtain hands-on experience working with historical materials, we should not overlook the opportunity for them to apply equally important critical thinking and research skills such as deep reading, higher order analysis and ongoing engagement with historical scholarship.

## Academic Programming

History, Media and Technology was most successful in fostering dynamic weekly discussions that tackled complex interdisciplinary theoretical issues. In spite of its modest success, the course was not without its setbacks. The idealism behind the course's inception conflicted with the unavoidable cold reality of the UCLA quarter system. Ten weeks was simply not enough time to cover three disciplinary areas with any degree of comprehensiveness.[12]

---

11  Two examples among several well-crafted courses that teach Digital History practices are Jeffrey McClurken's Adventures in Digital History (http://dh2010.umwblogs.org/) at the University of Mary Washington, which is one of several pioneering courses McClurken has developed, and Trevor Owen's History in the Digital Age (http://www.dighist.org/) taught at American University.

12  In their course evaluation, many students expressed a wish that more time had been spent on examining visual and digital representation, pointing out that the readings in Weeks 9 and 10 would have been more useful had they been assigned earlier in the semester. If given the luxury of additional weeks, as well as the benefit of hindsight and the publication of many wonderful new works of scholarship since the completion of the course, the following works would have been considered (in no particular order of preference): David J. Bodenhamer, John Corrigan, and Trevor M. Harris, *The Spatial Humanities: GIS and the Future of Humanities Scholarship* (Bloomington: Indiana University Press, 2010); Fiona Cameron and Sarah Kenderdine, ed., *Theorizing Digital Cultural*

The struggle to squeeze as much information into every reading and assignment proved that the cultivation of digital historiography must occur not through a single course, but at the programmatic level. At least for the short-term future, this will require a concerted effort to build trans-disciplinary relationships between history, information and media programs.

There are promising signs that programs are already moving in this direction. After an investigative period, New York University recently unveiled its revamped Archives and Public History program (described in detail in another chapter in this collection).[13] As its homepage proclaims, "the program emphasizes a solid grounding in historical scholarship, intense engagement with new media technologies, and close involvement with New York's extraordinary archival and public history institutions." A glance at their course offerings affirms the commitment to teaching archival theory alongside digital history practices with courses such as Advanced Archival Description and Creating Digital History. In short, we can see digital historiography principles inscribed at the programmatic level.

## Conclusion

The principles of digital historiography outlined in this chapter—including recognizing that all digital and new media histories are *representations*, infusing well-grounded historiography into the evaluation of representations and maintaining a constant eye on the use (or lack) of historical evidence in representations—should remind us of the need for digital history to communicate broader humanistic significance. We have always insisted that history teaching should instill students with a critical, inquisitive eye towards the past. The adoption of new technologies should not diminish this spirit of inquiry, but rather transform and enhance it.

A rigorous, digitally oriented pedagogical framework can have positive repercussions at all levels of historical learning and production from

---

Heritage: A Critical Discourse (Cambridge: MIT Press, 2007); Victoria Vesna, ed., *Database Aesthetics: Art in the Age of Information Overflow* (Minneapolis: University of Minnesota Press, 2007); Matthew G. Kirschenbaum, *Mechanisms: New Media and the Forensic Imagination* (Cambridge: MIT Press, 2008); Martin Hand, *Making Digital Cultures: Access, Interactivity, and Authenticity* (Burlington: Ashgate, 2008); Alan Liu, *Local Transcendence: Essays on Postmodern Historicism and the Database* (Chicago: University of Chicago Press, 2008); Matthew K. Gold, ed., *Debates in the Digital Humanities* (Minneapolis: University of Minnesota Press, 2012).

13  See the chapter on "Teaching Digital Skills in an Archives and Public History Curriculum" by Peter J. Wosh, Cathy Moran Hajo and Esther Katz, in this volume.

professional historians to students in the classroom. Scholars require professional standards in tenure review and publishing. Graduate students interested in pursuing digital-reliant research seek assurances that their work will receive appropriate accreditation by their departments and the wider academic community. Students at the undergraduate level and below require guidance in harnessing the power of digital technology to research, compose and peer review their work. In all of these scenarios, applying a few simple principles of digital historiography can ensure the integrity of historical work while at the same time accommodate diverse interdisciplinary objectives.

As implied in my brief discussion of the many hurdles that academic programs and departments face with regards to digital historical pedagogy, the need for collaboration is an unavoidable reality. Of course, in areas such as digital humanities research and tool development, collaboration has been deservedly embraced as a new model for academic productivity. This should be no different in the educational realm. Collaboration among instructors and students at the course, departmental or programmatic levels will breed the kind of cross-disciplinary dialogue that is necessary for expanding the intellectual scope of digital historiography. Recalling the impromptu discussion about metadata referenced at the opening of this chapter, the moments of terminological and theoretical uncertainty are precisely the points that breed the most rewarding knowledge. They require us all to reflect on our own disciplinary and technical training, to reassess accepted definitions and ultimately to inscribe new boundaries or draw commonalities that slowly build a sound theoretical and practical foundation.

# Appendix A: Fall 2008 Syllabus

# IS 289–1: History, Media and Technology

## Course Description

Welcome to History, Media and Technology! In this course we will explore the intersection of new media and technology — which can include documentaries, virtual exhibitions and archives, open source encyclopedias, television, GIS technologies, videogaming and much more — with contemporary historical representation. Scholars are currently struggling to devise a working set of evaluative criteria for these representations that still accounts for traditional historiographic methodology. Too often the rush to incorporate new technology has the detrimental effect of overshadowing historical content, which may jeopardize the progress of scholarship and education.

Rather than jump from one historical period to another, the core of this course will focus on modern 20th-century history, in particular, the Holocaust and the Cold War. Both periods have become points of contention in historical representation, not only for their sensitive subject matter, but also for the unprecedented availability of archival source materials such as oral testimonies, video and official records. The access (and at times critical restrictions) to this wealth of materials further complicates historical reconstruction.

This seminar will thus explore the intersection of scholastic, public and digital histories as they appear in contemporary society. It will pay close attention to applying basic historiographic principles to the evaluation of history-based media and new information technologies, considering both their scholarship and pedagogical value.

### Course Requirements

This is a discussion-based seminar, and as such, participation is critical for its success. I have selected a set of readings that should provide a working understanding of the current historiographic issues and debates; I strongly recommend, however, if you feel you need further background that you come see me and I will suggest further readings.

Class Participation: 20%

This not only includes in-class discussion, but also periodic submissions to our Moodle site according to discussion topics.

Assignments: 30%

The following assignments are intended to guide you through the process of composing a strong final paper, and to avoid drafting the paper at the last possible moment. Although it is not mandatory, I strongly recommend that you visit me during office hours to discuss your topic. This will provide me with an opportunity to approve your project, offer any guidance in sources to obtain and answer any questions you may have.

Assignment #1 (5%): Written proposal (at least 4 full pages), due Week 3 in class. In this paper, you will state the historical representation you wish to analyze, any background materials you have already obtained, questions you would like to explore, as well as possible arguments or conclusions you intend to draw.

Assignment #2 (5%): Critique of U.S. Holocaust Memorial Museum online exhibition (at least 3 full pages), due Week 5 in class. Select one exhibition (there are many to choose from!) and analyze its educational/ informational value in relation to its design elements, similar to the expectations of your final paper.

Assignment #3 (10%): Annotated Bibliography, at least 10 sources, due in class in Week 8. For your final paper you are expected to become fluent in three specific areas: your historical representation, the specific historical period or question that it addresses, and the design or format elements that contribute to the representation's composition (for example, a specific documentary filmmaking technique or a new technology or program such as Google Earth). For each source, please provide a brief summary along with how the particular source will be used to support your thesis argument. Do you agree with the argument(s) presented in the source, or do you plan to refute all or part of it? Sources need not all be full monographs, but may include journal articles, (credible) websites and other secondary *credible* materials—Wikipedia entries will not suffice! Your bibliography should be comprised accordingly:

- At least four secondary sources associated with your historical period. These works should represent the most recent literature on your topic, and cover multiple points of view. For example, if your representation covers the Auschwitz concentration camp, your secondary literature should reflect the historiographic arguments surrounding the camp. A general Holocaust reader in this case will probably not suffice; there are plenty of articles and monographs that delve specifically into all aspects of the camp. I would suggest beginning your search in electronic databases such as JSTOR, which will lead you to additional sources through the articles' footnotes and bibliographies.

- At least four secondary sources associated with your representation's format. If your representation is a documentary film, you may want to explore a particular film or editing technique that is employed by the film. If your film happens to be produced, for example, by CNN, you may want to explore the influence of CNN on communicating historical information. Be creative in your approach to your representation!
- Any sources directly linked to your representation. If there is literature or materials that directly reference your representation, you should include them in your analysis. This may include scholarly secondary literature, as well as news stories, user reviews/ comments or discussions by the authors or creators.

Assignment #4 (10%): Final Presentation, Week 10. This presentation should be no more than 10 minutes in length. The presentation should include a summary of your final paper's thesis argument. You may want show a brief clip or portion of your representation to illustrate your points to the class. Otherwise, the presentation should not be a fancy set of bells and whistles.

**Final Paper: 50%**

The final paper, at least 20 full pages, will be an evaluation of an historical representation of your choice. The representation you select must pertain to either the Holocaust or the Cold War, although this still leaves plenty of room for creativity. For example, your selection will likely cover a sub-period/topic within either period, such as a single battle or event during the Vietnam War or a particular concentration camp from the Holocaust. Please refer to the Paper Guidelines for details on the expectations for the paper. Ultimately, the paper should be an opportunity for you to explore an idea or topic that you find most interesting… and enjoyable!

## Course Materials

Required Books (Available at the Luvalle book store except the course reader)

Geis, Deborah R., ed., *Considering Maus: Approaches to Art Spiegelman's "Survivor's Tale" of the Holocaust.* Tuscaloosa: University of Alabama Press, 2003.

Knowles, Anne Kelly, ed., *Placing History: How Maps, Spatial Data, and GIS Are Changing Historical Scholarship.* Redlands: ESRI Press, 2008.

Linenthal, Edward T. *Preserving Memory: The Struggle to Create America's Holocaust Museum.* New York: Viking, 1995.

Spiegelman, Art. *The Complete Maus: A Survivor's Tale.* New York: Pantheon, 1996.

Stokes, Gale. *The Walls Came Tumbling Down: The Collapse of Communism in Eastern Europe.* New York: Oxford University Press, 1993.

Weissman, Gary. *Fantasies of Witnessing: Postwar Efforts to Experience the Holocaust.* Ithaca: Cornell University Press, 2004.


## Course Reader: Available at Course Reader Material on Westwood Blvd.


# Class Schedule


**Week 1:** Introduction: USHMM Google Earth

**Week 2:** Historical Information Science


### Historical Practice

Boonstra, Onno, Leen Breure, and Peter Doorn. "Past, Present and Future of Historical Information Science." (2004). This may be found online as a pdf.

### Holocaust and Cold War Historiography (Course Reader)

Bauer, Yehuda. *Rethinking the Holocaust*, Chapters 1–2, 1–38. New Haven: Yale University Press, 2001.

Gaddis, John Lewis. "On Starting All over Again: A Naive Approach to the Study of the Cold War." In *Reviewing the Cold War: Approaches, Interpretations and Theory,* edited by Odd Arne Westad, 27–42. London: Frank Cass, 2000.

Ferguson, Yale, and Rey Koslowski. "Culture, International Relations Theory, and Cold War History." *In Reviewing the Cold War: Approaches, Interpretations and Theory,* edited by Odd Arne Westad, 149–79. London: Frank Cass, 2000.

Leffler, Melvyn P. "Bringing It Together: The Parts and the Whole." *In Reviewing the Cold War: Approaches, Interpretations, and Theory,* edited by Odd Arne Westad, 43–63. London: Frank Cass, 2000.

## Week 3: Oral Testimony and the Documentary: Claude Lanzmann's Shoah

Liebman, Stuart, ed., *Claude Lanzmann's Shoah: Key Essays.* Oxford: Oxford University Press, 2007. Selections: 3–50, 113–124, 135–148, 191–230. (Course Reader)

Weissman, Gary. *Fantasies of Witnessing: Postwar Efforts to Experience the Holocaust,* 140–244. Ithaca: Cornell University Press, 2004.

VIEWING: Part I of *Shoah*

Assignment #1 due in class.

## Week 4: Graphic (Nonfiction) Storytelling: Maus: A Survivor's Tale

Geis, Deborah R., ed., *Considering Maus: Approaches to Art Spiegelman's "Survivor's Tale" of the Holocaust.* Tuscaloosa: University of Alabama Press, 2003.

READING: Spiegelman, Art. *The Complete Maus: A Survivor's Tale.* New York: Pantheon, 1996.

## Week 5: Memorializing the Past: The U.S. Holocaust Museum

Linenthal, Edward T. *Preserving Memory: The Struggle to Create America's Holocaust Museum.* New York: Viking, 1995.

VIEWING: http://www.ushmm.org/

Assignment #2 due in class.

**Week 6:** The 21st-Century Museum and Archive: The Wende
Museum

Stokes, Gale. *The Walls Came Tumbling Down: The Collapse of Communism in
Eastern Europe.* New York: Oxford University Press, 1993.

**TRIP**: Wende Museum

**Week 7:** Holiday (We will schedule a make-up session that will
be an opportunity to return to issues, representations,
topics that you would like to discuss).

**Week 8:** Web 2.0 Historical Education: Making the History of
1989 (Articles below are available either in the Course
Reader or online).

Barlow, Jeffrey G. "Historical Research and Electronic Evidence: Problems
and Promises." In *Writing, Teaching and Researching History in the Electronic
Age: Historians and Computers,* edited by Dennis A. Trinkle, 194–223.
Armonk: M. E. Sharpe, 1998.

   Staley, David J. "From Writing to Associative Assemblages: 'History' In
an Electronic Culture." In *Writing, Teaching, and Researching History in the
Electronic Age: Historians and Computers,* edited by Dennis A. Trinkle, 5–13.
Armonk: M. E. Sharpe, 1998.

   Kelly, T. Mills. "Using New Media to Teach East European History."
*Nationalities Papers* 29, no. 3 (2001), http://chnm.gmu.edu/resources/
essays/d/16.

   Rosenzweig, Roy. "Can History Be Open Source? Wikipedia and the
Future of the Past." *The Journal of American History* 93, no. 1 (2006): 117–46.
http://chnm.gmu.edu/resources/essays/d/42.

   Rosenzweig, Roy. "Digital Archives Are a Gift of Wisdom to Be Used
Wisely." *The Chronicle of Higher Education* 51, no. 42 (2005), http://chnm.gmu.
edu/resources/essays/d/32.

   Cohen, Daniel. "The Future of Preserving the Past." *The Journal of Heritage
Stewardship* 2, no. 2 (2005), http://chnm.gmu.edu/resources/essays/d/39.

   VIEWING: *Making the History of 1989.* http://chnm.gmu.edu/1989/.
   Assignment #3 due in class.

**Week 9:** GIS and Geotemporal Reconstructions: The UCLA Experiential Technologies Center

Knowles, Anne Kelly, ed., *Placing History: How Maps, Spatial Data, and GIS Are Changing Historical Scholarship*. Redlands: ESRI Press, 2008.

**TRIP:** UCLA Experiential Technologies Center

**Week 10:** Student Presentations (Assignment #4)

# Final Paper Guidelines

The following is a series of guidelines for composing your final paper. If you have any questions, please don't hesitate to come talk to me.

- You must include a title page that is separate from the final page count of your paper. The title should reflect your paper's thesis argument and it should grab the reader's attention. "Final Paper: IS 289" is unacceptable!
- Your paper should be at least 20 full pages, double-spaced, 1" margins all-around, Times Roman, 12 pt font.
- You should include page numbers in the header.
- Your introduction should grab the reader's attention. There are a number of techniques to do this: you may begin with an anecdote or passage from your representation, or even a single quote. The introductory paragraph(s) should not conclude with a thesis statement.
- You must conclude the introductory section with a thesis paragraph. This paragraph will contain the argument that you will prove in the rest of the paper. A thesis argument is not a statement of fact, your opinion or simply a summary of your historical representation. A thesis argument is provable with evidence that you acquired from your bibliographic sources.
- Your paper should be clearly marked with sections. Each section should in some way support your thesis argument. Section headings should be clearly marked in bold and should introduce the topic of the section.
- Your paper should not spend a copious amount of space summarizing or describing your representation. This is not a

satisfactory analysis. You should only summarize/describe those elements or aspects that go towards proving your larger argument.

- Your conclusion section should do more than simply restate your argument; it should also offer something new in terms of future analysis of the historical topic, representation, media format, or some combination of the three.

- All references should be cited as footnotes. You may use either MLA or Chicago style. All resources used must also be included in a bibliography (also not part of the final page count).

- Finally, your paper should give equal weight to both the historical issue and format elements relevant to your representation. The key to the paper, and the purpose of the course overall is to evaluate how historical information interacts with contemporary representational forms. This relationship should guide every aspect of your project from choosing a representation rich with analytical possibilities to the final framework of your paper and class presentation.

The more specific and focused you choose to make your argument, the better your paper will be. You may choose to analyze a single passage or element of your representation rather than cover the entire representation. This will enable you to select more specific bibliographic references which in turn will tighten and strengthen your overall thesis argument.

# 12. Nomadic Archives: Remix and the Drift to Praxis

*Virginia Kuhn and Vicki Callahan*

In opening our discussion of pedagogical strategies within the digital humanities, we begin by outlining what we see as the mission of the field. That is, while we often operate as if in agreement about what is included under the umbrella term of "digital humanities," it is unclear that our sense of this field or its objectives extends beyond a family resemblance. For our purposes, we first define the humanities quite broadly as disciplines concerned with the ongoing life of culture, and we note our firm belief in the value of humanities education. Indeed, in *Academically Adrift*, a recent book which paints a dismal picture of the state of undergraduate education, Richard Arum and Josipa Roksa argue that students in liberal arts majors "demonstrated significantly higher gains in critical thinking, complex reasoning and writing skills over time" than did their peers in majors such as business, education, social work and communications.[1] We further contend that the mission of the digital humanities is absolutely vital, given emergent technologies' imbrications in today's culture and the need to engage critically with digital culture, even as the field remains somewhat nebulous. In this we align ourselves with the authors of the "Digital Humanities Manifesto 2.0," who argue that the digital humanities "is not a unified field but an array of convergent practices," which are sensitive to the changes in the way knowledge is produced, expressed

---

1   Richard Arum and Josipa Roska, *Academically Adrift: Limited Learning on College Campuses* (Chicago: University of Chicago Press, 2011), 22.

and disseminated in a digital age.[2] Since the digital humanities are not a unified field, we feel its relative murkiness is rich with potential, and some of that potential will be actualized by sharing its "array of convergent practices" as we do here.

Therefore, we want to emphasize our view that digital humanities represents an opportunity for a new form of interdisciplinary engagement, a hybrid form of critical/creative expression that employs still and moving images, text, audio, and interactivity across and within media forms. Since current disciplinary boundaries were formed during the ascendancy of a print literate culture, we feel they must be re-imagined for a digital one. Indeed, the limitations of current disciplinary boundaries are often most evident when considering the role of *interdisciplinarity*. The term "interdisciplinary" typically refers to a kind of additive component, history plus literature, history plus art, and so forth. The perspective is essentially a horizontal one, linking fields without any fundamental change to the formal structures or logic of any one discipline. Generally speaking, in an interdisciplinary move, a narrative thread is enriched and enhanced by parallel yet still essentially linear story lines. This is evident in the case of a film industry discussion that combines economic, labor, gender, and aesthetic developments. The way in which that story is told is altered very little, although in some variations of the digital world that engage arts practice, we might get a more visually pleasing illustration of this history. Horizontal interdisciplinarity can be a productive endeavor, but it only takes us down one kind of pathway in the digital world, and may effectively block other possibilities.

We argue that the radicality of the digital humanities is the potential it offers to expand our understanding to the vertical plane, or more precisely, *planes* of research. In vertical interdisciplinarity, there is a rich layering in both the method and the practice of teaching and scholarship, and this poses challenges to the very discursive categories employed. The disruptive components are the creative, aesthetic and non-alphabetic elements, which once deployed vertically within a field radically transform its formal properties. If horizontal strategies make us imagine new narrative lines within a field, then the vertical approach forces us to rethink the narrator, what narrative form could be, and how we think, reflect, critique and express.

---

2    Todd Presner and Jeffrey Schnapp et al., "Digital Humanities Manifesto 2.0," University of California, Los Angeles, May 29, 2009, http://manifesto.humanities.ucla.edu/2009/05/29/the-digital-humanities-manifesto-20/.

A key roadblock to vertical interdisciplinarity is how we understand and implement our core materials. The difficulty is often that we operate under the assumption that information received from images (both still and moving) and audio materials is aligned almost exclusively with creative/ aesthetic expression and is seen as different or distinct from textual materials and critical thought/writing. Efforts that start from this point are inevitably doomed, or at best limited, as the two sides rarely speak to each other, or worse, simply repeat the same message in a different register. A successful vertically integrated praxis, however, uses these diverse materials and disciplinary strategies to engage across and within media, tools, formats, and philosophical categories, with each component in ruthless interrogation of every possible formal boundary. In other words, an approach to the digital humanities that is steeped in vertical interdisciplinarity is more a method than a field, and it can transform how we operate, what materials we engage, and with whom we work as academics.

With this in mind, we offer several possibilities for vertical strategies that engage text, sound, and image in ways that often conflict and compete, but always extend the conversation among the various elements or registers of meaning. We do this by adopting the stance of "electracy" proposed by Gregory Ulmer.[3] In the digital age, there is potential for more than the progression of "writing" from a text-driven literacy to multimedia electracy—what electracy signifies is a potential seismic shift between the structures of *writing* (object) and the *individual who writes* (subject). This means more than new tools in the toolbox—there is a new "organism" in place. As Ulmer notes, the "group subject" and a new public sphere become "writable."[4] Adopting Ulmer, we become digital curators combing nomadic archives as we assemble, dissolve and remake our work as scholars and as teachers.

How then, does this method work? A vertical strategy does not operate as an image or sonic substitution. It is not a metaphor, but an expression from within, which is not identical to, but rather relational or metonymic. Thus a gap or interval exists between word/image and word/sound (non-verbal or linguistic). The relative openness of the image/sound and the gap between word and image/sound create a space for shared or alternative perspectives. Since the vertical strategy offers new formal possibilities,

---

3  Gregory Ulmer, *Electronic Monuments* (Minneapolis: University of Minnesota Press, 2005).

4  Ulmer, *Electronic Monuments*, xviii.

the relationship among the elements is not *addition* or *replacement*, but *illumination* and *elaboration*.[5] Indeed, contrastive rhetoric and literacy studies have long used the disparate practices of discursive communities to shed light on each other; one can learn more about the assumptions that undergird any one academic discipline by placing it in conversation with the practices and discursive strategies of others. Likewise, we argue that one can learn more about the communicative and expressive possibilities of words when comparing them to the possibilities of images and vice versa.

It is instructive to remember a prior technological advance in media formats—the moving pictures—which for many artists and intellectuals appeared to augur for a parallel paradigm shift in language, thought and action. From Dziga Vertov to Gilles Deleuze, film was the machine of social and philosophical assemblage par excellence, capable of dismantling and reconfiguring the most intransigent of forms. Indeed, the cinema, as Jean-Luc Godard notes and as Robert B. Ray reminds us, is a combination of "spectacle and research" or construction/creativity and observation; it lies at the interstitial moment between the practical/physical and the intellectual/mental.[6] This mixture makes cinema—and now by extension, digital media—a "promise" of radical political intervention, a "promise" to imagine a new world unchained by past ways of singular, essentially linear thinking. In his epic video series, *Histoire(s) du Cinéma,* Godard acknowledges that cinema has not fulfilled this promise, and we recognize that digital media may well share a similar fate. In part, the failed promise of cinema (and media) is due to either spectacle or research dominating the enterprise.

If we follow Antonio Gramsci's definition, *praxis* means those two domains should not be discrete. Gramsci reminds us that we are all philosophers but we need a fluency of language, not simply knowledge of our particular dialectic, to transform those thoughts into political action. Fluency across "languages" is the key to praxis for Gramsci.[7] Incorporating this understanding of the term then, the opening and expansion of our critical and creative expression could be said to drift toward praxis.

---

5   For an excellent discussion about the difference between *illustration* and *illumination,* see Craig Stroupe, "Visualizing English: Recognizing the Hybrid Literacy of Visual and Verbal Authorship on the Web," *College English* 62, no. 5 (2000): 607–32.

6   Robert B. Ray, *How a Film Theory Got Lost and Other Mysteries in Cultural Studies* (Bloomington: Indiana University Press, 2001), 3.

7   Antonio Gramsci, *Selections from the Prison Notebooks,* ed. and trans. Quintin Hoare and Geoffrey Nowell-Smith (New York: International Publishers, 1972), 323–35.

This movement or "drift" is not endemic to any of the specific tools employed, but an outcome of the process outlined above. As such, our work here is necessarily contingent but strategically so, as we select and promote conversations across the boundaries of research and teaching, within academia and from the larger culture, willing to let our thinking be refreshed, reconfigured and remade.

# The Nomadic Archive

Like all scholarly remixes, the following exercises in sound sculpture, digital poster art, and filmed footage, are situated within, and dependent upon, a merger of art, critical investigation, and new digital collections that fall in the category of what has been called "participatory archives": collections characterized by their qualities of remix, distributed and networked authorship, and the realignment of objects and investigators in research. Participatory archives, as Isto Huvila notes, move away from the traditional "record-centric" or fixed artifact approach to archives and move toward more interactive and fluid roles for archivists and users.[8] Key to Huvila's approach is a focus on the *use of* and *conversation around* a record rather than a record as an object in itself, so that "a participatory archive is not a complementary layer, but a primary knowledge repository about records and their context."[9] But records—and what we define as "records"—are clearly the tip of the iceberg in the participatory archive: Huvila as well as Rick Prelinger and Terry Cook maintain that archives, archivists, and users are also well onto the path of transformation to essentially more transparent and democratic roles.[10] Both Cook and Prelinger point out that archives and archivists are rarely passive, objective entities but rather important historical agents that create new knowledge and, as Prelinger pointedly puts it, "archives make historical interventions. We intervene in the present by foregrounding the past and infusing contemporary culture

---

8   Isto Huvila, "Participatory Archive: Towards Decentralized Curation, Radical User Orientation, and Broader Contextualization of Records Management," *Archival Science* 8, no. 1 (2008): 17.

9   Huvila, "Participatory Archive," 27.

10  Terry Cook, "The Archive is a Foreign Country: Historians, Archivists and the Changing Archival Landscape," *The Canadian Historical Review* 90, no. 3 (2009): 497–534; and Rick Prelinger, "Points of Origin: Discovering Ourselves through Access," *The Moving Image* 9, no. 2 (2009): 164–75.

with historical record."[11] Prelinger's commentary reestablishes the link between past and present, a divide that Cook notes is a relatively new distinction, a creation of the nineteenth century whereby the past became "something to be collected, guarded, and venerated, as if on a pedestal."[12]

One example of the potential transformation within participatory archives can be found in Sally Potter's digital archive, SP-ARK (http://www.sp-ark.org/), a project still in its early stages of development but with several features of interest. Here the filmmaker has put materials from her film, *Orlando,* in an online and open archive, including pre-production sketches, script drafts, photographs of costumes and sets, information on distribution, and other "artifacts" related to the production. Digitizing and open-sourcing this sort of information provides a wealth of material to film scholars but the online collection is simply the first step of the enterprise. SP-ARK also features the ability to leave a research "trail" as well as engage in conversation with other researchers and their "trails" or pathways through the material. Forums allow teachers to pose questions to students or researchers to make commentaries that are then essentially "recorded" as part of the archive itself, thereby making new "artifacts" within the archive. While the objects "created" through the forums might, at first glance, not seem terribly significant, the larger historiographic process involved moves us away from the binary understanding of past and present since the artifacts of the recorded research trail and the dialogue via commentary are both inside and yet "freed" from history. The distributed researcher formed by SP-ARK is equally inside and outside history, plunged into the artifacts but also into a stream of other voices and perspectives, destabilizing singular and deterministic (or, indeed, random) paths through the material.

We argue that scholarly remix builds on the transformative qualities of distributed authorship by shifting the "site" of the archive itself, or at the very least *creating new mini archives* within each remix. Moreover, since the scholarly project *contains* a range of "artifacts" through the download process (sonic, visual, textual) and *circulates* through any number of venues (Internet Archive, Critical Commons, YouTube, Vimeo), we might well now argue that the participatory archive, through this transportable dynamic, becomes a mobile or *nomadic* entity: it lives nowhere and everywhere at once. Our choice of the term nomadic is, as might well be expected, not

---

11    Prelinger, "Points of Origin," 165.
12    Cook, "The Archive is a Foreign Country," 515.

accidental and references the structure and the purpose of the rhizome in Deleuze and Guattari's *A Thousand Plateaus*: "[A] rhizome ceaselessly establishes connections between semiotic chains, organizations, and power, and circumstances relative to the arts, sciences, and social sciences."[13]

Our rhizomatic connections might often be unexpected, but they are never random. Careful curation is vital, and indeed we underline our context as *scholarly* remix. As we will see in the "auto-tune" examples discussed below,[14] remixes can quickly fall into the domain of parody attendant alongside cynicism, passivity and political paralysis. While we encourage a resourceful—indeed, at times, hacktivist—approach to the collection of materials, these are accompanied by meticulous guidelines for citation, contextualization and reflection. Even here the process is still not complete for our students. Peer review plays a crucial role in our remix and students are encouraged to revise once the review is completed—in other words, yet another remix of their remix. Of course, students may choose not to do this, but by framing the assignment this way, we highlight the ongoing conversation or *process* of the participatory archive—that it is always open, fluid, and in motion, rather than a fixed entity.

The politics of remix, as performed within our scholarly context, integrates and builds on our history, but also moves us past tired ideological divides and is informed by what Elizabeth Grosz calls "thinking the new"—that is, thinking beyond established categories and boundaries, and thinking with "direction without destination, movement without prediction."[15] For Grosz, this entails thinking beyond our established *being* into a transformative *becoming*. We have now shifted from a time structure that associates past and present to one that propels both forward into the future, and becomes a change agent for public access that is *aligned with* thoughtful reflection of the media.

---

13 Gilles Deleuze and Félix Guattari, *A Thousand Plateaus: Capitalism and Schizophrenia*, trans. Brian Massumi (Minneapolis: University of Minnesota Press, 1987), 7.

14 For example, consider the sensation surrounding the "Bed Intruder Song," an "auto-tune" remix by the Gregory Brothers of a TV news story (aired July 29, 2010) about an attempted rape in Huntsville, Alabama, which went viral shortly after its release on YouTube. See Philip Kennicott, "Auto-Tune Turns the Operatic Ideal into a Shoddy Joke," *The Washington Post*, August 29, 2010, http://www.washingtonpost.com/wp-dyn/content/article/2010/08/27/AR2010082702197.html.

15 Elizabeth Grosz, "Thinking the New: Of Futures Yet Unthought," in *Becomings: Explorations in Time, Memory, and the Future*, ed. Elizabeth Grosz (Ithaca: Cornell University Press, 2000), 19.

In this chapter, we offer three examples of the nomadic archive emerging from classes we teach at the Institute for Multimedia Literacy (IML) at the University of Southern California. Founded in 1998 with the premise that contemporary students must "write" with images as well as they write with words, the IML has a long interdisciplinary history. Although IML practices are continually updated in response to shifts in the affordances of digital media, they remain founded in the principles of intellectual rigor and scholarly digital media. As such, IML research, scholarship, and pedagogy are closely intertwined. The course units we describe here are taken from foundational courses with the presumption of no previous experience with digital media.

## Sound, Montage, Remix

The drift to praxis is remarkably played out in a sound remix exercise that is assigned as part of a class on social media and remix culture. Aware that we are situated in a sonically saturated culture, students are challenged to de-familiarize the everyday soundscape and undertake a "Rhythm Science Sound Sculpture" or a "forensic investigation of sound as a vector of coded language,"[16] which then might generate new ideas and/or identities. This outcome becomes particularly challenging when audio/music is often reduced to an ambient or illustrative context, adding little more than restful or rhythmic backdrop to established narrative lines. But if familiarity is one problem, audio projects are further complicated by musical remixes that fall well on the spectacle side of Godard's equation. The Gregory Brothers' *Barely Political* site (http://www.barelypolitical.com/), featuring its "Auto-Tune the News," provides endless examples here. An infectious beat and catchy tune, alongside a voice altered to eliminate extreme pitch fluctuations flattens even the most serious subjects, from rape to robbery to historical events—as in "Martin Luther King, Jr. Sings 'I Have a Dream'"—into banal or laughable entertainment. Even apolitical mashups such as DJ Earworm's "United State of Pop" series (http://www.djearworm.com/) veers from the pop wallpaper to consumerist spectacle through seamless editing that dazzles the viewer through the sheer consistency of American pop music sonically and visually. Looking at these examples, one might think all is already lost for the remix aesthetic beyond a critique of late capitalism and post-modernism.

---

16    Paul D. Miller, *Rhythm Science* (Cambridge: MIT Press, 2004), 4–5.

Certainly a critique of these examples is a starting point, although students will quite rightly hold on to their pop culture pleasures. The key is to demonstrate the diversity and complexity of remixes and to move them past mere passive consumption or even "creative" reproduction (as content creators) of these spectacle variants. In other words, how do we ensure that providing the skills to mix generates and adds something new and not simply additional material for the consumer spectacle? In part, important distinctions can be made even within "suspect" sources. For example, the Gregory Brothers' later "Martin Luther King, Jr. Sings in Memphis" provides a pointed contrast to their "I Have a Dream" remix in that this later piece situates the speech visually in the larger civil rights history. Moreover, "Memphis" ends the sound track with King's authentic, un-doctored voice, concluding with an important reminder of the individual, unique presence and life's work behind the video. The simple act of ending with King's actual voice resituates the mix in history and retrospectively re-contextualizes the "auto-tune" segment as a pop culture homage formed in solidarity with the ideas expressed. It playfully but powerfully links past history with contemporary culture, something the "Dream" speech remix failed to do.

From this example, students see that context and richly nuanced detail can be employed on a number of levels, visually, musically, historically, with specific and distinct impact on narrative, voice, and authorship. In effect, when students take on their own sound sculptures, they are working *through* Michel Chion's three modes of listening, from "casual" (or "the most common," collecting information about a cause or source of sound) to "semantic" (coded language in need of interpretation) to "reduced" (close attention to "the traits of sound itself, independent of its cause or meaning").[17] For the "Rhythm Science" assignment, students are charged with crafting and thus listening to different registers of audio including at least one voice, two different music tracks, ambient sound, and one free track of their choice. The multiple yet distinct types of tracks required provide a pathway to think about context both in terms of content *and* form—in other words, both informational and aesthetic choices of "materials" are key. Students are thereby steered away from more mashup (two-track) strategies into deeper and more robust layering of sounds and ideas. At the same time, the engagement of materials using at least one musical element (as opposed

17  Michel Chion, *Audio-Vision: Sound on Screen*, trans. Claudia Gorbman (New York: Columbia University Press, 1994), 25–35.

to only voice and/or ambient materials) situates the exercise *in time*, that is, with a structured temporal component. Music thereby gives the sound sculpture a more jazz-like or improvisatory framework, which, as Vijay Iyer convincingly argues, is both an embodied and cognitive experience.[18] As Iyer notes, the successful jazz artist must *actively listen* to know what to add next, and since the event occurs "in time" the audience is equally an active and embodied participant.[19] In some ways, Iyer's commentary helps us understand the power of musical remixes (we must tap our feet, keep up the rhythm), but the *depth* of our participation as remixers and as listeners comes with the layering of sounds and contexts.

Students typically respond to the "Rhythm Science" assignment with some of the most inspired work of the semester (which includes photo, video, and social media remixes). This outcome is arguably the result of an approach that engages them not only with a new subject or technology, but also involves them in the complex layering and interaction of intellectual and physically embodied skills. The layering also deters or destabilizes the usual ideological formulas—the narrative lines of student work have a logic and arc but are rarely linear or didactic. The students seem to engage deeply with the reading for the assignment:

> This is a world where all meaning has been untethered from the ground of its origins and all signposts point to a road that you make up as you travel through the text. Rotate, reconfigure, edit and render the form. Contemporary sound composition is an involution machine.[20]

Perhaps this lack of fixed categories helps to make the peer review session for the project the most productive and heartfelt of all class meetings. Discussions are simultaneously passionate and respectful across sometimes difficult and sensitive terrain. The openness of students' responses might also be traced to their active and embodied listening practices, both as remix creators and audiences, and the very blurring of those roles itself. Our remix class begins the semester with William S. Burroughs's invocation from Tristan Tzara that "everyone is a poet" and the "Rhythm Science Sound Sculpture" provides a venue to enact this axiom of distributed authorship across diverse sonic planes.[21]

---

18   Vijay Iyer, "On Improvisation, Temporality, and Embodied Experience," in *Sound Unbound: Sampling Digital Music and Culture*, ed. Paul D. Miller (Cambridge: MIT Press, 2008), 273–92, 275–76.

19   Iyer, "On Improvisation," 276.

20   Miller, *Rhythm Science*, 5.

21   William S. Burroughs, "The Cut-Up Method of Brion Gysin," originally published in

# Image and the Praxis of Identity

In a culture that is increasingly visually mediated, the impact of images on identity formation is a topic that must be addressed in a praxis-based approach. Indeed, the same technologies that allow for the creation and dissemination of recorded images via digital cameras and digitized archives also allow for societal surveillance via cameras placed in the public sphere with no need for operators. These disembodied institutional agents serve as emblems to the distributed authority that bumps up against the liberatory potential of the nomadic archive.

We begin our unit on image editing by foregrounding the political nature of images as artwork, looking specifically to John Berger's *Ways of Seeing*, a BBC series based on Walter Benjamin's seminal essay, "The Work of Art in the Age of Mechanical Reproduction."[22] The benefit of using Berger's work, rather than what one might consider the "primary text" of Benjamin, lies in the enactment and translation of the concepts across both a book and a "filmic text."[23] Since *Ways of Seeing* is both a television series—which one can now find on YouTube—as well as a book,[24] its very form highlights the possibilities for expression across image, text, and sound and prepares students for the move to speaking with and in the language of images.

We move on to examining the work of graphic artists Barbara Kruger and Shepard Fairey. This has proven extremely productive in complicating notions of the politics of the image, the definition of a public personality and the veracity of visually mediated information. We explore Kruger's work in its historic, political and ethical contexts. We discuss the formal strategies Kruger uses, such as irony, scale, composition, and wordplay, in addition to the topics she addresses: gender, science, race, and corporate

---

*A Casebook on the Beat*, ed. Thomas Parkinson (New York: Crowell, 1961), 105–06, and published later in revised form in William S. Burroughs and Brion Gyson, *The Third Mind* (New York: Viking, 1978), 29–33.

22 *Ways of Seeing*, four-part TV mini-series, written by John Berger (London: British Broadcasting Corporation, 1972); and Walter Benjamin, "The Work of Art in the Age of Mechanical Reproduction," in *Illuminations: Essays and Reflections*, ed. Hannah Arendt and trans. Harry Zohn (New York: Schocken Books, 1969), 217–51.

23 The term "filmic text" implies one that was created in film but has since been digitized such that it shares more functions with a book than with a film. For a further discussion of this term, see Virginia Kuhn, "Filmic Texts and the Rise of the Fifth Estate," *International Journal of Learning and Media* 2, no. 2–3 (2010), http://ijlm.net/knowinganddoing/10.1162/IJLM_a_00057.

24 The series scripts were adapted into a book: John Berger, *Ways of Seeing* (Harmondsworth: Penguin, 1972).

culture. Students must choose one of the dozen or so photojournalistic images supplied to them, all of which have become iconic in US culture: from the World War II victory kiss to the Apollo moon landing; from the atomic bomb to the Wright Brothers' early flight; from the Kent state student shooting to the 9/11 attack on the World Trade Center. Using one of these seminal images, students apply Kruger-like techniques in order to reveal meanings that are submerged or to re-contextualize these meanings to say something new. The beauty of this assignment is that any re-contextualization necessarily includes research into the image's original context, as well as its subsequent iconic usages and meanings. The image of the Apollo astronaut, for example, was updated and popularized by the MTV logo.

While the meanings of many of these images may seem over-determined by their placement within Kruger's political landscape, students are surprisingly adept at shedding these constraints for the purposes of their own personal and political expression. Being required to mimic the formal elements of Kruger's work also reveals the communicative aspect of language. Whether verbal or image-based, graphic expression requires some form of agreement about its meaning, which shapes its communicative and expressive potential. Moreover, the constraint of designing like Kruger forces a degree of intentionality in students' use of image editing software, in this case Photoshop, rather than learning such tools in a strictly instrumental way. Indeed, we are always alert to the difference between teaching the tools and appreciating their historical and political contexts. Students do not have to adopt a particular political stance, but they do have to defend their own approach. Even the choice of de-politicization is a response to a particular ideology and therefore political in nature.

The second part of this image assignment loosens some of the constraints as it asks students to choose a contemporary political figure and work in the style of Shepard Fairey. We start with Fairey's prominent Obama Hope image, which became an important touchstone in the election of the first non-white US president. This image also represents a break with the artist's previous work, which has been described as political critique. The Hope poster represents a more productive piece in the sense that it offers a remedy and is optimistic. It also became the basis for a pivotal case of copyright and fair use when the Associated Press (AP) sued Fairey for copyright infringement, arguing that a photo taken by Mannie Garcia provided the root image for the Hope poster. The AP asserted its ownership of the photo taken by Garcia, an interesting aspect of current copyright conventions itself, particularly since Garcia also asserted ownership claiming that he was not a regular employee of the AP and, as such, need not relinquish his rights to the AP as an employer. Fairey maintained that the source image was a different photo, but subsequently confessed that the Garcia photo was in fact the source image. Fairey's legal counsel then dropped the case, noting that even though it still had merit, they could not defend a client who lies and conceals information. The extent to which Fairey remixed the photo becomes fodder for our discussion of the doctrine of fair use and the attendant legal drama offers rich opportunities for exploring all of the social, political and technological implications of an image-based culture. Since the implications of the case are ongoing,[25] students have the opportunity to explore these considerations in a way that seems particularly alive and grounded in the real world.

After this work on the Hope image, students create their own project by choosing a contemporary political figure and applying Fairey's techniques to transform a photorealistic image into their own visual statement. Students show great imagination in the political figures they choose as their subject, and they are told that as long as the choice is defensible, they are free to take liberties with their selection. Indeed, a course mantra is "challenge authority," so when students challenge any or all of the three descriptors of the assignment—"contemporary," "political," "figure"—by choosing, for example, J. Edgar Hoover, the Dalai Lama, and an oil rig respectively, their defense of choice proves gratifying in terms of its clear display of their critical skills. To date, the political figures students have submitted have included the usual suspects, such as Sarah Palin, John Boehner, and Iranian president Mahmoud Ahmadinejad, but they have also used personalities such as USC president Max Nikias, Facebook creator Mark Zuckerberg, pundit Stephen Colbert, and WikiLeaks founder Julian Assange, to name just a few. As such, this project requires an active engagement with key contemporary issues and demands consideration of their historic, political, social, and economic contexts and implications.

All image projects are peer reviewed in a structured way, adding

---

25   The parties settled out of court in January 2011; the settlement details remain confidential.

another layer of critical engagement. Students are assigned a colleague's piece to review and asked to comment on the following four aspects: the idea that informs the image, the extent to which the project follows the assignment (e.g. the creative constraints), the technical efficacy of the image editing and finally, the textual rationale that accompanies each image. This last component is important, for while we try not to allow the words to prevail—indeed a main goal of this project is to gain fluency with the language of images—we do recognize the dominance of verbal language in academic argument, even as we witness the emergence of new forms. This tension becomes a method for staying anchored in the past, while also anticipating the future.

The work with Kruger and Fairey necessarily includes an exploration of the ways in which the images that circulate in contemporary culture influence individual's subjectivity, and, indeed, their self-image. And while we often like to think that as enlightened and savvy media consumers we remain immune to the impossibly thin, flawlessly beautiful photos that grace the covers of magazines and advertising, the continued increase in eating disorders and plastic surgery in the US suggest that these images exert significant impact on individual's sense of self. To what extent does the ability to edit one's photographic image foster the sense that editing one's physical looks via plastic surgery is a natural path? To extend such questions, we shift the focus to images that move.

## Framing Reality: Camera Praxis

The role of surveillance on identity and citizenship is expanded when we work with moving images—specifically those that we frame by way of original footage that students record. Working in small groups of three or four, students create a three to five minute film, the subject of which is an aspect of the increase in surveillance culture brought about by emergent technologies. We begin by revisiting *Ways of Seeing* and Berger's argument that women are always aware of being surveyed, causing them to split their identity, since

> [f]rom earliest childhood she has been taught and persuaded to survey herself continually. And so she comes to consider the surveyor and the surveyed within her as the two constituent yet always distinct elements of her identity as a woman.[26]

---

26   Berger, *Ways of Seeing*, 46.

This link between identity and surveillance, as the assignment directions contend, is exacerbated by the increasing presence of surveillance cameras in public spaces. Furthermore, this type of surveillance is far more generalized and impacts on both men and women, and again we add, anyone whose appearance is somehow outside of the norm. To lend weight to this topic, Michel Foucault's discussion of the impact of the gaze is written directly into the assignment vis-à-vis a surveillance society in which

> [t]here is no need for arms, physical violence, material constraints. Just a gaze. An inspecting gaze, a gaze that each individual under its weight will end by interiorizing to the point that he is his own overseer, each individual thus exercising this surveillance over, and against, himself. A superb formula: power exercised continuously and for what turns out to be a minimal cost.[27]

Early discourse around computers and teaching used the panopticon metaphor to describe the potential for disciplining students with circular computer formations that left all screens open to the authority housed in the center—the all powerful instructor machine. Indeed, while this formation was often valorized as a way of calculating student engagement, humanists more often saw it as a way of scrutinizing student work and censoring their internet use by force rather than by actively engaging them in coursework. As Andrew Feenberg argues in his seminal book, *The Critical Theory of Technology*, technology is ultimately ambivalent—its functions can be used for more (or less) democratic purposes even as their reasons for being are ideologically imbued.[28]

But the more subtle ways in which the gaze exerts pressure on subjectivity can be enumerated by looking at other fields. During this unit, we read recent research on the impact of the gaze, which reveals the ways in which the practices of the social sciences can enhance and extend the theoretical models of humanities research. In "When What You See Is What You Get: The Consequences of the Objectifying Gaze for Women and Men," psychologists Sarah J. Gervais, Theresa K. Vescio, and Jill Allen report the findings of a research study in which undergraduate men and women were exposed to an objectifying gaze—interpersonal sexual objectification—by a member of the opposite sex. They found that women's math skills declined

---

27   Michel Foucault, *Power/Knowledge: Selected Interviews and Other Writings, 1972–1977*, ed. Colin Gordon (New York: Pantheon, 1980), 155.

28   Andrew Feenberg, *The Critical Theory of Technology* (Oxford: Oxford University Press, 1991).

when their bodies were sexualized by this gaze. Oddly enough, they also found that the women displayed more willingness to interact with those who had objectified them, and the authors hypothesize that this may be due to stereotype threat and women's desire to combat stereotypes, leading to a "vicious cycle where women underperform and then continue to interact with those who led them to underperform in the first place."[29] Although the authors did not find a direct correlation to body image or body surveillance in these interactions, it seems reasonable to speculate that the cumulative effect of sexual objectification and stereotyping would lead to such self surveillance. And, indeed, bringing these types of studies into the discussion of the camera project, we help students foster a more critical engagement with the materials they use for their own projects.

## The Nomadic Archive: A Caveat

Insofar as the public sphere becomes writable, the university classroom needs some protection; a certain contingent erasure from the public sphere. While students ought to do work that is alive in the world—indeed, they report feeling more engaged when they do so—there is also an important need for a buffer zone, since undergraduate education gives students the freedom to take risks, to experiment, and to fail. Moreover, part of being digital deeply means being discriminating about how, when and where one places one's work and information online. If students are using social networking extensively, they are free to post their work (and often do) but should demonstrate critical intentionality when they do so. As we have seen on sites like Facebook, students can share information that they are later sorry to have shared when it comes back to haunt them. Likewise, they may not want less than polished work persisting online when they apply for a job or to graduate school. It is the very assumption that all work ought to be public because it *can* be put online that allows contemporary culture to be monitored so thoroughly. To contribute to the notion that everything should be online simply because it can be demonstrates a lack of critical engagement with digital tools and, thus, it is a bad model. The line between the public and private is increasingly porous—social networking tools not only encourage the sharing of private information, their developers often harvest the information with convoluted

---

29   Sarah J. Gervais, Theresa K. Vescio, and Jill Allen, "When What You See Is What You Get: The Consequences of the Objectifying Gaze for Women and Men," *Psychology of Women Quarterly* 35, no. 1 (2011): 5.

security protocols. When Facebook shifted its default to public, forcing users to "opt in" to privacy, the sea change was most apparent.

Our classes address these concerns both practically and conceptually. Many of our assignments are posted to a closed site that ensures students' experimentation and expression. In some instances though, we do want to explore the potential of social media and the public space, but we initiate that process through a discussion of online privacy. We spend time on the variables of sharing within different platforms with the clarification that online need not exclusively mean public. The option of using an avatar or alias is certainly broached and always an option, but more profoundly, the question of personal privacy represents an opportunity for additional ethical concerns of online space to be examined, from issues of anonymous commentary to sharing/tagging of friends or third party images and speech. Privacy alongside questions of fair use is then linked into an important conversation regarding the responsible circulation and use of information in the digital age.

## Prolegomena to Any Future Remixes

The implications of digital humanities pedagogy are potentially revolutionary, for not only does this work disrupt monolithic truth claims, it challenges the hegemony of verbal language as the only avenue for the expression of sophisticated concepts and complex argument. While the written word is still highly valued, it is one register among many, each with its own set of potentials as semiotic resources. This method, and the student projects that result, uncovers more questions than answers. In order to counter the adoption of a preachy stance that attempts to have the last word on an issue and thus prevents a new remix even as it blocks circulation of the nomadic archive, we adopt Trinh T. Minh-ha's notion that her work does not lead to instant gratification on the part of either the viewer or the maker; rather, it contributes to long term change by impacting the way we view ourselves and each other. Thus, as she notes, disclosure of one's subject position is always the responsibility of the maker.[30]

Digital media praxis is not a utopian state (from which democracy will necessarily and inevitably flow) but a central skillful practice, an integration of analytical and creative process, which will serve as an

---

30  Trinh T. Minh-ha, *Cinema Interval* (New York: Routledge, 1999), 71.

essential foundation for an informed and participatory citizenry and public sphere. Fundamental to this idea of praxis is not just media literacy (recognition) but media fluency that reconfigures the tools of language not only in line with media age but in concert with a new social subject that is not isolated and insular but open and connected.

Perhaps the most salient aspect of teaching the digital humanities that binds its practitioners lies in the way that the expression of knowledge is in flux and we can no longer say with any confidence what an academic argument consists of, a fact that makes assigning student work a contested practice. Another result of sweeping technological change comes in the blurring of the boundary between scholarship and pedagogy. As the New London Group's watershed manifesto argued, contemporary teachers and learners are not only left with established patterns of meaning-making, we are also "active designers of meaning," and as such, we are "designers of social futures, public futures and community futures."[31] They outline six elements of the meaning-making process: "Linguistic Meaning, Visual Meaning, Audio Meaning, Gestural Meaning, Spatial Meaning and Multimodal patterns of meaning that relate the first five modes of meaning to each other."[32] We sample and mix practices employed by various fields and institutions in order to shed a more complete light on the systematically complex issues of a globally networked, digital world.

---

31  New London Group, "A Pedagogy of Multiliteracies: Designing Social Futures," *Harvard Educational Review* 66, no. 1 (1996): 65.

32  New London Group, "A Pedagogy of Multiliteracies," 65.

# III. Politics

# 13. They Have Come, Why Won't We Build It? On the Digital Future of the Humanities

*Jon Saklofske, Estelle Clements and Richard Cunningham*

> So many of [the] best-educated, best-placed people are too invested in old social models and old visions of history.
>
> Walter Russell Mead, "The Crisis of the American Intellectual" (2010)
>
> They seem to feast on technology and have an aptitude for all things digital.
>
> Don Tapscott, *Grown Up Digital* (2009)

In this chapter, we will suggest ways of implementing digital humanities instruction for students who, as Don Tapscott's research shows, comfortably "watch [...] movies on two-inch screens," "text incessantly, surf the Web," "make videos, collaborate" and *"have a natural affinity for technology"*.[1] These students came into a world in which the digital age was in a comparatively infantile state and have shared their adolescence with the adolescence of our culture's digital era.[2] We start from the premise that these hi-tech immersed students are the vast majority of current enrollees in post-secondary

---

1  Don Tapscott, *Grown Up Digital* (New York: McGraw-Hill, 2009), 9, my emphasis.
2  This characterization is based on the empirical data recently presented in Martin Hilbert and Priscila López, "The World's Technological Capacity to Store, Communicate, and Compute Information," *Science* 332, no. 6025 (2011): 60–65.

education in the developed world, and therefore it is past the time at which widespread introduction of digital humanities curricula would have been a timely intervention in their collective education. Our title plays off the apparitional voice heard in "Shoeless Joe Jackson Comes to Iowa," the W. P. Kinsella short story memorialized as the 1989 feature film *Field of Dreams*: "If you build it, he will come."[3] We hold the situation in higher education to be the inverse of that desire. Rather than simply needing to attract students, higher education needs to respond to the overwhelming presence of those who, as Gary Small and Gigi Vorgan argue, "multitask and parallel process with ease," "have shorter attention spans, especially when faced with traditional forms of learning", and "complain that books make them feel isolated".[4] As Tapscott so effectively documents in *Grown Up Digital*, "the Net Generation has arrived,"[5] so we ask: why have we not yet built what its members need and have every right to expect? Why have we not yet developed and implemented curricula more appropriate to today's digital reality and tomorrow's digital prospects than to the Gutenberg-era world in which most currently employed university faculty grew up?

Below, we begin with a discussion of at least some of the reasons for institutional resistance to change in the face of the explosive take-over by digital culture of what is variously called print or analogue culture. Following that, we introduce evidence that argues strongly for the recognition that the current post-secondary student generation has had a qualitatively different experience of technology from previous generations, and that they have been and are immersed in digital culture. From there, we will outline possible methods by which digital humanities could be integrated into existing programs and, in some cases, existing courses.

On the whole, we hope this chapter will be received as a call to action for those in the digital humanities, those wondering how to get involved in the digital humanities, and those who simply recognize that higher education needs to do *something* before the forces arguing in favor of home schooling, practical skills, and conformist ideologies in opposition to social engagement, theoretical sophistication and free, critical thinking convince our youth that higher education really is a waste of time. That call to action is a call to see the digital humanities as an opportunity rather than a threat,

---

3   W. P. Kinsella, *Shoeless Joe* (Boston: Houghton Mifflin, 1982), 6.
4   Gary Small and Gigi Vorgan, *iBrain: Surviving the Technological Alternation of the Modern Mind* (New York: Collins Living, 2008), 25.
5   Tapscott, *Grown Up Digital*, 6.

and as an opportunity to reinvigorate tertiary education in a manner that complements and participates in the "real" world of the student, rather than situating itself perpetually in opposition to the lived experiences of "the net generation."

## Institutional Resistance

Universities are by nature conservative entities. In the best understanding of conservation, universities preserve and profess Matthew Arnold's definition of culture as "the best that has been thought and uttered in the world."[6] Although Arnoldian notions of culture and of the role of the university have long been out of fashion, passing along to new generations "the best that has been thought and uttered" is, we think, a reasonable interpretation of what "conservative" should mean when applied to the humanities side of the university campus—and perhaps anywhere else. Unfortunately, there is a more bureaucratic conservatism awake and at work there. Too often, universities embrace the *status quo* simply because it is the *status quo*; far too many of those who work on university campuses around the world work to conserve the ways things are done simply because it is the way they have grown accustomed to doing things. Perhaps it is how, when they were undergraduates, they saw their professors do things. Perhaps it is how, in graduate school, their supervisors taught them to do things. Perhaps it is how mentors taught them when they were, or now that they are, junior faculty. This is not to say people consciously fight change or refuse to adapt simply because changing or adapting would result in new ways of doing and of being. While there may well be some for whom such motives are operative, most are probably motivated more by inertia, a simple desire to stay in a zone in which they have grown comfortable.

The fear of change is often threatening because it is a species of the fear of the unknown. This kind of conservatism—the kind that resists change because of an admixture of comfortable familiarity with the way things are, complacency, and fear of the unknown and untried—often seems more prevalent in the old than in the young. Older faculty members have worked their way through the processes of renewal, tenure, and promotion, have shepherded others through those processes and in so doing have become

---

6   Matthew Arnold, "Literature and Science," *Discourses in America* (London: Macmillan, 1885), 122.

invested in current systems, current structures, current ways of doing things, and the current state of the university. But in our experience, it is a mistake to believe a simple young/old dichotomy brings much explanatory force to the question of our title: "Why won't we build it?" If universities embrace change like nudists embrace hedgehogs—not willingly and not often—it is not simply because young faculty and young administrators have not yet had their chance to change the world.

If only the old were afflicted with ingrained resistance to change, solving the problem of reflexive resistance would be comparatively straightforward: take the old out of the offices of power (limited though such power always proves to be) and place youthful new hires in those offices. But in the words of Canadian novelist and academic Robertson Davies,

> The world is burdened with young fogies. Old men [and women] with ossified minds are easily dealt with. But [women and] men who look young, act young and everlastingly harp on the fact that they are young, but ... nevertheless think and act with a degree of caution that would be excessive in their grandfathers, are the curse of the world. Their very conservatism is secondhand, and they don't know what they are conserving.[7]

We fear merely replacing older office-holders and decision-makers with younger ones might simply create situations in which change is not merely shrugged off for reasons of comfort and complacency, but actively impeded out of a misguided sense of conservatism. Sometimes putting a younger person in an office with decision-making power only means more energy is available to oppose meaningful change. Thus, despite the fact that "the Net Generation has arrived," a digital humanities curriculum can often face more opposition than support even from younger members of faculty.

Resistance to change can also be an unintended consequence of the oppositional relationship that seems increasingly characteristic of relations between administrative personnel and faculty. The roles of administration and faculty often blur, largely because university administrators typically come out of the ranks of faculty. In this shadowy arena, each side becomes suspicious of the other: administrators still seem to think of themselves as researchers and educators but, given that their teaching and research activity are all but suspended due to the demands of their positions, they no longer are. On the other hand, faculty often think they need not concern themselves with the institution's financial

---

7    Robertson Davies, "The Table Talk of Robertson Davies," in *The Enthusiasms of Robertson Davies*, ed. Judith Skelton Grant (Toronto: McClelland and Stewart, 1979), 310–11.

health, when from an administrative perspective they are precisely the people best placed to help the university through trying financial times. Both sides claim that they have first right to the use of the university's name and, as a result, both sides question the loyalty of the other. The oppositional politics that emerge from these blurry contests offer very few occasions for significant change to be effected by either side. When one side proposes change, the other side too often opposes it on a matter of general principle—whatever "they" propose cannot be good for us and for "our" institution.

Administrative concerns certainly include budgetary concerns, and nothing closes off discussion of potential innovation faster than a fear that it will require more or new resources in addition to what is presently provided. In the words of Roger Rosenblatt's fictional but true-to-life character Professor Manning in the novel *Beet*, "The bottom line. As soon as that phrase crept into the language, [the] country was cooked."[8] More optimistically, Gordon Davies took a longer historical view when he reminded us that "there has always been a tension between the university and the funding source that could control the thought" from the church to the crown to the corporation, with the appropriate response being some version of insisting "that the earth goes around the sun even if it doesn't comport with what the Holy Father says."[9] But even those who know the sometimes-hardscrabble history of the university and celebrate its recurrent triumphs over adversity recognize the futility of proposing any innovation likely to raise the cost of program delivery, or likely to sweep funding from under the feet of established programs. Therefore, the introduction of a digital humanities curriculum, overdue though it is, must be feasible and unthreatening—at least on financial and pragmatic grounds—to existing curricula.

The conservatism of the old, the misguided conservatism of "young fogies," institutional inertia, and the perpetually present "current" financial climate all line up as formidable forces resisting the change digital humanities represents. But there is another reason why humanities faculty members might oppose what digital humanities so effectively represents. The humanities scholar has traditionally conducted their critical, analytical, and speculative inquiries into the human condition

---

8   Roger Rosenblatt, *Beet: A Novel* (New York: Ecco, 2008), 7.
9   Quoted in David L. Kirp, *Shakespeare, Einstein, and the Bottom Line: The Marketing of Higher Education* (Cambridge: Harvard University Press, 2003), 144–45.

from a position institutionally constructed to be, or to enable the scholar to pretend to be, outside the actual condition of humanity. To be human is to be part of a mob. By nature, humans are social beings. There is no such thing as one human. If ever we were to degenerate to there being only one of us, the extinction of the human species would already be complete.

Nonetheless, the university has allowed, enabled, and encouraged professors to conduct research and perform their teaching duties as though there were no one else involved, as though no help were required, as though the community of scholars with which even the most misanthropic professor engages were only a devoted audience waiting with baited breath for the profound utterances sure to come from the mouth or the pen of the solitary scholar. If the university and its professoriate find themselves undervalued by twenty-first-century society, at least some of the blame must be laid at the feet of these mock-individualists. But more importantly, the ideology of the lone scholar has a tenacious grip on our institutions of higher learning—except perhaps in the sciences, where the practice of collaboration has been normative for longer than the working life of current-generation scientists. The final form of institutional resistance to which we draw attention, therefore, is that of the "lone" scholar who sees the collaborative model of the digital humanities as a threat not merely to a way of working, but to a way of life. It is immaterial that the threatened state of being was always a chimera. People believed in it to such an extent that they were able to design their cycles of productivity to conform to it: when the office door is open, I am available; when it is closed, I am working.

To build a digital humanities program in answer to the fact that society and its university-age citizens have changed will not require us to confront and overpower all of these forces of resistance. However, we do need to be aware of them. And we should be aware, to the extent possible, of the motivations—conscious or not—of those who bring them to bear in department or faculty meetings, at meetings of university senates or other governing bodies, or in consultations or confrontations between faculty members and administrators or students or other faculty members. Awareness of the causes of resistance, and of the motivations behind them, can enable builders of digital humanities courses and programs to work strategically as we attempt to drag our most conservative of social institutions further into the digital age.

# Why the Net Gen *is* Different

In *Multiversities, Ideas, and Democracies*, George Fallis reminds us,

> We live in extraordinary times. We are living during a technological revolution. Advances in computing, communications and information technologies are so rapid, so extensive and so transforming as to constitute a revolution comparable to the industrial revolutions. This is changing the way things are made, *the way institutions are organized* and the way we communicate. The character of our age is defined by the information technology revolution.[10]

When we started our research for this chapter we would have disagreed with Fallis's characterization of our moment in history as "revolutionary." Indeed, we have not yet completed our own internal debate on whether the more accurate term is "*r*evolution" or "*e*volution." But much of the evidence gathered does indeed suggest that "revolution" is more than mere hyperbole.

Hilbert and López conclude their article on "The World's Technological Capacity to Store, Communicate, and Compute Information" with the assertion that "the world's technological information processing capacities" are "growing at clearly exponential rates".[11] Hilbert and López noted that during the two decades under examination, from 1986 to 2007, information that was previously stored in analog format (paper, vinyl records, and analog film formats) but had been migrated to digital formats increased from 0.8% to 94%. They point out that in 1986 the calculator "was still the dominant way to compute information" and as such it represented 41% of the $3 \times 10^8$ general-purpose million-instructions-per-second (MIPS) of computation. By the year 2000 the personal computer represented 86% of the $2.9 \times 10^{11}$ MIPS. Worthy of note is the fact that by 2007 videogame consoles represented 25% of the total of $6.4 \times 10^{12}$ MIPS of general-purpose computation taking place on the planet.[12] Hilbert and López distinguish between general-purpose computation as that which can be controlled, tasked, and re-tasked by humans interacting with the machine, and application-specific computation, such as is embedded in electronic appliances or visual interfaces. Their research shows that in the seven

---

10  George Fallis, *Multiversities, Ideas, and Democracy* (Toronto: University of Toronto Press, 2007), 178, my emphasis.

11  Hilbert and López, "The World's Technological Capacity," 5.

12  *Ibid.*, 4–5.

years from 2000 to the end of their study "the introduction of broadband Internet [...] multiplied the world's telecommunication capacity by a factor of 29, from 2.2 optimally compressed exabytes [...] to 65."[13]

This research makes it indisputable that there have been profound changes during the lifetime of most of the planet's current inhabitants: between 1986 and 2007, "general purpose computing capacity grew at an annual rate of 58%."[14] Seen in this context, the question of whether such profound change occurring in such a short historical period is revolutionary or not becomes almost a distraction. Consistent novelty amid constant change is merely the way things are for all students born into what Tapscott has labeled the "Net Generation." In this world of constant and continuing technological growth and adaptation, current students have no experience of a time when, with apologies to Bob Dylan, "the times [were not] a-changin.'" For them, technological change—and the power and control it affords—are as integral to reality as was political instability to a French peasant during the Hundred Years' War.

In *Grown Up Digital*, Tapscott reports the findings of an extensive data-collection exercise undertaken by his research team in a dozen developed and developing countries. The research on which Tapscott's book is founded was a four million dollar project "funded," as he writes, "by large companies."[15] As part of this research, data was collected from 9,442 people through interviews, surveys of Internet users, and ethnographic studies. His data set is large and his conclusions well founded. As noted above, he labels the current generation of students the "Net Gen," an abbreviation of "Net Generation." In Tapscott's scheme, Net Geners were born from January 1977 to December 1997. One of the observations made in Tapscott's industrial study is that "the Net Geners have grown up digital and they're living in the twenty-first century, but the educational system in many places is lagging 100 years behind."[16] This gap between what they find and what they want and need in education is due in part to the fact that Net Geners "want to customize things" and "make them their own,"[17] but institutional education is still mostly predicated on a capitalist model

---

13   *Ibid.*, 3. An exabyte or exibyte is the equivalent of $10^{18}$ bytes. It is the next order of magnitude in the quantification of data above petabyte, which in turn sites above terabyte.

14   *Ibid.*, "The World's Technological Capacity," 1.

15   Tapscott, *Grown Up Digital*, xi.

16   *Ibid.*, 122.

17   *Ibid.*, 6.

driven by an outmoded and centralized concept of copyright, institutional ownership, and professorial authority.

For Net Geners, "speed is normal. Innovation is part of life,"[18] while educational institutions—especially universities—innovate reluctantly and change slowly, and then only after extensive agitation, discussion, debate, revision (usually aimed at minimizing the impact of change), and prodding. Tapscott calls the model he considers to be an accurate description of too much of the present educational system "the sage-on-the-stage approach to instruction,"[19] and we find little basis to challenge this description. It is a model that has been practiced since the Middle Ages, since the earliest days of the university. (We might challenge Tapscott's assertion that the educational system is lagging only 100 years behind.) It is a model that was reinforced when books were handcrafted, expensive, and scarce. The one who had the book—or at least had the greatest sustained access to the book—was, reasonably enough, recognized as the authority on what the text had to offer. Those who wanted to learn would gather in a hall to glean what they could from the master's teachings.

When Gutenberg's moveable-type printing press came along, eventually the cost and relative scarcity of books became less significant factors. With this, perhaps we would expect the sage-on-the-stage model to have changed more than it did. From the vantage point of the early twenty-first century, there is much to be thankful for that the sage-on-the-stage model survived as long as it did; certainly we should be grateful for the retention of expertise to guide readers through the core texts. But the role of the expert can be retained even as control of content loosens, and the media, through which students encounter content, change. The sage must step off the stage and circulate in real and virtual realms where the reason for their authority lies not in their elevated position but in their ability to demonstrate the validity of whatever assertions they advance. Net Geners seek to replace the university's traditional "culture of control with a culture of enablement,"[20] and the digital humanities offer many opportunities for this to happen.

---

18  *Ibid.*, 7.
19  *Ibid.*, 8.
20  *Ibid.*, 6.

# Pedagogical Approach

The challenges of implementing digital humanities in pedagogy are complicated by what Luciano Floridi has dubbed the Infosphere: "the environment constituted by the totality of information entities—including all agents—processes, their proprieties, and mutual relations."[21] The blurring of boundaries between the analog and digital environments as they consolidate, coupled with the deterioration of borders between the learning space and the "outside world," require increased skills in self-regulation, discernment, and analysis of information (that is, critical thinking), and collaboration.[22]

Digital humanities pedagogy also raises fears—such as the easy ability to plagiarize "intellectual property" from online, or the requirement of student-centric learning in a mutable online environment—and concerns regarding how new technology can be provided for students. Educators must work together with both students and administrative powers to acknowledge the existence and consequences of the ubiquity of technology in the learning environment. The circumstances raised uniquely by the Infosphere must be addressed through numerous philosophical and technological provisions to ensure successful education in the tertiary-level classroom.

Philosophical requirements demand a number of creative methods and realistic ways of thinking about the consequences of the cultural shift into the digital age. Certainly, there is a need for openness to the inclusion of new technology and information exchange formats (such as social networking) implemented in new and unique ways. The elastic boundaries of the Infosphere insist on collaborative education models to provide students with the opportunity to access and to build upon new ideas collectively, whilst maintaining the ability to create new thoughts independently. Further, students need not only collaborate with academic colleagues, but also with their wider community. The mutable nature of the

---

21  Luciana Floridi, "Information Ethics: On the Philosophical Foundation of Computer Ethics," *Ethics and Information Technology* 1, no. 1 (1999): 44.

22  See Luciano Floridi, "A Look into the Future Impact of ICT on Our Lives," *The Information Society* 23, no. 1 (2007): 59–64; Roger Silverstone, "Regulation, Media Literacy and Media Civics," *Media, Culture & Society* 26, no. 3 (2004): 440–49; and Viviane Reding, "Media Literacy: Do People Really Understand How to Make the Most of Blogs, Search Engines, or Interactive TV?" press release by the Commissioner for Information Society and Media, European Commission, Brussels, December 20, 2007, http://europa.eu/rapid/pressReleasesAction.do?reference=IP/07/1970.

digital environment demands flexibility, so that students can be allowed to bring their own ideas, knowledge, questions, and topics into the learning environment, as opposed to the strict set of guidelines that might be imposed by an instructor or administration.

Initially such freedom may seem daunting, but it can also be a liberating experience if one considers that this allows educators to share their own passions with students. If educators' expectations are clearly outlined, students' own passion for a subject can flourish alongside those of their academic facilitators. The opportunity to self-regulate their research means students are free to explore what they love best about a subject; in turn, this liberates educators from having to "hand-hold" their students through a subject. Furthermore, we must recognize various means of knowledge contribution through unique and differing methods of communication. Students should push the boundaries of traditional communication to present their intentions as authors with clarity. Educators should create assignments designed to provoke original means of knowledge presentation. Assessment strategies should provide feedback that includes visual or aural material in addition to the written word.

Practically, such steps require equipment and call for technological requirements to be met, and these requirements are more easily handled at the tertiary level than in secondary schools. Policies designed to protect minors and to prevent legal action in primary and secondary institutions currently restrict the techniques and pedagogical tools that educators in these institutions might otherwise use. But such policy-driven restrictions are unnecessary in universities, where students are not minors (and are therefore accountable for their own actions) or, if they are minors, the institution is considered *in loco parentis* and has the authority to waive such restrictions as those that obtain in the pre-tertiary system. Consequently, at the post-secondary level, pre-existent online resources (e.g. Youtube, Facebook, and Twitter) can all be harnessed to assist in educational endeavors.

A second issue from which tertiary education is released is the need for uniform access to identical resources—a move necessary in pre-tertiary education in order to promote a fair and equal learning environment for all students. But if post-secondary students choose to use different tools than those offered by the institution they should be free to do so. While some students have access to computers better equipped for film editing, others may possess mobile phone technology with the ability to capture high quality digital video. This alleviates many of the financial obligations universities find prohibitive, while introducing new technological opportunities to both staff and students. In this model, learning is student-centric and individual, allowing students to provide feedback to—and communicate amongst— themselves, using a variety of media and hardware. Just as it might be ideal for universities to provide students with access to new forms of technology and means of communication, students should also be allowed to introduce new tools and technologies to one another. A move toward tertiary education inclusive of digital humanities does not necessarily call for more technological apparatus than currently can be found in universities; rather, what is required is a change in the way we engage with such tools, and the willingness to open the classroom to technologies suggested by the student.

The practice of a digital humanities philosophy such as the one outlined above can be established through engagement with online resources. Social networking sites, such as Facebook, have the potential to assist in educational organization—to create class groups, circulate assignment information, and entice student participation and group work. Facebook, for example, might also be employed to create alternative educational opportunities, such as role-playing scenarios. Youtube might be used to promote supplementary lectures in a subject area, or to create and share streams of video feedback for dissemination or assessment.[23] Weblogs provide students an opportunity to reflect on their thoughts and to gain new perspectives with classmates, while online resources such as the personal websites of professors or notable authorities grant access to new information in a subject area months before it appears in a print edition. The preprints of Luciano Floridi's work that appear on his website (http://www.philosophyofinformation.net/) offer an example of this method of accessing an author's most current thoughts on a topic. More experimentally, distance between academics and students with similar interests can be alleviated through the use of online environments such as *Second Life*.[24]

---

23    See, for example, the YouTube video created by Dr Michael Wesch and two-hundred students enrolled in his Introduction to Cultural Anthropology course at Kansas State University, Spring 2007: "A Vision of Students Today," *Digital Ethnography @ Kansas State University*, October 12, 2007, http://mediatedcultures.net/ksudigg/?p=119.

24    In April 2008, for example, Henry Jenkins, Provost's Professor of Communication, Journalism, and Cinematic Arts at the University of Southern California, gave a virtual lecture on Harry Potter fandom and social justice in *Teen Second Life*, a version of *Second Life* reserved for teenage users. For a video of the virtual lecture (and the impromptu dance party that followed), see "Henry Jenkins in Second Life Talks about Potter Fandom," *YouTube*, May 2, 2008, http://www.youtube.com/watch?v=sV7741jTOHc.

# Integrating Digital Humanities into Existing Programs

Integrating digital humanities into existing university programs and courses need not be a Herculean, much less a Sisyphean, task. However, various scales of adoption will require different levels of adaptation. Financial feasibility need be an issue only if a separate digital humanities department is considered. While this is possible, from our perspective it is not desirable: we assert digital humanities as a means of breaking down the exclusivity of disciplinary silos and encouraging exposure to technological opportunities across disciplines. Having a trans-disciplinary foundation, digital humanities operates somewhat antithetically to the established model of university organization into departments and faculties. Positing it as a "distinct society," as a new independent discipline, would distort the applicability and potential of the digital paradigm shift. Furthermore, it would only encourage competitive, insular, conservative reactions from existing departments.

Undergraduate programs are already ripe for the introduction and integration of digital humanities ideas and practices, since most already seek to establish networks of experience between disciplines, combining a breadth of knowledge acquisition with the focus provided through a declared major. Thus, developing a digital humanities curriculum might be more easily accomplished if it is presented as an evolutionary, rather than revolutionary, process. An initial step in such an evolution will be to work digital humanities into current curricula; such integration will require collaborative adoption. A persistent challenge to this will be ensuring that all involved are, and remain, on board. Digital humanities is not inherently about seeking new worlds or traveling in new directions, but exploring new methods of travel and considering new modes of cooperation—it is about reconfiguring the academic journey itself. Those involved need to be inspired and encouraged by solid leadership. Administrative understanding and support is therefore crucial. Such support can be as simple as acknowledging digital humanities as a priority in an institution's strategic plan, or as complex as working out a system of inducements and rewards to encourage professors to join digital humanities experiments in pedagogy (and in research).

To integrate digital humanities into existing curricula, it is important to remember that digital humanities is not a discipline, not a theoretical approach, and not an end in itself of research or teaching practices. Rather, it is a means of scholarship and pedagogy that embraces the digital frame as its knowledge *environment*, inclusively and self-consciously moving beyond the exclusive and often unacknowledged hegemony of print cultural paradigms. To enable this means, the integration of digital humanities perceptions into existing programs will require the co-ordination of collaborative relationships between existing humanities, social sciences, professional studies, and computer science programs. Essential disciplinary players are likely to include literature, computer science, political science, sociology, philosophy, art and media studies, communication, psychology, history, languages, the performing arts, religious studies, and economics.

## Faculty Participation

No matter how gradually it is done, changing universities into sites of digital engagement with both contemporary and traditional material requires that faculty be committed to exposing students to the most pertinent and useful processes and paradigms. But start small. Offer to guest lecture on digital humanities related topics or applications in colleagues' courses. Collaboratively create electronic resources and bibliographies and make such assets accessible university-wide. Arrange to integrate informational links and pages on personal, departmental, faculty, and library websites. Give lectures or sponsor visiting speakers at your university on digital humanities-related research. Such initiatives will create awareness and a place for digital humanities in your institution.

Following a coordinated effort to raise the visibility and awareness of digital humanities within institutions, initial integrative steps should involve populating, or at least peppering, a university curriculum with digital humanities-related content and practice. Introductory courses in the above-listed disciplines should be encouraged to contain a unit or module on digital humanities theory and praxis. Usefully, digital humanities reflections could be explored at the end of existing courses as a comparative way to consider some of the more traditional curricular structures to which students have been exposed in the rest of the course. For example, in the final few weeks of first-year English Literature courses—in which students typically develop a communicative and rhetorical awareness by studying examples drawn from 500 years of Western poetry, prose and drama—students can be exposed to digital humanities-related material and practices, such as digital archives, e-lit, digital games, text analysis, and data visualization. This complement to a historical and genre based introduction to literature will reveal the potential impact of the digital revolution on print-based traditions, born-digital materials, and digital opportunities for knowledge creation and criticism. This initial incorporation of digital humanities-inflected material into established introductory courses can expand to incorporate assignments throughout the year as the use of wikis, virtual narrative worlds, and collaborative data visualization find their way into other courses.

Upper-level undergraduate courses can draw on students' initial exposure in introductory courses and extend students' digital humanities understanding and practice by upgrading and diversifying assignment and participation opportunities. Enhancing pedagogical practices with digital humanities frameworks creates the possibility to experiment with "humanities labs." These digital spaces—akin to their scientific counterparts— can be procedural and process based environments where quantifiable experiments are done and the results of methodical processes related to larger hypotheses: one can explore the activated complex of literature and literary modes of analysis in a more participatory and networked way. One of the most desirable consequences of the collision between literary studies and digital humanities is the generation of these "humanities lab" spaces, experimental sandboxes where engineering and understanding can work in tandem. For example, in an upper-level romantic literature course taught by one of the authors of the present chapter, students both play and build interactive narrative spaces that are designed not simply to narrate or translate a book-bound story, but to construct a rhetorical argument about the book. These persuasive games are designed to offer a counterpoint to traditional essay argumentation, and students actually come to understand the all-too-often naturalized and unquestioned essay format in profound and useful ways after working through these alternatives. Roger Whitson, a romantic period scholar, teaches a course on William Blake and Media (http://media.blake2.org/) at the Georgia Institute of Technology, in which he engages his students via Twitter, Zotero and collaborative blogs.

Student engagement is the key advantage of such pedagogical evolutions, and what the implementation of digital humanities-related theory and praxis introduces into existing courses is an emphasis not on the *what*—the facts, histories, and artifacts of course content—but on the *how*, on the processes and the understanding of such processes related to the circulation and function of information in all its particular disciplinary incarnations.

Following from these initial integrations, digital humanities becomes less an unknown threat and more of a common denominator that will create its own opportunity to become an option for focused study at the upper-undergraduate level. To enable students to take advantage of this opportunity, universities could modify existing program requirements to enable undergraduates to declare majors that rely on a cooperative integration of courses offered through existing departments. Taking this further, graduate program possibilities raise the prospect of solid and unique co-supervisions, mutually influential mentorships between students and supervisors and, ultimately, the opportunity to prepare students for the next generation of innovation and progress beyond the first waves of digital humanities energies and speculations.

## Funding and Budgetary Commitments

What kind of institutional financial commitment will be necessary? Given that national granting agencies in North America and Europe already recognize digital scholarship and pedagogy as a primary funding and investment priority, it is not unreasonable to expect that institutional budgets ought to reflect such prioritization. However, in these times of perpetual financial crisis, our suggestion is that minimal impact on current funding formulae will be not only the best, but also the only realistic strategy to introduce and integrate digital humanities into existing post-secondary practice. While the establishment of new departments is neither desirable nor necessary, the hiring of new faculty members is also not strictly necessary, especially if hiring opportunities in existing departments are configured to encourage candidates with particular strengths in digital humanities-related areas and topics of research to apply. And even in the absence of hiring to fill existing vacancies, because teacher-scholar models encourage a feedback loop between cutting-edge research and classroom content and practice, existing faculty members are more than capable of integrating digital humanities perceptions and practices into their individual courses.

In addition, and perhaps most importantly, collaborative teams of existing faculty members from different disciplines should be encouraged to deliver course content. This can be as simple as organizing systems of guest lectures and exchanges (in which two or more faculty members agree to equally participate in, and contribute to, each other's courses during the term), or through infrequent combinations of two or more smaller classes into a larger integrated unit to host faculty roundtables, panels, or shared student activities (in real or virtual learning environments).[25] More ambitious opportunities include designing entire courses as a series of internal guest speakers from across campus invited to give their perspective on a given topic. Such an "umbrella" course could still be coordinated, administered, and evaluated by a single faculty member from a single department and remain as part of a department's core offerings. None of the above examples require additional administrative funding or faculty time commitment, and all serve as opportunities for modeling the cross-disciplinary conversations that digital humanities encourages.

Would any new technological resources or infrastructures be necessary? The short answer is "no," but this response is based on the assumption that most post-secondary institutions engaged in programs of higher learning have already established the necessary digital network infrastructures, resources, and access for their faculty and students. Assuming, then, that most campuses provide wired or wireless access to the internet, and that students either have their own computers or access to computer labs as a fundamental part of their post-secondary requirements, the integration of digital humanities into existing courses would not place unreasonable demands or strain on existing technological resources. Indeed, the relative ubiquity of digital media and hardware in the lived reality of the early twenty-first century is what justifies the need to engage with and explore digital humanities in the first place. When existing technological infrastructures are lacking at a particular institution, the integration and emphasis of digital humanities within existing pedagogical structures can provide the rationale necessary for upgrades toward a baseline standard of digital operation and access. Again, this can be supported administratively by a strategic and budgetary commitment to technological capability as a fundamental operational standard.

The most challenging economic hurdle to overcome could also result in the most useful and productive opportunities for the sustained development of university programs. Universities would be well-advised to consider alternative models for determining departmental budget allotments. Funding models that do not pit each department against all others—sometimes by dint of faculty complement, sometimes by counting

---

25  For a discussion of such a virtual pedagogical experiment across multiple campuses and countries, see Matthew K. Gold's chapter, "Looking for Whitman: A Multi-Campus Experiment in Digital Pedagogy."

the number of students who declare a particular discipline as their major, sometimes by counting the number of students who take courses offered by the department, whether or not they declare that discipline their major—would result in a healthier overall environment. Taking a cue from national and multi-national granting agencies that recognize, prioritize and promote collaborative research, university financial plans should be configured to encourage integration and exchange between its departments. In other words, departments could be rewarded for the amount of cross-campus engagement modeled by faculty members and made available to students.

One potential adjustment that could support inter- or multi-disciplinary programs (digital humanities or otherwise) could see different departments hosting required core (digital humanities) courses but no one department claiming those students who have declared (in our example, digital humanities) as a major concentration. An alternative to this could be to offer digital humanities as a minor concentration, or to allow specific departments to establish digital humanities as a mandatory minor concentration for particular majors. To encourage departments to participate in a cross-disciplinary digital humanities program, students who take a required course from a specific department toward a digital humanities major could contribute to that department's numbers/statistics used in determining budget allotments. Each department would receive credit for its particular course, eschewing the competitive strategy of departments fighting over or claiming majors as disciplinary possessions or economic bargaining chips.

Administratively, faculty members from different departments who plan to offer digital humanities-related courses would be expected to collectively determine program requirements for digital humanities majors, garner senate or governing-body approval for such curriculum modifications, and rotate advising responsibilities. While this might be met with resistance by faculty members who already feel overwhelmed with university-related service responsibilities, it reflects a decentralized program model that would require an initially larger time-commitment to establish, but not much more than a continuing committee responsibility to sustain.

# Conclusion

Ill-conceived, inflexible, conservative practices are likely to doom universities in the near and middle term. Resistance to change ought to be recognized as the suicidal attitude it is in today's post-secondary environment. Taking a wait-and-see attitude that cautiously preserves the *status quo* is akin to choosing an unnecessary slow death over the possibility of an innovative cure. In an era of budget crises, enrolment uncertainty, and an increasing lack of connections between university-level career preparation and professional practice, it would be foolish to ignore an opportunity to reinvent and reconsider existing paradigms and practices. Digital humanities represents an already-established movement away from the doom-inviting stasis of the secondhand conservatism of universities that know the Net Generation has come, and yet decline to build the education system Net Geners both want and need.

While it may seem unpleasant for many to envision universities other than as the medieval institutions they still resemble in so many ways, it may seem equally (or even more) unpleasant to imagine them as the corporations and businesses that others seem to expect them to be. The corporate model, as unpleasant as it is, has two things going for it: historically, this is the corporation's moment; and, practically, corporate success involves taking risks, embracing diversity, and attempting to lead trends rather than follow them.

Seeing universities fail is, fortunately or unfortunately, a very real possibility in the frightening (but also opportunity-laden) historical moment in which we find ourselves. We believe that failing to integrate digital humanities into higher education's collective consciousness will likely precipitate a large-scale failure of university-level humanities studies as the rest of the academy—indeed, the rest of the world—continues to move beyond knowledge systems that no longer account for significant chunks of a world already transformed by technological and communicative evolutions. This is not a doomsday scenario, but one that confirms the inevitable change in perception and the expansion of pedagogical possibilities that digital humanities affords. As Tapscott has demonstrated, "the Net Generation has arrived."[26] Whether the changes necessary to accommodate that generation's

---

26   Tapscott, *Grown Up Digital*, 6.

needs, desires, and proclivities is recognized as an opportunity, or resisted as yet another assault on the *status quo*, may depend on the success of digital humanists in convincing administrators and faculty colleagues that "they have come, it is high time we build it."

# 14.  Opening up Digital Humanities Education

*Lisa Spiro*

Suppose that you are an English graduate student who has become intrigued by digital humanities.[1] Your university lacks members of faculty with expertise in digital humanities, and you're too invested in your current graduate program to go somewhere else. You do your best to keep up with the developments happening in digital humanities by following blogs and Twitter streams, but you worry that you are being left behind. You would like to apply for a job with a digital humanities focus, but realize that you would need to develop the necessary scholarly and technical expertise.

Or perhaps you are a mid-career faculty member in history. In working on your current project, you think that you would be able to open up new possibilities for both analyzing data and presenting it to your readers by using GIS technologies. You have been diligently reading manuals and trying to pick up as much knowledge as you can on your own, but you suspect that you could learn much more efficiently through formal training. You might also be able to find collaborators interested in your project. However, you have existing obligations at your home institution, so you would need a flexible training program.

I would like to thank the anonymous peer reviewer for offering insightful questions and suggestions, as well as my colleagues Rebecca Davis and Bryan Alexander for exploring open education and MOOCs with me in ongoing conversations.

1   This scenario-based introduction was inspired by Peer 2 Peer University and The Mozilla Foundation's *An Open Badge System Framework*, https://docs.google.com/document/d/1xGuyK4h7DLVeOrFPeegB4ORMutblJf9xVRZCizgx_j8/edit?hl=en&authkey=CNarn4UJ.

Or maybe you are a programmer who is working on a humanities text-mining project. You are becoming increasingly fascinated by your work but you also are aware that you could take your work further if you had a deeper knowledge of the humanities. You would like to develop a keener understanding of digital humanities methods so that you can ultimately take a leadership role on digital humanities projects.

Each of these hypothetical would-be digital humanists faces the same problem: the lack of flexible opportunities to gain the knowledge and skills required for digital humanities researchers and professionals. As Geoffrey Rockwell argues, the digital humanities risk becoming too exclusive because "there are few formal ways that people can train."[2] In the past, many have entered the digital humanities by serving as informal apprentices on projects. But this approach is not scalable or equitable, since it essentially requires one to be in the right place at the right time. Aspiring digital humanists need a flexible, inexpensive way to develop key skills, demonstrate their learning and participate in the digital humanities community.

One lightweight solution is a certificate program, which is not as intensive as a master's or doctoral program but still prepares participants for professional work in the field. Although there are a few graduate certificate programs in the digital humanities, those that do exist face a central limitation: currently they serve only students already enrolled at the home institution. Furthermore, the instructors typically come from a local faculty. By developing an open certificate program, the digital humanities community can spark innovations in teaching and research, share educational practices and resources, open up learning opportunities, bring in new members, and cultivate a shared sense of mission.

Creating a networked, open digital humanities certificate program would engage the digital humanities community in larger efforts to build participatory, non-proprietary educational platforms and to explore the implications of digital technologies for knowledge creation:

- 'Networked' has both technological and cultural resonance, suggesting that participants would be connected through online networks and that they would participate in networked learning. Inspired by networked communities such as Wikipedia, such an

---

2   Geoffrey Rockwell, "Inclusion in the Digital Humanities," *philosophi.ca,* June 28, 2010, http://www.philosophi.ca/pmwiki.php/Main/InclusionInTheDigitalHumanities.

approach to learning "is committed to a vision of the social stressing cooperation, interactivity, mutuality, and social engagement for their own sakes and for the powerful productivity to which it more often than not leads."[3]

- 'Open' suggests that the curriculum and course content should be remixable and reusable so that instructors don't have to duplicate effort in developing educational materials but can share innovations. Additionally, openness means that the program should be as transparent as possible and engage the community in constructing learning opportunities.
- By focusing on the 'digital humanities', the certificate program would balance a strong grounding in humanities problems and methods with an understanding of technology, both as a maker and a theorist.
- 'Certificate' implies that the program would be more focused than a master's or PhD program.

As an initial foray into networked, open digital humanities education, a graduate certificate program makes sense. Since it is smaller in scale, it would likely require less work to develop and administer than a master's or PhD program (although the effort would still be significant).

By developing an open certificate program, the digital humanities community would forward several goals. First, it would offer more paths of entry and foster greater inclusiveness, bringing new members — and new ideas — into the profession and allowing established practitioners to take their work in new directions. As *Our Cultural Commonwealth* recognizes, building the humanities cyberinfrastructure will require "more formal venues and opportunities for training and encouragement."[4] Although the report specifically recommends brief one to three week workshops aimed at younger scholars, more systematic, intensive training would enable participants to do more sophisticated work. It makes sense for the digital humanities community, which focuses on innovative uses of technology in the humanities and embraces values of networked culture such as

---

3  Cathy N. Davidson and David Theo Goldberg, *The Future of Learning Institutions in a Digital Age*, John D. and Catherine T. MacArthur Foundation Reports on Digital Media and Learning (Cambridge: MIT Press, 2009), 30.

4  American Council of Learned Societies, *Our Cultural Commonwealth: The Report of the American Council of Learned Societies Commission on Cyberinfrastructure for the Humanities and Social Sciences* (New York: American Council of Learned Societies, 2006), 34.

openness and experimentation, to explore the implications of networked technologies for education. Developing an open digital humanities certificate program would likely unleash pedagogical innovation, as course leaders and students experiment with different approaches to building learning communities, designing effective assignments, and assessing and certifying learning. This program would not only teach participants how to operate as networked digital humanists, but also transmit the core values of collaboration, experimentation, and openness through its very structure.

The certificate program should display the following characteristics:

## 1. *Open*

There seems to be growing consensus that the digital humanities community should promote open source software and open access to scholarly information.[5] As Gideon Burton argues, openness can enhance teaching, as it makes the research process transparent, fosters collaboration (including with students), and reveals "best practices."[6] Just as open scholarship builds our collective knowledge and provides access to information, so open education promotes opportunity, trains researchers, and builds a larger appreciation of the scholarly mission. By adopting open licenses, the community can make available curricula and educational resources that can be reused and adapted in other contexts. Moreover, open education makes learning transparent (or as Mark Sample puts it, "naked"[7]), increasing accountability and replicability.

## 2. *Global*

Rather than being restricted to a local institution, a digital humanities certificate program would be global, bringing together learners around the

---

5   Dan Cohen, "Open Access Publishing and Scholarly Values," *Dan Cohen's Digital Humanities Blog*, May 27, 2010, http://www.dancohen.org/2010/05/27/open-access-publishing-and-scholarly-values/; Stephen Ramsay, "Open Access Publishing and Scholarly Values (Part Two)," *Stephen Ramsay*, March 28, 2010, http://lenz.unl.edu/wordpress/?p=190; and Kathleen Fitzpatrick, "Open Access Publishing and Scholarly Values (Part Three)," *Planned Obsolescence*, May 28, 2010, http://www.plannedobsolescence.net/open-access-publishing-and-scholarly-values-part-three/.

6   Gideon Burton, "The Open Scholar," *Academic Evolution*, August 11, 2009, http://www.academicevolution.com/2009/08/the-open-scholar.html.

7   Mark Sample, "The Open Source Professor: Teaching, Research, and Transparency" (paper presented at the Maryland Institute for Technology in the Humanities [MITH], College Park, Maryland, October 27, 2009), http://www.slideshare.net/samplereality/the-open-source-professor-teaching-research-and-transparency.

world to work towards a common goal and share their diverse knowledge.[8] Taking a global approach would include more perspectives, expand access and strengthen the community. Of course, running a global program would entail challenges—including negotiating linguistic and cultural differences and dealing with differences in time zones.[9]

### 3. *Modular*

Although the program would require completion of a foundation course and practicum project, the curriculum would be modular, so that a participant could design a program that matches particular objectives and builds on prior knowledge. The program should experiment with different ways of organizing learning, such as courses that follow a set schedule and more focused modules that facilitate self-directed or small group learning. Serious attention would need to be paid to how best to sequence the modules, since some might build on previous knowledge.

### 4. *Community-driven*

This program would take what John Seeley Brown and Richard P. Adler call a "demand-pull" approach to education, which provides students "access to rich (sometimes virtual) learning communities built around a practice" and is driven by students' passion to become members of that community of practice (as opposed to supply-push, where the objective is to pour knowledge into the student's head).[10] Much of the learning would take place through participation in virtual communities such as online forums and project teams, and the curriculum itself would be developed through community effort.

### 5. *Technological*

As befits its focus on the digital humanities, the certificate program would explore how technologies can be harnessed to enhance learning.

---

8   Connie Moon Sehat and Erika Farr likewise recommend "cross-campus cooperation" in developing digital humanities education, imagining courses taught by faculty at different universities; see *The Future of Digital Scholarship: Preparation, Training, Curricula. Report of a Colloquium on Education in Digital Scholarship, April 17–18, 2009* (Washington: Council on Library and Information Resources, 2009), http://www.clir.org/pubs/archives/SehatFarr2009.pdf.

9   Matthew K. Gold's chapter in this collection, "Looking for Whitman: A Multi-Campus Experiment in Digital Humanities Pedagogy," offers a detailed discussion of these issues.

10  John Seely Brown and Richard P. Adler, "Minds on Fire: Open Education, the Long Tail and Learning 2.0," *EDUCAUSE Review* 43, no. 1 (2008): 16–32.

For example, the program could employ social technologies to support interactive, dynamic learning communities and use gaming to motivate and structure learning. It could experiment with the approach used by the Open Learning Initiative (http://oli.web.cmu.edu/openlearning/initiative) and build online courses that incorporate intelligent tutoring systems, simulations, and continuous assessment and targeted feedback to make learning flexible and responsive (or make use of existing interactive open content, given the expense of developing such systems).[11] Further, it could enable students to hone their skills as *producers* of digital resources and tools, whether by creating databases, visualizations, multimedia essays, or software applications.

## 6. *Experimental*

Rather than taking a set approach to education, the certificate program could experiment with different ways of structuring learning, building communities, creating educational content, and guiding learners, assessing and reporting back on what works and what does not. Indeed, part of the program's mission could be to study learning in open environments. Assessment might include levels of participation by learners, performance on exams and exercises, evaluation of portfolios, and longer-term studies of the career and personal outcomes of those who complete the certificate program.

In some ways, this certificate program entails rethinking higher education so that it is comparable to a "wiki-ized university." A "wiki-ized university" enables students and faculty to self-organize and co-design the curriculum, makes class content openly available and editable, and engages the course facilitator in setting up a learning environment that students can then navigate and modify.[12] Likewise, this model extends

---

11  A study of an online statistics course offered by the Open Learning Initiative found that "the learning gains of students were at least as good as in a traditional, instructor-led course" and that students in a hybrid course combining online learning with face-to-face tutorials learned the material better and more quickly than they would in a traditional course. Marsha Lovett, Oded Meyer, and Candace Thille, "The Open Learning Initiative: Measuring the Effectiveness of the OLI Statistics Course in Accelerating Student Learning," *Journal of Interactive Media in Education* 14 (2008), http://jime.open.ac.uk/jime/article/view/2008-14.

12  David J. Staley, "Managing the Platform: Higher Education and the Logic of Wikinomics," *EDUCAUSE Review* 44, no. 1 (2009): 36–47. See also Don Tapscott and Anthony D. Williams, "Innovating the 21st-Century University: It's Time!" *EDUCAUSE Review* 45, no. 1 (2010): 16–29, and Davidson and Goldberg, *The Future of Learning Institutions in a Digital Age*.

the community-driven, participatory nature of THATCamp (http://www.thatcamp.org/) to more in-depth professional training. Like THATCamp, the digital humanities certificate program would allow participants from all levels to shape the program, focus on experimentation and conversation rather than the one-way transmission of knowledge, promote collaboration and play, be low cost, and encourage participants to make their work freely and openly available. For a comparison between traditional graduate certificate programs with the proposed open, networked program, see Table 1.

| | **Traditional** | **Networked, Open** |
|---|---|---|
| Place | Campus-based | Available anywhere; primarily online |
| Administration | Overseen by a single institution | Engages multiple institutions and organizations |
| Curriculum | Departments and schools set the curriculum | Digital humanities community defines the curriculum |
| Access | Closed; content, curriculum, and student work typically behind wall | Open; content, curriculum, and student work accessible and visible |
| Organization | Organized around courses | Organized around competencies |
| Certification | Certified by a department within an accredited university | Certified by professional organization or community |
| Development | Educational content developed by course faculty | Content developed by larger digital humanities community |
| Focus | Individual work | Collaborative work |

**Table 1.** Comparison between the traditional graduate certificate program and the open, networked program proposed in this chapter.

In this chapter, I make the case for an open digital humanities certificate program, sketch its potential components, and imagine how it might be run. Certainly establishing an open digital humanities certificate program would be an ambitious undertaking. However, it would not face the same financial, institutional, and cultural barriers as would completely transforming a university toward an open model, since it is smaller in scale and more focused in its aspiration to prepare participants for work in the digital humanities community. Implementing a digital humanities certificate program would require engaging the community in developing a curriculum, creating course content, connecting students and mentors, honing participants' skills through a practicum project or internship, coaching students by providing feedback on their work, and certifying knowledge. This open digital humanities certificate program could emerge iteratively, perhaps first through the creation of curriculum and course content, then through building learning communities, and finally by providing formalized means of certification.

## Curriculum

To establish an open digital humanities certificate program, the community would need to develop an academic program that would strengthen students' core knowledge and skills. As Melissa Terras suggests, curriculum reveals the core identity and "hidden history" of a disciplinary community—what it values and how it trains the next generation of scholars.[13] Although there are an increasing number of digital humanities graduate programs, the community has not yet reached wide consensus on what the digital humanities curriculum should include, nor has much research been published on digital humanities education (although there is growing interest in DH pedagogy).[14] Since I believe that the *community* should shape the curriculum for the digital humanities program, I will suggest a process for creating it rather than detailing its specific content. The digital humanities community could design a flexible, focused curriculum both by reviewing existing programs (including curriculum documents

---

13  Melissa Terras, "Disciplined: Using Educational Studies to Analyse 'Humanities Computing,'" *Literary and Linguistic Computing* 21, no. 2 (2006): 229–46.

14  Brett D. Hirsch and Meagan Timney, "The Importance of Pedagogy: Towards a Companion to Teaching Digital Humanities" (poster presented at Digital Humanities 2010, King's College London, London, July 7–10, 2010).

and syllabi) and engaging in a broader conversation about what constitutes knowledge in the digital humanities. This conversation could take place in different contexts, such as the annual Digital Humanities conference, through a survey of and interviews with digital humanities practitioners[15] and via online forums. Indeed, this conversation is already underway, as the Digital Humanities 2012 conference featured a workshop that aimed to determine "common elements of digital humanities curricula."[16] Based on such analysis and discussion, the community could devise a flexible, dynamic structure for a digital humanities certificate program. This evolving curriculum could be shared through a wiki, which could also aggregate resources (syllabi, learning modules, readings, exercises, assessments) that support it.

In designing the open certificate program, we can look to existing graduate certificate programs in the digital humanities. Several US universities, including Texas A&M, UCLA, Emory, University of Nebraska, and Tulane, recently began offering digital humanities certificate programs aimed primarily at their current graduate students.[17] These programs typically require fewer courses than a master's program. Common elements of the curriculum include a foundation course, a project/internship, and two to three additional courses focused on topics such as book history, computer-human interaction, visualization, Geographic Information Systems, media studies, and research methods. Reflecting the diverse nature of knowledge in the digital humanities, these programs often involve interdisciplinary collaborations, bringing in faculty from departments such as literature, history, computer science,

---

15  I have launched a Zotero group (http://www.zotero.org/groups/digital_humanities_ education) to collect syllabi and other information relevant to digital humanities education. At the 2011 Digital Humanities conference, I presented an initial study of these syllabi; see Lisa Spiro, "Knowing and Doing: Understanding the Digital Humanities Curriculum" (paper presented at Digital Humanities 2011, Stanford University, Stanford, California, July 19–22, 2011).

16  Manfred Thaller, "Towards a Reference Curriculum for the Digital Humanities" (paper presented at Digital Humanities 2012, Hamburg, 2012), http://www.dh2012. uni-hamburg.de/conference/programme/abstracts/towards-a-reference-curriculum-for-the-digital-humanities/.

17  Others have likewise recognized the need for a digital humanities certificate program. For instance, Margie McLellan envisions a certificate program for graduate and undergraduate students at Wayne State that would train students in digital literacy and include a number of online classes. Pointing to MIT's Open Courseware model, McLellan suggests making course content available online; see Marjorie McLellan, "Digital Humanities Certificate," *Digital Humanities Forum*, July 11, 2010, http://webapp3. wright.edu/web2/digitalhumanities/2010/07/11/digital-humanities-certificate/.

information studies, film and media studies, and educational technology; several involve collaborations among academic departments and libraries or archives.

Typically, digital humanities certificate programs aim to give their students an edge in an intensely competitive job market, arguing that skills in producing digital scholarship will help them distinguish themselves. A few programs require students to create electronic portfolios that can be used in assessing (and demonstrating) knowledge. Some, such as Texas A&M's Digital Humanities Certificate and Tulane's Certificate in Archival and Digital Humanities, strive to prepare students for careers not only in traditional academic jobs, but also in alt-academic jobs such as at libraries, archives, and museums. Although these programs offer a compelling model for training digital humanists, they follow a fairly traditional model of higher education, in that they are only open to students at the home institution, typically divide learning into semester-long courses, and are taught by local faculty. In contrast, the curriculum for an open, networked certificate program could engage people from around the world as students and mentors and offer a more flexible, modular approach to learning.

As the digital humanities community explores what students need to learn, it tends to emphasize honing skills by working on projects and understanding key concepts rather than developing fluency in particular applications. For instance, THATCamp 2010 featured a session on digital humanities teaching that suggested students should learn technical skills (coding, scripting, database development), design skills (user-centered design, game design), management skills (collaboration, project management, sustainability, assessment, marketing), and theoretical understanding (information vs. knowledge).[18] According to participants in a 2009 CLIR Workshop on education in digital scholarship, programs should aim "to educate students on how to teach themselves new software and technical skills; to develop peer-to-peer support among both faculty and students; and to prepare students to work without the support of well-staffed centers."[19] Since digital humanities work often demands a range of skills and since many lack deep institutional support, digital humanists need to develop a base of knowledge upon which they can build, learn how to learn, and understand how to reach

---

18    The notes from the "THATCamp 2010 Session on DH teaching/curriculum" were made available on GoogleDocs following the session in May 2010, https://docs.google.com/Doc?id=ddz3r8kz_65ggjm74f3&pli=1.

19    Sehat and Farr, *The Future of Digital Scholarship*, 4.

out to and work with collaborators. Further, educational programs should balance theory and practice, so that participants understand both the core research problems and the technical and methodological approaches used to approach them. Finally, the certificate program should reflect the multi- and inter-disciplinary nature of the digital humanities, integrating computer science, statistics, library and information science, design, and other disciplines as well as traditional humanities fields. The program could be flexible enough to encompass multiple perspectives, enabling the certificate candidates to pursue the paths that make sense to them.

To qualify for this certificate in digital humanities, the student might be required to complete or participate in:

- *An introductory online course on digital humanities*, which might cover the history of digital humanities, core principles, theoretical approaches, and methods such as visualization, modeling, and text analysis.[20]
- *A practicum or internship* that would enable participants to learn first-hand how to frame, execute, and manage a project.[21]
- *A series of virtual seminars on issues in digital humanities*, which might cover topics such as project management, grant writing, user design, sustainability, and collaboration. The larger community would be welcome to participate to foster a larger conversation and the sharing of knowledge.
- *A required number of digital humanities learning modules*, which the participant could select based on area of specialization. Some modules might be self-paced; others might bring together a cohort group for discussion or collaborative projects. In some cases, participation in related educational activities, such as the Digital Humanities Summer Institute, Digital Humanities Observatory workshops, Nebraska Digital Workshop or a National Endowment

---

20  See, for instance, the University of Virginia's plan for its first year master's course in digital humanities, which though somewhat outdated nevertheless breaks down core knowledge in compelling ways. Johanna Drucker, John Unsworth, and Andrea Laue, "Final Report for Digital Humanities Curriculum Seminar," University of Virginia, August 10, 2002, http://jefferson.village.virginia.edu/hcs/dhcs/.

21  Martyn Jessop describes the benefits of capstone digital humanities projects for undergraduates, including the ability to learn independently, develop multidisciplinary approaches and contribute knowledge to the growing field of digital humanities; see Martyn Jessop, "Teaching, Learning and Research in Final Year Humanities Computing Student Projects," *Literary and Linguistic Computing* 20, no. 3 (2005): 295–311.

for the Humanities seminar on the digital humanities, would count for module credit. Taken together, these modules would be roughly equivalent to three courses.

- *Occasional face-to-face meetings of cohort groups*, perhaps at the annual Digital Humanities conference. These meetings might be modeled on the JCDL Doctoral Consortium, where graduate students present their work and receive feedback and mentoring from leaders in the community.
- *An electronic portfolio* documenting what the student has learned. This portfolio would be opened up to peer commentary from the larger digital humanities community.

# Content

In support of the curriculum, the digital humanities community could develop open educational content, such as online tutorials, readings, exercises, simulations, videos, and quizzes. As Julie Meloni proposes, the community can create bite-sized modules that teach core skills, such as basic web development, an introduction to Python, fundamentals of geospatial scholarship, and so forth. The modules could be hosted using open educational platforms such as Connexions (http://www.cnx.org/), which employs XML to provide the technological capacity for reuse and Creative Commons licenses to establish the legal framework for sharing. To facilitate discovering open learning materials, the OER Commons (http://www.oercommons.org/) provides a portal to content in Connexions and other open repositories. In developing online educational content, we could build on and aggregate existing resources, such as The Programming Historian 2 (http://programminghistorian.org/), TEI By Example (http://tbe.kantl.be/TBE/), and materials developed for THATCamp BootCamps, such as the GIS resources offered at Virginia BootCamp 2010.[22]

As much as possible, digital humanities educational resources should be released with Creative Commons attribution licenses so that they are credited to the original author and can easily be adapted, remixed, and re-used. Ethan Watrall makes a compelling case for open educational

---

22   Chris Gist and Kelly Johnston, "Virginia BootCamp 2010: GIS Short Courses," Scholars' Lab, University of Virginia Library, December 17, 2010, http://www.lib.virginia.edu/scholarslab/resources/class/bootCamp2010/.

content: it benefits society by making knowledge widely available, the institution by enhancing its reputation and by providing resources to students that may help them succeed, and faculty by documenting their pedagogical innovations and allowing them to see how others are approaching similar courses.[23] If works on the digital humanities come with open licenses, instructors can more easily put together open textbooks using tools such as the open source software Anthologize (http://www. anthologize.org/). Certainly not every reading that will be assigned in a digital humanities class will have an open license. However, the digital humanities community should embrace open licenses whenever possible, as it is already doing with journals such as *Digital Humanities Quarterly* and books published by Michigan's Digital Culture Books (which often use an Attribution-Noncommercial-No Derivative Works 3.0 Creative Commons License). Just as grant agencies are beginning to recommend that software developed with grant funds be made available as an open source,[24] they could call for learning materials developed for institutes and other educational programs to be made freely available online under Creative Commons licenses.

To ensure both that the best resources rise to the top and that their authors get the credit, there should be peer review for educational materials. For instance, users of the materials (both course facilitators and students) could provide ratings or comments describing how the materials were used. Alternatively, the digital humanities certificate community could curate collections of materials. For example, Connexions allows communities to create a "lens" that gathers endorsed learning modules, such as the lens created by the IEEE Digital Signal Processing Society (http://cnx.org/lenses/ ieeesps/endorsements).

# Community

Beyond offering open content, proponents of open education are now promoting "open courses," enabling people around the world to participate

---

23  Ethan Watrall, "Developing a Personal Open Courseware Strategy," ProfHacker, *The Chronicle of Higher Education*, June 11, 2010, http://chronicle.com/blogs/profhacker/ developing-a-personal-open-courseware-strategy/.

24  For example, the NEH Digital Humanities Start-Up Grant application "strongly encourages" projects "to employ open-source and fully accessible software;" see "Digital Humanities Start-Up Grants," National Endowment for the Humanities, August 6, 2010, http://www.neh.gov/grants/guidelines/digitalhumanitiesstartup.html.

in networked, online classes, typically for free (unless they want academic credit).[25] As Dave Cormier and George Siemens observe, "the true benefit of the academy is the interaction, the access to the debate, to the negotiation of knowledge—not to the stale cataloging of content."[26] Whereas open content provides the raw material of learning, instructors (working in collaboration with learners) set expectations, structure learning, and shape communities that interact with and produce knowledge. Learning is social—we learn *with* others by explaining what we know, having our gaps in understanding questioned and filled in by others, and working through problems together. Through social learning, we learn *how* to learn and how to *be* a practitioner, coming to understand the norms, vocabulary and methods of a community of practice.[27] As Brown and Adler observe, we can see social learning at work in the open source development community, where newcomers initially work on smaller projects and gradually take on more responsibility as they learn the norms and demonstrate their capabilities. Not only has the Internet provided a means of freely sharing learning materials, but also a participatory platform that enables people to share ideas and work together to build knowledge.[28]

New models for education are emerging, driven by the ability to transcend the campus and create online courses that engage participants around the world. With the rise of Coursera, MIT-X, and Udacity in 2011 and 2012, Massive Open Online Courses (MOOCs) have gained much notice. They have also stirred up backlash from those who scorn the hype, dispute the underlying pedagogy and worry about the implications for universities and academic labor from free or low-cost, distributed online education. I share some of these concerns, but I also think MOOCs have the potential to expand access to education, foster experimentation in online pedagogy, and facilitate participatory networks focused on building and sharing knowledge. MOOC can refer to a range of approaches to learning, from watching short video lectures and taking automatically graded quizzes to contributing to online discussions and working on group or individual projects. As Audrey Watters points out, each of the key terms in "MOOC" can take on different

25  Marc Parry, "Online, Bigger Classes May Be Better Classes," *The Chronicle of Higher Education*, August 29, 2010, http://chronicle.com/article/Open-Teaching-When-the-W/124170/.

26  Dave Cormier and George Siemens, "Through the Open Door: Open Courses as Research, Learning and Engagement," *EDUCAUSE Review* 45, no. 4 (2010): 30–39.

27  Brown and Adler, "Minds on Fire."

28  *Ibid.*

meanings that reflect the course's overall approach.[29] What size constitutes "massive"? Does "open" imply open enrollment, open content, transparency in how the course is conducted, or something else? Does "C" stand for course, community, or certification? For the digital humanities, the emphasis would be on open, online and course/community rather than massive: OOCs, not MOOCs. Given the relatively small size of the DH community and its fairly specialized focus, it is unlikely that DH specific courses on, say, text markup or geospatial humanities would attract more than a few hundred participants. Certainly not every course in the digital humanities certificate program would include more than twenty or thirty people, but the certificate program could offer some open courses on topics of broad interest to encourage participation by the community.

Two main models of MOOCs have emerged as of summer 2012: the connectivist model, which seems to emphasize "openness" over course, and the Udacity/ Coursera model (the UC MOOC?), which seems to focus on "massive" and "course" over "openness." The earlier, connectivist model developed by George Siemens, Stephen Downes, and others is based on the theory "that knowledge is distributed across a network of connections, and therefore that learning consists of the ability to construct and traverse those networks."[30] A connectivist MOOC provides "an ecosystem from which knowledge can emerge," in which the syllabus offers a "starting point" and the outcomes are determined by the participants as they build knowledge networks.[31] Connectivist MOOCs do not aim to impart particular knowledge, but rather ask the learner to *aggregate* content, selecting what is compelling to them; *remix* that content, whether through a blog post, tweet or online discussion; *repurpose* that content, crafting their own understanding through creation and critique; and *feed forward*, sharing work with the course and in public.[32]

In designing open online courses for the digital humanities, we can learn about effective practices and potential pitfalls from connectivist MOOCs, where there is a greater body of publicly available research than for the

29  Audrey Watters, "The Language of MOOCs," *Inside Higher Ed*, 7 June 2012, http://www.insidehighered.com/blogs/hack-higher-education/language-moocs.

30  Stephen Downes, "What Connectivism Is," *Half an Hour*, February 3, 2007, http://halfanhour.blogspot.com/2007/02/what-connectivism-is.html.

31  Dave Cormier and Neal Gillis, "Knowledge in a MOOC," *YouTube*, December 1, 2010, http://www.youtube.com/watch?v=bWKdhzSAAG0.

32  Stephen Downes and George Siemens, "How This Course Works," *Connectivism and Connective Knowledge 1,1* (2011), http://cck11.mooc.ca/how.htm.

newer Udacity/Coursera MOOCs. In a study of Siemens, Downes, Cormier and Kop's Personal Learning Environments Networks and Knowledge course (PLENK2010, http://connect.downes.ca/)[33] and Downes and Siemens' Connectivism and Connective Knowledge course (CCK11, http://cck11. mooc.ca/), Kop, Fournier and Mak argue (perhaps not surprisingly) that students learned more by producing content and interacting with others rather than by passively absorbing content, although most registrants did not participate actively. MOOC students faced some significant barriers that impeded their participation, including "time zone differences, language differences, difficulties in connecting with others in different spaces, lack of skills in the use of tools, difficulties in making connections with facilitators and/or learners, and power relations."[34] Another study of participants' views of an earlier iteration of Connectivism and Connective Knowledge, CCK08, found: "The more autonomous, diverse and open the course, and the more connected the learners, the more the potential for their learning to be limited by the lack of structure, support and moderation normally associated with an online course, and the more they seek to engage in traditional groups as opposed to an open network."[35] While some appreciated having the autonomy to focus on what mattered to them and determine their own level of commitment, others felt disoriented by the multiple venues for connection and interaction, particularly novices and non-English speakers. Some participants in course forums used inflammatory discourse ("trolling"), diminishing trust and participation. Perhaps such problems could be avoided if the course were smaller (as would be likely with DH OOCs), course facilitators more actively set norms and moderated discussions, and participants received more consistent feedback and direction, while still having room to explore their interests.

In contrast, the Coursera/Udacity approach currently seems to focus more on bringing elements of the traditional university classroom to the digital environment.[36] In many such MOOCs, students follow a set schedule laid out in the syllabus, watch brief video lectures, test their comprehension

33   I signed up for PLENK 2010, but was not an active participant due to lack of time.

34   Rita Kop, Hélène Fournier, and Sui Fai John Mak, "A Pedagogy of Abundance or a Pedagogy to Support Human Beings? Participant Support on Massive Open Online Courses," *The International Review of Research in Open and Distance Learning*, 12 (2011): 86.

35   Jenny Mackness, Sui Fai John Mak, and Roy Williams, "The Ideals and Reality of Participating in a MOOC," in *7th International Conference on Networked Learning 2010* (Lancaster: University of Lancaster, 2010), 266.

36   Doug Holton, "What's the 'Problem' with MOOCs?" *EdTechDev*, May 4, 2012, http://edtechdev.wordpress.com/2012/05/04/whats-the-problem-with-moocs/.

through automatically graded quizzes, and complete exercises and exams. However, some UC MOOCS do engage students in more active, project-based learning. For example, Coursera's Human Computer Interaction MOOC takes students through a series of design-based assignments, and Stanford's Technology Entrepreneurship (Venture Lab) class employs team projects that teach the principles of entrepreneurship and challenge collaborators to create a start-up.[37]

The rise of MOOCs has sparked some significant concerns about their implications for learning and for the future of higher education. As Clark Quinn points out, while the Coursera model of MOOCs err in depending too much on the facilitator guiding learning rather than in fostering social learning, the connectivist MOOCs may err in providing not enough facilitator support, requiring a high level of "self-learning" skills.[38] Further, we simply don't know enough about the effectiveness of MOOCs, particularly in the case of the MITx/Udacity/ Coursera model. Completion rates for MOOCs tend to be low; for example, around 35,000 out of 160,000 registrants completed Sebastian Thrun and Peter Norvig's Artificial Intelligence Course, 7,157 out of 154,763 registrants passed MITx's "Circuits and Electronics" course, and 3,500 out of 50,000 registrants finished Dave Patterson's Coursera course on software engineering.[39] While Rebecca Rosen views the dropout rate as an encouraging sign that people are willing to try out this new approach to learning, Audrey Watters worries that it indicates problems with the pedagogy or the platform.[40] With such a massive scale, it is much more difficult to form human connections between teacher and student and with fellow students, which may weaken the students' motivation to learn and the instructor's ability to mentor students and understand their needs (although this weakness can also characterize large lecture courses at traditional universities). In addition to challenging the pedagogy of Udacity and Coursera MOOCs, critics point out that they are not truly open. Indeed, both companies claim copyright

---

37  I was a student in both courses (although I did not complete them due to a lack of time).
38  Clark Quinn, "MOOC Reflections," *Learnlets*, February 29, 2012, http://blog.learnlets.com/?p=2562.
39  Rebecca J. Rosen, "Overblown-Claims-of-Failure Watch: How Not to Gauge the Success of Online Courses," *The Atlantic*, July 22, 2012, http://www.theatlantic.com/technology/archive/2012/07/overblown-claims-of-failure-watch-how-not-to-gauge-the-success-of-online-courses/260159/.
40  Audrey Watters, "Dropping Out of MOOCs: Is It Really Okay?" *Inside Higher Ed*, July 23, 2012, http://www.insidehighered.com/blogs/hack-higher-education/dropping-out-moocs-it-really-okay.

over all course content and provide access only to enrolled students.[41] In contrast, MIT asserts its plans to make MITx content and software available through open content licenses, although it also states that course materials "are for your personal use in connection with those courses only."[42] If a MOOC is not truly open, then it cannot involve the broader community in explorations of key ideas covered in the course, nor does it allow content to be used and remixed by anyone. Terran Lane articulates broader concerns in worrying that MOOCs will lead to a decline in the academic labor force (in which just a few professors teach the masses), the dominance of just a few leading institutions, and the destruction of the human bond among teachers and students.[43]

Yet open online courses can offer an interactive educational experience to learners around the world at a relatively low cost and with significant flexibility. Open courses in DH would not set out to disrupt traditional education. Rather, they would expand post-graduate learning opportunities for (alt-) academics, professionals and enthusiasts who otherwise lack the time, money, or opportunity to participate in more traditional educational options. They would also share educational resources that could be used and adapted by instructors and students regardless of their enrollment status. As the DH community seeks to internationalize, MOOCs can connect students across the world, enabling them to collaborate on projects, exchange ideas, and together build a learning community.

In designing and implementing open online DH modules (shorter, more focused learning experiences) and courses, developers should consciously reflect on how to confront the challenges that arise when you extend the scale of a class so that it engages a couple hundred rather than a couple dozen students and is distributed across the network rather than consolidated in a single location. [44] How do you (as a facilitator) foster a sprit of community when people don't meet face to face? How can you

41    Josh Baron, "Are Coursera Courses Really MOOCs?" *Educause CIO Constituent Group Listserv*, July 20, 2012, http://listserv.educause.edu/cgi-bin/wa.exe?A2=ind1207&L=CIO& T=0&F=&S=&P=67921; "Terms of Service", *Udacity*, March 31, 2012, http://www.udacity. com/legal/.

42    "MITx Terms of Service," *MITx*, February 20, 2012, http://mitx.mit.edu/t/tos.html.

43    Terran Lane, "On Leaving Academia," *Ars Experientia*, July 23, 2012, http://cs.unm. edu/~terran/academic_blog/?p=113.

44    Terje Väljataga, Hans Põldoja, and Mart Laanpere, "Open Online Courses: Responding to Design Challenges," in *Proceedings of the 4th International Network-Based Education 2011 Conference: The Social Media in the Middle of Nowhere* (Rovaniemi: University of Lapland, 2011), 68.

reduce the dropout rates known to plague MOOCs? How can you assess the work of such a large group of students? How can you offer guidance and mentoring? Below I sketch out possible approaches to these questions, but deeper insights will come through experimentation. The design principles I've already articulated should inform the development of DH open online courses, no matter what the size: openness, a global orientation, modularity, a community-driven, experimental approach, and the use of technologies to support learning.

Although there are already compelling models for networked education, the certificate program would need to figure out how best to build and maintain a community that only rarely, if ever, meets face to face. As Clifford Lynch observes, the internet enables groups of people with similar interests to collaborate, but much work needs to be done to figure out the most suitable way to organize and run cohort groups, including determining the ideal size, duration, and timing (when a class begins, and whether people can join in process) and fostering diversity (linguistic, skill level, geographic, etc).[45] Perhaps the best way to address these questions is to experiment with different approaches and adapt existing models.

The certificate program can foster active learning communities through online forums (perhaps using web-based video conferencing to facilitate face-to-face connection), cohort groups, group projects, and peer commentary and assessment. DH has already succeeded to some extent in creating networked communities through Twitter, blogs, and other means, although more needs to be done to cultivate a welcoming climate. Diverse cohort groups could be organized so that participants can navigate a course or the entire certificate program with a small group of people, turning to them for help, conversation and support. Whereas classes of students (sophomores, seniors, etc) typically go through an educational experience together, at the Open University cohort groups form around individual modules, which provides more flexibility and thus fosters broader participation.[46]

---

45   Clifford Lynch, "Digital Libraries, Learning Communities, and Open Education," in *Opening Up Education: The Collective Advancement of Education through Open Technology, Open Content, and Open Knowledge*, ed. Toru Iiyoshi and M. S. Vijay Kumar (Cambridge: MIT Press, 2008), 105–18.

46   Andy Lane, "Widening Participation in Education through Open Educational Resources," in *Opening Up Education: The Collective Advancement of Education through Open Technology, Open Content, and Open Knowledge*, ed. Toru Iiyoshi and M. S. Vijay Kumar (Cambridge: MIT Press, 2008), 149–64.

Group projects can introduce students to different perspectives, enable them to pursue more ambitious projects, build relationships, and help them to learn how to collaborate more effectively. However, virtual group projects can face the same challenges that can confront traditional classes, potentially magnified because students cannot meet face-to-face and may not be fully committed to the course: poor group dynamics, the failure of some members to contribute, the loss of motivation, and lack of consensus. Thus care would need to be taken in setting expectations, providing mechanisms for communication among the group and with the course facilitator or project mentor, and addressing low levels of participation. Although most of the certificate program would take place online, it should offer occasional opportunities for participants to come together face-to-face so that they can build relationships and put together plans that can then be implemented as they work separately.

The certificate program could also build community by:

- Holding face-to-face gatherings at events such as the Digital Humanities conference.
- Building local networks of digital humanists, expanding on THATCamps and ThinkDrinks.[47]
- Creating interest groups around topics of shared interest.
- Reaching out to the larger digital humanities community through open class sessions and social networking.

By providing greater support, community, feedback, and structure, open online courses may cut dropout rates. Given the DH program's smaller size, specific focus on a more specialized area of knowledge and community, and pathway to certification, I would expect that there would be a more committed group of students who would be more likely to engage. At the same time, the program could be flexible enough to recognize that learners have different goals, so there should be an option for declaring from the start one's intent to audit a course. (I say this as someone who has signed up for several MOOCs, more out of curiosity and a desire to graze than a commitment to complete them or a need for certification.)

---

47  For example, establishing a local Decoding Digital Humanities (http://www.ucl.ac.uk/dh/ddh) chapter to host informal monthly meetings. Founded at University College London, chapters have now been launched in Bloomington (US), Lisbon (Portugal), and Melbourne (Australia).

Although MOOCs raise issues such as protecting privacy, negotiating intellectual property, sustaining participation, preventing spamming and bad behavior, and managing (and evaluating) information coming from so many people, they also offer a networked (and in some cases decentralized) model of education that can place greater responsibility on learners, foster collaboration, expand access to learning, and enable knowledge to be shared more widely.[48] By exploring open courses, the DH community can help to shape this emerging educational paradigm in a way consistent with its practices and values, emphasizing participation, sharing, inquiry, learning by doing, play and collaboration.

## Contributions

Education is not so much about absorbing knowledge as producing it, whether through essays, projects, or other demonstrations of mastery. The digital humanities certificate program should require participants to complete either a capstone project or a substantial internship contributing to a significant digital humanities project. These projects should be openly available and reveal the student's mastery of key digital humanities skills. Further, reflective essays that describe the process of building the project, the pitfalls encountered, and the scholarly value of the work should accompany them. Students should also review projects produced by fellow members of the certificate program, learning from the experiences of others and offering more in-depth information about these projects to the larger community.[49] As students work on projects, they develop key knowledge about how to do research, plan a project, manage it, and assess its impact. Not only would students gain the authentic, embedded knowledge that comes with grappling with the problems that inevitably come up with project work, but they could also make substantial contributions to the digital humanities community.

To help students find internship opportunities, the certificate program, working with the Association for Computers and the Humanities (ACH) or a similar organization, could create a database or even a "matchmaking"

---

48   Cormier and Siemens, "Through the Open Door."

49   I take this idea in part from a May 2010 THATCamp session on digital humanities education, where participants proposed "partnerships where students are looking at each other's work across institutions" ("THATCamp 2010 Session on DH teaching/ curriculum").

service. Perhaps the DHCommons platform (http://dhcommons.org/), which matches projects and collaborators, could be adapted for this purpose.[50] Further, the digital humanities certificate program could pursue formal partnerships with organizations—such as libraries and archives, digital humanities centres, and community organizations—that want to produce or support digital scholarship.[51] Some of these internships could be primarily virtual, supplemented with occasional face-to-face meetings with clients and project teams. Alternatively, students could work on independent projects, although the certificate program may need to broker access to hardware, software, programming support and/ or a small budget.

Students could also contribute to crowd-sourced and participatory digital humanities projects. For instance, they could learn transcription and editing skills by contributing to projects like Transcribe Bentham (http://www.ucl.ac.uk/transcribe-bentham/), and hone their skills in evaluating and responding to arguments by participating in peer-to-peer review projects such as those sponsored by MediaCommons (http://mediacommons.futureofthebook.org/). Further, they would learn how these communities operate, gaining tacit knowledge of the field and of online communities. We might think of such an approach to volunteer work as "(near-) expert crowd-sourcing." Citing Wikipedia, Christopher Blackwell and Gregory Crane argue that students can cumulatively make significant contributions to community-based projects, providing training data, producing tree-banks and diplomatic editions, and finding patterns in large amounts of data.[52] In addition to working on projects, participants in the digital humanities certificate programs could also contribute modules to the digital humanities learning commons, "paying it forward" and demonstrating their own learning.

---

50  Disclosure: I am on the DH Commons Board and ACH Executive Council.
51  Several existing digital humanities certificate programs partner with libraries and archives to give students the opportunity to contribute to projects, so the networked certificate program would extend that idea. See, for example, the discussion of such partnerships at work in New York University's archives and public history curriculum in Peter J. Wosh, Cathy Moran Hajo, and Esther Katz's chapter, "Teaching Digital Skills in an Archives and Public History Curriculum."
52  Christopher Blackwell and Gregory Crane, "Conclusion: Cyberinfrastructure, the Scaife Digital Library and Classics in a Digital Age," *Digital Humanities Quarterly* 3, no. 1 (2009), http://www.digitalhumanities.org/dhq/vol/3/1/000035/000035.html.

# Coaching

As participants make their way through the certificate program, they would need more senior members of the community to guide them on particular modules or projects and on broader career-related and intellectual questions. Inevitably, learners make mistakes or get confused, but mentors can help them become aware of these errors, correct them, and clarify their knowledge. Mentors could be facilitators of courses as well as members of a larger network of digital humanities professionals willing to participate in occasional conversations with program participants. One of the key benefits offered by formal degree programs is becoming part of an alumni network; the certificate program could expand that network beyond a single institution.

In developing a mentor program, we can look to existing models both within and outside of the community. Currently the ACH offers a mentoring program where veteran digital humanities professionals provide guidance to newcomers. Perhaps this program could be expanded and formalized so that mentors work with their advisees throughout the year on specific learning goals, connecting via Skype, chat and other tools. Digital Humanities Questions & Answers (http://www.digitalhumanities.org/answers/), a collaborative project of the ACH and the Chronicle of Higher Education's *ProfHacker* blog, provides a channel for informal mentoring and advice, as people offer guidance on topics ranging from the best way to teach oneself XML to what should be included on a digital history curriculum to "reading recommendations for a GIS newbie."

Beyond the digital humanities community, Wikipedia supplies a model for mentoring, both informally through its talk pages, chat sessions, and review processes,[53] and formally through its Ambassador program. To support lecturers who want to incorporate Wikipedia assignments into the curriculum and students who are working on editing assignments, Wikipedia provides both Campus Ambassadors (who provide in-person training) and Online Ambassadors (who serve as virtual mentors) to help newcomers understand Wikipedia's culture

---

53 Susan L. Bryant, Andrea Forte, and Amy Bruckman, "Becoming Wikipedian: Transformation of Participation in a Collaborative Online Encyclopedia," in *Proceedings of the 2005 International ACM SIGGROUP Conference on Supporting Group Work*, ed. Kjeld Schmidt, Mark Pendergast, Mark Ackerman, and Gloria Mark (New York: ACM, 2005), 1–10.

and editing processes.[54] Likewise, the Free and Open Software (FOSS) community mentors students through programs such as the Google Summer of Code (http://code.google.com/soc/), which partners students with FOSS projects. Mentors play a vital role in this program as they help students set priorities, get to know others in the community and learn the culture as well as evaluate their work. Mentors have also supported open education classes. For instance, when Alec Couros called for network mentors for his open graduate course Social Media and Open Education, over 120 people responded, offering to follow students' blog and Twitter posts, provide guidance and support via Skype and other media and help students work through their assessments.[55] All of these programs suggest that people need not be physically co-located to build mentoring relationships. In some MOOCs, students themselves provides peer mentoring by answering questions on online forums and developing structures for support, such as spin-off groups focused on particular languages.

Whereas in most universities faculty members do the bulk of the teaching (at least for graduate students), the certificate program could also draw on the expertise of the broader alternative academic career (alt-ac) community of librarians, information technologists, museum professionals, and others. Perhaps collaborative teams of scholars and technical experts could lead some modules. Indeed, the certificate program could help to address the frustration of those who pursue alt-ac careers (I include myself in this crowd): the lack of opportunities to teach. Further, when people complete the certificate program they could become mentors; their recent experiences as students may make them more aware of difficulties newcomers may encounter.

## Assessment and Certification

For some in the digital humanities community, the knowledge, community engagement, and experience gained through the certificate program will be rewarding in itself, but others will need formal certification to get a job or a

---

54  Wikimedia Foundation, "Wikipedia Ambassador Program," *Wikimedia Outreach*, May 14, 2011, http://outreach.wikimedia.org/wiki/Wikipedia_Ambassador_Program. Disclosure: I served as a Wikipedia Campus Ambassador.

55  Alec Couros, "Call for Network Mentors—Follow-Up," *Open Thinking*, September 27, 2010, http://educationaltechnology.ca/couros/1877.

promotion. One of the biggest challenges facing open education programs is determining how to recognize, assess, and accredit learning, but the open education community is actively working to address it.[56] Several models for certifying open education are emerging, including awarding "badges" that symbolize skills or knowledge; requiring students to create online portfolios documenting their accomplishments; providing feedback from the community through ratings, comments, and other measures of reputation; and working through accredited institutions to offer course credits for open learning.[57] The Mozilla Foundation has developed the Open Badge Infrastructure (http://openbadges.org/en-US/) to enable organizations to issue badges and learners to manage them. Badges can mark the "learning path" that a learner has pursued, signify learning achievements at a granular level, motivate learners to pursue particular milestones, and build learning communities by making explicit one's identity as a learner.[58] However, the idea of badges has stirred up significant controversy, as critics contend that badges could cheapen and commodify learning (making it a quest for trinkets), are too easily gamed, and may be difficult to contextualize and evaluate.[59] As Alex Halavais cautions, badges carry with them multiple significances (sometimes complementary, sometimes clashing) that derive from the ways that they have been used historically, often connoting both achievement and trust (reflecting a commercial ethos) and rank and authority (reflecting a "guardian" ethos identified with the military and government officials).[60] Badges can thus be used to exclude others and reinforce privilege. Yet badges can also provide a mechanism for those outside the traditional educational system to validate their learning and signify that they have acquired some level

---

56  "Recognizes" suggests applauding the achievements of a learner, "assess" means measuring what he or she has learned and "accredited" means "formal certification by a third party or intermediary;" see Jan Philipp Schmidt, Christine Geith, Stian Håklev, and Joel Thierstein, "Peer-To-Peer Recognition of Learning in Open Education," *The International Review of Research in Open and Distance Learning* 10, no. 5 (2009), http://www.irrodl.org/index.php/irrodl/article/view/641.

57  Schmidt et al., "Peer-To-Peer Recognition of Learning in Open Education."

58  Peer 2 Peer University and The Mozilla Foundation, "An Open Badge System Framework" (Badge Paper 4.0), working paper, Google Docs, 2011, http://bit.ly/badgepaper4.

59  Jeffrey R. Young, " 'Badges' Earned Online Pose Challenge to Traditional College Diplomas," *Chronicle of Higher Education*, January 8, 2012, http://chronicle.com/article/Badges-Earned-Online-Pose/130241.

60  Alexander M. C. Halavais, "A Genealogy of Badges: Inherited Meaning and Monstrous Moral Hybrids," *Information, Communication, and Society*, 15 (2012), 354–73. Thanks to the anonymous peer reviewer for this reference.

of expertise valued by a professional or intellectual community. The DH community could develop meaningful, authentic ways of certifying the knowledge represented by a badge. Halavais recommends that the developers of badge systems make clear the badges' functions (whether to signify authority or identity), use "stable and recognizable" visual symbolism so that they carry meaning in the community, openly define the process of evaluating and awarding badges, and "point" to more detailed documentation. Badges and portfolios can be used together to provide different views of a learner's accomplishments, so that badges offer a quick visual representation of learning and community validation, whereas portfolios document the learning behind the badges.[61]

Not only can assessment be important in certifying students' learning, but also in enabling them to check their understanding, evaluate their progress (often in collaboration with an instructor), and push their ideas to the next level. Traditionally, assessment is bundled into the course, but perhaps it would be even more effective to disaggregate instruction from assessment, so that peers could help to evaluate student work.[62] "Peer" could imply fellow participants in the certificate program or the larger digital humanities community. Perhaps a review committee could evaluate capstone projects using standard rubrics for digital scholarship, such as those developed by NINES (http://www.nines.org/). Alternatively, the program could foster peer-to-peer review of work. For example, Cathy Davidson assigns student teams to lead different course modules and gives them the responsibility of evaluating fellow students' blog posts. As Davidson comments, "Digital thinking is a mode of thinking together, online, through a process of peer evaluation and peer contribution, using a form of 'participatory learning' that blurs the lines between work and play, intellectual and social life."[63] Peer-to-peer review of work makes everyone responsible for learning, prepares participants for their professional duties of reviewing their colleagues' work and helps students develop first-hand knowledge of how to distinguish good work from bad. Peer evaluation typically works better if the instructor provides a clear rubric so that the

---

61    Peer 2 Peer University and The Mozilla Foundation, "An Open Badge System Framework."

62    Patrick McAndrew, Eileen Scanlon, and Doug Clow, "An Open Future for Higher Education," *EDUCAUSE Quarterly* 33, no. 1 (2010), http://www.educause.edu/EDUCAUSE+Quarterly/ EDUCAUSEQuarterlyMagazineVolum/AnOpenFutureforHigherEducation/199388.

63    Cathy N. Davidson, "Crowdsourcing Grading: Follow-Up," *HASTAC*, August 9, 2009, http://www.hastac.org/blogs/cathy-davidson/crowdsourcing-grading-follow.

evaluators know what to focus on and how to weight the evaluation.[64] As a participant in a Coursera sociology course reported, peer evaluation encourages the evaluators to pay closer attention to core concepts and exposes them to different perspectives.[65] Yet a student in Coursera's Human-Computer Interaction (HCI) course noted that anonymous peer grading seems to face some obstacles, including student resistance and worries that evaluators might breach students' privacy.[66] Perhaps an open approach to peer review would give students access to models, foster more conversations about their work, and provide concrete evidence of a student's learning and participation in a community.

In addition to external assessment, the digital humanities certificate program should cultivate self-assessment, or reflection on learning goals to assess how successful one has been in meeting them. To document their work and knowledge, participants could create online portfolios along with reflective essays. Portfolios are required by some digital humanities certificate programs, such as Tulane's. For models of portfolios, we can look to those created by digital humanities graduate students, such as Jentery Sayers (http://www.jenterysayers.com/portfolio/), now an assistant professor) and Jason Heppler (http://www.jasonheppler.org/portfolio/). Prospective employers could use these portfolios to evaluate job candidates, while tenure committees could use them in making advancement decisions.[67] Making transparent one's work also provides models for other aspiring digital humanists.

Traditionally, people receive certification by satisfactorily completing a sequence of classes (as in graduate certificates) or by passing a comprehensive exam (as in professional certificates). In establishing the digital humanities curriculum, an advisory committee could come to a consensus about what it would take be to "certified" in different areas, specifying skills, knowledge and content that should be mastered and rubrics that can be used to assess that mastery. Ideally, the certificate would receive official sanction from an accredited institution. Alternatively,

---

64  Debbie Morrison, "Peer Grading in Online Classes: Does It Work?" *Online Learning Insights*, July 6, 2012, http://onlinelearninginsights.wordpress.com/2012/07/06/peer-grading-in-online-classes-does-it-work/.

65  Morrison, "Peer Grading."

66  Katy Jordan, "HCI—Interesting Issues with Peer Grading," *MoocMoocher*, July 12, 2012, http://moocmoocher.wordpress.com/2012/07/18/hci-interesting-issues-with-peer-grading/.

67  By way of further example, professor Kathleen Fitzpatrick compiled an electronic dossier in preparation for her promotion review at Pomona College. Although prepared in 2009, it remains publically accessible on her website (http://machines.pomona.edu/dossier/).

perhaps a professional organization could provide validation for the certificate, like the Professional Archivist exam certified by the Academy of Certified Archivists. In some cases, exams might be an appropriate way to test knowledge of particular modules, but the certificate program should offer a more holistic approach, looking also at specific projects and at students' ability to articulate what they have learned. Whichever method is chosen as the basis to certify knowledge, the evaluation approaches should be trustworthy, relevant, scalable and transparent.[68]

## How Could a Digital Humanities Certificate Program Be Implemented?

Implementing this admittedly ambitious program would require confronting several challenges, including providing administrative oversight, developing a viable funding model, and fostering participation. Some may worry that a certificate program might replace a "Do It Yourself" ethic with systematization, standardization, and bureaucracy. But it is hoped that the "hacker ethos"[69] of digital humanities could infuse the certificate program. Throughout this essay, I have referred to the power of the "digital humanities community" to build an open certificate program, reflecting my own optimism about its creativity, collaborative disposition, and commitment to openness and peer support. Successful digital humanities initiatives such as THATCamp, *ProfHacker*, and Digital Humanities Questions & Answers were launched when a group of motivated people had a good idea, got organized, and built an appropriate platform for community participation.

Although a certificate program may be larger in scope, launching it would likewise require a group to provide the organizational spark and structure for participation, and then invite the community to supply the energy and effort to make the project succeed. Given that this approach is new, it is likely that not everything will work, but failure comes with experimentation and can lead to new wisdom. The program could be approached, as many digital humanities projects are, iteratively. Even if it is not possible at this time to run a complete certificate program, many of

---

68  Schmidt et al., "Peer-To-Peer Recognition of Learning in Open Education."

69  Melissa Terras, "Hacking the Career: Digital Humanities as Academic Hackerdom," *Melissa Terras' Blog*, May 24, 2010, http://melissaterras.blogspot.com/2010/05/hacking-career-digital-humanities-as.html.

these components—such as creating open content, collaborative curriculum, and learning communities—could be implemented without much funding. Other components could be added as the program grows.

## Management

Who would manage a digital humanities certificate program? While the program would be decentralized, it would need a group to coordinate it, develop curriculum and course materials, recruit course facilitators and mentors, set up project and internship opportunities, manage admissions, oversee assessment and certification and communicate with the community. The certificate program would likely be managed through strategic partnerships among key stakeholders, including professional organizations, digital humanities centers, and educational programs, and/or open education providers. Perhaps a consortium of digital humanities educational programs and centres could oversee the program. Different digital humanities centres could offer training in their unique areas of specialization, such as Virginia on geospatial scholarship and methodological training (as offered by the Praxis program), Stanford on text mining, and King's College on visualization and modeling.

Furthermore, the community could partner with library schools that offer online education programs and have strengths in the digital humanities to provide core informatics training and perhaps oversee the program. Although an open certificate program might seem to compete with existing graduate programs, it could help these programs identify and recruit students with potential to do further work in a more traditional master's or PhD program. The program could also increase the visibility and reputation of participating organizations. When Open University launched its Open Learn program (http://openlearn.open.ac.uk/) to give free access to learning materials, learning clubs and learning tools, it gained key strategic benefits, including enhancing its reputation, reaching new users, recruiting students, widening participation, fostering collaboration and catalyzing experimentation.[70] Perhaps, most importantly, the program would support the community's overarching aim to train the next generation of digital humanities leaders.

---

70   McAndrew, Scanlon, and Clow, "An Open Future for Higher Education."

Alternatively, the digital humanities program could be overseen by organizations like the ACH or the Alliance of Digital Humanities Organizations (ADHO), which have a vested interest in providing professional development opportunities. In order to take on this responsibility, professional organizations would need additional resources as well as a mechanism for providing certification. Finally, an existing open education provider such as Peer 2 Peer University (http://www.p2pu.org/) or University of the People (http://www.uopeople.org/) could administer the certificate program. By doing so, the program could take advantage of their established technical and administrative infrastructure. No matter what approach is taken, the digital humanities certification program would need to develop an appropriate governance structure, perhaps modeled on open source software projects. The community would elect a board to oversee the certificate program as a whole; additional boards might focus on particular aspects of the program, such as curriculum, certification and community development.

# Funding

Running an open certificate program requires money. Presumably the costs of an open source certificate program would be lower than traditional education, since students would not be in residence and would not demand the same degree of user services such as library, IT and the like (although how to provide such services might be another challenge). While some of this work—such as sharing syllabi, creating open textbooks, and taking part in a virtual symposium—could be done through a largely volunteer effort, it would take some funding to pay a small staff to coordinate the program, reward honoraria to module facilitators, cover travel, and provide the technical infrastructure. To meet its core goal of increasing access to training in the digital humanities, the certificate program should be low cost. However, those pursuing a certificate degree should have to pay a small fee if they are able, not only to provide financial support to the program but also to signify and solidify their commitment. As the developers of many training programs have learned, if people have a financial stake in training, they are often more likely to remain committed to the program. Like the University of the People, which charges modest application fees and a $100 exam processing fee (per exam), perhaps the program could make the education freely available, but charge application and exam fees.[71] While the courses themselves should remain free, students could be given opportunities to contribute what they can, in the same way that free museums encourage visitors to donate.

In charging addition to tuition and fees, the program could raise start-up funds from foundations and grant agencies. Historically, foundations such as the Hewlett Foundation and Mellon Foundation have provided much of the support for open education and open source software development in higher education—although governmental agencies such as the Joint Information Systems Committee (JISC) in the UK and, more recently, the US government, have also provided support. The digital humanities community could seek support from such organizations to launch an open certificate program. Foundations and grant agencies would benefit in several ways from investing in open education. First, they would help to train new digital humanists who could play leadership roles in academic departments, libraries, museums and other cultural heritage organizations. Second, they would support a focused experiment in developing networked, open ways to provide professional education. This experiment would likely produce important insights into open education and networked pedagogy.

Since continuing education is important to the development of the digital humanities, the broader DH community could provide some support. For instance, libraries, digital humanities centers, and other organizations already pay for their employees to attend workshops such as the Digital Humanities Summer Institute. Could they not also offer funding or in-kind support to help sustain open online educational programs? Likewise, the broader community can be encouraged to provide financial backing through crowdfunding mechanisms such as Kickstarter campaigns. Granted, crowdsourcing funding may entail instability and uncertainty, since there is no guarantee that a campaign will be funded and the community's willingness to contribute likely has limits. However, it may work on a per course level or for specific programs. For example, Jim Groom successfully raised funds for his DS 106 Digital Storytelling MOOC through a Kickstarter campaign, exceeding his $4200 goal by $8,443, with 164 backers chipping in over the course of the two-week campaign.[72]

---

71   Tamar Lewin, "On the Internet, a University Without a Campus," *New York Times*, February 5, 2009, http://www.nytimes.com/2009/01/25/technology/25iht-university.4.19660731.html.

72   Jim Groom, "DS106: The Open Online Community of Digital Storytellers," *Kickstarter*, March 29, 2012, http://www.kickstarter.com/projects/jimgroom/ds106-the-open-online-community-of-digital-storyte.

Other educational projects that have successfully raised $10,000 or more through Kickstarter include SmartHistory, Punk Mathematics, and Open Educational Resources for Typography.[73]

# Participation

One of the major challenges facing a digital humanities open education initiative would be persuading members of the digital humanities community to contribute content and exercises, as well as to serve as mentors. While there would likely be good will toward an open certificate program, many in the digital humanities community are already overextended. However, making it easy to participate, enabling a diversity of people to contribute, offering incentives, and creating a culture of participation could overcome this challenge. Instructors who are already teaching digital humanities classes could, without too much additional effort, contribute their syllabi, exercises, assignments, and other instructional content to the community, whether by using a simple upload form at a centralized repository or by making their content available to be harvested. As Christopher Mackie suggests, students could develop content — including advanced students who are helping to train less experienced students and beginning students who are cementing their own learning.[74]

Further, digital humanities organizations could recognize and reward contribution to open educational initiatives, such as through a prize for best module, exercise, mentor and so forth. Most importantly, the certificate program could cultivate a culture of participation. Through participatory projects such as Wikipedia, people seek credit, acknowledgement of one's contributions, or more clout and a position of greater trust in the community.[75] The digital humanities certificate program could create

73  Jeffrey R. Young, "Professor Hopes to Support Free Course With Kickstarter, the 'Crowd Funding' Site," *The Wired Campus*, March 29, 2012, http://chronicle.com/blogs/wiredcampus/professor-hopes-to-support-free-course-with-kickstarter-the-crowd-funding-site/35864.

74  Christopher Mackie, "Open Source in Open Education: Promises and Challenges," in *Opening Up Education: The Collective Advancement of Education through Open Technology, Open Content, and Open Knowledge*, ed. Toru Iiyoshi and M. S. Vijay Kumar (Cambridge: MIT Press, 2008), 119-32.

75  Andrea Forte and Amy Bruckman, "Why Do People Write for Wikipedia? Incentives to Contribute to Open-Content Publishing" (paper presented at Sustaining Community: The Role and Design of Incentive Mechanisms in Online Systems, GROUP 2005 International Conference on Supporting Group Work, Sanibel Island, Florida, November 6, 2005), http://www.andreaforte.net/ForteBruckmanWhyPeopleWrite.pdf.

a structure whereby contributors build their reputations and take on positions of increasing responsibility.

## Conclusion

By connecting learners to educational content and learning communities, the Internet has unlocked new possibilities for learning. As John Seely Brown observes,

> The networked age might be the "silver bullet" that will provide a way to both improve education and to set the stage for a necessary culture of learning. In the digital age, communities self-organize around the Internet, which has created a global "platform" that has vastly expanded access to all sorts of resources including formal and informal educational materials.[76]

Launching an open digital humanities certificate program would offer several benefits. Aspiring digital humanists would gain more flexible yet rigorous opportunities to develop key skills and knowledge in the field. Given digital humanities' focus on digital knowledge production, engaging in an open, mostly online program would enable participants to develop an embedded knowledge of digital pedagogy and best practices in open education. By building open resources, the digital humanities community would create materials of benefit to all institutions with digital humanities programs, open or not. The community would likely develop a stronger sense of identity and purpose as it comes together to formulate an open certificate program, and it would meet the core goal of training the next generation of digital humanists. As the digital humanities certificate program experiments with different approaches, it could produce both a community of trained digital humanists and broader knowledge about open education.

---

76 John Seely Brown, "Foreword: Creating a Culture of Learning," in *Opening Up Education: The Collective Advancement of Education through Open Technology, Open Content, and Open Knowledge*, ed. Toru Iiyoshi and M. S. Vijay Kumar (Cambridge: MIT Press, 2008), xi-xiii, xii.

# 15. Multiliteracies in the Undergraduate Digital Humanities Curriculum: Skills, Principles, and Habits of Mind

*Tanya Clement*

Mark Baeurlein complains that undergraduates are passive consumers because they convert "history, philosophy, literature, civics, and fine art into information" as "material to retrieve and pass along."[1] In contrast, scholarship in digital humanities suggests that inquiry enabled by modes of research, design, preservation, dissemination, and communication that rely on information systems—algorithms or online networks for processing data—deepen and advance knowledge in the humanities. Dubbing teens and twenty-somethings "the dumbest generation" and "mentally agile" but "culturally ignorant," Bauerlein decrees that "The Web hasn't made them better writers and readers, sharper interpreters and more discerning critics, more knowledgeable citizens and tasteful consumers."[2] Yet, truth

---

1 Mark Bauerlein, "Online Literacy Is a Lesser Kind," The Chronicle Review, *The Chronicle of Higher Education,* September 19, 2008, http://chronicle.com/article/Online-Literacy-Is-a-Lesser/28307.

2 Mark Bauerlein, *The Dumbest Generation: How the Digital Age Stupefies Young Americans and Jeopardizes Our Future (Or, Don't Trust Anyone Under 30)* (New York: Jeremy P. Tarcher; Penguin, 2008), 110.

be told books haven't done that either. Like pedagogy intended to teach students to read more critically, project-based learning in digital humanities demonstrates that when students learn how to study digital media, they are learning how to study knowledge production as it is represented in symbolic constructs that circulate within information systems that are themselves a form of knowledge production. A curriculum infused with the pedagogical concerns of digital humanities is a curriculum in which undergraduates learn to think about the cultural work done by and through digital media. Baeurlein is right: "The Web" has not taught students anything. But digital humanities can improve students' abilities to write and read the Web, to interpret, discern, and critique the Web, and ultimately, to be more engaged citizens in the world.

Because the "DH" field[3] is burgeoning, opponents and proponents inevitably slide into discussions about definitions of work (the *what*) and therefore knowledge production (the *why*) of digital humanities. At the same time, these conversations have been only loosely tied with broader discussions in the fields of education, information science, and communications that concern the *how* of pedagogy in a digital age, especially as it pertains to undergraduate education. In 2012, digital humanities has multiple established and emerging centers, tenured professors, programs, and initiatives, its own book series and journals, and its own funding office at the National Endowment for the Humanities. *The New York Times* and robust Twitter, Facebook and blogging communities host fervent debates about defining the field and the nature of digital humanities work and considering *who*—computer scientists, new media critics, tenured English and history professors, undergraduates, graduates, alternative career scholars, women, queer, transgender, people of color— takes advantage of these new and limited resources.[4] In all regards, in

---

3  I use the word "field" purposefully and broadly to denote "An area or sphere of action, operation, or investigation; a (wider or narrower) range of opportunities, or of objects, for labour, study or contemplation; a department or subject of activity or speculation" (*OED*, "field, n." III.15.a.) This broad term, in my use, includes notions of digital humanities as a discipline and digital humanities as a set of methodologies.

4  These include, but are not limited to, Patricia Cohen, "Digital Keys for Unlocking the Humanities' Riches," *The New York Times*, November 16, 2010; Patricia Cohen, "Analyzing Literature by Words and Numbers," *The New York Times*, December 3, 2010; Matthew G. Kirschenbaum, "The (DH) Stars Come Out in LA," *Matthew G. Kirschenbaum*, January 13, 2011, http://mkirschenbaum.wordpress.com/2011/01/13/the-dh-stars-come-out-in-la-2/; Bethany Nowviskie, "#alt-ac: Alternative Academic Careers for Humanities Scholars," *Bethany Nowviskie*, January 3, 2010, http://nowviskie.org/2010/alt-ac/; Stephen Ramsay, "Who's In and Who's Out," *Stephen Ramsay*, January 8, 2011,

discussing how we define the field and who or what we include in it, we must also consider what students should do and should learn in a digital humanities program. This chapter will explore this question (the why, the how, and the what students should learn) by discussing three interconnected topics that influence the development of undergraduate digital humanities curricula: the history of digital humanities as a history tied to curriculum development; the role that institutional infrastructure is playing in program development; and current notions of "digital literacy" in undergraduate education.

# Digital Humanities and Undergraduate Curriculum Development: A Brief History

## The origins of a name

The turn from calling the field "humanities computing" in the 1980s and 1990s to calling it "digital humanities" in recent years, mirrors a significant turn in the kinds of work that undergraduate students are expected to engage in. This reflection is due to various factors including, but not limited to, changing and emerging technologies. In other respects, however, very little has changed in digital humanities. For instance, the field is and has always been defined by pedagogical concerns. Much like today's digital humanities educators, twenty-five years ago scholars debated whether computing could serve as a way to deepen inquiry in the humanities. In a 1986 article titled a "Workshop on Teaching Computers and the Humanities Courses" held at Vassar College in July of the same year, Susan Hockey points out that there was much discussion in the workshop concerning "whether programming should be taught;" she found "There was no consensus on this."[5] She notes on the one hand that "The main argument for programming was that it gives the right mental approach [...] of stretching the minds of humanists to think about humanists' problems;" on the other hand, she says, participants

---

http://lenz.unl.edu/wordpress/?p=325; Geoffrey Rockwell, "Inclusion in the Digital Humanities," *philosophi.ca*, June 28, 2010, http://www.philosophi.ca/pmwiki.php/Main/InclusionInTheDigitalHumanities; and Alexis Lothian, "THATCamp and Diversity in Digital Humanities," *Queer Geek Theory*, January 18, 2011, http://www.queergeektheory.org/2011/01/thatcamp-and-diversity-in-digital-humanities/.

5   Susan Hockey, "Workshop on Teaching Computers and the Humanities Courses," *Literary and Linguistic Computing* 1, no. 4 (1986): 228.

"noted that this kind of programming is only amateur programming" or an academic adventure rather than an activity that results in a professional-level product.[6] More than ten years later at the 2001 symposium "The Humanities Computing Curriculum / The Computing Curriculum in the Arts and Humanities," Hockey asks similar questions about curriculum development, but in 2001 they are couched (as is indicated by the title of the symposium) in terms of defining the field: "How far," she asks, "can the need for analytical and critical thinking in the humanities be reconciled with the practical orientation of much work in humanities computing?"[7] Certainly, Hockey's concerns are the concerns we have in defining the field now, ten years later: what does learning computing in terms of the humanities entail? What is the pedagogical value of digital humanities?

Value is clearly dependent on venue. Other conversations were happening at approximately the same time in the United States. As the result of a multi-institutional yearlong NEH-funded seminar organized around the question "Is humanities computing an academic discipline?" John Unsworth reported that the University of Virginia would start offering a master's degree in digital humanities as part of its New Media program. The rationale was to create "trained professionals who understand both the humanities and information technology" and who could "take advantage of the new intellectual and creative possibilities" that digital forms offer. "The program," he explained, "aims to provide students with experience in recognizing and articulating problems in humanities computing and working collaboratively to solve them, as well as providing hands-on experience in designing and creating digital media."[8] Unsworth's talk, which lays out the curriculum for these students, makes plain the extent to which questions concerning why, what, and how students learn in digital humanities was a central aspect of defining the field. Specifically,

---

6  Hockey, "Workshop on Teaching Computers and the Humanities Courses," 228.

7  Susan Hockey, "Towards a Curriculum for Humanities Computing: Theoretical Goals and Practical Outcomes" (paper presented at The Humanities Computing Curriculum / The Computing Curriculum in the Arts and Humanities, Malaspina University College, Nanaimo, British Columbia, November 9–10, 2001).

8  John Unsworth, "A Masters Degree in Digital Humanities at the University of Virginia" (paper presented at the 2001 Congress of the Social Sciences and Humanities, Université Laval, Québec, Canada, May 25, 2001), http://www3.isrl.illinois.edu/~unsworth/laval.html.

Unsworth recalls why the term "digital humanities" was chosen as the title for the degree:

> The name of the program ("Digital Humanities") is a concession to the fact that "Humanities Informatics" (which would probably be a more accurate name) sounds excessively technocratic, at least to American ears. The other obvious alternative—"Humanities Computing"—sounded too much like a computer support function.[9]

Unsworth's proposal for the master's in digital humanities at the University of Virginia, delivered at the 2001 Congress of the Social Sciences and Humanities, links the conversation about the name "digital humanities" to a larger conversation about curriculum development.[10]

## Considering building—or project-based learning in digital humanities

In 2011, the debate about what digital humanities students should learn becomes a nexus around which some scholars are still attempting to define the field—and the point against which others are resisting essentialist definitions. At the 2011 Modern Language Association (MLA) panel "History and Future of Digital Humanities," for example, Steve Ramsay and Alan Liu (among others) discuss the extent to which the skills students learn in digital humanities project development changes hermeneutics. In terms of whether students should learn programming, Ramsay answers a resounding "yes" so long as we consider that work as part of a larger set of skills that encompass "building." In a blog post of the same name, he writes:

> DH-ers insist—again and again—that this process of creation yields insights that are difficult to acquire otherwise [...] People who mark up texts say it, as do those who build software, hack social networks, create visualizations, and pursue the dozens of other forms of haptic engagement that bring DH-ers to the same table. Building is, for us, a new kind of hermeneutic— one that is quite a bit more radical than taking the traditional methods of humanistic inquiry and applying them to digital objects.[11]

---

9   Unsworth, "A Masters Degree in Digital Humanities at the University of Virginia."
10  Matthew G. Kirschenbaum dates the origins of the name "digital humanities" to an April-November time period in 2001 when Unsworth and others were in conversation about their seminal collection, *A Companion to Digital Humanities.* Matthew G. Kirschenbaum, "What is Digital Humanities and What's It Doing in English Departments?" *ADE Bulletin* 150 (2010): 55–61. The collection was subsequently published as Susan Schreibman, Ray Siemens, and John Unsworth, eds., *A Companion to Digital Humanities* (Malden: Blackwell, 2004).
11  Stephen Ramsay, "On Building," *Stephen Ramsay,* January 11, 2011, http://lenz.unl.edu/wordpress/?p=340.

Liu responds to both Ramsay's talk and his corresponding blog post by broadening the definition of building further to include multiple roles:

> So, I'm okay with the thesis that the differentia specifica of the digital humanities is that its "knowing" includes a robust element of "building" — so long as we recognize the multiplicity of builder roles (including the importance of interpreters, critics, and theorists in the enterprise, many of them the same people as the coders, etc.); and so long as we also recognize that it takes a village or, as Bruno Latour puts is, an actor-network.[12]

In a post by Geoffrey Rockwell from which Ramsay quotes, Rockwell also notes the pedagogical importance of building project teams and project workflows:

> We should be able to be clear about the importance of project management and thing knowledge—the tacit knowledge of fabrication and its cultures— even if the very nature of that *poesis* (knowledge of making) itself cannot easily (and shouldn't have to) be put into words. We should be able to welcome theoretical perspectives without fear of being swallowed in postmodernisms that are exclusive as our craft knowledge.[13]

On a certain level, the point in most of these debates goes back to a point that Father Roberto A. Busa made in 1980—this work that digital humanists do "can help us to be more humanistic than before."[14] Ramsay, Liu, and Rockwell are doing what humanists always do: they are analyzing and critiquing knowledge production in the humanities. On another level, these debates reflect updated concerns in higher education in general that educators must constantly evolve their curricula to reflect new developments in technology and in the constant changes at higher education institutions.

## Examples of building- or project-based learning in undergraduate digital humanities curricula

In light of this continued interest in "meta" conversations about defining digital humanities, discussions concerning specific examples of curriculum development within undergraduate programs remain disparate and few. A search for the word "undergraduate" in the abstracts from the annual Digital Humanities conference (or the joint ACH/ALLC conference)

---

12   Alan Liu, Response to "On Building," *Stephen Ramsay*, January 12, 2011, http://lenz.unl.edu/wordpress/?p=340#comment-9144.

13   Rockwell, "Inclusion in the Digital Humanities."

14   Roberto Busa, "The Annals of Humanities Computing: The Index Thomisticus," *Computers and the Humanities* 14 (1980): 89.

between the years 2004 and 2009 shows that there were only three presentations specifically concerning undergraduate pedagogy.[15] Searching the preceding twenty years of the journal *Literary and Linguistic Computing* produces a more complete picture that reflects a prevailing notion: an undergraduate curriculum in humanities computing or digital humanities is skills-based rather than research-based. In 1991, Thomas N. Corns wrote in an article entitled "Computers in the Humanities: Methods and Applications in the Study of English Literature" that "[t] he computer skills most useful to literature undergraduates are word-processing skills."[16] Twenty years later, the conversation has in some ways evolved minimally. For instance, in an exchange on the *Humanist* Listserv in April 2010, Alexander Hay asks, "What would be the bare minimum any would-be Humanities Computing researcher should have in terms of skills? By that, I mean what should you know in order to be eligible for most jobs, funding opportunities, etc.?"[17] Willard McCarty replies that a question concerning skills "is a question implicitly at least asked and answered by those who set up programmes in the field, *especially undergraduate programmes*," since a question of skills "becomes less important the more academic and the less professional the training becomes."[18] He continues,

> Undergraduate training provides two paths: (1) basic training for those who have bought into the notion that education is for full-time employment, who want the degree in order to get a job; (2) a highly simplified starting point for those who will go on to dwell on the questions that make for a life worth living.[19]

---

15   These include Martyn Jessop, "In Search of Humanities Computing in Teaching, Learning, and Research" (paper presented at The 17th Joint International Conference of the Association for Computers and the Humanities [ACH] and the Association for Literary and Linguistic Computing [ALLC], Victoria, British Columbia, June 15–18, 2005); Simon Mahony, "An Interdisciplinary Perspective on Building Learning Communities Within the Digital Humanities" (paper presented at Digital Humanities 2008, Oulu, Finland, June 25–29, 2008); and John G. Keating, Aja Teehan, and Thomas Byrne, "Delivering a Humanities Computing Module at Undergraduate Level: A Case Study" (paper presented at Digital Humanities 2009, College Park, Maryland, June 22–25, 2009).

16   Thomas N. Corns, "Computers in the Humanities: Methods and Applications in the Study of English Literature," *Literary and Linguistic Computing* 6 (1991): 130.

17   Alexander Hay, "What Would Be A Good Basic Skill-set For Humanities Computing Jobs?" *Humanist Discussion Group* 23, no. 758 (2010), April 8, 2010, http://lists.digitalhumanities. org/pipermail/humanist/2010-April/001181.html.

18   Willard McCarty, "Basic Skills?" *Humanist Discussion Group* 23, no. 760 (2010), April 10, 2010, http://lists.digitalhumanities.org/pipermail/humanist/2010-April/001183.html, my emphasis.

19   McCarty, "Basic Skills?"

McCarty delineates the difference between undergraduate and graduate work as one determined by learning technical skills and professional training on the one hand (undergraduate), and learning to think or do academic research on the other (graduate). Similarly, in describing their work on formal methods in the humanities in *Computing in Humanities Education: A European Perspective* (1999), the authors differentiate between "the two levels of studies common in European universities (undergraduate vs. postgraduate; licence vs. maîtrise; etc.)": they explain their choice to "pay more attention to the former" as one that reflects the notion that "the presence of humanities computing in the second level is more closely tied to research and raises fewer problems concerning educational methods and organization."[20] In general, over the last decade or so, many scholars in digital humanities have relegated "basic" technical or "computer skills" to undergraduate pedagogy.

Beginning to address *what* and *how* undergraduate students can learn to become "builders" and to engage the "actor-network" that scholars are arguing is essential to digital humanities is a crucial step in determining a role that digital humanities can play in higher education that is beyond basic skills. History shows us that the rigorous attention that scholars are paying to the theory and practice of the digital humanities in recent years is compatible with questions scholars and educators have always asked concerning what students should learn in a humanities program. At the same time, debates on defining the theory and practice of digital humanities have so far failed to adequately define *what* students should learn and *how* students should immerse themselves in these theoretical perspectives. Until we consider digital humanities undergraduate pedagogy in terms other than training, and rather as a pursuit that enables all students to ask valuable and productive questions that make for "a life worth living," digital humanities will remain unrelated to and ill defined against the goals of higher education.

---

20   Tito Orlandi, Joseph Norment Bell, Lou Burnard, Dino Buzzetti, Koenraad de Smedt, Ingo Kropac, Jacques Souillot, and Manfred Thaller, "European Studies on Formal Methods in the Humanities," in *Computing in Humanities Education: A European Perspective*, ed. Koenraad de Smedt, Hazel Gardiner, Espen Ore, Tito Orlandi, Harold Short, Jacques Souillot, and William Vaughan (Bergen: University of Bergen, 1999), 16.

# *Why* digital humanities

## The risks of reading

Before discussing *what* undergraduates learn in digital humanities and *how* they learn it, it is useful to return to Bauerlein's argument that undergraduates today are "the dumbest" and to consider *why* digital humanities is important in this context. First, Bauerlein is not alone in his thinking. In 2004, the National Endowment for the Arts (NEA) published *Reading at Risk: A Survey of Literary Reading in America* in order to "provide an invaluable snapshot of the role of literature in the lives of Americans."[21] The report poses three main premises of concern to this discussion:

1. Literacy is "the baseline for participation in social life [...] and reading of literary work in particular—is essential to a sound and healthy understanding of, and participation in, a democratic society";
2. Now is "a critical time, when electronic media are becoming the dominant influence in young people's worlds"; and,
3. Electronic media "have increasingly drawn Americans away from reading."[22]

The crux of the supposed "risk" to literacy lies in the link that the NEA, Bauerlein, and others such as Sven Birkerts make between reading print or static text and critical thinking: NEA chairman Dana Gioai laments that "print culture affords irreplaceable forms of focused attention and contemplation that make complex communications and insights possible,"[23] while Bauerlein reports ominously that "the relationship between screens and books isn't benign."[24] Like Bauerlein and the authors of the NEA report, Sven Birkerts maintains that book readers learn more because the book is a system that "evolved over centuries in ways that map our collective

---

21  National Endowment for the Arts, *Reading at Risk: A Survey of Literary Reading in America*, Research Division Report #46, ed. Tom Bradshaw and Bonnie Nichols (Washington: National Endowment for the Arts, 2004), ix.
22  *Reading at Risk*, 1, ix, xii.
23  Dana Gioia, Preface to *Reading at Risk*, vii.
24  Bauerlein, "Online Literacy Is a Lesser Kind."

endeavor to understand and express our world" while "the electronic book, on the other hand, represents—and furthers—a circuitry of instant access."[25] Seemingly foreboding, these arguments against the digital are built on definitions of literacy that preclude the kinds of *multiliteracies* that others argue are essential to undergraduate student learning outcomes in the twenty-first century.

## Multiculturalism, Multimodalities and Multimedia

In contrast to the perspective forwarded by the NEA and others, scholars in education, information studies, literacy studies, and literary studies have been working from data that informs other twenty-first century approaches to literacy , including multiculturalism, multimodalities, and multimedia. For instance, *Reading at Risk* reports that electronic media is a "dominant influence" in young people's lives that, because of its availability and accessibility, increasingly draws them away from reading and therefore advanced literacy skills.[26] In contrast, "A Pedagogy of Multiliteracies: Designing Social Futures" by the New London Group (comprised of ten academics including James Gee and Allan Luke) addresses how literacy pedagogy in a digital age can reflect societal changes such as globalization, technology and increasing cultural and social diversity.[27] In particular, the New London Group focuses on access and availability as key factors in "multiliteracies" that empower students to achieve the authors' goals of literacy learning, including "creating access to the evolving language of work, power, and community, and fostering the critical engagement necessary for them to design their social futures and achieve success through fulfilling employment."[28] The New London group specifically refers to students learning "modes of representation much broader than language alone" such as virtual representations. The authors argue that this broader set of representations shows students that multiliteracies are situational as well as global, that they differ "according to culture and context," and that multiliteracies can have "specific cognitive, cultural, and social effects" since "in some cultural contexts—in an Aboriginal community or in a

---

25   Sven Birkerts, "Resisting the Kindle," *Atlantic Monthly,* March 2, 2009, http://www. theatlantic.com/magazine/archive/2009/03/resisting-the-kindle/7345/.

26   *Reading at Risk,* ix.

27   New London Group, "A Pedagogy of Multiliteracies: Designing Social Futures," *Harvard Educational Review* 66, no. 1 (1996): 60–92.

28   New London Group, "A Pedagogy of Multiliteracies," 60.

multimedia environment, for instance—the visual mode of representation may be much more powerful."[29]

Similarly, the "Digital Humanities Manifesto 2.0" launched by the UCLA Mellon Seminars in the Digital Humanities in 2009, reminds us that a notion of "literacy" in the digital humanities is not necessarily a concept pertaining to "universal" literacies: "It is not about the emergence of a new general culture, Renaissance humanism/Humanities, or universal literacy. On the contrary, it promotes collaboration and creation across domains of expertise."[30] A notion of multiliteracies that incorporates and anticipates difference is useful to digital humanities scholars who herald shared expertise and collaborative practices as a primary outcome of teaching students to use online networks and computational methodologies in the humanities.[31]

## Participatory cultures

Further, there is clear evidence that students are not dominated by new media (as the NEA reports), but instead feel an increased sense of creative control and therefore a desire to participate in society and actively engage in "generative practices" that herald social change. A 2009 Pew Research Center report titled "The Internet and Civic Engagement" reveals that the kinds of civic activities that bloggers and gamers engage with "in traditional realms of political and nonpolitical participation" are directly related to how they "use blogs and social networking sites as an outlet for civic engagement." In fact, the Pew report finds that these Internet users "are far more active than other internet users. In addition, they are even more active than those who do not use the internet at all."[32] Further, it is because of their active engagement that Henry Jenkins defines Bauerlein's "dumbest generation" in a different fashion, as a "participatory culture" with

---

29  New London Group, "A Pedagogy of Multiliteracies," 64.
30  Todd Presner and Jeffrey Schnapp et al., "Digital Humanities Manifesto 2.0," University of California, Los Angeles, May 29, 2009, http://manifesto.humanities.ucla.edu/2009/05/29/the-digital-humanities-manifesto-20/.
31  See Busa, "The Annals of Humanities Computing," 89; Koenraad de Smedt, "Some Reflections on Studies in Humanities Computing," *Literary and Linguistic Computing* 17, no. 1 (2002): 90; and Willard McCarty, "'Knowing True Things by What Their Mockeries Be': Modelling in the Humanities," *TEXT Technology* 12, no. 1 (2003): 43–58.
32  Aaron Smith, Kay Lehman Schlozman, Sidney Verba, and Henry Brady, "The Internet and Civic Engagement," *Pew Internet and American Life Project*, September 1, 2009, http://www.pewinternet.org/Reports/2009/15--The-Internet-and-Civic-Engagement.

[...] relatively low barriers to artistic expression and civic engagement, strong support for creating and sharing one's creations, and some type of informal mentorship whereby what is known by the most experienced is passed along to novices. A participatory culture is also one in which members believe their contributions matter, and feel some degree of social connection with one another (at the least they care what other people think about what they have created).[33]

Certainly, the fact that accessibility and availability barriers are lowered in our increasingly globalized and digitized twenty-first century culture means that students think and engage differently in culture and scholarship. The "Digital Humanities Manifesto 2.0" declares that "Digital Humanities = Big Humanities = Generative Humanities" because "Digital Humanities is about integration and generative practices: the building of bigger pictures out of the *tesserae* of expert knowledge."[34] Additionally—given the nature of participatory culture and the desire to encourage a sense of "multiliteracies" in the classroom—teaching digital humanities students to become "builders" and to engage the "actor-network" means more than simply incorporating a different kind of pedagogy that allows for more access to more information or even more creative engagements or remixings. Underlying this work is a fundamental shift in our definitions of literacies, which now must account for multiculturalism and a diversity of perspectives that require multimodal and multimedia knowledge production; it is a shift in which "language and other modes of meaning are dynamic representational resources, constantly being remade by their users as they work to achieve their various cultural purposes."[35]

# Digital humanities how?

## Digital humanities inflected programs

*What* and *how* digital humanities students learn in order to achieve these multiliteracies is under considerable debate from a variety of perspectives. Simply listing examples of existing programs called "digital humanities" is problematic. In fact, in the fall of 2009, the website at King's College

---

33  Henry Jenkins, *Confronting the Challenges of Participatory Culture: Media Education for the 21st Century,* John D. and Catherine T. MacArthur Foundation Reports on Digital Media and Learning (Cambridge: MIT Press, 2009), 3.

34  Presner and Schnapp et al., "Digital Humanities Manifesto 2.0."

35  New London Group, "A Pedagogy of Multiliteracies," 64.

still touted itself as "one of the very few academic institutions in the world where the digital humanities may be pursued as part of a degree" in undergraduate studies—a fact complicated now that they have cut the program. There are a few programs that currently use the phrase "digital humanities" in either a course title such as the Introduction to Digital Humanities at Bloomsburg University in Pennsylvania and at the University of Victoria or as a specialization or certificate such as that offered by Michigan State University. There is also a brand-new digital humanities bachelor of arts minor at the University of California, Los Angeles,[36] and a digital humanities Bachelor of Science degree in professional communication and emerging media at the University of Wisconsin-Stout. This (at times) wide and disparate variety of degree names and types could explain why Willard McCarty and Matthew Kirschenbaum's list of institutional models for humanities computing— though extensive—does not include an account of specifically undergraduate programs.[37]

The fact that such a list[38] would immediately include a broad range of programs encompassing information science, digital cultures, new media, and computer science reflects the fact that there are a variety of methods by which we are attempting to guide undergraduate study in what McCarty calls the "methodological commons" of digital humanities.[39] It also reflects the provocative nature of asking scholars to describe their pedagogical methodologies within an interdisciplinary space. Further, because digital humanities is a field that engages a wide range of disciplinary perspectives, it is a field that is represented by programs of study that are inflected by, but

---

36  For a discussion of the programs in digital humanities at UCLA, see Chris Johanson and Elaine Sullivan, with Janice Reiff, Diane Favro, Todd Presner, and Willeke Wendrich, "Teaching Digital Humanities through Digital Cultural Mapping," another chapter in this collection.

37  Willard McCarty and Matthew G. Kirschenbaum, "Institutional Models for Humanities Computing," *Literary and Linguistic Computing* 18, no. 4 (2003): 465-89. More recently, Lisa Spiro has made 134 digital humanities syllabi freely available at citeline: http://citeline.mit.edu/fd86695ba2977553d1d40baa97b310a1ae64e10b/. It is not clear, however, without reading each one and knowing the context whether a class is for undergraduate or graduate students.

38  To see how this list might develop, I started an online list of undergraduate programs generated through an informal survey conducted on Twitter, the *Humanist* Discussion List, and my blog *U+2E19*; see Tanya Clement, "Digital Humanities Inflected Undergraduate Programs," *U+2E19* November 4, 2009, http://tanyaclement.org/2009/11/04/digital-humanities-inflected-undergraduate-programs-2/.

39  Willard McCarty, *Humanities Computing* (New York: Palgrave, 2005), 131.

not necessarily called, "digital humanities."[40] Certainly, just as Unsworth (and others) asking the question "[w]hat is Humanities Computing and what is not?" generated more questions than answers about defining the field, asking the community to identify programs inflected by the digital humanities provokes more discussion concerning existing models.

## A diversity of methodologies

In an attempt to gather information about the formation of various undergraduate programs, I conducted a survey (advertised on Twitter, the *Humanist* listserv and the 2010 Digital Humanities Conference in London) titled "Designing for Digital Literacy Survey" open to anyone who self-identified with an undergraduate program inflected by the digital humanities. In the survey, I asked some basic questions concerning how an undergraduate program inflected by the digital humanities has been and might be developed within a variety of university settings. These questions were based on similar questions posed by scholars ten years previous,[41] but this previous work had focused primarily on graduate (or post-graduate) work. My intention was to make these same matters surrounding undergraduate pedagogy transparent and to broaden discussion about the range of issues that underpin the formation of an undergraduate curriculum. With my questions, I was interested in two aspects of how digital humanities curricula are developed for undergraduates: (1) how definitions of "digital humanities" manifest in a particular curriculum and (2) how this is the result of infrastructural freedoms and constraints at the home institution. At the time of this writing, eight respondents completed the nine questions. Some of the respondents were from large research universities; others were from small liberal arts colleges. Respondents reflected a range of nationalities, representing universities in Canada, Germany, the United Kingdom, and the United States.

---

40  At the time of this writing, Martyn Jessop has written to clarify: "Sadly the ... minor at King's College London has been closed down," though they "still operate 'standalone' modules in digital humanities for 1st and 2nd year students;" see "Undergraduate Programmes," *Humanist Discussion Group* 23, no. 398 (2009), October 27, 2009, http://lists. digitalhumanities.org/pipermail/humanist/2009-October/000825.html. For a discussion of previous and current digital humanities training at King's College, see Willard McCarty's chapter, "The PhD in Humanities Computing," and Simon Mahony and Elena Piezzaro's chapter, "Teaching Skills or Teaching Methodology?"

41  Hockey, "Towards a Curriculum for Humanities Computing," and John Unsworth and Terry Butler, "A Masters Degree in Digital Humanities at the University of Virginia" (paper presented at ACH-ALLC 2001, New York University, June 13–16, 2001).

One of the first questions was "What are the aims and objectives of your undergraduate curriculum? What are the main learning outcomes?" Of the eight respondents, a few said their curriculum is focused on teaching digital methodologies as technical skills or "to provide practical technical skills within a humanistic framework." Specifically, another responded, "[t]he courses teach computer skills and methods as applied to disciplines in the College of Humanities with different sets of courses oriented toward different typical career paths for humanities majors: teaching, editing, publishing, writing, graduate study and research, etc." Other respondents remarked that the courses were focused on analyzing culture or "provid[ing] students with a critical understanding of the uses and impact of technologies in society." A third type of respondent focused on interdiscplinarity: "It is an interdisciplinary degree that combines theory and practice in the study of the latest communication technologies." Another question asked, "How is the academic content of the curriculum structured? What are the core modules/courses and how are they sequenced?" Respondents described programs that include historical and theoretical classes, core or mandatory coursework, as well as "hands-on" classes or labs and capstone projects. Only one mentioned programming while many mentioned "multimedia" classes. Some mentioned a core course that covers a wide variety of topics while others described core courses that can lead students to a wide variety of directions. Whether digital skills, cultural analysis, or interdisciplinary theory and practice, the respondents remained focused on developing active and productive citizens.

## A diversity of subject areas

It is not surprising that there is such a wide range of existing models: digital humanities is as diverse as the humanities. For instance, Patrik Svensson sees work in the digital humanities as part of a spectrum "from textual analysis of medieval texts and establishment of metadata schemes to the production of alternative computer games and artistic readings of nanotechnology."[42] From another perspective, John Unsworth asserts that "the semantic web is our future, and it will require formal representations of the human record" requiring "training in the humanities, but also [...]

---

42  Patrik Svensson, "Humanities Computing as Digital Humanities," *Digital Humanities Quarterly* 3, no. 3 (2009): paras. 1–62.

elements of mathematics, logic, engineering, and computer science."[43] The "competences" that students would achieve in the proposed University of Virginia (UVa) master's curriculum highlight the significance that all of the participants placed on programming skills:

> Successful completion of this MA program requires students to have, or to acquire, a working familiarity with major computer operating systems (PC, Macintosh, Unix) and software more specialized than the usual office applications (e.g., visual programming software, multimedia authoring tools, databases), as well as with markup languages (e.g., SGML, XML) and programming languages (e.g., Perl, Java).[44]

While Unsworth noted that UVA's MA was proscribed, in part, by institutional resources, the Advanced Computing in the Humanities Working Group on Formal Methods in the Humanities limit their definition of undergraduate programs in humanities computing in Europe based on disciplinary boundaries: they chose "to concentrate on *computing* and to avoid the fields of information, communication, media, and multimedia since these are generally considered as social sciences rather than as humanities."[45] From a final perspective, students at Bloomsburg University of Pennsylvania note in their "Manifesto" on digital humanities, "The science major approaches things differently than the literature major—this diversity is foundational to Digital Humanities."[46] The small sample of various perspectives in my more recent survey tells plainly what these other examples reflect: different contexts require different pedagogies and digital humanities is a meeting house for these many minds.

## A diversity of institutions

Just as simply listing examples of existing programs would leave many digital humanities inflected programs out, simply listing any one program as a model for others would also belie the extent to which scholars and administrators have shaped and are shaping these curricula according to the needs of their specific experiences, disciplines, and communities.

---

43  John Unsworth, "What is Humanities Computing and What is Not?" *Jahrbuch für Computerphilologie* 4 (2002): 82-83.
44  Unsworth, "A Masters Degree in Digital Humanities at the University of Virginia."
45  Orlandi et al., "European Studies on Formal Methods in the Humanities," 16.
46  "Bloomsburg U. Undergraduate 'Manifesto' on Digital Humanities," *4Humanities*, December,2010,http://humanistica.ualberta.ca/bloomsburg-u-undergraduate-manifesto-on-digital-humanities/.

Accordingly, with the "Designing for Digital Literacy Survey," I was interested in discerning the extent to which a particular digital humanities instantiation is the result of the home institution's infrastructure. In a third question I asked, "How does the program fit into the overall structure of the institution? Is it a program in a department or is it interdepartmental? It is certificate or degree granting? If a degree program, what are/were the key issues in establishing a certificate or degree for students in your program?" The respondents come from a wide range of institutional situations. They reported that their programs were in departments such as the Department of Communication Studies and Multimedia, the English Department, and the Computing Department, with a small overlap with the Music Department. Another program was administered directly at the college level (although historically it was part of the Department of Linguistics) and another was described as interdepartmental. Overall, one program granted a bachelor of arts degree, one granted a bachelor of science degree, the others gave BA minors, a "designation," or certificates. Again, the variety of responses speaks to the culture of a particular institute but it also speaks to the varieties of disciplinary cultures represented in digital humanities, a multiplicity that Geoffrey Rockwell, for one, embraces: "I am no longer confident that we want to take the route of forming a discipline with all its attendant institutions."[47]

Another question I asked in the survey that pertains to institutional infrastructures was "What technical facilities are needed for the curriculum and how are these supported?" Respondents reported a wide range of facilities. On one end of the spectrum, one respondent said that their program had two computer classrooms, two open labs ("priority is given to our students, and other students throughout the Humanities are let in as space permits"), a collaborative space for group projects, a sound recording studio, video editing stations, and two SMARTboard-equipped rooms. Another respondent had a multimedia wing with two labs of computers and some specialized hardware and software. Others had one or two labs. One had laptops. Some just had technical support. Another responded with measured levity and emoticons saying, "No facilities needed :-)" and then explained: "I flee the computer pools, but force students to bring along and use their laptops in class, in addition we have some laptops to lend for a term; there is WLAN in every room, I provide them with multi-plugs and extension cables."

---

47  Rockwell, "Inclusion in the Digital Humanities."

Finally, I asked in the "Designing for Digital Literacy" survey "What are other important infrastructural issues and challenges arose in setting up your curriculum within your institution?" There were three types of responses to this question. First, respondents mention monetary expense. One said, "This is a relatively expensive program to run (both in terms of hardware/software, in terms of faculty who can teach these intensive courses, and in terms of space)." A second response mentioned the general attitude or mindset of colleagues who do not see the relationship between digital humanities and their home disciplines; this respondent cited "[j]ustification to the academic departments in our college" as an issue: "we find it difficult to build awareness of our program because many of the departments don't see how we can augment their curriculum." A third respondent mentioned the fact that interdisciplinary work in the academy poses an issue when it was time to grant degrees: "Initially, there were many concerns over the curriculum due to the potential overlap with other degree areas at the university (since many have a digital media component, such as Communication Studies and Fine Art)." In general, these responses point to the inherently interdisciplinary nature of digital humanities. Where does one program start and another program end when we are talking about the digital and the humanities?

The fact is that any program that identifies itself as digital humanities is in fact inflected by a version of digital humanities that is situational and irreproducible. In his talk "A Master's Degree in Digital Humanities," Unsworth notes that the faculty, graduate students, and library staff who came together and concluded from their year-long seminar that digital humanities was a discipline drew their experiences from programs that

> [...] differed from one another in various interesting ways—some leaned more toward media studies, some more toward linguistics, some more toward informatics. The model that seemed to fit best with the interests and resources already in evidence at Virginia was somewhere between media studies and informatics, as you'll see in what follows. I should note that UVA has no library science program, no journalism program, no communications program—so the potential for overlap between this new MA and existing graduate programs was effectively nil.[48]

In this talk, Unsworth points out a significant aspect that concerns the *why*, *what* and *how* of the possible UVA master's degree program that also affects

---

48   Unsworth, "A Masters Degree in Digital Humanities at the University of Virginia."

the development of undergraduate programs—that is, the institutional and infrastructural issues that are specific to certain universities. These same issues—faculty experience, academic infrastructures, and available resources—affect how curriculum in undergraduate programs is developed today. At the same time, in order to understand what it means to educate undergraduates in digital humanities, it is crucial that we have examples and models to draw from as the field and the nature of study in general evolves.

## What digital humanities: skills, principles and habits of mind

While the survey's anecdotal responses give us a glimpse into the diverse nature of undergraduate digital humanities programs, it is useful to step back, finally, from the particularities of each program to take a look at more general student learning outcomes and at possible steps forward. To this end and in lieu of listing every possible perspective from the many fields from which digital humanities draws, I am including here a Table of Multiliteracies (Table 1) that includes four perspectives: one from new media studies;[49] one from humanities and science;[50] one from gaming and literacy studies;[51] and one from education scholars.[52] Each of these contributions discusses the kinds of multiliteracies that are engaged within undergraduate humanities curricula through general skills, principles and habits of mind that allow students to progress within and engage society in the twenty-first century.

Further, each list comes from a different disciplinary perspective and is assembled and disseminated differently. In the 2006 white paper *Confronting the Challenges of Participatory Culture: Media Education for the 21st Century*, Henry Jenkins and his researchers generated a list of the

---

49  Jenkins, *Confronting the Challenges of Participatory Culture.*
50  Cathy Davidson, "21st Century Literacies: Syllabus, Assignments, Calendar," *HASTAC*, December 31, 2010, http://www.hastac.org/blogs/cathy-davidson/21st-century-literacies-syllabus-assignments-calendar.
51  James Paul Gee, *What Video Games Have to Teach Us About Learning and Literacy* (New York: Palgrave, 2003).
52  Arthur L. Costa and Bena Kallick, "Describing 16 Habits of Mind," *The Institute for Habits of Mind*, n.d., http://www.instituteforhabitsofmind.com/resources/pdf/16HOM.pdf. The article is adapted from a series of books by the authors—*Discovering and Exploring Habits of Mind; Activating and Engaging Habits of Mind; Assessing and Reporting Growth in Habits of Mind;* and *Integrating and Sustaining Habits of Mind*—published by the Association for Supervision and Curriculum Development as *Habits of Mind: A Developmental Series.*

kinds of skills that participatory practices generally engage.[53] For her Spring 2011 undergraduate English class Twenty-first Century Literacies, HASTAC founder and English professor Cathy Davidson designates twenty "interrelated skills (literacies) that were defined in a specific way for over a century and that beg redefinition." Complicating earlier definitions of literacies by posing questions based on the complexities of new forms of literacies, Davidson argues, that "in the Information Age, English departments should be central, helping all of us to understand the complexities of new forms of reading, writing, communicating using this new form of interactive, iterative publication."[54] In his book, *What Video Games Have to Teach Us about Learning and Literacy*, literacy scholar James Paul Gee argues that multiliteracies are formed in relation to specific semiotic domains such as videogames. Asserting that bestselling videogames reflect "the theory of human learning built into good videogames," Gee establishes thirty-six key learning principles that are intrinsic to "good" games.[55] Finally, the fourth column is a list of "Habits of Mind," developed by education scholars Arthur L. Costa and Bena Kallick to encourage educators to consider "a composite of many skills, attitudes, cues, past experiences and proclivities" when creating curricula. This list is particularly useful in the context of digital humanities because the habits, which focus on "value," "inclination," "sensitivity," "capability," and "commitment," were generated from Costa and Kallick's interest in exploring the idea that "the critical attribute of intelligent human beings is not only having information, but also knowing how to act on it."[56]

---

53    Jenkins, *Confronting the Challenges of Participatory Culture.*

54    Davidson, "21st Century Literacies."

55    Gee, *What Video Games Have to Teach Us About Learning and Literacy*, 6.

56    Costa and Kallick, "Describing 16 Habits of Mind." For a thorough investigation of Costa and Kallick's "Habits of Mind" in relation to Learning Theory, including theories on the nature of intelligence, information processing models of learning, metacognitive models, cognitive styles, constructivism, social learning theory, and emotional intelligence, see John Campbell, "Theorising Habits of Mind as a Framework for Learning" (paper presented at the Australian Association for Research in Education Conference, Adelaide, November, 2006), http://www.aare.edu.au/06pap/cam06102.pdf.

| Davidson | Gee | Jenkins | Costa & Kallick |
|---|---|---|---|
| Attention | Active, Critical Learning Principle | Play | Persisting |
| Participation | Design Principle | Performance | Thinking and Communicating with Clarity and Precision |
| Collaboration | Semiotic Principle | Simulation | Managing Impulsivity |
| Network awareness | Semiotic Domains Principle | Appropriation | Gathering Data Through all Senses |
| Global Consciousness | Meta-level thinking about Semiotic Domain Principle | Multitasking | Listening with Understanding and Empathy |
| Design | "Psychosocial Moratorium" Principle | Distributed Cognition | Creating, imagining and Innovation |
| Narrative, Storytelling | Committed Learning Principle | Collective Intelligence | Thinking Flexibly |
| Procedural (Game) Literacy | Identity Principle | Judgment | Responding with Wonderment and Awe |
| Critical consumption of information | Self-Knowledge Principle | Transmedia Navigation | Thinking about Thinking (Metacognition) |
| Digital Divides, Digital Participation | Amplification of Input Principle | Networking | Taking Responsible Risks |
| Ethics | Achievement Principle | Negotiation | Striving for Accuracy |
| Assessment | Practice Principle | | Finding Humor |
| Preservation | Ongoing Learning Principle | | Questioning and Posing Problems |

| Davidson | Gee | Costa & Kallick |
|---|---|---|
| Sustainability | "Regime of Competence" Principle | Thinking Interdependently |
| Learning, Unlearning, and Relearning | Probing Principle | Applying Past Knowledge to New Situations |
| | Multiple Routes Principle | Remaining Open to Continuous Learning |
| | Situated Meaning Principle | |
| | Text Principle | |
| | Intertextual Principle | |
| | Multimodal Principle | |
| | "Material Intelligence" Principle | |
| | Intuitive Knowledge Principle | |
| | Subset Principle | |
| | Incremental Principle | |
| | Concentrated Sample Principle | |
| | Bottom-up Basic Skills Principle | |
| | Explicit Information On-Demand and Just-in-Time Principle | |
| | Discovery Principle | |
| | Transfer Principle | |
| | Cultural Models about the World Principle | |
| | Cultural Models about Learning Principle | |
| | Cultural Models about Semiotic Domains Principle | |
| | Distributed Principle | |
| | Dispersed Principle | |
| | Affinity Group Principle | |
| | Insider Principle | |

**Table 1.** Table of Multiliteracies

What is significant about these lists is not necessarily where they differ, but rather the points at which they converge. They all include skills that require critical thinking, commitment, community, and play. These represent student-learning outcomes that not only gesture towards essential multiliteracies, but also methods for thinking about how we define digital humanities in the undergraduate curriculum. In a recent online article that is responding in part to conversations about defining and disciplining digital humanities, Geoffrey Rockwell considers the complex nature of interdisciplinarity within the previously marginalized world of digital humanities—or what he is calling the "discipline of the refused." He asks, "[i]s there some way to maintain both the permeability of an interdisciplinary commons where the perspectives of different disciplines are welcome in the commons while encouraging appropriate skills and rigour? Can we have it both ways—have both the commons and well-articulated onramps?"[57] Posing this query, Rockwell points out the difficult questions that the digital humanities community must face, especially as it continues to grow and expand. In particular, the fact that the three lists on the left (by Davidson, Gee, and Jenkins respectively) in Table 1 fit comfortably within the list of "Habits of Mind" suggests that digital humanities undergraduate curriculum development could be considered less as "a common methodological outlook"[58] or "methodological commons,"[59] but more fruitfully and productively as "a disposition toward behaving intelligently when confronted with problems, the answers to which are not immediately known."[60] As a result, if we consider digital humanities as a space that requires "multiliteracies," which are learned through "habits of mind" then we may begin to see how the work of digital humanities allows for a commons to which we could take many roads.

## Conclusion

The undergraduate curricula are an integral part of higher education. As such it reaches a community that is essential to the continued work of digital humanities. In 2001, Steven Tötösy de Zepetnek observed that because undergraduates begin their research online, scholars should create

---

57  Rockwell, "Inclusion in the Digital Humanities."
58  Kirschenbaum "What Is Digital Humanities and What's It Doing in English Departments?," 2.
59  McCarty, *Humanities Computing*, 131.
60  Costa and Kallick, "Describing 16 Habits of Mind."

more and better online resources for academic study.[61] A glance just at the last ten years of the journal *Literary and Linguistic Computing*, the abstracts from the annual Digital Humanities conference, the first issues of the *Digital Humanities Quarterly*, and the daily news prove that the digital humanities community has worked hard to produce these resources. Scholars in the digital humanities are already teaching the next generation of students not only how to use electronic resources, but how to create them, expand them, and preserve them. Certainly, the digital humanities has its fair share of manifestos that seek, as manifestos do, to revolutionize the way we think about the digital and the humanities:

> We wave the banner of "Digital Humanities" for tactical reasons (think of it as "strategic essentialism"), not out of a conviction that the phrase adequately describes the tectonic shifts embraced in this document. But an emerging transdisciplinary domain without a name runs the risk of finding itself defined less by advocates than by critics and opponents.[62]

The work that digital humanities has done concerning how we define "digital humanities" provides a good example for the work we need to do in defining *why, what* and *how* we teach digital humanities. Part and parcel with the work that is engaged in defining and redefining the field should be the work we need to do to consider how the logistics of departments, the crossing paths of curricula development, and the allocation and reallocation of essential resources shapes how we teach undergraduate programs inflected by digital humanities. Now is the time to make that work transparent and to provide a resource for others who wish to continue, broaden, and support this work.

---

61  Steven Tötösy de Zepetnek, "The New Knowledge Management and Online Research and Publishing in the Humanities," *CLCWeb: Comparative Literature and Culture* 3, no. 1 (2001), http://docs.lib.purdue.edu/clcweb/vol3/iss1/8/.
62  Presner and Schnapp et al., "Digital Humanities Manifesto 2.0."

# 16. Teaching Digital Rhetoric: Wikipedia, Collaboration, and the Politics of Free Knowledge

*Melanie Kill*

The vast majority of the undergraduates we teach will not become professional scholars, but all will be educated citizens with a responsibility to put their knowledge and abilities to use for the common good. Our work with them, then, is not only about exposing them to the critical methods and modes of thinking that are central to knowledge-making in our fields, but also about helping them to map humanist questions and approaches onto an always complex and changing world. Wikipedia (http://www. wikipedia.org/) provides students with a range of opportunities to work as intermediaries between the disciplinary expertise they are studying, a public system of knowledge curation, and a global audience of readers. In this chapter, I present a case for Wikipedia as an environment not only for the collaborative compilation of knowledge, but also for collaborative inquiry into knowledge-making practices and resources across disciplines and cultures. We can engage students in humanist thinking about the technologies through which digital communities and collaborations are supported by involving them in Wikipedia content development and by directing critical attention to the ways that established institutions of knowledge inform and interact with the tools and resources of the digital public sphere. My focus here is not on descriptions of specific assignments,[1] but rather on expanding attention to the wide range of pedagogical affordances presented by the resources and interactions that Wikipedia's texts, tools, and community make available.

On their way toward the greater responsibilities of educated citizens, students in the humanities need experiences and opportunities that will help them to develop both understanding of the collaborative nature of knowledge-making and skill in learning and working collaboratively. These are not just marketable traits that will serve graduates in the work force; they are also essential skills for citizens as generative producers and critical consumers of cultural products.[2] The analytical lenses of digital rhetorics open up a range of possibilities for prompting students to see the humanities as allowing them to make meaningful interventions in the world and lasting connections between their humanist training and public engagement. Wikipedia in particular provides opportunities for investigation of, and participation in, public knowledge curation with attention to the ways particular community norms and values are encoded in its discourse practices and digital tools. This kind of work stands to help college students to integrate their generally well-developed understandings of writing as a platform for individual expression with their often still developing understandings of writing as an arena of social action. By designing assignments that engage students in complex collaborative composing processes with civic-minded goals and public audiences, we teach digital rhetoric and we offer motivations for writing far beyond that of a grade.

As one of the ten most-visited websites in the world, Wikipedia is a well-known success story of the web. As the only site among that top ten built by volunteers and backed by a non-profit,[3] it is also an important

---

1   For a detailed description and discussion of a Wikipedia writing assignment sequence, see Robert Cummings, *Lazy Virtues: Teaching Writing in the Age of Wikipedia* (Nashville: Vanderbilt University Press, 2009). A range of resources is also available at http://outreach.wikimedia.org/wiki/Education/For_educators.

2   For a critical discussion of the place of digital humanities in teaching, writing and composition, see Olin Bjork's chapter, "Digital Humanities and the First-Year Writing Course."

3   Wikipedia, along with nine sister projects, is supported by the Wikimedia Foundation, a non-profit with the stated mission to "empower and engage people around the world to collect and develop educational content under a free license or in the public domain, and to disseminate it effectively and globally." The Foundation asserts that it will "make and keep useful information from its projects available on the Internet free of charge, in perpetuity." Wikimedia Foundation, "Our Projects," http://wikimediafoundation.org/wiki/Our_projects. Wikimedia Foundation, "Mission Statement," http://wikimediafoundation.org/wiki/Mission_statement.

reminder of early visions for free networked information exchange on the web. It is generally a revelation to students that, as Tim Berners-Lee articulated in his 1991 newsgroup announcement of the WorldWideWeb, "the project started with the philosophy that much academic information should be freely available to anyone."[4] Understood in this context, Wikipedia represents a powerful vision of knowledge sharing that can be passed along to grow in the hands of students working as intermediaries between academia, other institutions of knowledge-making, and the diverse publics to which they belong. Moreover, classroom discussions of free knowledge and information open space to address with students the politics of the web as a complex generative space for negotiating social progress built on shared resources—that is, a digital public sphere— rather than simply a set of proprietary tools and products for business and social activities.

Making visible to students the various forms and functions of rhetoric online can pose challenges. The rhetorical tradition itself benefits from a very long and complex history rife with definitions, redefinitions, and various institutional politics, as well as re-mediations from the oral tradition to writing, print, and now the digital. When presenting *digital rhetorics* to students I begin with the idea that studying rhetoric is about exploring the ways that people use symbol systems to establish and maintain shared social realities, and so it addresses all manner of texts as well as the issues of identity and power at stake between the individuals, communities, and institutions that produce them. I then explain that rhetoric pays attention to both analysis and production—it insists on both interpretation and intervention as critical moves. Finally, I add the digital, which has not only expanded the formal range in which we compose, but has also both blurred the boundary between medium and text and reengaged questions of intention and agency as programmers write programs that become others' rhetorical environments and sometimes produce unforeseen and humanly unforeseeable actions.

In the sections that follow, I begin with an introduction to the rhetorical situation Wikipedia presents as an encyclopedia developed on a wiki by a community of volunteers. Next, I turn to the ways that the New London Group's multiliteracies pedagogy along with ideas about genre awareness can be used to structure assignments that include varying

---

4   Tim Berners-Lee, "WorldWideWeb: Summary," *alt.hypertext* (August 6, 1991), http:// groups.google.com/group/alt.hypertext/msg/395f282a67a1916c.

degrees of attention to developing content for Wikipedia and studying Wikipedia's knowledge curation practices.[5] In conclusion, I suggest that this type of teaching involves our students as agents in questions of the unequal distribution of wealth and opportunity by asking them to learn by drawing on research resources available to them while they are on college campuses, and sharing some of that privilege with the networked world. By no means an answer to the inequities of life chances, such an approach to this work is a motivator for our students, and us, and it has some positive potential at the global level.

## The Rhetorical Situation of Wikipedia

In her foreword to the edited collection *Rhetorics and Technologies*, Carolyn Miller describes rhetoric and technology as "arts of design," pointing out that they are "both in the business of balancing innovation with tradition," that is, of "initiating change and then compensating for it."[6] Described by Yochai Benkler as "a radically new form of encyclopedia writing,"[7] Wikipedia is a fascinating example of such rhetorical and technological change taking place on computer screens in front of us. Wikipedia is an encyclopedia; its all-volunteer community of editors works hard to see to that. But, while strongly Diderotian in genre norms and values, its wiki-based creation and free distribution under a Creative Commons license are decidedly born of internet culture. The genre, wiki, and license together are the mechanisms that coordinate, support, and motivate people to participate in the encyclopedia's collaborative creation, and so they are a careful balance of tradition and innovation that have made Wikipedia by some measures astoundingly successful and by others wildly controversial.

---

5    New London Group, "A Pedagogy of Multiliteracies: Designing Social Futures," *Harvard Educational Review* 66, no. 1 (1996): 60-92. See also Amy J. Devitt, "Teaching Critical Genre Awareness," in *Genre in a Changing World*, eds., Charles Bazerman, Adair Bonini and Débora C. Figueiredo (West Lafayette: Parlor Press, 2009), 337-51, and *Writing Genres* (Carbondale: Southern Illinois University Press, 2004); Anne M. Johns, *Genre in the Classroom: Multiple Perspectives* (Mahwah: L. Erlbaum, 2002); and, Charles Bazerman, "The Life of Genre, the Life in the Classroom," in *Genre and Writing: Issues, Arguments, Alternatives*, eds., Wendy Bishop and Hans A. Ostrom (Portsmouth: Heinemann, 1997), 19-26.

6    Carolyn R. Miller, "Foreword: Rhetoric, Technology, and the Pushmi-Pullyu," in *Rhetorics and Technologies: New Directions in Writing and Communication*, ed., Stuart A. Selber (Columbia: University of South Carolina Press, 2010), ix-xii (x).

7    Yochai Benkler, *The Wealth of Networks: How Social Production Transforms Markets and Freedom* (New Haven: Yale University Press, 2006), 70.

Wikipedia is by far the most visited wiki on the web, but it is by no means the first. The wiki concept of allowing users to collaboratively create and edit web content online using only a web browser was created by Ward Cunningham, who wrote the first wiki software and put the first wiki application on the web in 1994. There are now hundreds of wiki programs, and countless wiki applications online for all kinds of purposes. The wiki software on which Wikipedia runs, MediaWiki (http://www.mediawiki.org/), has been designed and developed specifically for Wikimedia projects and so provides both common and tailor-made wiki affordances. Unlike most wikis, Wikipedia pages separate user discussion from page content with a separate "Talk" tab on which contributors plan and discuss an article's development. More common to wiki software, in addition to the option to click "Edit," is the "View history" tab on which all revisions to an article are archived and available for comparison so that users can see a detailed record of every change made.[8] Wikipedia not only makes content creation interactive but also makes editorial process transparent. These common and uncommon wiki features are non-traditional as encyclopedic features, but they allow Wikipedia to represent the process of arriving at a consensus in an open and clear in a way that print media simply could not. In this way, Jonathan Zittrain points out,

> Wikipedia has… come to stand for the idea that involvement of people in the information they read — whether to fix a typographical error or to join a debate over its veracity or completeness — is an important end itself.[9]

Wikipedia provides the digital tools that make such interventions possible and by making them possible, encourages a mode of thinking and engagement that moves beyond critical thinking to critical engagement in producing solutions.

Operating alongside this technological infrastructure for developing and distributing free content is a legal one. Wikipedia works on a model that respects copyright for legal reasons, but generates and circulates free content for global ethical reasons, and so provides an opportunity to educate students about both systems. Wikipedia's content was distributed under a GNU General Public License until 2009 and so inherits many of the

---

8   Exceptions include rare cases of removal of "certain defamations and privacy breaches" deemed to be "grossly improper." See Wikipedia, "Revision Delete," Wikipedia, http://en.wikipedia.org/wiki/Wikipedia:Revision_deletion."

9   Jonathan Zittrain, *The Future of the Internet and How to Stop It* (New Haven: Yale University Press, 2008), 147.

ideals developed through the free software movement. As software became corporatized and copyrighted, Richard Stallman, a product of MIT's hacker culture in the 1970s and 80s, fought for the right to collaborate freely with other developers by founding the GNU project and authoring the GNU General Public License, the first copyleft license which used copyright to reserve the right to share and to require that users of a work do the same. As Stallman explains, "Free software is a matter of liberty, not price."[10] His free software definition specifies four freedoms:

Freedom 0.   The freedom to run the program, for any purpose.

Freedom 1.   The freedom to study how the program works, and adapt it to your needs. (Access to the source code is a precondition for this.)

Freedom 2.   The freedom to redistribute copies so you can help your neighbor.

Freedom 3.   The freedom to improve the program, and release your improvements to the public, so that the whole community benefits. (Access to the source code is a precondition for this.)[11]

Central here is the idea of access to source code, and while an encyclopedia is not a computer program, there are clear parallels in source code in editable text and cited research sources. Also useful if your goal is not simply to adapt prior work to your individual purposes, but to improve work to meet the needs of a broad audience, is the record of discussion among contributors and all prior revisions to the article content. The echoes of the free software movement within Wikipedia call for liberty, reuse, adaptation, and the affordances of the wiki buttress transparency, community, and collaboration.

But far from being all technology and licenses, Wikipedia is first and foremost an encyclopedia developed by a dedicated community of volunteers. The project has an extensive and proliferating set of help resources covering policies and guidelines. However, you can get a long way knowing Wikipedia's three core content policies—Neutral Point of View, Verifiability, and No Original Research—and five fundamental principles, known as the "five pillars" of Wikipedia.[12] These policies for practice and declarations of

---

10   Richard M. Stallman, "Free Software Definition," in *Free Software, Free Society: Selected Essays of Richard M. Stallman,* ed., Joshua Gray (Boston: GNU Press, 2002), 41-43 (41).

11   *Ibid.,* 41.

12   Wikipedia, "Five Pillars," *Wikipedia,* http://en.wikipedia.org/wiki/Wikipedia:Five_pillars. Wikipedia, "Core Content Policies," *Wikipedia,* http://en.wikipedia.org/wiki/Wikipedia:Core_content_policies.

purpose coordinate contributions in clear relation to both the tradition of the encyclopedia genre and the new possibilities of networked collaboration. The first pillar begins, "Wikipedia is an encyclopedia" and so explicitly identifies the project with its genre tradition. The second begins, "Wikipedia is written from a neutral point of view" and thus reinforces Wikipedia's genre identity with a difference. Rather than aiming for objectivity, Wikipedia strives for neutrality, and as Benkler points out, it does so "within the limits of substantial self-awareness as to the difficulty of such an enterprise."[13] In other words, editorial policy aims to frame articles that offer a fair representation of the current state of knowledge, rather than presenting an explanation that has been pared back to a simplistic point of agreement.

The remaining pillars address the license and medium, the community, and the spirit of the project. The third begins, "Wikipedia is free content that anyone can edit, use, modify, and distribute." This principle identifies characteristics of the project made possible by the wiki-foundation and release of content under a Creative Commons license. The fourth pillar begins, "Editors should interact with each other in a respectful and civil manner," and so declares a behavioral ideal for the community. The final, and certainly most curious, pillar begins: "Wikipedia does not have firm rules." I find this final declaration particularly remarkable because it parallels a dynamic, rhetorical vision of genre. It suggests that rules coordinate practices but won't necessarily help writers achieve the purposes of a genre more effectively than thinking through the genre's aims and figuring out how best to meet them.

This openness to the possibility of innovation fits well with the academic approach to genre studies developed in rhetoric and writing studies over the past few decades. In 1984, Carolyn Miller broke new ground with her article "Genre as Social Action" and her effort to determine a rhetorically sound basis for analyzing texts, grouping them by social function rather than by formal regularities.[14] This approach allowed others to see the ways that genre organizes communities, aligning individual purposes with

---

13  Benkler, *The Wealth of Networks*, 70. Wikipedia's core policy on neutral point of view currently states that editors must represent "fairly, proportionately, and as far as possible without bias, all *significant* views that have been *published by reliable sources*" (Wikipedia, "Neutral Point of View," *Wikipedia*, http://en.wikipedia.org/wiki/Wikipedia:Neutral_point_of_view, my emphasis) and so has more carefully articulated this policy such that it no longer suggests editors must represent "*sympathetically all* views on a subject" (Benkler, *The Wealth of Networks*, 71, my emphasis).

14  Carolyn R. Miller, "Genre as Social Action," *Quarterly Journal of Speech* 70, no. 2 (1984): 151-67.

social motives so that writers are what Anis Bawarshi has called "double agent[s],"[15] and genres offer what Anne Freadman has called "rules for play,"[16] but all with very real ideological and material outcomes. As John Frow writes, "[f]ar from being merely 'stylistic' devices, genres create effects of reality and truth, authority and plausibility, which are central to the different ways the world is understood."[17] Catherine Schryer has offered two influential definitions of genre, first in 1994 when she described them as "stabilized-for-now or stabilized-enough sites for social and ideological action,"[18] and then in 2000 when she defined genres as constellations of "regulated, improvisational strategies triggered by the interaction between individual socialization and an organization." [19] David Russell has contributed that,

> Genres are ways of recognizing and predicting how certain tools (including vocalizations and inscriptions), in certain typified—typical, reoccurring—conditions, may be used to help participants act together purposefully.[20]

This re-conceptualization of genres as dynamic, socio-cognitive frameworks present genre as a concept with tremendous potential for exploring how texts shape, organize, and perpetuate modes of human interaction, especially in discourse-based contexts like many of those we find online.

As Benkler observes,

> The important point is that Wikipedia requires not only mechanical cooperation among people, but a commitment to a particular style of writing and describing concepts that is far from intuitive or natural to people.[21]

This "particular style" includes that of the encyclopedic genre, but it is also the case that Wikipedia depends on "self-conscious use of open-discourse, usually aimed at consensus" in its editorial discussions and

---

15   Anis S. Bawarshi, *Genre and the Invention of the Writer: Reconsidering the Place of Invention in Composition* (Logan: Utah State University Press, 2003), 50.

16   Anne Freadman, "Anyone for Tennis?" in *Genre and the New Rhetoric*, eds., Aviva Freedman and Peter Medway (London: Taylor & Francis, 1994), 43-66 (47).

17   John Frow, *Genre* (New York: Routledge, 2006), 2.

18   Catherine F. Schryer, "The Lab vs. the Clinic: Sites of Competing Genres," in *Genre and the New Rhetoric*, eds., Aviva Freedman and Peter Medway (London: Taylor & Francis, 1994), 105-24 (108).

19   Catherine F. Schryer, "Walking a Fine Line: Writing Negative Letters in an Insurance Company," *Journal of Business and Technical Communication* 14, no. 4 (2000): 445-97 (445).

20   David R. Russell, "Rethinking Genre in School and Society: An Activity Theory Analysis," *Written Communication* 14, no. 4 (1997): 504-54 (513).

21   Benkler, *The Wealth of Networks*, 73.

community processes to make decisions about what innovations might be appropriate.[22] The interesting thing is that, for Wikipedia, this balance between attention to genre and openness to potential innovation results in a community that is aligned both by its genre tradition and by the public, communal processes of modifying that tradition. Having no firm rules does not result in chaos or anarchy because anyone wanting to break with established best practices must articulate their reasons for doing so and seek consensus before they proceed, which means writing reasoned and well-argued statements of their positions and engaging with any who disagree in a "respectful and civil manner."[23]

Depending on the pedagogical goals of a given course, Wikipedia assignments can be designed to focus primarily on small improvements to or significant development of articles in areas of course content knowledge, but perhaps the richest and most unique opportunities of Wikipedia assignments are concerned with also engaging in the culture of Wikipedia. For success with any significant interventions, students will want to understand the values and ideological assumptions informing common practices in order to participate with deep effectiveness, rather than just working to follow the rules. In the next section, I will sketch out a structure for facilitating such participation that blends the New London Group's multiliteracies pedagogy with a genre awareness approach to writing pedagogy advocated by scholars in the field of rhetorical genre studies.

## Beyond Received Knowledge: Learning Through Argument and Genre

Students are generally familiar with Wikipedia as readers, but few are likely to have given much thought to Wikipedia from the perspective of its writers. While it is true, as Wikipedia's tagline asserts, that "anyone can edit," much can be learned from understanding the ways and means of the Wikipedian discourse community and the variety of genres and tools through which its volunteers work. Participation can vary from simply clicking the edit button and fixing typos, to copy-editing well-researched but untidy prose, to learning how to integrate not only one's research and writing but also one's editorial input into the vast body of work and

---

22   *Ibid.*, 70.
23   Wikipedia, "Five Pillars."

community of volunteers already dedicated to the project.[24] Deciding how to lead students into this experience is not without challenges, but I have found the structure offered by the New London Group's multiliteracies pedagogy to be flexible enough to address the needs of a wide range of courses with small and large Wikipedia-based assignments.

Developed in response to the question, "What constitutes appropriate literacy teaching in the context of the ever more critical factors of local diversity and global connectedness?,"[25] the four central components of multiliteracies pedagogy are *situated practice, overt instruction, critical framing,* and *transformed practice.* The New London Group is careful to point out that these are neither stages nor a linear hierarchy, but rather that "elements of each may occur simultaneously, while at different times one or the other will predominate, and all of them are repeatedly revisited at different levels."[26] One of the primary challenges of multiliteracies pedagogy is that it represents a distinct break with much contemporary education in the United States. While its conclusions and goals resonate strongly with those dedicated to teaching toward progressive social change, it is a demanding task to reflect for these students a vision of themselves as "active designers of meaning" and "designers of social futures" as they step beyond a K-12 education currently characterized by standardized testing and back-to-basics curriculums. But while multiliteracies pedagogy may not overlay readily onto US students' prior educational experience, it does resonate at a very significant level with everyday experiences of language diversity and new media technologies, and so I see tremendous potential for instructors in higher education to draw creatively and consistently on the range of relevant skills and knowledge that students develop both inside and outside the classroom.

Situated practice draws on students' expertise and discourses and it involves "immersion in meaningful practices" with both experts and *novice experts,* that is "people who are experts at learning new domains in

---

24  There is practical guidance available for new contributors not only on Wikipedia's help pages but also in books like *How Wikipedia Works: And How You Can Be a Part of It* by Phoebe Ayers, Charles Matthews, and Ben Yates (San Francisco: No Starch Press, 2008) and John Broughton's *Wikipedia: The Missing Manual* (Sebastopol: O'Reilly Media, 2008).

25  Bill Cope and Mary Kalantzis, "Introduction: Multiliteracies: The Beginnings of an Idea," in *Multiliteracies: Literacy Learning and the Design of Social Futures,* eds., Bill Cope and Mary Kalantzis (New York: Routledge, 2000), 3-8 (3).

26  New London Group, "A Pedagogy of Multiliteracies," 85.

some depth."[27] On Wikipedia, the environment for making use of currently developing and existing areas of expertise and immersing students in a new discourse community is readymade. The instructor can take on the role of novice expert, learning as she introduces students to editing tasks and facilitates interactions with expert Wikipedian editors. As discussed above, Wikipedia offers students both hard and soft infrastructure through which they can work as intermediaries between areas of disciplinary expertise, the specialized discourse community of Wikipedia, and a potentially massive general audience of readers. Incorporating research, translating across Wikipedias, editing prose, linking to the digital resources of cultural heritage organizations, participating in editorial discussions and in community processes, and so on—all provide environments for participatory production and rhetorical skill building with potential to enrich student learning across the humanities while at the same time improving humanities content on Wikipedia as a free, global resource.

Overt instruction includes the range of "active interventions" on the part of the instructor and experts that (1) scaffold learning activities, (2) focus students' attention on the features of their experience and activities that are most central to their learning, and (3) give students access to explicit information "at times when it can most usefully organize and guide practice."[28] One of the initially astounding things about Wikipedia is that other editors will give students feedback on their efforts. At times, it will be almost instantaneous, but it will also be uneven. Some students will receive thoughtful, supportive, and detailed feedback. For others, the feedback will come in harsher forms; for example, they may submit edits in good faith only to find them reverted without explanation, or with only a boilerplate warning left on their user talk page. Essential here, and called for in multiliteracies pedagogy, is the development and use of meta-languages, both within Wikipedia and in the classroom. Wikipedia is structured to allow editors to leave explanations of their actions. If students leave edit summaries—brief notes that show up on the article history page indicating the nature of each edit—and explanations of major revisions on the article talk page, other editors are far more likely to engage with them and be respectful of their efforts. In the classroom, because students tend to have a variety of experiences with different editors on Wikipedia, shared reflective writing excercises and class discussions can be

---

27   *Ibid.*, 85.
28   *Ibid.*, 86.

essential to knowing what kinds of overt instruction an instructor might offer to complement that of expert editors. Help to ensure that everyone benefits from the most supportive expert feedback and can understand productively any feedback offered without adherence to the Wikipedian guideline commonly expressed as "Don't bite the newbies."[29]

Critical framing opens up a wide range of possibilities. In writing courses or those interested in disciplinarity and knowledge construction, I find it useful to explore the overlap and resonance between multiliteracies pedagogy and pedagogies of genre awareness developed by scholars in the field of rhetorical genre studies. As students first engage with Wikipedia, or any new discourse community, the types of writing and ways of interacting on the wiki may seem very natural or they may seem very strange. This will depend largely on their prior experiences and is an important discussion to raise because learning to write in particular ways is not purely instrumental; it involves participation in ways of thinking and understanding. As Charles Bazerman puts it, "[i]n perceiving an utterance as being of a certain kind or genre, we become caught up in a form of life, joining speakers and hearers, writers and readers, in particular relations of a familiar and intelligible sort."[30] In Thomas Helscher's words, "[t]o do business within a specific community, we occupy the subject position offered by the genre or genres at hand."[31] And, as I have written elsewhere, "[i]t is by engaging in the generic actions and interactions that are valued in particular communities that we perform and develop identities appropriate to the places and spaces we want to occupy."[32] The goal of critical framing in multiliteracies pedagogy is to denaturalize the skills students have mastered through situated practice and the conscious control and understanding of that learning they have developed with

29  Wikipedia, "Please Do Not Bite the Newcomers," *Wikipedia,* http://en.wikipedia.org/wiki/Wikipedia:Please_do_not_bite_the_newcomers.

30  Charles Bazerman, "Genre and Identity: Citizenship in the Age of the Internet and the Age of Global Capitalism," in *The Rhetoric and Ideology of Genre: Strategies for Stability and Change,* eds., Richard M. Coe, Lorelei Lingard, and Tatiana Teslenko (Cresskill: Hampton Press, 2002), 13-37 (13).

31  Thomas P. Helscher, "The Subject of Genre," in *Genre and Writing: Issues, Arguments, Alternatives,* eds., Wendy Bishop and Hans A. Ostrom (Portsmouth: Heinemann, 1997), 27-36 (29).

32  Melanie Kill, "Acknowledging the Rough Edges of Resistance: Negotiation of Identities for First-Year Composition," *College Composition and Communication* 58, no. 2 (2006): 213-35 (217).

the help of overt instruction. With very similar aims in mind, rhetorical genre theorists have tended to emphasize that it is crucial not to teach students genres *per se* but to teach them to be aware of the ways that genre conventions structure expectations between writers and readers and to think through the implications of these expectations.

Genre scholars Ann Johns, Charles Bazerman, and Amy Devitt, among others, have proposed genre-based approaches to teaching writing that combine practice in manipulating genres with smart awareness of generic power.[33] Johns has explored the challenges posed by contradictions between theoretical understandings of the dynamic nature of genres and the classroom tendency "to emphasize regularities and to search for stability."[34] She concludes simply, yet insightfully, that this tendency should be resisted, as "student genre theories need to be destabilized, enriched, and expanded" if they are to be flexible and adaptable.[35] Bazerman has contributed to this vision of the teaching of genre awareness by pointing out that if we take into account the important role of student motivation in student learning, it is perhaps less important to identify ideal antecedent genres already in students' repertoires than it is to tap into students' interests. He observes, "[o]nce students learn what it is to engage deeply and write well in any particular circumstance, they have a sense of the possibilities of literate participation in any discursive arena."[36] The critical framing offered by rhetorical genre theory provides ways of talking about writing and discourse as historical, social, cultural, political, and ideological, while Wikipedia offers an opportunity to look at the genre of the encyclopedia article as it has been, as it has changed, and as it could be.

In 1993's *The Electronic Word*, Richard A. Lanham suggests that while the computer is traditionally associated with logic and reason, it in practice "often turns out to be a rhetorical device as well as a logical

---

33   Amy J. Devitt, "Teaching Critical Genre Awareness," in Genre in a Changing World, eds., Charles Bazerman, Adair Bonini and Débora C. Figueiredo (West Lafayette: Parlor Press, 2009), 337–51, and Writing Genres (Carbondale: Southern Illinois University Press, 2004); Anne M. Johns, Genre in the Classroom: Multiple Perspectives (Mahwah: L. Erlbaum, 2002); and, Charles Bazerman, "The Life of Genre, the Life in the Classroom," in Genre and Writing: Issues, Arguments, Alternatives, eds., Wendy Bishop and Hans A. Ostrom (Portsmouth: Heinemann, 1997), 19–26.

34   Johns, *Genre in the Classroom*, 238.

35   *Ibid.*, 246.

36   Bazerman, "The Life of Genre," 26.

one."[37] Now that the computer is well established as an everyday tool for communication in a vast array of forms, the challenge we are negotiating is how we might use the logical capacity of the device to aid in our identification of digital textual patterns significant to the interpretation and understanding of rhetorical effects. From this perspective one might also approach critical framing by drawing on any of a wide range of analytical methods.

Wikipedia is a windfall of text. It offers big data in the form of XML data dumps,[38] as well as a wide range of more familiar types of digital texts—articles, editorial discussion, policy, community deliberation, etc.—that can be compiled into small human-readable datasets. Using Wikipedia as an heuristic, we can teach not only methods of textual analysis, but also the ways that we arrive at questions and the ways we select texts for analysis, and then also the kinds of claims that we can and cannot make about what our evidence shows. Perhaps the greatest pedagogical possibility of this variety is that we can customize questions and datasets for particular purposes, or invite students to do the same. I suggest that involving students in the methodological issues of devising questions, constructing datasets and conducting analysis as elements of an iterative process helps to demystify what research is in the humanities. Helping students think through why we ask the kinds of questions we do, why we look to texts at all, even most broadly defined, and why we look to particular texts to make particular arguments, not only teaches them about our disciplines but about the ways those disciplines construct knowledge.

For students working on Wikipedia, then, the ability to recognize patterns across larger bodies of texts and to connect and correlate those patterns with additional contextual information offers new ground to develop research questions and interpret results in ways that account for larger and multiple resonant patterns. The goals of analyses are always to focus attention in different ways to see new patterns, connections, and resonance. As always what matters is the strength of the questions one asks and the interpretations one offers. Rhetorical analysis is enhanced by computing, not replaced by it.

This work of thinking through the implications of existing practices, of knowledge curation on Wikipedia and in knowledge-making methods in

---

37    Richard A. Lanham, *The Electronic Word: Democracy, Technology, and the Arts* (Chicago: University of Chicago Press, 1993), 31.
38    Wikimedia project database dumps are available at http://dumps.wikimedia.org/.

academia, and the possibilities of innovation brings students to the point of transformed practice. Ideally, we have helped them develop skills such that they have both mastery of practice and enough critical distance to make decisions about when change is called for and how they might advocate for such changes. Key to transformed practice in multiliteracies pedagogy is the idea of juxtaposition and integration of different discourses, and in a Wikipedia assignment this has been essential from the start as students must reframe expert knowledge and expert discourses for public audiences and new genres.

One of the major rewards is that the exchange-value (work for grade) dynamic that characterizes many classroom assignments is altered by the public audience and the use-value (work for purpose) of the work that students produce. Some students, though admittedly not all, are able to transform their understanding of the activity from grade-making into knowledge-sharing and so to genuinely see themselves as designers of meaning.

In a larger frame, we as instructors and researchers have something to learn as well. Collaboration is among the major promises, lessons, and challenges of work in the digital humanities today. The complexity and scope of problem-solving as well as modes of project presentation made possible by networked computing have inspired humanists not only to read and draw on scholarship across disciplinary lines but also to draw other scholars and technologists into cooperative efforts that cross boundaries of disciplinary and professional communities, discourses, and knowledge-making practices. The challenges involved in the planning and execution of such work involve learning to listen for new possibilities in ways we would not have thought to do things and to communicate our ideas to those who don't share our backgrounds. We don't need to be neo-Sophists to recognize that our fundamentals vary: we analyze different types and sizes of datasets, ask different questions, select and define key terms differently, argue from different types of evidence, and present different stakes and goals. We rarely see our own assumptions and expectations except when they are offset by those of others.

The lessons we learn about collaboration through our research and scholarship clearly have a place in our classrooms. Fortunately, even if it doesn't make sense to involve students directly in our own research or to invent classroom-scale projects, students can learn a great deal about effective collaboration in practical and real world terms, and reflect on the diversity of contemporary knowledge-making methods and practices, by participating in existing public digital humanities projects like Wikipedia.

## Final Considerations: Creating Knowledge and Designing Social Futures

On his satirical news program, *The Colbert Report*, US comedian Steven Colbert declared, "Wikipedia is the first place I go when I am looking for knowledge, or when I want to create some."[39] The joke reflects a common concern about the collaboratively written encyclopedia: namely, by making the representation of knowledge an explicitly collaborative project, that truth is put up for negotiation. It is often the case that Wikipedia is among the first places students end up when they are looking for information, but seldom do they imagine they might be in a position to curate knowledge. This lack of recognition of their ability and responsibility should be the real cause for concern. Clearly, we do not want students spreading misinformation about elephants online *a la* Colbert,[40] but we do want to educate students as citizens capable and responsible to share what they know about the world around them. In the humanities, we know that what counts as knowledge is the result of complex social negotiation, not on the result of whim, but responsive to social change and shifting cultural and technological contexts. To engage students in the midst of this negotiation is a pedagogical feat and a gift that Wikipedia enables.

In teaching digital rhetoric, there is a strong connection to be made between our humanist roots and our digital daily lives that we can yoke creatively in our pedagogy and pass on to our students. The encyclopedia is a humanist reference genre, and students pursuing higher education, whatever their background, are in a position of privilege in relation to the millions of the world's inhabitants with variable access to educational materials. In engaging Wikipedia, they have authentic and practical

---

39   Stephen Colbert, interview with Jimmy Wales, *The Colbert Report*, Comedy Central (May 24, 2007), http://www.colbertnation.com/the-colbert-report-videos/87528/may-24-2007/jimmy-wales.

40   In his interview with Wales, Colbert admitted to changing the Wikipedia entry for "Elephant" in 2006 to read that "the population of elephants in Africa had tripled," only to note that the entry had been corrected shortly after.

opportunities to act as humanists in an arena of digital humanities that is nudging forward the vision of Wikipedia's founder, Jimmy Wales, of "a world in which every single human being can freely share in the sum of all knowledge."

Our work is not to educate students to reproduce the specific genres in exchange for which they might expect to make a living; the fact of the matter is that we cannot possibly anticipate what they will need to know even a few years in advance. What we offer is the long view of the humanities and the critical skills of analysis and communication. In aspiring to the transformed practices of multiliteracies pedagogies for ourselves and our students, in thinking through the value of engaging with Wikipedia, I like to recall the advice of the New London Group: "Our job is not to produce docile, compliant workers. Students need also to develop the capacity to speak up, to negotiate, and to be able to engage critically with the conditions of their working lives."[41]

---

41   New London Group, "A Pedagogy of Multiliteracies," 67.

# Select Bibliography

*#alt-academy: Alternate Academic Careers*, edited by Bethany Nowviskie, MediaCommons, http://mediacommons.futureofthebook.org/alt-ac/.

*#transformDH: Transformative Digital Humanities.* #transformDH Collective. http://transformdh.org/.

Abelson, Harold, and Gerald Jay Sussman. *Structure and Interpretation of Computer Programs*, 2nd edn. Cambridge: MIT Press, 1996.

Adolphs, Svenja. *Introducing Electronic Text Analysis: A Practical Guide for Language and Literary Studies.* New York: Routledge, 2006.

Allen, Gay Wilson, and Ed Folsom, ed. *Walt Whitman and the World.* Iowa City: University of Iowa Press, 1995.

American Council of Learned Societies. *Our Cultural Commonwealth: The Report of the American Council of Learned Societies Commission on Cyberinfrastructure for the Humanities and Social Sciences.* New York: American Council of Learned Societies, 2006.

Anderson, Lorin W., David R. Krathwohl, and Benjamin S. Bloom. *A Taxonomy for Learning, Teaching, and Assessing: A Revision of Bloom's Taxonomy of Educational Objectives.* New York: Longman, 2001.

Arnold, Matthew. "Literature and Science." *Discourses in America.* London: Macmillan, 1885.

Arum, Richard, and Josipa Roska. *Academically Adrift: Limited Learning on College Campuses.* Chicago: University of Chicago Press, 2011.

Ayers, Phoebe, Charles Matthews, and Ben Yates. *How Wikipedia Works: And How You Can Be a Part of It.* San Francisco: No Starch Press, 2008.

Ball, Cheryl E., Douglas Eyman, Julie Klein, Alex Reid, Virginia Kuhn, Jentery Sayers, and N. Katherine Hayles. "Are You a Digital Humanist?" Town Hall Session, 2011 Computers & Writing Conference, Ann Arbor, Michigan, May 21, 2011, http://vimeo.com/24388021.

Bauerlein, Mark. *The Dumbest Generation: How the Digital Age Stupefies Young Americans and Jeopardizes Our Future (Or, Don't Trust Anyone Under 30).* New York: Jeremy P. Tarcher/Penguin, 2008.

—. "Online Literacy Is a Lesser Kind." The Chronicle Review, *The Chronicle of Higher Education*, September 19, 2008. http://chronicle.com/article/Online-Literacy-Is-a-Lesser/28307.

Bawarshi, Anis S. *Genre and the Invention of the Writer: Reconsidering the Place of Invention in Composition.* Logan: Utah State University Press, 2003.

Bazerman, Charles. "Genre and Identity: Citizenship in the Age of the Internet and the Age of Global Capitalism." *The Rhetoric and Ideology of Genre: Strategies for Stability and Change,* edited by Richard M. Coe, Lorelei Lingard, and Tatiana Teslenko. Cresskill: Hampton Press, 2002. 13-37.

—. "The Life of Genre, the Life in the Classroom." *Genre and Writing: Issues, Arguments, Alternatives,* edited by Wendy Bishop and Hans A. Ostrom. Portsmouth: Heinemann, 1997. 19-26.

Benkler, Yochai. *The Wealth of Networks: How Social Production Transforms Markets and Freedom.* New Haven: Yale University Press, 2006.

Benjamin, Walter. *Charles Baudelaire: A Lyric Poet in the Era of High Capitalism,* translated by Harry Zohn. London: Verso, 1983.

—. "The Work of Art in the Age of Mechanical Reproduction." *Illuminations: Essays and Reflections,* edited by Hannah Arendt and translated by Harry Zohn. New York: Schocken Books, 1969. 217-51.

Bennett, Sue, Karl Maton, and Lisa Kervin. "The 'Digital Natives' Debate: A Critical Review of the Evidence." *British Journal of Educational Technology* 39, no. 5 (2008): 775-86.

Berger, John. *Ways of Seeing.* London: British Broadcasting Corporation, 1972; Harmondsworth: Penguin, 1972.

Bernard-Donals, Michael. "It's Not about the Book." *Profession* (2008): 172-84.

Berners-Lee, Tim. "WorldWideWeb: Summary." *alt.hypertext,* August 6, 1991, http://groups.google.com/group/alt.hypertext/msg/395f282a67a1916c.

Bernstein, Rachel, and Paul Mattingly. "The Pedagogy of Public History." *Journal of American Ethnic History* 18, no. 1 (1998): 77-92.

Birkerts, Sven. "Resisting the Kindle." *Atlantic Monthly,* March 2, 2009, http://www.theatlantic.com/magazine/archive/2009/03/resisting-the-kindle/7345/.

Bjork, Olin, and John Pedro Schwartz. "What Composition Can Learn from the Digital Humanities." Paper presented at the MLA Annual Convention, Philadelphia, Pennsylvania, December 29, 2009.

Blackwell, Christopher, and Gregory Crane. "Conclusion: Cyberinfrastructure, the Scaife Digital Library and Classics in a Digital Age." *Digital Humanities Quarterly* 3, no. 1 (2009), http://www.digitalhumanities.org/dhq/vol/3/1/000035/000035.html.

Bloom, Benjamin S. *Taxonomy of Educational Objectives, Handbook I: The Cognitive Domain.* New York: David McKay, 1956.

"Bloomsburg U. Undergraduate 'Manifesto' on Digital Humanities." *4Humanities,* December, 2010, http://humanistica.ualberta.ca/bloomsburg-u-undergraduate-manifesto-on-digital-humanities/.

Bodenhamer, David J., John Corrigan, and Trevor M. Harris, ed. *The Spatial Humanities: GIS and the Future of Humanities Scholarship.* Bloomington: Indiana University Press, 2010.

Bogost, Ian. *Persuasive Games: The Expressive Power of Videogames.* Cambridge: MIT Press, 2007.

Borgman, Christine L. "The Digital Future is Now: A Call to Action for the Humanities." *Digital Humanities Quarterly* 3, no. 4 (2009), http://digitalhumanities. org/dhq/vol/3/4/000077/000077.html.

Bradshaw, Tom, and Bonnie Nichols, ed. *Reading at Risk: A Survey of Literary Reading in America.* NEH Research Division Report 46. Washington: National Endowment for the Arts, 2004.

Brooke, Colin Gifford. *Lingua Fracta: Toward a Rhetoric of New Media.* Cresskill: Hampton Press, 2009.

Brown, John Seely. "Foreword: Creating a Culture of Learning." *Opening Up Education: The Collective Advancement of Education through Open Technology, Open Content, and Open Knowledge,* edited by Toru Iiyoshi and M. S. Vijay Kumar. Cambridge: MIT Press, 2008. xi-xiii.

Brown, John Seely, and Richard P. Adler. "Minds on Fire: Open Education, the Long Tail, and Learning 2.0." *EDUCAUSE Review* 43, no. 1 (2008): 16-32.

Broszat, Martin, and Saul Friedländer. "A Controversy About the Historicization of National Socialism." *New German Critique* 44 (1988): 85-126.

Broughton, John. *Wikipedia: The Missing Manual.* Sebastopol: O'Reilly Media, 2008.

Bryant, Susan L., Andrea Forte, and Amy Bruckman. "Becoming Wikipedian: Transformation of Participation in a Collaborative Online Encyclopedia." *Proceedings of the 2005 International ACM SIGGROUP Conference on Supporting Group Work,* edited by Kjeld Schmidt, Mark Pendergast, Mark Ackerman, and Gloria Mark. New York: ACM, 2005. 1-10.

Burghart, Marjorie, and Malte Rehbein. "The Present and Future of the TEI Community for Manuscript Encoding." *Journal of the Text Encoding Initiative* 2 (2012), http://jtei.revues.org/372.

Burroughs, William S. "The Cut-Up Method of Brion Gysin." *A Casebook on the Beat,* edited by Thomas Parkinson. New York: Crowell, 1961. 105-6.

Burroughs, William S., and Brion Gysin. *The Third Mind.* New York: Viking, 1978.

Burton, Gideon. "The Open Scholar." *Academic Evolution,* August 11, 2009, http:// www.academicevolution.com/2009/08/the-open-scholar.html.

Busa, Roberto. "The Annals of Humanities Computing: The Index Thomisticus." *Computers and the Humanities* 14 (1980): 83-90.

Cameron, Fiona, and Sarah Kenderdine, ed. *Theorizing Digital Cultural Heritage: A Critical Discourse.* Cambridge: MIT Press, 2007.

Campbell, John. "Theorising Habits of Mind as a Framework for Learning." Paper presented at the Australian Association for Research in Education Conference, Adelaide, November, 2006, http://www.aare.edu.au/06pap/cam06102.pdf.

Cecire, Natalia. "In Defense of Transforming DH," *Works Cited,* January 8, 2012, http://nataliacecire.blogspot.com/2012/01/in-defense-of-transforming-dh.html.

Chen, Peter Pin-Shan. "The Entity-Relationship Model: Toward a Unified View of Data." *ACM Transactions on Database Systems* 1, no. 1 (1976): 9-36.

Chion, Michel. *Audio-Vision: Sound on Screen,* translated by Claudio Gorbman. New York: Columbia University Press, 1994.

Classen, Christoph. "Balanced Truth: Steven Spielberg's *Schindler's List* Among History, Memory, and Popular Culture." *History and Theory* 48, no. 2 (2009): 77-102.

Clement, Tanya. "Digital Humanities Inflected Undergraduate Programs." *U+2E19*, November 4, 2009, http://tanyaclement.org/2009/11/04/digital-humanities-inflected-undergraduate-programs-2/.

Cohen, Daniel J. "Open Access Publishing and Scholarly Values." *Dan Cohen's Digital Humanities Blog*, May 27, 2010, http://www.dancohen.org/2010/05/27/open-access-publishing-and-scholarly-values/.

Cohen, Daniel J., and Tom Scheinfeldt, ed. *Hacking the Academy: The Edited Volume.* Ann Arbor: University of Michigan Press, 2012.

Cohen, Daniel J., and Roy Rosenzweig. *Digital History.* Philadelphia: University of Pennsylvania Press, 2006.

Cohen, Patricia. "Analyzing Literature by Words and Numbers." *The New York Times*, December 3, 2010.

—. "Digital Keys for Unlocking the Humanities' Riches." *The New York Times*, November 16, 2010.

Committee for the Workshops on Computational Thinking. *Report of a Workshop on The Scope and Nature of Computational Thinking.* Washington: National Academies Press, 2010.

Conn, Peter. "We Need to Acknowledge the Realities of Employment in the Humanities." *The Chronicle of Higher Education*, April 4, 2010, http://chronicle.com/article/We-Need-to-Acknowledge-the/64885/.

Cook, Terry. "The Archive is a Foreign Country: Historians, Archivists and the Changing Archival Landscape." *The Canadian Historical Review* 90.3 (2009): 497-534.

Cooper, Alan. *The Inmates Are Running the Asylum.* Indianapolis: Sams Publishing, 2004.

Cope, Bill, and Mary Kalantzis. "Introduction: Multiliteracies: The Beginnings of an Idea." *Multiliteracies: Literacy Learning and the Design of Social Futures*, edited by Bill Cope and Mary Kalantzis. New York: Routledge, 2000. 3-8.

Cormier, Dave, and George Siemens. "Through the Open Door: Open Courses as Research, Learning, and Engagement." *EDUCAUSE Review* 45, no. 4 (2010): 30-39.

Corns, Thomas N. "Computers in the Humanities: Methods and Applications in the Study of English Literature." *Literary and Linguistic Computing* 6 (1991), 127-30.

Costa, Arthur L., and Bena Kallick. "Describing 16 Habits of Mind." *The Institute for Habits of Mind*, no date, http://www.instituteforhabitsofmind.com/resources/pdf/16HOM.pdf.

Couros, Alec. "Call for Network Mentors—Follow-Up." *open thinking*, September 27, 2010, http://educationaltechnology.ca/couros/1877.

Cummings, Robert. *Lazy Virtues: Teaching Writing in the Age of Wikipedia.* Nashville: Vanderbilt University Press, 2009.

Czmiel, Alexander. "Editio ex machina: Digital Scholarly Editions out of the Box." Paper presented at Digital Humanities 2008, University of Oulu, Oulu, Finland, June 25–28, 2008.

Davidson, Cathy N. "21st Century Literacies: Syllabus, Assignments, Calendar." *HASTAC*, December 31, 2010, http://www.hastac.org/blogs/cathy-davidson/21st-century-literacies-syllabus-assignments-calendar.

—. "Crowdsourcing Grading: Follow-Up." *HASTAC*, August 9, 2009, http://www.hastac.org/blogs/cathy-davidson/crowdsourcing-grading-follow.

—. "Research is Teaching." *ADE Bulletin* 149 (2010): 53-60.

—. "What If Scholars in the Humanities Worked Together, in a Lab?" *The Chronicle of Higher Education*, May 28, 1999, http://chronicle.com/article/What-If-Scholars-in-the/24009.

Davidson, Cathy N., and David Theo Goldberg. *The Future of Learning Institutions in a Digital Age.* John D. and Catherine T. MacArthur Foundation Reports on Digital Media and Learning. Cambridge: MIT Press, 2009.

Davies, Robertson. "The Table Talk of Robertson Davies." *The Enthusiasms of Robertson Davies*, edited by Judith Skelton Grant. Toronto: McClelland and Stewart 1979. 310-15.

Dearing, Ron, et al. *Higher Education in the Learning Society: The Report of the National Committee of Inquiry into Higher Education.* London: Her Majesty's Stationary Office, 1997.

Deegan, Marilyn, and Willard McCarty, ed. *Collaborative Research in the Digital Humanities.* Farnham: Ashgate, 2012.

Deleuze, Gilles, and Félix Guattari. *A Thousand Plateaus: Capitalism and Schizophrenia*, translated by Brian Massumi. Minneapolis: University of Minnesota Press, 1987.

Denning, Peter J. "Beyond Computational Thinking." *Communicaions of the ACM* 52, no. 6 (2009): 28-30.

Devitt, Amy J. "Teaching Critical Genre Awareness." *Genre in a Changing World*, edited by Charles Bazerman, Adair Bonini, and Débora C. Figueiredo. West Lafayette: Parlor Press, 2009. 337-51.

—. *Writing Genres.* Carbondale: Southern Illinois University Press, 2004.

De Smedt, Koenraad. "Some Reflections on Studies in Humanities Computing." *Literary and Linguistic Computing* 17, no. 1 (2002): 89-101.

Donoghue, Frank. "An Open Letter from a Director of Graduate Admissions." *The Chronicle of Higher Education*, April 4, 2010, http://chronicle.com/article/An-Open-Letter-From-a-Director/64882/.

Drucker, Johanna. "Humanities Approaches to Graphical Display." *Digital Humanities Quarterly* 5, no. 1 (2011), http://digitalhumanities.org/dhq/vol/5/1/000091/000091.html.

Drucker, Johanna, John Unsworth, and Andrea Laue. "Final Report for Digital Humanities Curriculum Seminar." University of Virginia, August 10, 2002, http://jefferson.village.virginia.edu/hcs/dhcs/.

Ess, Charles. "Wag the Dog? Online Conferencing and Teaching." *Computers and the Humanities* 34, no. 3 (2000): 297-309.

Edwards, Charlie. "The Digital Humanities and Its Users." *Debates in the Digital Humanities*, edited by Matthew K. Gold. Minneapolis: University of Minnesota Press, 2012. 213-32.

Fallis, George. *Multiversities, Ideas, and Democracy.* Toronto: University of Toronto Press, 2007.

Favro, Diane. "In the Eye of the Beholder: Virtual Reality Re-Creations and Academia." *Journal of Roman Archaeology*, Supplementary Series 61 (2006): 321-34.

Feenberg, Andrew. *The Critical Theory of Technology.* Oxford: Oxford University Press, 1991.

Fish, Stanley. "The Digital Humanities and the Transcending of Morality." Opinionator, *New York Times*, January 9, 2012, http://opinionator.blogs.nytimes.com/2012/01/09/the-digital-humanities-and-the-transcending-of-mortality.

—. *How to Write a Sentence and How to Read One.* New York: Harper, 2011.

—. "Mind Your P's and B's: The Digital Humanities and Interpretation." Opinionator, *New York Times*, January 23, 2012, http://opinionator.blogs.nytimes.com/2012/01/23/mind-your-ps-and-bs-the-digital-humanities-and-interpretation.

—. *Save the World on Your Own Time.* Oxford: Oxford University Press, 2008.

Fitzpatrick, Kathleen. "Open Access Publishing and Scholarly Values (Part Three)." *Planned Obsolescence*, May 28, 2010, http://www.plannedobsolescence.net/open-access-publishing-and-scholarly-values-part-three/.

Floridi, Luciana. "Information Ethics: On the Philosophical Foundation of Computer Ethics." *Ethics and Information Technology* 1, no. 1 (1999): 33-52.

—. "A Look into the Future Impact of ICT on Our Lives." *The Information Society* 23, no. 1 (2007): 59-64.

Fogu, Claudio. "Digitalizing Historical Consciousness." *History and Theory* 48, no. 2 (2009): 103-21.

Folsom, Ed, and Kenneth M. Price. *Re-Scripting Walt Whitman: An Introduction to His Life and Work.* Malden: Blackwell, 2005.

Forest, James J. F. *I Prefer to Teach: An International Study of Faculty Preferences for Teaching.* New York: Routledge, 2002.

Forte, Andrea, and Amy Bruckman. "Why Do People Write for Wikipedia? Incentives to Contribute to Open-Content Publishing." Paper presented at Sustaining Community: The Role and Design of Incentive Mechanisms in Online Systems, GROUP 2005 International Conference on Supporting Group Work, Sanibel Island, Florida, November 6, 2005, http://www.andreaforte.net/ForteBruckmanWhyPeopleWrite.pdf.

Foucault, Michel. *Power/Knowledge: Selected Interviews and Other Writings, 1972–1977*, edited by Colin Gordon. New York: Pantheon, 1980.

Freadman, Anne. "Anyone for Tennis?" *Genre and the New Rhetoric*, edited by Aviva Freedman and Peter Medway. London: Taylor & Francis, 1994. 43-66.

Friedländer, Saul, ed. *Probing the Limits of Representation: Nazism and the "Final Solution".* Cambridge: Harvard University Press, 1992.

Frow, John. *Genre.* New York: Routledge, 2006.

Gancarz, Mike. *Linux and the Unix Philosophy*. Amsterdam: Elsevier-Digital, 2003.

Gee, James Paul. "New People in New Worlds: Networks, the New Capitalism and Schools." *Multiliteracies: Literacy Learning and the Design of Social Futures*, edited by Bill Cope and Mary Kalantzis. New York: Routledge, 2000. 43-68.

—. *What Video Games Have to Teach Us About Learning and Literacy*. New York: Palgrave, 2003.

Gervais, Sarah J., Theresa K. Vescio, and Jill Allen. "When What You See Is What You Get: The Consequences of the Objectifying Gaze for Women and Men." *Psychology of Women Quarterly* 35, no. 1 (2011): 5-17.

Gibbs, Fred. "Critical Discourse in Digital Humanities." *Journal of Digital Humanities* 1, no. 1 (2012), http://journalofdigitalhumanities.org/1-1/articles/critical-discourse-in-digital-humanities-by-fred-gibbs/.

Giroux, Henry A. "Rethinking the Boundaries of Educational Discourse: Modernism, Postmodernism, and Feminism." *Margins in the Classroom: Teaching Literature*, edited by Kostas Myrsiades and Linda S. Myrsiades. Minneapolis: University of Minnesota Press, 1994. 1-51.

Gist, Chris, and Kelly Johnston. "Virginia BootCamp 2010: GIS Short Courses." Scholars' Lab, University of Virginia Library, December 17, 2010, http://www.lib.virginia.edu/scholarslab/resources/class/bootCamp2010/.

Gold, Matthew K., ed. *Debates in the Digital Humanities*. Minneapolis: University of Minnesota Press, 2012.

—. "Whose Revolution? Towards a More Equitable Digital Humanities." *The Lapland Chronicles*, January 10, 2012, http://mkgold.net/blog/2012/01/10/whose-revolution-toward-a-more-equitable-digital-humanities/.

Goodwin, Charles. "Professional Vision." *American Anthropologist* 96 (1994): 606-33.

Google Books Team, et al. "Quantitative Analysis of Culture Using Millions of Digitized Books." *Science* 331, no. 6014 (2011): 176-82.

Gouglas, Sean, Stéfan Sinclair, and Aimée Morrison. "Coding Theory: Balancing Technical and Theoretical Requirements in a Graduate-Level Humanities Computing Programme." *Mind Technologies: Humanities Computing and the Canadian Academic Community*, edited by Raymond G. Siemens and David Moorman. Calgary: University of Calgary Press, 2006. 245-56.

Gramsci, Antonio. *Selections from the Prison Notebooks*, edited and translated by Quintin Hoare and Geoffrey Nowell-Smith. New York: International Publishers, 1972.

Grosz, Elizabeth. "Thinking the New: Of Futures Yet Unthought." *Becomings: Explorations in Time, Memory, and the Future*, edited by Elizabeth Grosz. Ithaca: Cornell University Press, 2000. 15-28.

Grünzweig, Walter. "Whitman and the Cold War: The Centenary Celebration of *Leaves of Grass* in Eastern Europe." *Leaves of Grass: The Sesquicentennial Essays*, edited by Susan Belasco, Ed Folsom, and Kenneth M. Price. Lincoln: University of Nebraska Press, 2007. 343-60.

Guillory, John. "Professionalism: What Graduate Students Want." *Profession* (1996): 91-99.

Guldi, Joanna. "What is the Spatial Turn?" *Spatial Humanities*, Institute for Enabling Geospatial Scholarship, http://spatial.scholarslab.org/spatial-turn/.

Guzdial, Mark. "Paving the Way for Computational Thinking." *Communications of the ACM* 51, no. 8 (2008): 25-27.

Hand, Martin. *Making Digital Cultures: Access, Interactivity, and Authenticity*. Burlington: Ashgate, 2008.

Hart, James Morgan. *German Universities: Narrative of Personal Experience*. New York: G. P. Putnam's Sons, 1874.

Hawisher, Gail E., Paul LeBlanc, Charles Moran, and Cynthia L. Selfe. *Computers and the Teaching of Writing in American Higher Education, 1979–1994: A History*. Norwood: Ablex, 1996.

Hay, Alexander. "What Would Be A Good Basic Skill-set For Humanities Computing Jobs?" *Humanist Discussion Group* 23, no. 758 (2010), http://lists.digitalhumanities. org/pipermail/humanist/2010-April/001181.html.

Hayles, N. Katherine. "How We Think: The Transforming Power of Digital Technologies." Lecture presented at the School of Literature, Communication, and Culture's Distinguished Speaker Series on Minds, Machines, and Media, Georgia Institute of Technology, Atlanta, Georgia, January 15, 2009.

—. *My Mother Was a Computer: Digital Subjects and Literary Texts*. Chicago: University of Chicago Press, 2005.

Heidegger, Martin. "The Question Concerning Technology." *The Question Concerning Technology and Other Essays*, translated by William Lovitt. New York: Harper & Row, 1977. 3-35.

Helscher, Thomas P. "The Subject of Genre." *Genre and Writing: Issues, Arguments, Alternatives*, edited by Wendy Bishop and Hans A. Ostrom. Portsmouth: Heinemann, 1997. 27-36.

Hilbert, Martin, and Priscila López. "The World's Technological Capacity to Store, Communicate, and Compute Information." *Science* 332, no. 6025 (2011): 60-65.

Hirsch, Brett D., and Meagan Timney. "The Importance of Pedagogy: Towards a Companion to Teaching Digital Humanities." Poster presented at Digital Humanities 2010, King's College London, London, July 7–10, 2010.

Hockey, Susan. "Some Perspectives on Teaching Computers and the Humanities." *Computers and the Humanities* 26, no. 4 (1992): 261-66.

—. "Towards a Curriculum for Humanities Computing: Theoretical Goals and Practical Outcomes." Paper presented at *The Humanities Computing Curriculum / The Computing Curriculum in the Arts and Humanities*, Malaspina University College, Nanaimo, British Columbia, November 9–10, 2001.

—. "Workshop on Teaching Computers and the Humanities Courses." *Literary and Linguistic Computing* 1, no. 4 (1986): 228-29.

Hoffman, Stephen J., ed. *Teaching the Humanities Online: A Practical Guide to the Virtual Classroom*. New York: M. E. Sharpe, 2011.

Holm, Ulla M., and Mia Liinason. "Disciplinary Boundaries between the Social Sciences and the Humanities: Comparative Report on Interdisciplinarity." Report for the Research Integration: Changing Knowledge and Disciplinary Boundaries Through Integrative Research Methods in the Social Sciences and the Humanities Project, University of York, May 2005.

Hunter, Lynette. "Alternative Publishing in Canada." *Difference and Community: Canadian and European Cultural Perspectives*, edited by Peter Easingwood, Konrad Gross, and Lynette Hunter. Amsterdam: Editions Rodopi, 1996. 35-56.

Huvila, Isto. "Participatory Archive: Towards Decentralized Curation, Radical User Orientation, and Broader Contextualization of Records Management." *Archival Science* 8, no. 1 (2008): 15-36.

Hyland, Terry. "Competency, Knowledge and Education." *Journal of Philosophy of Education* 27, no. 1 (1993): 57-68.

Irvine, Colin. "Moving Beyond the Binaries: A Learning-Centered Approach to Pedagogy." *Pedagogy* 6, no. 1 (2006): 149-53.

Iyer, Vijay. "On Improvisation, Temporality, and Embodied Experience." *Sound Unbound: Sampling Digital Music and Culture*, edited by Paul D. Miller. Cambridge: MIT Press, 2008. 273-92.

Jannidis, Fotis. "Digitale Editionen." *Literatur im Medienwechsel*, edited by Andrea Geier and Dietmar Till. Bielefeld: Aisthesis, 2008. 317-32.

Jaschik, Scott. "What Direction for Rhet-Comp?" *Inside Higher Ed*, December 30, 2009, http://www.insidehighered.com/news/2009/12/30/comp.

Jenkins, Henry. *Confronting the Challenges of Participatory Culture: Media Education for the 21st Century*. John D. and Catherine T. MacArthur Foundation Reports on Digital Media and Learning. Cambridge: MIT Press, 2009.

Jessop, Martyn. "In Search of Humanities Computing in Teaching, Learning and Research." Paper presented at The 17th Joint International Conference of the Association for Computers and the Humanities (ACH) and the Association for Literary and Linguistic Computing (ALLC), Victoria, British Columbia, June 15–18, 2005.

—. "Teaching, Learning and Research in Final Year Humanities Computing Student Projects." *Literary and Linguistic Computing* 20, no. 3 (2005): 295-311.

—. "Undergraduate Programmes." *Humanist Discussion Group* 23, no. 398 (2009), http://lists.digitalhumanities.org/pipermail/humanist/2009-October/000825.html.

Johanson, Christopher. "Visualizing History: Modeling in the Eternal City." *Visual Resources: An International Journal of Documentation* 25, no. 4 (2009): 403-18.

Johns, Anne M. *Genre in the Classroom: Multiple Perspectives*. Mahwah: L. Erlbaum, 2002.

Johnson, Larry, Alan Levine, Rachel S. Smith, and Sonja Stone. *The 2010 Horizon Report*. Austin: The New Media Consortium, 2010.

Jones, Diane Auer. "Are the Humanities Dead, or Are Academic Programs Just Too Narrow?" *The Chronicle of Higher Education*, April 9, 2010, http://chronicle.com/blogs/brainstorm/are-the-humanities-dead-or-are-academic-programs-just-too-narrow/22454.

Jones, John M. "Algorithmic Rhetoric and Search Literacy." Paper presented at the 2011 Humanities, Arts, Science, and Technology Advanced Collaboratory Conference, Ann Arbor, Michigan, December 13, 2011, http://www.slideshare.net/johnmjones/algorithmic-rhetoric-and-search-literacy-hastac2011

Kansteiner, Wulf. "Success, Truth, and Modernism in Holocaust Historiography: Reading Saul Friedländer Thirty-Five Years After the Publication of Metahistory." *History and Theory* 48, no. 2 (2009): 25-53.

Kaplan, Justin. *Walt Whitman: A Life.* New York: Simon and Schuster, 1980.

Keating, John G., Aja Teehan, and Thomas Byrne. "Delivering a Humanities Computing Module at Undergraduate Level: A Case Study." Paper presented at Digital Humanities 2009, College Park, Maryland, June 22–25, 2009.

Keilbach, Judith. "Photographs, Symbolic Images, and the Holocaust: On the (Im) Possibility of Depicting Historical Truth." *History and Theory* 48, no. 2 (2009): 54-76.

Kennicott, Philip. "Auto-Tune Turns the Operatic Ideal into a Shoddy Joke." *The Washington Post*, August 29, 2010, http://www.washingtonpost.com/wp-dyn/content/article/2010/08/27/AR2010082702197.html.

Kill, Melanie. "Acknowledging the Rough Edges of Resistance: Negotiation of Identities for First-Year Composition." *College Composition and Communication* 58, no. 2 (2006): 213-35.

Kinsella, W. P. *Shoeless Joe.* Boston: Houghton Mifflin, 1982.

Kirp, David L. *Shakespeare, Einstein, and the Bottom Line: The Marketing of Higher Education.* Cambridge: Harvard University Press, 2003.

Kirschenbaum, Matthew G. "The (DH) Stars Come Out in LA." *Matthew G. Kirschenbaum*, January 13, 2011, http://mkirschenbaum.wordpress.com/2011/01/13/the-dh-stars-come-out-in-la-2/.

—. *Mechanisms: New Media and the Forensic Imagination.* Cambridge: MIT Press, 2008.

—. "What is Digital Humanities and What's It Doing in English Departments?" *ADE Bulletin* 150 (2010): 55-61.

Knuth, Donald E. "Literate Programming." *The Computer Journal* 27, no. 2 (1984): 97-111.

Koch, Christian. "On the Benefits of Interrelating Computer Science and the Humanities: The Case of Metaphor." *Computers and the Humanities* 25, no. 5 (1991): 289-95.

Kolowich, Steve. "Massive Courses, Sans Stanford." *Inside Higher Ed*, January 24, 2012, http://www.insidehighered.com/news/2012/01/24/stanford-open-course-instructors-spin-profit-company.

Kuhn, Virginia. "Filmic Texts and the Rise of the Fifth Estate." *International Journal of Learning and Media* 2, no. 2-3 (2010), http://ijlm.net/knowinganddoing/10.1162/IJLM_a_00057.

Lancashire, Ian. *Forgetful Muses: Reading the Author in the Text.* Toronto: University of Toronto Press, 2010.

Lancashire, Ian, ed. *Teaching Literature and Language Online.* New York: Modern Language Association of America, 2009.

Lane, Andy. "Widening Participation in Education through Open Educational Resources." *Opening Up Education: The Collective Advancement of Education through Open Technology, Open Content, and Open Knowledge*, edited by Toru Iiyoshi and M. S. Vijay Kumar. Cambridge: MIT Press, 2008. 149-64.

Lane, Lisa M. "Insidious Pedagogy: How Course Management Systems Affect Teaching." *First Monday* 14, no. 10 (2009), http://firstmonday.org/htbin/cgiwrap/bin/ojs/index.php/fm/article/view/2530/2303.

Langmann, Pete. "Einführung in die Datenmodellierung in den Geisteswissenschaften." *xlab,* http://www.xlab.at/wordbar/definitionen/datenmodellierung.html.

Lanham, Richard A. *The Electronic Word: Democracy, Technology, and the Arts.* Chicago: University of Chicago Press, 1993.

Laurillard, Diana. *Rethinking University Teaching,* 2nd edn. New York: Routledge, 2002.

Levine, Felice J. "Professionalization, Certification, Labor Force: United States." *International Encyclopedia of the Social and Behavioral Sciences,* edited by Neil J. Smelser and Paul B. Bates. Oxford: Elsevier, 2001. 12146-2154.

Levy, Daniel, and Natan Sznaider. *The Holocaust and Memory in the Global Age,* translated by Assenka Oksiloff. Philadelphia: Temple University Press, 2006.

Lewin, Tamar. "On the Internet, a University Without a Campus." *New York Times,* February 5, 2009, http://www.nytimes.com/2009/01/25/technology/25iht-university.4.19660731.html.

Lewis, Lionel S. *Marginal Worth: Teaching and the Academic Labor Market.* New Brunswick: Transaction, 1996.

Liebman, Stuart, ed. *Claude Lanzmann's Shoah: Key Essays.* Oxford: Oxford University Press, 2007.

Linenthal, Edward T. *Preserving Memory: The Struggle to Create America's Holocaust Museum.* New York: Viking, 1995.

Liu, Alan. "Digital Humanities and Academic Change." *English Language Notes* 47, no. 1 (2009): 17-35.

—. *Local Transcendence: Essays on Postmodern Historicism and the Database.* Chicago: University of Chicago Press, 2008.

—. Response to "On Building." *Stephen Ramsay,* January 12, 2011, http://lenz.unl.edu/wordpress/?p=340#comment-9144.

—. "The State of the Digital Humanities: A Report and a Critique." *Arts and Humanities in Higher Education* 11, no. 1-2 (2012): 1-34.

—. "Where Is Cultural Criticism in the Digital Humanities?" *Debates in the Digital Humanities,* edited by Matthew K. Gold. Minneapolis: University of Minnesota Press, 2012. 490-509.

Lothian, Alexis. "Conference Thoughts: Queer Studies and the Digital Humanities." *Queer Geek Theory,* October 18, 2011, http://www.queergeektheory.org/2011/10/conference-thoughts-queer-studies-and-the-digital-humanities/.

—. "THATCamp and Diversity in Digital Humanities." *Queer Geek Theory,* January 18, 2011, http://www.queergeektheory.org/2011/01/thatcamp-and-diversity-in-digital-humanities/.

Lovett, Marsha, Oded Meyer, and Candace Thille. "The Open Learning Initiative: Measuring the Effectiveness of the OLI Statistics Course in Accelerating Student Learning." *Journal of Interactive Media in Education* 14 (2008), http://jime.open.ac.uk/jime/article/view/2008-14.

Lynch, Clifford. "Digital Libraries, Learning Communities, and Open Education." *Opening Up Education: The Collective Advancement of Education through Open Technology, Open Content, and Open Knowledge*, edited by Toru Iiyoshi and M. S. Vijay Kumar. Cambridge: MIT Press, 2008. 105-18.

Lyon, Arabella. "Composition and the Preservation of Rhetorical Traditions in a Global Context." Paper presented at the MLA Annual Convention, Philadelphia, Pennsylvania, December 29, 2009.

Mactavish, Andrew, and Geoffrey Rockwell. "Multimedia Education in the Arts and Humanities." *Mind Technologies: Humanities Computing and the Canadian Academic Community*, edited by Raymond G. Siemens and David Moorman. Calgary: University of Calgary Press, 2006. 225-43.

Mahony, Simon. "An Interdisciplinary Perspective on Building Learning Communities within the Digital Humanities." Paper presented at Digital Humanities 2008, Oulu, Finland, June 25–29, 2008.

—. "Using Digital Resources in Building and Sustaining Learning Communities." *Body, Space & Technology Journal* 7, no. 2 (2007), http://people.brunel.ac.uk/bst/vol0702/simonmahony/.

Mackie, Christopher. "Open Source in Open Education: Promises and Challenges." *Opening Up Education: The Collective Advancement of Education through Open Technology, Open Content, and Open Knowledge*, edited by Toru Iiyoshi and M. S. Vijay Kumar. Cambridge: MIT Press, 2008. 119-32.

Mannion, John Martin. *History Teaching with Moodle 2*. Birmingham: Packt Publishing, 2011.

McAndrew, Patrick, Eileen Scanlon, and Doug Clow. "An Open Future for Higher Education." *EDUCAUSE Quarterly* 33, no. 1 (2010), http://www.educause.edu/EDUCAUSE+Quarterly/EDUCAUSEQuarterlyMagazineVolum/AnOpenFutureforHigherEducation/199388.

McBreen, Pete. *Software Craftsmanship: The New Imperative*. Boston: Addison, 2002.

McCarty, Willard. "Basic Skills?" *Humanist Discussion Group* 23, no. 760 (2010), http://lists.digitalhumanities.org/pipermail/humanist/2010-April/001183.html.

—. *Humanities Computing*. New York: Palgrave, 2005.

—. "'Knowing true things by what their mockeries be': Modelling in the Humanities." *TEXT Technology* 12, no. 1 (2003): 43-58.

—. "Modeling: A Study in Words and Meanings." *A Companion to Digital Humanities*, edited by Susan Schreibman, Ray Siemens, and John Unsworth. Malden: Blackwell, 2004. 254-70.

McCarty, Willard, and Matthew G. Kirschenbaum. "Institutional Models for Humanities Computing." *Literary and Linguistic Computing* 18, no. 4 (2003): 465-89.

McIlroy, M. D., E. N. Pinson, and B. A. Tague. "Unix Time-Sharing System: Forward." *The Bell System Technical Journal* 57, no. 6 (1978): 1899-904.

McLellan, Marjorie. "Digital Humanities Certificate." *Digital Humanities Forum*, July 11, 2010, http://webapp3.wright.edu/web2/digitalhumanities/2010/07/11/digital-humanities-certificate/.

McLuhan, Marshall. *Understanding Media: The Extensions of Man.* London: Routledge & Kegan Paul, 1964.

McPherson, Tara. "Why Are the Digital Humanities So White? Or Thinking the Histories of Race and Computation." *Debates in the Digital Humanities,* edited by Matthew K. Gold. Minneapolis: University of Minnesota Press, 2012. 139-60.

Meloni, Julie. "Wordles, or The Gateway Drug to Textual Analysis." ProfHacker, *The Chronicle of Higher Education,* October 21, 2009, http://chronicle.com/blogs/profhacker/wordles-or-the-gateway-drug-to-textual-analysis/.

Melville, David, Cliff Allan, Julian Crampton, and John Fothergill, et al. "Higher Education in a Web 2.0 World." Report of the Committee of Inquiry into the Changing Learner Experience to the Joint Information Systems Committee, May 12, 2009, http://www.jisc.ac.uk/media/documents/publications/heweb20rptv1.pdf.

Miller, Carolyn R. "Foreword: Rhetoric, Technology, and the Pushmi-Pullyu." *Rhetorics and Technologies: New Directions in Writing and Communication,* edited by Stuart A. Selber. Columbia: University of South Carolina Press, 2010. ix-xii.

—. "Genre as Social Action." *Quarterly Journal of Speech* 70, no. 2 (1984): 151-67.

Miller, Marla. "Playing to Strength: Teaching Public History at the Turn of the 21st-Century." *American Studies International* 42 (2004): 174-212.

Miller, Paul D. *Rhythm Science.* Cambridge: MIT Press, 2004.

Minh-ha, Trinh T. *Cinema Interval.* New York: Routledge, 1999.

Monmonier, Mark. *How to Lie with Maps,* 2nd edn. Chicago: University of Chicago Press, 1996.

Moretti, Franco. "Conjectures on World Literature." *New Left Review* 1 (2000): 54-68.

—. "Graphs, Maps, Trees: Abstract Models for Literary History—1." *New Left Review* 24 (2003): 67-93.

—. "Graphs, Maps, Trees: Abstract Models for Literary History—2." *New Left Review* 26 (2004): 79-103.

—. "Graphs, Maps, Trees: Abstract Models for Literary History—3." *New Left Review* 28 (2004): 43-63.

Morton, Donald, and Mas'ud Zavarzadeh, ed. *Theory/Pedagogy/Politics: Texts for Change.* Urbana: University of Illinois Press, 1991.

Mott, Jon, and David Wiley. "Open for Learning: The CMS and the Open Learning Network." *In Education* 15, no. 2 (2009), http://ineducation.ca/article/openlearning-cms-and-open-learning-network.

New London Group. "A Pedagogy of Multiliteracies: Designing Social Futures." *Harvard Educational Review* 66, no. 1 (1996): 60-92.

Nørmark, Kurt. "Literate Programming: Issues and Problems." Department of Computer Science, Aalborg University, August 13, 1998, http://www.cs.aau.dk/~normark/litpro/issues-and-problems.html.

Nowviskie, Bethany. "#alt-ac: Alternative Academic Careers for Humanities Scholars." *Bethany Nowviskie,* January 3, 2010, http://nowviskie.org/2010/alt-ac/.

—. "The #alt-ac Track: Negotiating Your 'Alternative Academic' Appointment." ProfHacker, *The Chronicle of Higher Education,* August 31, 2010, http://chronicle.com/blogs/profhacker/the-alt-ac-track-negotiating-your-alternative-academic-appointment-2/26539.

—. "What Do Girls Dig?" *Bethany Nowviskie*, April 7, 2011, http://nowviskie.org/2011/what-do-girls-dig/.

Oakman, Robert L. "Perspectives on Teaching Computing in the Humanities." *Computers and the Humanities* 21, no. 4 (1987): 227-33.

Orlandi, Tito. "The Scholarly Environment of Humanities Computing: A Reaction to Willard McCarty's Talk on The Computational Transformation of the Humanities." http://rmcisadu.let.uniroma1.it/~orlandi/mccarty1.html.

Orlandi, Tito, Joseph Norment Bell, Lou Burnard, Dino Buzzetti, Koenraad de Smedt, Ingo Kropac, Jacques Souillot, and Manfred Thaller. "European Studies on Formal Methods in the Humanities." *Computing in Humanities Education: A European Perspective*, edited by Koenraad de Smedt, Hazel Gardiner, Espen Ore, Tito Orlandi, Harold Short, Jacques Souillot, and William Vaughan. Bergen: University of Bergen, HIT Centre, 1999. 13-62.

Palfrey, John, and Urs Gasser. *Born Digital: Understanding the First Generation of Digital Natives.* New York: Basic Books, 2008.

Parry, Marc. "Online, Bigger Classes May Be Better Classes." *The Chronicle of Higher Education*, August 29, 2010, http://chronicle.com/article/Open-Teaching-When-the-W/124170/.

Phelps, Louise Wetherbee. "Practical Wisdom and the Geography of Knowledge in Composition." *College English* 53, no. 8 (1991): 836-85.

Phillips, Amanda. "#transformDH – A Call to Action Following ASA 2011." *HASTAC*, October 26, 2011, http://hastac.org/blogs/amanda-phillips/2011/10/26/transformdh-call-action-following-asa-2011/.

Plachta, Bodo. "Teaching Editing—Learning Editing." *editio* 13 (1999): 18-32.

Polack, Katharine. "A Letter from a Graduate Student in the Humanities." *The Chronicle of Higher Education*, April 4, 2010, http://chronicle.com/article/A-Letter-From-a-Graduate/64889/.

Posner, Miriam. "Some Things to Think About Before You Exhort Everyone to Code." *Miriam Posner*, February 29, 2012, http://miriamposner.com/blog/?p=1135.

Prelinger, Rick. "Points of Origin: Discovering Ourselves Through Access." *The Moving Image* 9, no. 2 (2009): 164-75.

Presner, Todd, and Jeffrey Schnapp, et al. "Digital Humanities Manifesto 2.0." University of California, Los Angeles, May 29, 2009, http://manifesto.humanities.ucla.edu/2009/05/29/the-digital-humanities-manifesto-20/.

Ramsay, Stephen. "On Building." *Stephen Ramsay*, January 11, 2011, http://lenz.unl.edu/wordpress/?p=340.

—. "Open Access Publishing and Scholarly Values (Part Two)." *Stephen Ramsay*, March 28, 2010, http://lenz.unl.edu/wordpress/?p=190.

—. "Toward an Algorithmic Criticism." *Literary and Linguistic Computing* 18, no. 2 (2003): 167-74.

—. "Who's In and Who's Out." *Stephen Ramsay*, January 8, 2011, http://lenz.unl.edu/wordpress/?p=325.

Ray, Robert B. *How a Film Theory Got Lost and Other Mysteries in Cultural Studies.* Bloomington: Indiana University Press, 2001.

Raymond, Eric S. *The Art of UNIX Programming.* Boston: Addison, 2003.

Reding, Viviane. "Media Literacy: Do People Really Understand How to Make the Most of Blogs, Search Engines or Interactive TV?" Press release, Commissioner for Information Society and Media, European Commission, Brussels, December 20, 2007, http://europa.eu/rapid/pressReleasesAction.do?reference=IP/07/1970.

Renear, Allen H. "Text Encoding." *A Companion to Digital Humanities,* edited by Susan Schreibman, Ray Siemens, and John Unsworth. Malden: Blackwell, 2004. 218-39.

Reynolds, David S. *Walt Whitman.* Oxford: Oxford University Press, 2004.

Rhem, James. "Problem-Based Learning: An Introduction." *National Teaching & Learning Forum* 8, no. 1 (1998): 1-4.

Rice, Jeff. *The Rhetoric of Cool: Composition Studies and New Media.* Carbondale: Southern Illinois University Press, 2007.

—. "Writing about Cool: Teaching Hypertext as Juxtaposition." *Computers and Composition* 20, (2003): 221-36.

Ridolfo, Jim, and Dànielle Nicole DeVoss. "Composing for Recomposition: Rhetorical Velocity and Delivery." *Kairos* 13, no. 2 (2009), http://www.technorhetoric.net/13.2/topoi/ridolfo_devoss/.

Rockwell, Geoffrey. "Inclusion in the Digital Humanities." *philosophi.ca,* June 28, 2010, http://www.philosophi.ca/pmwiki.php/Main/InclusionInTheDigitalHumanities.

—. "Is Humanities Computing an Academic Discipline?" Presented at the University of Virginia, Charlottesville, November 1999, http://jefferson.village.virginia.edu/hcs/rockwell.html.

—. "Multimedia, is it a Discipline? The Liberal and Servile Arts in Humanities Computing." *Jarhbuch für Computerphilologie* 4 (2002): 59-70.

—. "What Is Text Analysis? A Very Short Answer." *WikiTADA,* Text Analysis Developers Alliance, April 30, 2005, http://tada.mcmaster.ca/Main/WhatTA.

Rockwell, Geoffrey, and Andrew Mactavish. "Multimedia." *A Companion to Digital Humanities,* edited by Susan Schreibman, Ray Siemens and John Unsworth. Malden: Blackwell, 2004. 108-20.

Rockwell, Geoffrey, Graham Passmore, and John Bradley. "TACTweb: The Intersection of Text-Analysis and Hypertext." *Journal of Educational Computing Research* 17, no. 3 (1997): 217-30.

Rockwell, Geoffrey, Stéfan Sinclair, Stan Ruecker, and Peter Organisciak. "Ubiquitous Text Analysis." *The Poetess Archive Journal* 2, no. 1 (2010), http://paj.muohio.edu/paj/index.php/paj/article/view/13/.

Rosen, Jeffrey. "The Web Means the End of Forgetting." *The New York Times Magazine,* July 21, 2010, http://www.nytimes.com/2010/07/25/magazine/25privacy-t2.html.

Rosenblatt, Roger. *Beet: A Novel.* New York: Ecco, 2008.

Rumsey, David, and Meredith Williams. "Historical Maps in GIS." *Past Time, Past Place: GIS for History,* edited by Anne Kelly Knowles. San Diego: ESRI Press, 2002. 1–18.

Rushkoff, Douglas. *Program or Be Programmed: Ten Commands for the Digital Age.* New York: O/R Books, 2010.

Russell, David R. "Rethinking Genre in School and Society: An Activity Theory Analysis." *Written Communication* 14, no. 4 (1997): 504-54.

Ryle, Gilbert. *The Concept of Mind.* Chicago: University of Chicago Press, 1949.

Sahle, Patrick. "Zwischen Mediengebundenheit und Transmedialisierung. Anmerkungen zum Verhältnis von Edition und Medien." *editio* 24 (2010): 23-36.

Salus, Peter H. *A Quarter Century of UNIX.* Reading: Addison-Wesley, 1994.

Sample, Mark. "The Open Source Professor: Teaching, Research, and Transparency." Paper presented at the Maryland Institute for Technology in the Humanities (MITH), College Park, Maryland, October 27, 2009, http://www.slideshare.net/samplereality/the-open-source-professor-teaching-research-and-transparency.

Schlib, John L. "Turning Composition toward Sovereignty." Paper presented at the MLA Annual Convention, Philadelphia, Pennsylvania, December 29, 2009.

Schmidt, Jan Philipp, Christine Geith, Stian Håklev, and Joel Thierstein. "Peer-To-Peer Recognition of Learning in Open Education." *The International Review of Research in Open and Distance Learning* 10, no. 5 (2009), http://www.irrodl.org/index.php/irrodl/article/view/641.

Scholz, Trebor, ed. *Learning Through Digital Media: Experiments in Technology and Pedagogy.* New York: Institute for Distributed Creativity, 2011. http://www.learningthroughdigitalmedia.net/.

Schreibman, Susan, Ray Siemens, and John Unsworth, ed. *A Companion to Digital Humanities.* Malden: Blackwell, 2004.

Schryer, Catherine F. "The Lab vs. the Clinic: Sites of Competing Genres." *Genre and the New Rhetoric,* edited by Aviva Freedman and Peter Medway. London: Taylor & Francis, 1994. 105-24.

Searle, John R. "Minds, Brains, and Programs." *Behavioral and Brain Sciences* 3, no. 3 (1980): 417-57.

Sehat, Connie Moon, and Erika Farr. *The Future of Digital Scholarship: Preparation, Training, Curricula. Report of a Colloquium on Education in Digital Dcholarship, April 17–18, 2009.* Washington: Council on Library and Information Resources, 2009. http://www.clir.org/pubs/archives/SehatFarr2009.pdf.

Selwyn, Neil. "The Digital Native: Myth and Reality." *Aslib Proceedings* 61, no. 4 (2009): 364-79.

Shell, Duane F., and Jenefer Husman. "Control, Motivation, Affect, and Strategic Self-Regulation in the College Classroom: A Multidimensional Phenomenon." *Journal of Educational Psychology* 100, no. 2 (2008): 443-59.

Shillingsburg, Peter. *From Gutenberg to Google: Electronic Representations of Literary Texts.* Cambridge: Cambridge University Press, 2006.

Short, Harold. "The Digital Humanities: A Collaborative Discipline." Presented at the Oxford e-Research Centre, May 18, 2010.

Siemens, Ray, and Susan Schreibman, ed. *A Companion to Digital Literary Studies.* Malden: Blackwell, 2007.

Silverstone, Roger. "Regulation, Media Literacy and Media Civics." *Media, Culture & Society* 26, no. 3 (2004): 440-49.

Simon, Roger. "Empowerment as a Pedagogy of Possibility." *Language Arts* 64 (1988): 370-82.

Sinclair, Stéfan, and Sean Gouglas. "Theory into Practice: A Case Study of the Humanities Computing Master of Arts Programme at the University of Alberta." *Arts and Humanities in Higher Education* 1, no. 2 (2002): 167-83.

Small, Gary, and Gigi Vorgan. *iBrain: Surviving the Technological Alternation of the Modern Mind*. New York: Collins Living, 2008.

Smith, Aaron, Kay Lehman Schlozman, Sidney Verba, and Henry Brady. "The Internet and Civic Engagement." *Pew Internet and American Life Project*, September 1, 2009, http://www.pewinternet.org/Reports/2009/15--The-Internet-and-Civic-Engagement.

Smith John B. "Image and Imagery in Joyce's Portrait: A Computer-Assisted Analysis." *Directions in Literary Criticism: Contemporary Approaches to Literature*, edited by Stanley Weintraub and Philip Young. University Park: Pennsylvania State University Press, 1973. 220-27.

Spiro, Lisa. "Collaborative Authorship in the Humanities." *Digital Scholarship in the Humanities*, April 21, 2009, http://digitalscholarship.wordpress.com/2009/04/21/collaborative-authorship-in-the-humanities/.

Soh, Leen-Kiat, Ashok Samal, Stephen Scott, Stephen Ramsay, Etsuko Moriyama, George Meyer, Brian Moore, William G. Thomas, and Duane F. Shell. "Renaissance Computing: An Initiative for Promoting Student Participation in Computing." *Proceedings of the 40th ACM Technical Symposium on Computer Science Education, SIGCSE 2009*, Chatanooga, 4–7 March 2009, edited by Sue Fitzgerald, Mark Guzdial, Gary Lewandowski, and Steven A. Wolfman. New York: ACM, 2009. 59-63.

Spiegelman, Art. *Maus: A Survivor's Tale*. Vol. 1. New York: Pantheon Books, 1986.

—. *Maus: A Survivor's Tale*. Vol. 2. New York: Pantheon Books, 1991.

Spool, Jared M. "The Essence of a Successful Persona Project." *User Interface Engineering*, February 17, 2010, http://www.uie.com/articles/essence_personas/.

Stachowiak, Herbert. *Allgemeine Modelltheorie*. Wien: Springer, 1973.

Stäcker, Thomas. "Creating the Knowledge Site—elektronische Editionen als Aufgabe einer Forschungsbibliothek." *Digital Edition und Forschungsbibliothek*, edited by Franz Fischer, Christiane Fritze, Patrick Sahle, and Malte Rehbein. Forthcoming.

Staley, David J. "Managing the Platform: Higher Education and the Logic of Wikinomics." *EDUCAUSE Review* 44, no. 1 (2009): 36-47.

Stallman, Richard M. "Free Software Definition." *Free Software, Free Society: Selected Essays of Richard M. Stallman*, edited by Joshua Gray. Boston: GNU Press, 2002. 41-43.

Stenberg, Shari. *Professing and Pedagogy: Learning the Teaching of English*. Urbana: National Council of Teachers of English, 2005.

Stenberg, Shari, and Amy Lee. "Developing Pedagogies: Learning the Teaching of English." College English 64, no. 3 (2002): 326-47.

Stephenson, Neal. *In the Beginning Was the Command Line*. New York: Avon, 1999.

Sternfeld, Joshua. "Archival Theory and Digital Historiography: Selection, Search, and Metadata as Archival Processes for Assessing Historical Contextualization." *The American Archivist* 74, no. 2 (2011): 544-75.

Stokes, Peter A. "Teaching Manuscripts in the Digital Age." *Kodikologie & Paläographie im Digitalen Zeitalter 2 / Codicology & Palaeography in the Digital Age 2*, edited by Franz Fischer, Christiane Fritze, and Georg Vogeler. Norderstedt: Books on Demand, 2011. 231-47.

Stokes, Peter A., and Elena Pierazzo. "Encoding the Language of Landscape: XML and Databases at the Service of Anglo-Saxon Lexicography." *Perspectives on Lexicography in Italy and Europe*, edited by Silvia Bruti, Roberta Cella, and Marina Foschi Albert. Newcastle-upon-Tyne: Cambridge Scholars Publishing, 2009. 203-38.

Stroupe, Craig. "Visualizing English: Recognizing the Hybrid Literacy of Visual and Verbal Authorship on the Web." *College English* 62, no. 5 (2000): 607-32.

Suitor, Tad. "Why 'Hacking'?" *Hacking the Academy: The Edited Volume,* edited by Dan Cohen and Tom Scheinfeldt. Ann Arbor: University of Michigan Press, 2012.

Svensson, Patrik. "Humanities Computing as Digital Humanities." *Digital Humanities Quarterly* 3, no. 3 (2009), http://digitalhumanities.org/dhq/vol/3/3/000065/000065.html.

TAPoR Project. http://portal.tapor.ca/.

Tapscott, Don. *Grown Up Digital.* New York: McGraw-Hill, 2009.

Tapscott, Don, and Anthony D. Williams. "Innovating the 21st-Century University: It's Time!" *EDUCAUSE Review* 45, no. 1 (2010): 16-29.

TEI Consortium. *TEI P5: Guidelines for Electronic Text Encoding and Interchange.* Version 1.9.1, March 5, 2011, http://www.tei-c.org/release/doc/tei-p5-doc/en/html/.

Terras, Melissa. "Disciplined: Using Educational Studies to Analyse 'Humanities Computing.'" *Literary and Linguistic Computing* 21, no. 2 (2006): 229-46.

—. "Hacking the Career: Digital Humanities as Academic Hackerdom." *Melissa Terras' Blog*, May 24, 2010, http://melissaterras.blogspot.com/2010/05/hacking-career-digital-humanities-as.html.

Theimer, Kate. *Web 2.0 Tools and Strategies for Archives and Local History Collections.* New York: Neal-Schuman, 2010.

Thomas, Douglas. *Hacker Culture.* Minneapolis: University of Minnesota Press, 2002.

Tötösy de Zepetnek, Steven. "The New Knowledge Management and Online Research and Publishing in the Humanities." *CLCWeb: Comparative Literature and Culture* 3, no. 1 (2001), http://docs.lib.purdue.edu/clcweb/vol3/iss1/8/.

Townsend, Robert B. "How Is New Media Reshaping the Work of Historians?" *Perspectives on History* 48, no. 8 (2010): 36-39.

Tufte, Edward R. *Visual Explanations: Images and Quantities, Evidence and Narrative.* Cheshire, Connecticut: Graphics Press, 1997.

Turing, Alan. "Computing Machinery and Intelligence." *Mind* 59, no. 236 (1950): 433-60.

Turrini, Joseph M. "The Historical Profession and Archival Education." *AHA Perspectives* 45, no. 5 (2007): 47-49.

Ulmer, Gregory L. *Electronic Monuments*. Minneapolis: University of Minnesota Press, 2005.

—. *Heuretics: The Logic of Invention*. Baltimore: Johns Hopkins University Press, 1994.

—. *Internet Invention: From Literacy to Electracy*. New York: Longman, 2003.

Unsworth, John. "A Masters Degree in Digital Humanities at the University of Virginia." Paper presented at the 2001 Congress of the Social Sciences and Humanities, Université Laval, Québec, Canada, May 25, 2001, http://www3.isrl. illinois.edu/~unsworth/laval.html.

—. "What is Humanities Computing and What is Not?" *Jahrbuch für Computerphilologie* 4 (2002): 71-83.

Unsworth, John, and Terry Butler. "A Masters Degree in Digital Humanities at the University of Virginia." Paper presented at ACH-ALLC 2001, New York University, June 13–16, 2001.

Vanhoutte, Edward. "Traditional Editorial Standards and the Digital Edition." *Learned Love: Proceedings of the Emblem Project Utretch Conference on Dutch Love Emblems and the Internet (November 2006)*, edited by Els Stronks and Peter Boot. The Hague: DANS Symposium Publications, 2007. 157-74.

Vesna, Victoria, ed. *Database Aesthetics: Art in the Age of Information Overflow*. Minneapolis: University of Minnesota Press, 2007.

Watrall, Ethan. "Developing a Personal Open Courseware Strategy." ProfHacker, *The Chronicle of Higher Education*, June 11, 2010, http://chronicle.com/blogs/ profhacker/developing-a-personal-open-courseware-strategy/.

Whitson, Roger T. "Does DH Really Need to be Transformed? My Reflections on #mla12." *Roger T. Whitson, Ph.D.*, January 8, 2012, http://www.rogerwhitson. net/?p=1358.

Wicke, Jennifer. "I Profess: Another View of Professionalism." Profession (2001): 52-57.

Wieseltier, Leon. "Shoah." *Claude Lanzmann's Shoah: Key Essays*, edited by Stuart Liebman. Oxford: Oxford University Press, 2007. 89-93.

Williams, George H. "Disability, Universal Design, and the Digital Humanities." *Debates in the Digital Humanities*, edited by Matthew K. Gold. Minneapolis: University of Minnesota Press, 2012. 202-12.

Wilson, Matthew W., Curtis Hisayasu, Jentery Sayers, and J. James Bono. "Standards in the Making: Composing with Metadata in Mind." *The New Work of Composing*, edited by Debra Journet, Cheryl E. Ball, and Ryan Trauman. Logan: Computers and Composition Digital Press/Utah State University Press, forthcoming.

Wosh, Peter J. "Research and Reality Checks: Change and Continuity in NYU's Archival Management Program." *The American Archivist* 63, no. 2 (2000): 271-83.

Wysocki, Anne Frances, and Johndan Johnson-Eilola. "Blinded by the Letter: Why Are We Using Literacy as a Metaphor for Everything Else?" *Passions, Pedagogies, and 21st Century Technologies*, edited by Gail E. Hawisher and Cynthia L. Selfe. Logan: Utah State University Press, 1999. 349-68.

Young, Jeffrey R. " 'Badges' Earned Online Pose Challenge to Traditional College Diplomas." *Chronicle of Higher Education*, January 8, 2012, http://chronicle.com/article/Badges-Earned-Online-Pose/130241.

Ziman, John. *"Puzzles, Problems and Enigmas." Puzzles, Problems and Enigmas: Occasional Pieces on the Human Aspects of Science.* Cambridge: Cambridge University Press, 1981.

Zittrain, Jonathan. *The Future of the Internet and How to Stop It.* New Haven: Yale University Press, 2008.

# This book does not end here...

At Open Book Publishers, we are changing the nature of the traditional academic book. The title you have just read will not be left on a library shelf, but will be accessed online by hundreds of readers each month across the globe. We make all our books free to read online so that students, researchers and members of the public who can't afford a printed edition can still have access to the same ideas as you.

Our digital publishing model also allows us to produce online supplementary material, including extra chapters, reviews, links and other digital resources. Find *Digital Humanities Pedagogy* on our website to access its online extras. Please check this page regularly for ongoing updates, and join the conversation by leaving your own comments:

http://www.openbookpublishers.com/product/161

If you enjoyed this book, and feel that research like this should be available to all readers, regardless of their income, please think about donating to us. Our company is run entirely by academics, and our publishing decisions are based on intellectual merit and public value rather than on commercial viability. We do not operate for profit and all donations, as with all other revenue we generate, will be used to finance new Open Access publications.

For further information about what we do, how to donate to OBP, additional digital material related to our titles or to order our books, please visit our website: www.openbookpublishers.com.

Knowledge is for sharing

www.ingramcontent.com/pod-product-compliance
Lightning Source LLC
LaVergne TN
LVHW052124070326
832902LV00038B/1743